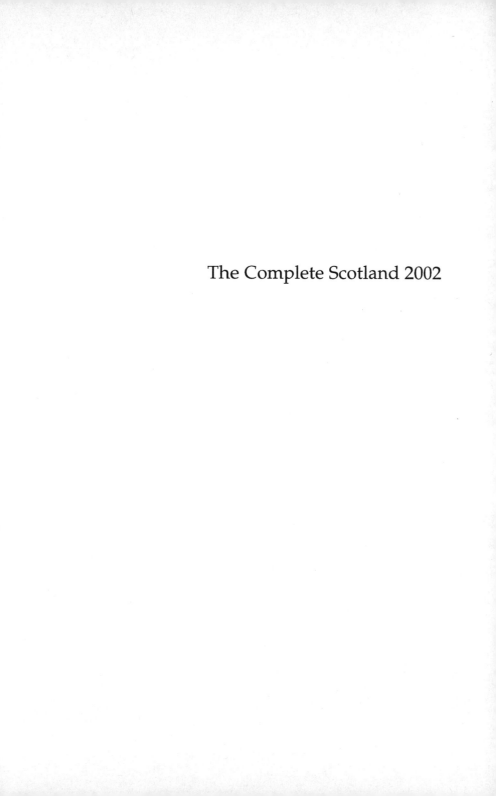

The Complete Scotland 2002

The Complete Scotland
2002

Carrick Media

The information in The Complete Scotland, in particular the statistical material, has been gathered from a vast range and number of sources, and space does not permit us to credit all concerned, but we must single out the Government information services and their annual publications, the Scottish Abstract of Statistics and the Annual Report of the Registrar General for Scotland, both of which we recommend to serious students of Scottish public affairs.

Published by Carrick Media
1/4 Galt House, 31 Bank Street, Irvine KA12 0LL
01294 311322

Copyright 2002 Carrick Media

Printed in England by Bookcraft Limited

British Library Cataloguing-in-Publication Data
A catalogue record for this book is available from the British Library

ISBN 0 946724 49 0

Contents

Preface

The first editions of *The Complete Scotland* co-incided with a period of momentous change in Scottish life: preparations for and elections to the Scottish Parliament, followed by ministerial appointments and the assumption of devolved power by the Scottish Executive. In this, the fourth edition, the framework of the new Scotland having been established, we continue to devote a generous section of the book to a detailed exposition of the Parliament and the Executive, while maintaining our coverage of the UK Government and, in particular, The Scotland Office, which now has a page of its own. A new feature of the book is the section on the growing number of consulates in Scotland.

Elsewhere, through dedicated sections such as "People" and "Compendium", the book offers the same eclectic range of knowledge, practical and curious, for readers who need to know all there is to know about Scotland and would prefer to have the facts at their fingertips. The heart of *The Complete Scotland* is "The Directory", in which we list more than 1,000 organisations influential in the life of the nation, with a mass of detailed information (including historical background) about a good many of them. Reflecting the increasing use of new technology in everyday communication, we include in many entries, as well as telephone numbers, fax, e-mail and web details.

The Complete Scotland would not be possible without the active co-operation of many organisations and individuals. We thank them for their help.

The Editors
Irvine
February 2002

Government

The Scottish Parliament

Background

On 24 July 1997 the Secretary of State (Donald Dewar) presented a White Paper to Parliament outlining a scheme for the establishment of a Scottish Parliament, provided the Government's policy on devolution was supported in a referendum. The White Paper proposed a 129-member parliament to be elected in 1999, 73 members of which would each represent a constituency elected by majority vote, the remaining 56 members to be elected by proportional representation on the basis of lists submitted by political parties. Elections would be held every four years. The Scottish Parliament would have powers to raise or reduce the basic rate of income tax by up to 3p, provided that this specific proposal was supported in the referendum.

On 11 September 1997 there was a decisive endorsement both of the Parliament and of the tax varying power, 74.3% of those who voted supporting the Parliament and 63.5% declaring in favour of the tax varying power. The electorate in only two of the 32 unitary authorities registered disapproval of either proposition, those being Orkney and Dumfries and Galloway, which voted against the tax varying power.

On 6 May 1999 the first election to the Scottish Parliament produced no overall majority for the largest single party, Labour, which subsequently entered a coalition with the Liberal Democrats.

The Parliament was opened by the Queen on 1 July 1999.

Devolved Powers

The Parliament has "legislative competence" to make primary legislation – Acts of the Scottish Parliament – on a wide range of devolved matters, including:

Agriculture	Health
Economic development	Housing
Education	Local government
Environment	Planning
Fisheries	Social work
Food standards	Transport (some aspects)
Forestry	Tourism

Acts of the Scottish Parliament will require to comply with rights under the European Convention on Human Rights and with European community law.

Reserved Powers

The UK Parliament continues to be the sovereign parliament of the UK and retains the power to legislate about any matter. However, the convention has been established that the UK Parliament does not normally legislate on devolved matters in Scotland without the consent of the Scottish Parliament.

The Scottish Parliament is not able to legislate about certain reserved matters, including: the constitution; defence; foreign affairs; electricity, coal, oil and gas, nuclear energy; employment; financial and economic affairs; social security.

There are provisions in the Scotland Act to ensure that the Scottish Parliament can legislate on devolved matters even if this has an ancillary effect on reserved matters. The Parliament can also legislate to apply certain general rules of Scots law consistently to reserved and devolved matters. Questions about whether the Scottish Parliament can legislate about a matter can be referred to the judicial committee of the Privy Council.

The UK Government has a limited power to intervene to prevent the submission of a Scottish bill for royal assent if it has reasonable grounds to believe that it contains provisions which would be incompatible with an international obligation, or the interests of defence or national security, or that it would have an adverse effect on the operation of the law as it applies to reserved matters.

The Scottish Executive

The Scottish Parliament nominates one of its number to be the First Minister, who is appointed by the Queen. With the Parliament's agreement, the First Minister in turn appoints or nominates to the Queen the other members of the Scottish Executive.

The Scottish Executive is the government of Scotland for all devolved matters. The members of the Executive, collectively referred to as "the Scottish Ministers" are:

The First Minister (Jack McConnell); the Lord Advocate and the Solicitor General for Scotland (the Scottish Law Officers); and other ministers appointed by the First Minister. The First Minister also appoints junior ministers to assist the Scottish Ministers.

The Scottish Parliament and the Scottish Executive assumed their full powers on 1 July 1999. On that date, the powers and duties exercised by UK ministers in Scotland relating to devolved matters transferred to the Scottish Ministers.

The Permanent Secretary to the Scottish Executive is Sir Muir Russell.

Secretary of State for Scotland

Before devolution, the Secretary of State for Scotland was responsible to the UK Parliament for the operations of the Scottish Office, which formerly discharged most of the functions of the UK government in Scotland, excluding defence, foreign policy, taxation, and social security. After devolution, a Secretary of State continues to be appointed as a member of the UK Government. He or she is not a member of the Scottish Executive but remains a member of the UK cabinet, representing Scottish interests in matters that are reserved to the UK Parliament.

Programme for Government

In autumn 1999, the Scottish Executive published its programme for government. Included are the following commitments, each with a target date for accomplishment:

Advertising
Ban tobacco advertising, end 1999

Agriculture
Package of measures to "assist the integration of agriculture with a wider and more diverse rural economy", early 2000
Introduce independent appeals mechanism for farmers suffering penalties in relation to EU subsidy claims, autumn 2000

Business
Introduce business mentoring scheme, 2000
Set up the Scottish University for Industry, 2000
Develop a manufacturing strategy and start to implement it, 2000
Support the establishment of a Scottish Institute of Enterprise, 2001, to encourage the transformation of ideas from laboratories into successful businesses
Create 100,000 new Scottish businesses, 2009

Childcare
Set up a new National Childcare Information Line, end 1999
Set up a new independent regulatory body to ensure high quality care for children, 2001
Ensure a nursery place for every 3-year-old whose parents want it, 2002
Out of school care places for 100,000 children, 2003

Community Care
Introduce a Carers' Strategy to help unpaid carers, 2000

Culture
National Culture Strategy, summer 2000

Drugs
Set up a Scottish Drug Enforcement Agency to target dealers and the supply of drugs, summer 2000

Education
Increase student numbers by 42,000, 2002
Double loan funding for mature part-time students on low incomes, 2001

Environment
New urban wastewater treatment systems in Edinburgh and Glasgow, end 2000

Food and food standards
Introduce a Butchers' Licensing Scheme for Scotland, 2000
New schemes to help Scottish food and drink industry, autumn 2000

Football
Set up a Scottish Football Academy, 2002

Health
Launch Scottish NHS Direct to provide 24-hour telephone health advice service, early 2000
Create network of Healthy Living Centres to improve health in areas of poverty and deprivation, 2002

Hospitals
Ensure that patients know the time of their hospital appointment before leaving their local surgery, 2002
Launch walk-in/walk-out hospitals in which patients will be assessed and treated by specialist staff offering same day treatment, 2002
80 One-Stop Clinics where patients will get diagnosis and treatment in the same day, 2002
Deliver biggest-ever hospital building programme in Scotland and provide 8 major new modern hospital developments, 2003

Housing
Empty Homes Initiative to bring 900 empty houses back into use for people in need, 2000
Three-year programme to build 18,000 houses for affordable renting or low-cost owner occupation, 2002
New accommodation and better support services for homeless so that "no one has to sleep rough", 2003
Large-scale investment to improve council houses through schemes to encourage community ownership, 2003
Improve 100,000 houses suffering from dampness and condensation through Healthy Homes Initiative, 2003

Land
Legislation to abolish feudal tenure, 1999
Legislation to provide a community right of purchase when land comes to be sold, spring 2000
Legislation to provide a right of responsible access to the land, spring 2000
Legislation to modernise crofting tenure, autumn 2000

Local Government

Set up Community Leadership Forum to encourage modernisation of local government, end 1999
Set up Scottish Standards Commission and a code of conduct for local government, summer 2000

Museums

Free admission to National Museums of Scotland, spring 2001

National Parks

Establish first National Park for Scotland, in Loch Lomond and the Trossachs, summer 2001

Policing

Use information technology to free up police officers for front-line duties and develop a Scottish Police Information Strategy, end 1999

Poverty

New Social Inclusion Partnerships supporting the regeneration of Scotland's most deprived neighbourhoods, end 1999
60,000 children "raised out of poverty", 2002

Schools

New framework for continuing professional development of teachers, 2000
Reduce class sizes in P1, P2 and P3 to 30 or fewer, summer 2001
60 new Community Schools, 2002
1,000 additional teachers and 5,000 classroom assistants, 2002
e-mail address for every school child, 2002
Build or substantially renovate 100 schools, 2003
Four modern computers for each class, 2003
Personal Learning Plan for every school age child, 2003

Skills

Initiate a Scottish Labour Market Unit to highlight the skills the country needs, end 1999
Create 20,000 Modern Apprenticeships, 2003

Stalking

Review the law on harassment and stalking, 2001

Transport

Legislation to invest in transport and encourage bus use, early 2000
Implement national transport timetable system, end 2000
Public Transport Fund to provide alternatives to car use, 1999-2002
Increase Freight Facilities Grant with aim of moving freight off the roads, spring 2002

Ministers of the Scottish Executive

First Minister
Jack McConnell, MSP
Ministerial responsibilities
Head of the Scottish Executive. With the Deputy First Minister, responsible for the development, implementation and presentation of Scottish Executive policies.
Biographical notes
Labour Member for Motherwell and Wishaw; b 1960, Irvine; educ Arran High School and Stirling University; married; 1 son; 1 daughter; teacher of mathematics, 1983-92; Member, Stirling District Council, 1984-92, Leader of the Council, 1990-92; General Secretary, Scottish Labour Party, 1992-98; formerly Minister for Finance and Minister for Education, Europe and External Affairs.

Deputy First Minister and Minister for Justice
Jim Wallace, QC, MSP
Ministerial responsibilities
With the First Minister, responsible for the development, implementation and presentation of Scottish Executive policies. Responsible for external relations, especially development and implementation of links with Europe. Responsible for home affairs, including civil law and criminal justice, criminal justice social work services, police, fire, prisons and courts, law reform and freedom of information.
Biographical notes
Liberal Democrat Member for Orkney; b 1954, Annan; educ Annan Academy, Downing College Cambridge, and Edinburgh University; married; 2 daughters; lives in Orkney; called to the Scottish Bar, 1979; MP, Orkney and Shetland, since 1983.

Minister for Education and Young People
Cathy Jamieson, MSP
Ministerial responsibilities
Responsible for pre-school and school education, children and young people.
Biographical notes
Labour and Co-operative Member for Carrick, Cumnock and Doon Valley; b 1956, Kilmarnock; educ James Hamilton Academy, Kilmarnock, Glasgow Art School and Glasgow University; married; 1 son; former Principal Officer, Who Cares? Scotland, developing policy and legislation for young people in care.

Minister for Enterprise, Transport and Lifelong Learning
Wendy Alexander, MSP

Ministerial responsibilities
Responsible for the economy, transport, business and industry including Scottish Enterprise, Highlands and Islands Enterprise, trade and inward investment, energy, further and higher education, public transport, roads, lifeline air and ferry services, lifelong learning and training. Minister for Science.
Biographical notes
Labour Member for Paisley North; b 1963, Glasgow; educ Park Mains High School (Erskine), Glasgow University, Warwick University, INSEAD Business School, France; worked as a management consultant, Europe, America, and Asia; also worked as a research officer for the Labour Party; former Special Adviser to Secretary of State for Scotland; former Minister for Communities.

Minister for Environment and Rural Development
Ross Finnie, MSP
Ministerial responsibilities
Responsible for the environment and natural heritage, renewable energy, land reform, water, sustainable development, rural development including aquaculture and forestry. Responsible for agriculture and fisheries.
Biographical notes
Liberal Democrat Member for West of Scotland; b 1947, Greenock; educ Greenock Academy; married; 1 son; 1 daughter; chartered accountant; Member, Inverclyde District Council and Inverclyde Council, 1977-99; Chairman, Scottish Liberal Party, 1982-86; formerly Minister for Rural Affairs.

Minister for Tourism, Culture and Sport
Mike Watson, MSP
Ministerial responsibilities
Responsible for tourism, sport, culture and the arts, the built heritage, architecture, Historic Scotland, lottery funding and Gaelic.
Biographical notes
Labour Member for Glasgow Cathcart; b 1949, Cambuslang; educ Dundee High School and Heriot-Watt University; former Development Officer, WEA; Regional Officer, ASTMS (latterly MSF) union, 1979-89; Member, Scottish Executive Committee, Labour Party, 1987-90; author of official history of Dundee United FC.

Minister for Social Justice
Iain Gray, MSP
Ministerial responsibilities
Responsible for social inclusion, housing and area regeneration including the promotion of sustainable urban development, cities, the land use planning system and building standards, equality issues and the voluntary sector.
Biographical notes

Labour Member for Edinburgh Pentlands; b 1957, Edinburgh; educ Inverness Royal Academy and Edinburgh University; married; 1 daughter; 2 step-daughters; former physics and maths teacher; Campaign Manager, Oxfam in Scotland, 1986-99; formerly Deputy Minister for Community Care.

Minister for Finance and Public Services
Andy Kerr, MSP
Ministerial responsibilities
Responsible for the Scottish Budget, better public service delivery, modernising government including civil service reform, local government and European Structural Funds. Responsible for overseeing strategic communications.
Biographical notes
Labour Member for East Kilbride; b 1962, East Kilbride; educ Claremont High School and Glasgow College; married; 3 daughters; Research Officer, Strathkelvin District Council, 1987-90; Achieving Quality Consultancy, 1990-93; worked for Glasgow City Council, 1993-99.

Minister for Health and Community Care
Malcolm Chisholm, MSP
Ministerial responsibilities
Responsible for health policy; the National Health Service in Scotland, community care and food safety.
Biographical notes
Labour Member for Edinburgh North and Leith; b 1949; married; 2 sons; 1 daughter; former teacher; Parliamentary Under-Secretary of State, Scottish Office; former Labour MP for Edinburgh North and Leith.

Minister for Parliamentary Business
Patricia Ferguson, MSP
Ministerial responsibilities
Responsible for Parliamentary affairs and the management of Executive business in the Parliament and Parliamentary liaison, public appointments policy and quango governance. Responsible for the co-ordination of Executive policy and the management of cross-cutting issues.
Biographical notes
Labour Member for Glasgow Maryhill; b 1958, Glasgow; married; educ Garnethill Convent Secondary School, Glasgow; former Deputy Presiding Officer.

Junior Ministers of the Scottish Executive

Deputy Minister for Justice: Richard Simpson, MSP
Special responsibility for co-ordination of Executive policy on drugs.
Biographical notes
Labour Member for Ochil; b 1942, Edinburgh; educ Trinity College and Edinburgh University; married; 2 sons; GP and psychiatrist; former Chair, Strathcarron Hospice; former Director, Forth Valley Primary Care Research Group.

Deputy Minister for Education, Europe and External Affairs: Nicol Stephen, MSP
Specific responsibility for teachers and schools.
Biographical notes
Liberal Democrat Member for Aberdeen South; b 1960; educ Robert Gordon's College, Aberdeen, Aberdeen Univ-ersity and Edinburgh University; married; 2 children; qualified as a solicitor; Member, Grampian Regional Council, 1982-92; MP, Kincardine and Deeside, 1991-92; former Deputy Minister for Enterprise and Lifelong Learning.

Deputy Minister for Enterprise, Transport and Lifelong Learning: Lewis Macdonald, MSP
Ministerial responsibilities
Specific responsibility for transport.
Biographical notes
Labour Member for Aberdeen Central; b 1957, Stornoway; educ Inverurie Academy and Aberdeen University; married; 2 daughters; former Parliamentary researcher, office of Frank Doran, MP; former Shadow Cabinet Adviser to Tom Clarke, MP.

Deputy Minister for Environment and Rural Development: Allan Wilson, MSP
Biographical notes
Labour Member for Cunninghame North; b 1954, Glasgow; educ Spiers School, Beith; married; 2 sons; former Head of Higher Education (Scotland), UNISON.

Deputy Minister for Tourism, Culture and Sport: Elaine Murray, MSP
Specific responsibility for arts and culture.
Biographical notes
Labour Member for Dumfries; b 1954, Hitchin; educ Mary Erskine School, Edinburgh University and Cambridge University; married; 2 sons; 1 daughter; former Senior Scientific Officer, Institute of Food Research, Reading.

Deputy Minister for Social Justice: Margaret Curran, MSP
Specific responsibility for housing.
Biographical notes
Labour Member for Glasgow Baillieston; educ Glasgow University; former Lecturer in Community Education.

Deputy Minister for Finance and Public Services: Peter Peacock, MSP
Specific responsibility for budgetary monitoring and control.
Biographical notes
Labour Member for Highlands and Islands; b 1952, Edinburgh; educ Hawick High School, Jordanhill College of Education; married; 2 sons; former community worker; former area officer, Citizens Advice Bureau; self-employed consultant; elected to Highland Regional Council, 1982; Convener, Highland Council.

Deputy Minister for Health and Community Care: Hugh Henry, MSP
Biographical notes
Labour Member for Paisley South; b 1952, Glasgow; married; 1 s.; 2 daughters; former Leader, West Renfrewshire Council.

Deputy Minister for Health and Community Care: Mary Mulligan, MSP
Biographical notes
Labour Member for Linlithgow; b 1960, Liverpool; educ Notre Dame High School and Manchester University; married; 2 sons; 1 daughter; retail and personnel management, 1981-86; former Edinburgh City councillor.

Deputy Minister for Parliamentary Business: Euan Robson, MSP
Particular responsibility for the Parliamentary handling of the legislative programme and management of cross-cutting priorities. Assists with the oversight of strategic communications.
Biographical notes
Liberal Democrat Member for Roxburgh and Berwickshire; b 1954, Northumberland; educ Trinity College, Glenalmond, Newcastle-upon Tyne University and Strathclyde University; married; 2 daughters; former Scottish Manager, Gas Consumers' Council.

Law Officers

Lord Advocate
Colin Boyd, QC
Lord Advocate, since 1997; b 1953, Falkirk; educ Wick High School, George Watson's College (Edinburgh), Manchester University, Edinburgh University; married; 2 sons, 1 daughter; called to the Bar, 1983; Advocate Depute, 1993-95; former Solicitor General.

VOTING SYSTEM
The Scottish Parliament was elected using the Additional Member System, a type of proportional representation intended to ensure that the share of seats each party received would reflect as closely as possible its level of support among voters. Each voter had two votes, the first to elect a constituency member by the traditional "first past the post" method, the second for a polical party, or candidate standing as an individual, within a larger electoral area

Solicitor General
Elish Angiolini, QC
Solicitor General, since 2002; b 1960; educ Strathclyde University; married; 2 children; former Regional Procurator Fiscal, Grampian, Highland and Islands

Presiding Officers of the Scottish Parliament

Presiding Officer
Rt Hon Sir David Steel, KBE, MSP
Liberal Democrat Member for Lothians; b 1938, Kirkcaldy; educ George Watson's College, Edinburgh, and Edinburgh University; married; 3 children; former MP for Roxburgh, Selkirk and Peebles and, later, Tweeddale, Ettrick and Lauderdale; Leader of the Liberal Party, 1976-88; returned to (UK) Parliament, 1997, as Lord Steel of Aikwood.

Deputy Presiding Officer
George Reid, MSP
Scottish National Party Member for Mid Scotland and Fife; b 1939, Tullibody; married; 2 daughters; former MP, Clackmannan and East Stirling; journalist and television producer; former Director of Public Affairs, Intrenational Red Cross.

Deputy Presiding Officer
Murray Tosh, MSP
Conservative Member for South of Scotland; b 1950, Ayr; married; 2 sons; 1 daughter; former history teacher.

called a Scottish Parliament region. Each of the eight regions was allocated seven additional seats, the members chosen to fill these additional seats being known as "regional members".

CONSTITUENCY (FIRST) VOTE

Labour	908,346
Scottish National Party	672,768
Scottish Conservative	364,425
Liberal Democrat	333,269
Others	63,770

The Scottish Executive and its Departments

The Scottish Executive

Address: St Andrews House, Regent Road, Edinburgh EH1 3DG
Telephone: 0131-556 8400
Permanent Secretary: Sir Muir Russell

Development Department (SEDD)

Address: Victoria Quay, Edinburgh EH6 6QQ
Telephone: 0131-556 8400
Head of Department: Mrs N S Munro

Administers a wide range of Government responsibilities, including social inclusion, housing and area regeneration, local government and finance, land use planning, building control, European Structural Funds management, roads and transport, and planning and building control. The department also provides economic and statistical advice for various parts of the Scottish Executive.

SEDD's primary housing aim is to ensure an adequate supply of housing in Scotland, with choice and effective use of resources, in particular by encouraging private finance. The department sponsors Scottish Homes, the national housing agency. SEDD provides advice and guidance to local authorities and other housing agencies on securing an adequate supply of housing for community care groups as part of the Government's policy for Care in the Community, and for homeless people in priority need. Improvements in Scotland's housing stock are promoted through targeting local authority and Scottish Homes resources. SEDD promotes improvements in housing management and in rights of tenants.

SEDD is responsible for social justices policies, including area regeneration: i.e., the economic, social and environmental improvement of disadvantaged urban areas. The department manages the Social Inclusion Partnership, a special grant scheme which targets resources into these areas, to help to achieve sustainable regeneration and improve the conditions in which people live.

It is further responsible for developing and administering policy on local government: its structure, powers, conduct and finance (including Council Tax and non-domestic rates). SEDD sponsors the Local Government Boundary Commission for Scotland and the Accounts Commission for Scotland.

SEDD advises the First Minister on national planning guidance and advice, local authority structure plans, and on development proposals of national importance, and deals with planning appeals. It is also responsible for policies on building control which ensure that the construction, use and demolition of buildings pose no threat to health and safety.

SEDD has responsibility for transport policy in Scotland, including the trunk road network, shipping and air services in the Highlands and Islands, rail, ports and canals, and liaison with local authorities on transport matters.

It provides economic advice and statistical information to some other departments in the Scottish Executive, and prepares the Scottish Abstract of Statistics and other economic and statistical publications.

Education Department (SEED)

Address: Victoria Quay, Edinburgh EH6 6QQ
Telephone: 0131-556 8400
Head of Department: John Elvidge
Works to give children the best start in life and to promote tourism, culture and sport. Its aims are: to ensure that every child or young person is able to develop to his or her fullest potential; to ensure all children have access to early learning and quality care; to promote social justice for children and young people; to raise standards and broaden achievement in education; to modernise Scottish schools, strengthen leadership in schools and reward professionalism in teaching; to increase the success of Scotland's tourism industry; to broaden access to and involvement in the arts, culture and sport and enhance the contribution they make to Scotland's well-being; to contribute to the physical environment through preserving Scotland's built heritage and promoting and encouraging better architecture.

SEED is responsible for administering policy on pre-school and school education; children and young people; and tourism, culture and sport. It promotes the education service for 830,000 pupils in more than 5,000 pre-school centres, primary and secondary schools, and special schools and units.

There are four main areas of responsibility within SEED, each managed by a member of the Departmental management board.

Children and Young People's Group has a remit to promote effective co-ordination and integration across the Executive of policies and resources affecting children and young people. It develops and administers the policies for children's rights, support for families, child protection, regulation of childcare centres and pre-school education and looked-after children. The Group also has responsibility for producing statistics, promoting international links, managing the Department's research programme and carrying out economic analysis and evaluation of policy.

The Social Work Services Inspectorate (SWSI) provides an annual evaluation of social services in each local authority and undertakes thematic inspections and reviews of services, often working jointly with other Inspectorates. The Inspectorate also carries responsibility for social work education and training.

Schools' Group is responsible for policy covering the national priorities in education, teachers and schools, New Community Schools, social justice, school ethos and pupil welfare, health education, special educational needs, support and inclusion, new educational developments and qualifications, assessment and curriculum.

Tourism, Culture and Sport Group, which is in the process of formation, is responsible for policy covering tourism, the arts, film, architecture, the cultural heritage, sport, Gaelic and liaison with the UK government on broadcasting and the lottery; and promotes the widest possible involvement with Scotland's sporting and cultural life.

There are two Executive Agencies linked to the Department.

HM Inspectorate of Education (HMIE) began operating as an Executive Agency of the Scottish Executive on 1 April 2001. HMIE operates independently and impartially. Its mission is to promote improvements in standards, quality and attainment in Scottish education. It conducts independent inspections and reviews of educational establishments, community learning and the education functions of local authorities.

Historic Scotland is directly responsible to Scottish ministers for safeguarding the nation's built heritage and promoting its understanding and enjoyment.

SEED's main partners are Scotland's 32 unitary local authorities. It also sponsors and works with a wide range of non-Departmental public bodies, including Learning and Teaching Scotland, the General Teaching Council for Scotland, the Scottish Qualifications Authority, the Scottish Children's Reporters' Administration, Community Learning Scotland, VisitScotland, the Scottish Arts Council, Scottish Screen, the National Museums of Scotland, the Royal Commission on Ancient and Historic Monuments in Scotland, Ancient Monuments Board, the Historic Buildings Council, the Royal Fine Art Commission for Scotland and sportscotland.

Enterprise and Lifelong Learning Department (ELLD)

Address: Meridian Court, Cadogan Street, Glasgow G2 6AT
Telephone: 0141-248 4774
Head of Department: Eddie Frizzell
Created from the pre-devolution Scottish Office Education and Industry Department, ELLD supports Scottish ministers in the achievement of their objectives in economic and industrial development, further and higher education, skills and lifelong learning. It also co-ordinates the delivery of the New Deal in Scotland.

Grant-aid for business

ELLD supports Scottish ministers in developing and promoting an environment that encourages business and enterprise to flourish in

Scotland. It provides assistance directly to a wide range of businesses. Two schemes exist to attract investment and create and safeguard jobs in Assisted Areas: Regional Selective Assistance and Invest for Growth. Qualifying projects generally involve purchase of fixed assets, including opening of a new plant or modernising or adding new facilities to existing plants. Invest for Growth can offer grants of up to £100million, while Regional Selective Assistance is available for projects that need higher levels of assistance.

The Smart:Scotland competition helps individuals planning to start a business, and existing small enterprises located in Scotland, to develop highly innovative products and processes. Scottish medium-sized enterprises developing similar products can benefit from the Spur grant scheme.

Enterprise Network: the Scottish Executive's economic development and skills objectives are promoted in collaboration with Scottish Enterprise and Highlands and Islands Enterprise through a network of Local Enterprise Companies (LECs). LECs provide support to business start-ups, venture capital, and a range of business services. The LECs also deliver training programmes, including Youth Training and Skillseekers/Modern Apprenticeships for young people, and Training for Work for unemployed adults.

Export Promotion: Help is available to Scottish-based businesses from Scottish Trade International (STI).

Inward Investment: ELLD works jointly with Scottish Enterprise to fund and staff Locate in Scotland, a "single door" agency responsible for attracting investment projects.

Lifelong Learning: ELLD promotes lifelong learning through policy development and funding for further and adult education, and higher education, promoting and supporting training for people at every stage in life beyond school age. A Scottish University for Industry has been established. ELLD also funds the Scottish Further Education Council and the Scottish Higher Education Funding Council, and the higher and further education institutions.

Student Support: Financial support for eligible Scottish-domiciled students on higher education courses is provided by the Scottish Students Awards Agency. SAAS is an Executive Agency of ELLD, whose remit includes the determination of students' eligibility for loans paid through the Student Loans Company. ELLD also contracts with the 17 careers service companies in Scotland.

Health Department (SEHD)

Address: St Andrew's House, Regent Road, Edinburgh EH1 3DG
Telephone: 0131-556 8400
Chief Executive: Trevor Jones; Chief Medical Officer: Dr E Armstrong
Responsible for health policy and the administration of the National

Health Service in Scotland.

The Chief Executive of the Scottish Executive Health Department leads the central management of the NHS, is accountable to ministers for the efficiency and performance of the service, and heads a management executive which oversees the work of 15 area health boards responsible for planning health services for people in their area, and 28 self-governing NHS Trusts responsible for providing services to patients and to the community.

The Public Health Policy Unit of the Health Department is responsible for promoting the health of the people of Scotland.

The department has a further responsibility for the State Hospital, which cares for patients who require treatment under conditions of special security, and the Health Education Board for Scotland, which promotes positive attitudes to health and encourages healthy lifestyles.

It is also responsible for social work policy and in particular for community care and voluntary issues.

Justice Department (SEJD)

Address: Saughton House, Broomhouse Drive, Edinburgh EH11 3XD
Telephone: 0131-556 8400
Head of Department: Jim Gallagher

Brings together the Scottish Office Home Department and the Scottish Court Administration. Responsible for: police and fire services; criminal justice, including criminal justice social work; aspects of civil law; courts administration; legal aid; liaison with the legal profession in Scotland.

The department, in partnership with chief constables and local police authorities, discharges the First Minister's responsibilities for administration of the police service, including provision of training at the Scottish Police College. It has similar responsibilities for the fire service, including provision of training at the Scottish Fire Service Training School. The department promotes emergency planning by both government and local authorities, and co-ordinates preparation for civil emergencies.

SEJD is responsible for criminal justice policy and procedure in Scotland, including the early release of prisoners, and such civil law matters as matrimonial and family law, policy on victims of crime, and regulation of charities.

It is further responsible for the legal aid system and aspects of the work of District Courts. It supports the operations of a number of courts and tribunals, including the Scottish Land Court and the VAT and Duties Tribunal. It also has a role in administering the system of appointments of the judiciary in Scotland (other than appointments to the District Courts).

The department deals with electoral procedures, including registration of electors, and with Royal, church and ceremonial matters.

There are two agencies within the department: the Scottish Prison Service, which was established as an executive agency in 1993, and the

Scottish Court Service, which was established as an executive agency in 1995.

Environment and Rural Affairs Department (SEERAD)

Address: Pentland House, 47 Robb's Loan, Edinburgh EH14 1TY
Telephone: 0131-556 8400
Head of Department: John Graham
Responsible for advising ministers on policy relating to agriculture, rural development, food, the environment and fisheries, and for ensuring the implementation of these policies in Scotland. The Department also supports and promotes the agricultural and biological science base in Scotland.

The department's main aims are: to help improve the economic performance of Scotland's agriculture, aquaculture, fishing and food industries within the wider context of sustainable exploitation of our land, sea and freshwater resources and rural development, while safeguarding the interests of consumers, protecting and enhancing the environment, and ensuring a fair deal for taxpayers; and to support ministers in helping the people of Scotland to secure a high quality of life through sensitive stewardship and sustainable development of the natural resources of Scotland, in particular by securing a clean, healthy and safe environment, ensuring a safe and effective water industry, and improving people's enjoyment of the environment.

SEERAD aims to promote rural development and ensure that the needs and interests of rural Scotland are reflected in the Executive's policies and priorities.

It aims to improve the agricultural, food and fisheries industries' economic performance by effective implementation of the EC Common Agricultural Policy and Common Fisheries Policy obligations, and by promotion of further reform of policies at UK and EU level.

The department is responsible for assisting the development and structural adjustment of the agriculture, aquaculture and fishing industries; regulating the sustainable exploitation of fish stocks and promoting fisheries conservation measures; and taking action against plant diseses and pests, and animal and fish diseases within the overarching controls of EU Single Market requirements. SEERAD also encourages high animal welfare standards on farms and in transport.

It aims to protect and enhance the environment by promoting environmentally sensitive farming, farm woodlands and fishing, by securing the conservation and enhancement of Scotland's natural heritage and by improving scientific understanding of our terrestrial and aquatic environment.

The department is responsible for ensuring that UK and EC objectives for pollution control and drinking water are met, including appropriate control over the use and disposal of radioactive substances, and the regulation of environmental aspects of nuclear installations.

SEERAD is responsible for ensuring safe, effective and efficient water and sewerage services in Scotland. It sponsors three public water authorities: North of Scotland Water, West of Scotland Water and East of Scotland Water.

It promotes nature conservation and the public's enjoyment of the natural heritage by ensuring compliance with EU and international nature conservation requirements and the positive management of designated areas. It is introducing National Parks in Scotland, and is preparing legislation to establish a right of responsible access to the countryside. In support of these aims it sponsors and works through Scottish Natural Heritage, the Executive's statutory advisor on natural heritage and nature conservation matters.

SEERAD is assisted by three Executive Agencies: the Scottish Agricultural Science Agency, Fisheries Research Services, and the Fisheries Protection Agency. It is also responsible for a range of scientific research establishments, and sponsors several non-departmental public bodies, including the Royal Botanic Garden Edinburgh, the Crofters Commission, and the Deer Commission for Scotland.

From April 2000, the Department's responsibilities for food safety and standards were transferred to the Food Standards Agency.

In addition to the main departments, the Scottish Executive has three other departments:

Corporate Services
Principal Establishment Officer: Agnes Robson
Provides central support for ministers and staff of the Executive, covering such matters as human resources, employee relations, training and development, equal opportunities, accommodation and estate management, communications and information, and security.

Finance and Central Services Department (FCSD)
Chief Executive: Robert Gordon, CB
Responsible for parliamentary liaison, the legislative programme, co-ordination of relations with the UK government and Europe, local government relations. Provides support to the Scottish Cabinet. The Finance Group within FCSD advises ministers on the allocation of the Scottish Budget and accounts for the budget, and advises other departments of the Scottish Executive on financial matters.

Finance Department
Principal Finance Officer: Dr Peter Collings
Advises ministers on the allocation of the Scottish budget. Advises other departments on financial matters, and issues guidance to the Executive, non-departmental public bodies, and other public bodies on propriety and regularity in financial affairs. It includes the internal audit of the Executive.

The Scottish Parliamentary Constituencies

May 1999

CENTRAL SCOTLAND

AIRDRIE AND SHOTTS
Electorate 58,481 Poll 56.79%

K Whitefield, Lab	18,338
G Paterson, SNP	9,353
P Ross-Taylor, Con	3,177
D Miller, LD	2,345
Lab majority	8,985

COATBRIDGE AND CHRYSTON
Electorate 52,178 Poll 57.87%

E Smith, Lab	17,923
P Kearney, SNP	7,519
G Lind, Con	2,867
J Hook, LD	1,889
Lab majority	10,404

CUMBERNAULD AND KILSYTH
Electorate 49,395 Poll 61.97%

C Craigie, Lab	15,182
A Wilson, SNP	10,923
H O'Donnell, LD	2,029
R Slack, Con	1,362
K McEwan, SSP	1,116
Lab majority	4,259

EAST KILBRIDE
Electorate 66,111 Poll 62.49%

A Kerr, Lab	19,987
L Fabiani, SNP	13,488
C Stevenson, Con	4,465
E Hawthorn, LD	3,373
Lab majority	6,499

FALKIRK EAST
Electorate 57,345 Poll 61.40%

C Peattie, Lab	15,721
K Brown, SNP	11,582
A Orr, Con	3,399
G McDonald, LD	2,509
R Stead	1643
Others	358
Lab majority	4,139

FALKIRK WEST
Electorate 53,404 Poll 63.04%

D Canavan, Falkirk W	18,511
R Martin, Lab	6,319
M Matheson, SNP	5,986
G Miller, Con	1,897
A Smith, LD	954
Falkirk W majority	12,192

HAMILTON NORTH AND BELLSHILL
Electorate 53,992 Poll 57.82%

M McMahon, Lab	15,227
K McAlorum, SNP	9,621
S Thomson, Con	3,199
J Struthers, LD	2,105
K McGavigan, Soc Lab	1,064
Lab majority	5,606

HAMILTON SOUTH
Electorate 46,765 Poll 55.43%

T McCabe, Lab	14,098
A Ardrey, SNP	6,922
M Mitchell, Con	2,918
J Oswald, LD	1,982
Lab majority	7,176

KILMARNOCK AND LOUDOUN
Electorate 61,454 Poll 64.03%

M Jamieson, Lab	17,345
A Neil, SNP	14,585
L McIntosh, Con	4,589
J Stewart, LD	2,830
Lab majority	2,760

MOTHERWELL AND WISHAW
Electorate 52,613 Poll 57.71%

J McConnell, Lab	13,955
J McGuigan, SNP	8,879
W Gibson, Con	3,694
J Milligan, Soc Lab	1,941
R Spillane, LD	1,895
Lab majority	5,076

ADDITIONAL MEMBERS ELECTED BY PR
L McIntosh, Con
D Gorrie, LD
A Neil, SNP
M Matheson, SNP
L Fabiani, SNP
A Wilson, SNP
G Paterson, SNP

GLASGOW

GLASGOW ANNIESLAND
Electorate 54,378 Poll 52.37%

D Dewar, Lab	16,749

K Stewart, SNP	5,756
W Aitken, Con	3,032
I Brown, LD	1,804
A Lynch, SSP	1,000
Others	139
Lab majority	10,993

GLASGOW BAILLIESTON
Electorate 49,068 Poll 48.32%

M Curran, Lab	11,289
D Elder, SNP	8,217
J McVicar, SSP	1,864
K Pickering, Con	1,526
J Fryer, LD	813
Lab majority	3,072

GLASGOW CATHCART
Electorate 51,338 Poll 52.55%

M Watson, Lab	12,966
M Whitehead, SNP	7,592
M Leishman, Con	3,311
C Dick, LD	2,187
Others	920
Lab majority	5,374

GLASGOW GOVAN
Electorate 53,257 Poll 49.52%

G Jackson, Lab	11,421
N Sturgeon, SNP	9,665
T Ahmed-Sheikh, Con	2,343
M Aslam Khan, LD	1,479
C McCarthy, SSP	1,275
Others	190
Lab majority	1,756

GLASGOW KELVIN
Electorate 61,207 Poll 46.34%

P McNeill, Lab	12,711
S White, SNP	8,303
M Craig, LD	3,720
A Rasul, Con	2,253
H Ritchie, SSP	1,375
Lab majority	4,408

GLASGOW MARYHILL
Electorate 56,469 Poll 40.75%

P Ferguson, Lab	11,455
B Wilson, SNP	7,129
C Hamblen, LD	1,793
G Scott, SSP	1,439
M Fry, Con	1,194
Lab majority	4,326

GLASGOW POLLOK
Electorate 47,970 Poll 54.37%

J Lamont, Lab Co-op	11,405
K Gibson, SNP	6,763
T Sheridan, SSP	5,611
R O'Brien, Con	1,370
J King, LD	931
Lab Co-op majority	4,642

GLASGOW RUTHERGLEN
Electorate 51,012 Poll 56.89%

J Hughes, Lab	13,442
T Chalmers, SNP	6,155
R Brown, LD	5,798
I Stewart, Con	2,315
W Bonnar, SSP	832
Others	481
Lab majority	7,287

GLASGOW SHETTLESTON
Electorate 50,592 Poll 40.58%

F McAveety, Lab Co-op	11,078
J Byrne, SNP	5,611
R Kane, SSP	1,640
C Bain, Con	1,260
L Clarke, LD	943
Lab Co-op majority	5,467

GLASGOW SPRINGBURN
Electorate 55,670 Poll 43.77%

P Martin, Lab	14,268
J Brady, SNP	6,375
M Roxburgh, Con	1,293
M Dunnigan, LD	1,288
J Friel, SSP	1,141
Lab majority	7,893

ADDITIONAL MEMBERS ELECTED BY PR
W Aitken, Con
R Brown, LD
D Elder, SNP
S White, SNP
N Sturgeon, SNP
K Gibson, SNP
T Sheridan, SSP

HIGHLANDS AND ISLANDS

ARGYLL AND BUTE
Electorate 49,609 Poll 64.86%

G Lyon, LD	11,226
D Hamilton, SNP	9,169
H Raven, Lab	6,470
D Petrie, Con	5,312
LD majority	2,057

CAITHNESS, SUTHERLAND AND EASTER
ROSS
Electorate 41,581 Poll 62.60%

J Stone, LD	10,691
J Hendry, Lab	6,300
J Urquhart, SNP	6,035
R Jenkins, Con	2,167
Others	836
LD majority	4,391

INVERNESS EAST, NAIRN AND LOCHABER
Electorate 66,285 Poll 63.10%

F Ewing, SNP	13,825
J Aitken, Lab	13,384
D Fraser, LD	8,508
M Scanlon, Con	6,107
SNP majority	441

MORAY
Electorate 58,388 Poll 57.50%

M Ewing, SNP	13,027
A Farquharson, Lab	8,898
A Findlay, Con	8,595
P Kenton, LD	3,056
SNP majority	4,129

ORKNEY
Electorate 15,658 Poll 56.95%

J Wallace, LD	6,010
C Zawadzki, Con	1,391
J Mowat, SNP	917
A Macleod, Lab	600
LD majority	4,619

ROSS, SKYE AND INVERNESS WEST
Electorate 55,845 Poll 63.42%

J Farquhar-Munro, LD	11,652
D Munro, Lab	10,113
J Mather, SNP	7,997
J Scott, Con	3,351
D Briggs, Ind	2,302
LD majority	1,539

SHETLAND
Electorate 16,978 Poll 58.77%

T Scott, LD	5,435
J Wills, Lab	2,241
W Ross, SNP	1,430
G Robinson, Con	872
LD majority	3,194

WESTERN ISLES
Electorate 22,412 Poll 62.26%

A Morrison, Lab	7,248

A Nicholson, SNP	5,155
J MacGrigor, Con	1,095
J Horne, LD	456
Lab majority	2,093

ADDITIONAL MEMBERS ELECTED BY PR
J MacGrigor, Con
M Scanlon, Con
M MacMillan, Lab
P Peacock, Lab
R Grant, Lab
W Ewing, SNP
D Hamilton, SNP

LOTHIANS

EDINBURGH CENTRAL
Electorate 65,945 Poll 56.73%

S Boyack, Lab	14,224
I McKee, SNP	9,598
A Myles, LD	6,187
J Low, Con	6,018
K Williamson, SSP	830
Others	555
Lab majority	4,626

EDINBURGH EAST AND MUSSELBURGH
Electorate 60,167 Poll 61.48%

S Deacon, Lab	17,086
K MacAskill, SNP	10,372
J Balfour, Con	4,600
M Thomas, LD	4,100
D White, SSP	697
Others	134
Lab majority	6,714

EDINBURGH NORTH AND LEITH
Electorate 62,976 Poll 58.19%

M Chisholm, Lab	17,203
A Dana, SNP	9,467
J Sempill, Con	5,030
S Tombs, LD	4,039
R Brown, SSP	907
Lab majority	7,736

EDINBURGH PENTLANDS
Electorate 60,029 Poll 65.97%

I Gray, Lab	14,343
D McLetchie, Con	11,458
S Gibb, SNP	8,770
I Gibson, LD	5,029
Lab majority	2,885

EDINBURGH SOUTH
Electorate 64,100 Poll 62.61%

A MacKay, Lab	14,869
M MacDonald, SNP	9,445
M Pringle, LD	8,961
I Whyte, Con	6,378
Others	482
Lab majority	5,424

EDINBURGH WEST
Electorate 61,747 Poll 67.34%

M Smith, LD	15,161
J Douglas-Hamilton, Con	10,578
C Fox, Lab	8,860
G Sutherland, SNP	6,984
LD majority	4,583

LINLITHGOW
Electorate 54,262 Poll 62.26%

M Mulligan, Lab	15,247
S Stevenson, SNP	12,319
G Lindhurst, Con	3,158
J Barrett, LD	2,643
Others	415
Lab majority	2,928

LIVINGSTON
Electorate 62,060 Poll 58.93%

B Muldoon, Lab	17,313
G McCarra, SNP	13,409
D Younger, Con	3,014
M Oliver, LD	2,834
Lab majority	3,904

MIDLOTHIAN
Electorate 48,374 Poll 61.51%

R Brankin, Lab Co-op	14,467
A Robertson, SNP	8,942
J Elder, LD	3,184
G Turnbull, Con	2,544
Others	618
Lab Co-op majority	5,525

ADDITIONAL MEMBERS ELECTED BY PR
J Douglas-Hamilton, Con
D McLetchie, Con
D Steel, LD
K MacAskill, SNP
M MacDonald, SNP
F Hyslop, SNP
R Harper, Green

MID SCOTLAND AND FIFE

DUNFERMLINE EAST
Electorate 52,087 Poll 56.94%

H Eadie, Lab Co-op	16,576
D McCarthy, SNP	7,877
C Ruxton, Con	2,931
F Lawson, LD	2,275
Lab Co-op majority	8,699

DUNFERMLINE WEST
Electorate 53,112 Poll 57.75%

S Barrie, Lab	13,560
D Chapman, SNP	8,539
E Harris, LD	5,591
J Mackie, Con	2,981
Lab majority	5,021

FIFE CENTRAL
Electorate 58,850 Poll 55.82%

H McLeish, Lab	18,828
T Marwick, SNP	10,153
JA Liston, LD	1,953
K Harding, Con	1,918
Lab majority	8,675

FIFE NORTH EAST
Electorate 60,886 Poll 59.03%

I Smith, LD	13,590
E Brocklebank, Con	8,526
C Welsh, SNP	6,373
C Milne, Lab	5,175
Others	2,277
LD majority	5,064

KIRKCALDY
Electorate 51,640 Poll 54.88%

M Livingstone, Lab Co-op	13,645
S Hosie, SNP	9,170
M Scott-Hayward, Con	2,907
J Mainland, LD	2,620
Lab Co-op majority	4,475

OCHIL
Electorate 57,083 Poll 64.58%

R Simpson, Lab	15,385
G Reid, SNP	14,082
N Johnston, Con	4,151
J Mar and Kellie, LD	3,249
Lab majority	1,303

PERTH
Electorate 61,034 Poll 61.27%

R Cunningham, SNP	13,570
I Stevenson, Con	11,543
J Richards, Lab	8,725
C Brodie, LD	3,558
SNP majority	2,027

STIRLING
Electorate 52,904 Poll 67.68%

S Jackson, Lab	13,533
A Ewing, SNP	9,552
B Monteith, Con	9,158
I Macfarlane, LD	3,407
Others	155
Lab majority	3,981

TAYSIDE NORTH
Electorate 61,795 Poll 61.58%

J Swinney, SNP	16,786
M Fraser, Con	12,594
M Dingwall, Lab	5,727
P Regent, LD	2,948
SNP majority	4,192

ADDITIONAL MEMBERS ELECTED BY PR
N Johnston, Con
B Monteith, Con
K Harding, Con
K Raffan, LD
B Crawford, SNP
G Reid, SNP
T Marwick, SNP

NORTH-EAST SCOTLAND

ABERDEEN CENTRAL
Electorate 52,715 Poll 50.26%

L Macdonald, Lab	10,305
R Lochhead, SNP	7,609
E Anderson, LD	4,403
T Mason, Con	3,655
A Cumbers, SSP	523
Lab majority	2,696

ABERDEEN NORTH
Electorate 54,553 Poll 51.00%

E Thomson, Lab	10,340
B Adam, SNP	9,942
J Donaldson, LD	4,767
I Haughie, Con	2,772
Lab majority	398

ABERDEEN SOUTH
Electorate 60,579 Poll 57.26%

N Stephen, LD	11,300
M Elrick, Lab	9,540
N Milne, Con	6,993
I McGugan, SNP	6,651
Others	206
LD majority	1,760

ABERDEENSHIRE WEST AND KINCARDINE
Electorate 60,702 Poll 58.87%

M Rumbles, LD	12,838
B Wallace, Con	10,549
M Watt, SNP	7,699
G Guthrie, Lab	4,650
LD majority	2,289

ANGUS
Electorate 59,891 Poll 57.66%

A Welsh, SNP	16,055
R Harris, Con	7,154
I McFatridge, Lab	6,914
D Speirs, LD	4,413
SNP majority	8,901

BANFF AND BUCHAN
Electorate 57,639 Poll 55.06%

A Salmond, SNP	16,695
D Davidson, Con	5,403
M Mackie, LD	5,315
M Harris, Lab	4,321
SNP majority	11,292

DUNDEE EAST
Electorate 57,222 Poll 55.33%

J McAllion, Lab	13,703
S Robison, SNP	10,849
I Mitchell, Con	4,428
R Lawrie, LD	2,153
H Duke, SSP	530
Lab majority	2,854

DUNDEE WEST
Electorate 55,725 Poll 52.19%

K MacLean, Lab	10,925
C Cashley, SNP	10,804
G Buchan, Con	3,345
E Dick, LD	2,998
J McFarlane, SSP	1,010
Lab majority	121

GORDON
Electorate 59,497 Poll 56.51%

N Radcliffe, LD	12,353
S Stronach, SNP	8,158
A Johnstone, Con	6,602
G Carlin-Kulwicki, Lab	3,950
Others	2,559
LD majority	4,195

ADDITIONAL MEMBERS ELECTED BY PR
D Davidson, Con
A Johnstone, Con

B Wallace, Con
R Lochhead, SNP
S Robison, SNP
B Adam, SNP
I McGugan, SNP

SOUTH SCOTLAND

AYR
Electorate 56,338 Poll 66.48%
I Welsh, Lab	14,263
P Gallie, Con	14,238
R Mullin, SNP	7,291
E Morris, LD	1,662
Lab majority	25

CARRICK, CUMNOCK AND DOON VALLEY
Electorate 65,580 Poll 62.66%
C Jamieson, Lab Co-op	19,667
A Ingram, SNP	10,864
J Scott, Con	8,123
D Hannay, LD	2,441
Lab Co-op majority	8,803

CLYDESDALE
Electorate 64,262 Poll 60.61%
K Turnbull, Lab	16,755
A Winning, SNP	12,875
C Cormack, Con	5,814
S Grieve, LD	3,503
Lab majority	3,880

CUNNINGHAME SOUTH
Electorate 50,443 Poll 56.06%
I Oldfather, Lab	14,936
M Russell, SNP	8,395
M Tosh, Con	3,229
S Ritchie, LD	1,717
Lab majority	6,541

DUMFRIES
Electorate 63,162 Poll 60.93%
E Murray, Lab	14,101
D Mundell, Con	10,447
S Norris, SNP	7,625
N Wallace, LD	6,309
Lab majority	3,654

EAST LOTHIAN
Electorate 58,579 Poll 60.74%
J Home Robertson, Lab	19,220

C Miller, SNP	8,274
C Richard, Con	5,941
J Hayman, LD	2,147
Lab majority	10,946

GALLOWAY AND UPPER NITHSDALE
Electorate 53,057 Poll 66.56%
A Morgan, SNP	13,873
A Fergusson, Con	10,672
J Stevens, Lab	7,209
J Mitchell, LD	3,562
SNP majority	3,201

ROXBURGH AND BERWICKSHIRE
Electorate 47,639 Poll 58.52%
E Robson, LD	11,320
A Hutton, Con	7,735
S Crawford, SNP	4,719
S McLeod, Lab	4,102
LD majority	3,585

TWEEDDALE, ETTRICK AND LAUDERDALE
Electorate 51,577 Poll 65.37%
I Jenkins, LD	12,078
C Creech, SNP	7,600
G McGregor, Lab	7,546
J Campbell, Con	6,491
LD majority	4,478

ADDITIONAL MEMBERS ELECTED BY PR
P Gallie, Con
D Mundell, Con
M Tosh, Con
A Fergusson, Con
M Russell, SNP
A Ingram, SNP
C Creech, SNP

WEST SCOTLAND

CLYDEBANK AND MILNGAVIE
Electorate 52,461 Poll 63.55%
D McNulty, Lab	15,105
J Yuill, SNP	10,395
R Ackland, LD	4,149
D Luckhurst, Con	3,688
Lab majority	4,710

CUNNINGHAME NORTH
Electorate 55,867 Poll 59.95%
A Wilson, Lab	14,369
K Ullrich, SNP	9,573

M Johnston, Con	6,649	
C Irving, LD	2,900	
Lab majority	4,796	

DUMBARTON
Electorate 56,090 Poll 61.86%

J Baillie, Lab	15,181
L Quinan, SNP	10,423
D Reece, Con	5,060
P Coleshill, LD	4,035
Lab majority	4,758

EASTWOOD
Electorate 67,248 Poll 67.51%

K Macintosh, Lab	16,970
J Young, Con	14,845
R Findlay, SNP	8,760
A McCurley, LD	4,472
Others	349
Lab majority	2,125

GREENOCK AND INVERCLYDE
Electorate 48,584 Poll 58.95%

D McNeil, Lab	11,817
R Finnie, LD	7,504
I Hamilton, SNP	6,762
R Wilkinson, Con	1,699
D Landels, SSP	857
Lab majority	4,313

PAISLEY NORTH
Electorate 49,020 Poll 56.61%

W Alexander, Lab	13,492
I Mackay, SNP	8,876
P Ramsay, Con	2,242
T Mayberry, LD	2,133
F Macdonald, SSP	1,007
Lab majority	4,616

PAISLEY SOUTH
Electorate 53,637 Poll 57.15%

H Henry, Lab	13,899
B Martin, SNP	9,404
S Callison, LD	2,974
S Laidlaw, Con	2,433
Others	1,946
Lab majority	4,495

RENFREWSHIRE WEST
Electorate 52,452 Poll 64.89%

P Godman, Lab	12,708
C Campbell, SNP	9,815
A Goldie, Con	7,243
N Ascherson, LD	2,659

Others	1,612
Lab majority	2,893

STRATHKELVIN AND BEARSDEN
Electorate 63,111 Poll 67.17%

S Galbraith, Lab	21,505
F McLeod, SNP	9,384
C Ferguson, Con	6,934
A Howarth, LD	4,144
Others	423
Lab majority	12,121

ADDITIONAL MEMBERS ELECTED BY PR

A Goldie, Con
J Young, Con
R Finnie, LD
L Quinan, SNP
F McLeod, SNP
K Ullrich, SNP
C Campbell, SNP

By-elections since 1999

AYR

J Scott, Con	12,580
J Mather, SNP	9,236
R Miller, Lab	7,054
J Stewart, SSP	1,345
S D Ritchie, Lib Dem	800
Others	885
Con majority	3,344

GLASGOW ANNIESLAND

W Butler, Lab	9,838
T Chalmers, SNP	4,462
K Pickering, Con	2,148
R Kane, SSP	1,429
J Fryer, Lib Dem	1,384
Others	960
Lab majority	5,376

BANFF AND BUCHAN

S Stevenson, SNP	15,386
T Brocklebank, Con	6,819
M Harris, Lab	4,597
Canon K Wright, LD	3,231
P Anderson, SSP	682
SNP majority	8,567

STRATHKELVIN AND BEARSDEN

B Fitzpatrick, Lab	15,401
J M Turner, Ind	7,275
J Morrison, LD	7,147
J E Law, SNP	6,457
C Ferguson, Con	5,037
Lab majority	8,126

Members of The Scottish Parliament

Address: The Scottish Parliament, Edinburgh EH99 1SP
Telephone (Switchboard): 0131-348 5000
Telephone (General Enquiries): 0845 278 1999
web: www.scottish.parliament.uk/

Name	Party	Constituency
denotes Additional Member elected by PR		
*Adam, Brian	SNP	North East Scotland
*Aitken, Bill	Con	Glasgow
Alexander, Wendy	Lab	Paisley North
Baillie, Jackie	Lab	Dumbarton
Barrie, Scott	Lab	Dunfermline West
Boyack, Sarah	Lab	Edinburgh Central
Brankin, Rhona	Lab	Midlothian
*Brown, Robert	LD	Glasgow
Butler, Bill	Lab	Glasgow Anniesland
*Campbell, Colin	SNP	West of Scotland
Canavan, Dennis	Ind	Falkirk West
Chisholm, Malcolm	Lab	Edinburgh North & Leith
Craigie, Cathie	Lab	Cumbernauld & Kilsyth
*Crawford, Bruce	SNP	Mid Scotland & Fife
Cunningham, Roseanna	SNP	Perth
Curran, Margaret	Lab	Glasgow Baillieston
*Davidson, David	Con	North East Scotland
Deacon, Susan	Lab	Edinburgh East & Musselburgh
*Douglas-Hamilton, Lord James	Con	Lothians
Eadie, Helen	Lab	Dunfermline East
*Elder, Dorothy-Grace	SNP	Glasgow
Ewing, Fergus	SNP	Inverness East, Nairn & Lochaber
Ewing, Margaret	SNP	Moray
*Ewing, Dr Winnie	SNP	Highlands and Islands
*Fabiani, Linda	SNP	Central Scotland
Ferguson, Patricia	Lab	Glasgow Maryhill
*Fergusson, Alex	Con	South of Scotland
*Finnie, Ross	LD	West of Scotland
Fitzpatrick, Brian	Lab	Strathkelvin & Bearsden
*Fraser, Murdo	Con	Mid-Scotland & Fife
*Gallie, Phil	Con	South of Scotland
*Gibson, Kenneth	SNP	Glasgow
Gillon, Karen	Lab	Clydesdale
Godman, Trish	Lab	West Renfrewshire
*Goldie, Annabel	Con	West of Scotland

*Gorrie, Donald, OBE	LD	Central Scotland
*Grahame, Christine	SNP	South of Scotland
*Grant, Rhoda	Lab	Highlands & Islands
Gray, Iain	Lab	Edinburgh Pentlands
*Hamilton, Duncan	SNP	Highlands and Islands
*Harding, Keith	Con	Mid Scotland & Fife
*Harper, Robin	Green	Lothians
Henry, Hugh	Lab	Paisley South
Home Robertson, John	Lab	East Lothian
Hughes, Janis	Lab	Glasgow Rutherglen
*Hyslop, Fiona	SNP	Lothians
*Ingram, Adam	SNP	South of Scotland
Jackson, Gordon, QC	Lab	Glasgow Govan
Jackson, Dr Sylvia	Lab	Stirling
Jamieson, Cathy	Lab	Carrick, Cumnock & Doon Valley
Jamieson, Margaret	Lab	Kilmarnock & Loudoun
Jenkins, Ian	LD	Tweeddale, Ettrick & Lauderdale
*Johnstone, Alex	Con	North East Scotland
Kerr, Andy	Lab	East Kilbride
Lamont, Johann	Lab	Glasgow Pollok
Livingstone, Marilyn	Lab	Kirkcaldy
*Lochhead, Richard	SNP	North East Scotland
Lyon, George	LD	Argyll and Bute
McAllion, John	Lab	Dundee East
*MacAskill, Kenny	SNP	Lothians
McAveety, Frank	Lab	Glasgow Shettleston
McCabe, Tom	Lab	Hamilton South
McConnell, Jack	Lab	Motherwell & Wishaw
Macdonald, Lewis	Lab	Aberdeen Central
*MacDonald, Margo	SNP	Lothians
*McGrigor, Jamie	Con	Highlands & Islands
*McGugan, Irene	SNP	North East Scotland
Macintosh, Kenneth	Lab	Eastwood
*McIntosh, Lyndsay	Con	Central Scotland
MacKay, Angus	Lab	Edinburgh South
MacLean, Kate	Lab	Dundee West
McLeish, Henry	Lab	Central Fife
*McLeod, Fiona	SNP	West of Scotland
*McLetchie, David	Con	Lothians
McMahon, Michael	Lab	Hamilton North & Bellshill
*Macmillan, Maureen	Lab	Highlands & Islands
McNeil, Duncan	Lab	Greenock & Inverclyde
McNeill, Pauline	Lab	Glasgow Kelvin
McNulty, Des	Lab	Clydebank & Milngavie
Martin, Paul	Lab	Glasgow Springburn
*Marwick, Tricia	SNP	Mid Scotland & Fife
*Matheson, Michael	SNP	Central Scotland

*Monteith, Brian	Con	Mid Scotland & Fife
Morgan, Alasdair	SNP	Galloway & Upper Nithsdale
Morrison, Alasdair	Lab	Western Isles
Muldoon, Bristow	Lab	Livingston
Mulligan, Mary	Lab	Linlithgow
*Mundell, David	Con	South of Scotland
Munro, John Farquhar	LD	Ross, Skye & Inverness West
Murray, Dr Elaine	Lab	Dumfries
*Neil, Alex	SNP	Central Scotland
Oldfather, Irene	Lab	Cunninghame South
*Paterson, Gil	SNP	Central Scotland
*Peacock, Peter	Lab	Highlands & Islands
Peattie, Cathy	Lab	Falkirk East
*Quinan, Lloyd	SNP	West of Scotland
Radcliffe, Nora	LD	Gordon
*Raffan, Keith	LD	Mid Scotland & Fife
*Reid, George	SNP	Mid Scotland & Fife
*Robison, Shona	SNP	North East Scotland
Robson, Euan	LD	Roxburgh & Berwickshire
Rumbles, Mike	LD	West Aberdeenshire & Kincardine
*Russell, Michael	SNP	South of Scotland
*Scanlon, Mary	Con	Highland & Islands
Scott, John	Con	Ayr
Scott, Tavish	LD	Shetland
*Sheridan, Tommy	SSP	Glasgow
Simpson, Dr Richard	Lab	Ochil
Smith, Elaine	Lab	Coatbridge & Chryston
Smith, Iain	LD	North East Fife
Smith, Margaret	LD	Edinburgh West
*Steel, Rt Hon Sir David	LD	Lothians
Stephen, Nicol	LD	Aberdeen South
Stevenson, Stewart	SNP	Banff & Buchan
Stone, Jamie	LD	Caithness, Sutherland & Easter Ross
*Sturgeon, Nicola	SNP	Glasgow
Swinney, John	SNP	North Tayside
Thomson, Elaine	Lab	Aberdeen North
*Tosh, Murray	Con	South of Scotland
*Ullrich, Kay	SNP	West of Scotland
*Wallace, Ben	Con	North East Scotland
Wallace, Jim, QC	LD	Orkney
Watson, Mike	Lab	Glasgow Cathcart
Welsh, Andrew	SNP	Angus
*White, Sandra	SNP	Glasgow
Whitefield, Karen	Lab	Airdrie & Shotts
Wilson, Allan	Lab	Cunninghame North
*Wilson, Andrew	SNP	Central Scotland
*Young, John, OBE	Con	West of Scotland

Parliamentary Committees

Audit
Convener: Andrew Welsh (Scottish National Party)
Deputy Convener: David Davidson (Conservative); *Members:* Scott Barrie, Margaret Jamieson, Paul Martin, Lloyd Quinan, Keith Raffan
Remit – to consider and report on: any accounts laid before the Parliament; any report laid before the Parliament by the Auditor General for Scotland; any other documents laid before the Parliament concerning financial control, accounting and auditing in relation to public expenditure.

Education, Culture and Sport
Convener: Karen Gillon (Labour)
Members: Jackie Baillie, Ian Jenkins, Frank McAveety, Irene McGugan, Brian Monteith, Michael Russell
Remit – to consider and report on: matters relating to school and pre-school education which fall within the responsibility of the Minister for Education, Europe and External Affairs; and on matters relating to the arts, culture and sport which fall within the responsibility of the Minister for Environment, Sport and Culture.

Enterprise and Lifelong Learning
Convener: Alex Neil (Scottish National Party)
Deputy Convener: Annabel Goldie (Conservative); *Members:* Rhona Brankin, Brian Fitzpatrick, Duncan Hamilton, Marilyn Livingstone, Kenny MacAskill, Kenneth Macintosh, David Mundell, Tavish Scott, Elaine Thomson
Remit – to consider and report on: matters relating to the Scottish economy, industry, tourism, training and further and higher education and other matters within the remit of the Minister for Enterprise and Lifelong Learning. This remit relies upon a definition of the responsibility of the Minister for Enterprise and Lifelong Learning. At present this is understood to be: the economy, business and industry, including tourism, trade and inward investment, further and higher education, the science base, lifelong learning, training and the New Deal, and co-ordination of Executive policy in relation to the Highlands and Islands and Gaelic.

Equal Opportunities
Convener: Kate MacLean (Labour)
Deputy Convener: Kay Ullrich (Scottish National Party); *Members:* Lyndsay McIntosh, Michael McMahon, Gil Paterson, Cathy Peattie, Tommy Sheridan, Elaine Smith, Jamie Stone
Remit – to consider and report on matters relating to equal opportunities and upon the observance of equal opportunities within the Parliament.

"Equal opportunities" includes the prevention, elimination or regulation of discrimination between persons on grounds of sex or marital status, on racial grounds, or on grounds of disability, age, sexual orientation, language or social origin, or of other personal attributes, including beliefs or opinions, such as religious beliefs or political opinions.

European
Convener: Irene Oldfather (Labour)
Deputy Convener: John Home Robertson (Labour); *Members:* Sarah Boyack, Colin Campbell, Dennis Canavan, Helen Eadie, Lloyd Quinan, Nora Radcliffe, Ben Wallace
Remit – to consider and report on: proposals for European Communities legislation; the implementation of European Communities legislation; any European Communities or European Union issue.

Finance
Convener: Des McNulty (Labour)
Deputy Convener: Elaine Thomson (Labour); *Members:* Brian Adam, David Davidson, Donald Gorrie, Tom McCabe, Alasdair Morgan
Remit – to consider and report on: any report or other document laid before the Parliament by members of the Scottish Executive containing proposals for, or budgets of, public expenditure or proposals for the making of a tax-varying resolution, taking into account any report or recommendations concerning such documents made to them by any other committee with power to consider such documents or any part of them; any report made by a committee setting out proposals concerning public expenditure; Budget Bills; any other matter relating to or affecting the expenditure of the Scottish Administration or other expenditure payable out of the Scottish Consolidated Fund. The Committee may also consider and, where it sees fit, report to the Parliament on the timetable for the Stages of Budget Bills and on the handling of financial business. "Public expenditure" means expenditure of the Scottish Administration, other expenditure payable out of the Scottish Consolidated Fund and any other expenditure met out of taxes, charges and other public revenue.

Health and Community Care
Convener: Margaret Smith (Liberal Democrat)
Deputy Convener: Margaret Jamieson (Labour); *Members:* Bill Butler, Dorothy-Grace Elder, Janis Hughes, John McAllion, Shona Robison, Mary Scanlon, Nicola Sturgeon
Remit – to consider and report on issues relating to the health policy and the National Health Service in Scotland and such other matters as fall within the responsibility of the Minister for Health and Community Care.

Justice 1
Convener: Christine Grahame (Scottish National Party)

Deputy Convener: Gordon Jackson (Labour); *Members*: Lord James Douglas-Hamilton, Donald Gorrie, Maureen Macmillan, Paul Martin, Michael Matheson
Remit – to consider and report on matters relating to the administration of civil and criminal justice, the reform of the civil and criminal law and such other matters as fall within the responsibility of the Minister for Justice.

Justice 2
Convener: Pauline McNeill (Labour)
Deputy Convener: Bill Aitken (Conservative); *Members:* Scott Barrie, Margaret Ewing, George Lyon, Alasdair Morrison, Stewart Stevenson
Remit – same as Justice 1

Local Government
Convener: Trish Godman (Labour)
Deputy Convener: Dr Sylvia Jackson (Labour); *Members*: Keith Harding, Michael McMahon, Tricia Marwick, Iain Smith, Sandra White
Remit – to consider and report on matters relating to local government and which fall within the responsibility of the Minister for Finance and Local Government.

Procedures
Convener: Murray Tosh (Conservative)
Deputy Convener: Kenneth Macintosh (Labour); *Members*: Susan Deacon, Donald Gorrie, Fiona Hyslop, Frank McAveety, Gil Paterson
Remit – to consider and report on the practice and procedures of the Parliament in relation to its business.

Public Petitions
Convener: John McAllion (Labour)
Deputy Convener: Helen Eadie (Labour); *Members*: Dorothy Grace-Elder, Dr Winnie Ewing, Phil Gallie, Rhoda Grant, John Farquhar Munro
Remit – to consider and report on: whether a public petition is admissible; and what action is to be taken upon the petition.

Rural Development
Convener: Alex Fergusson (Conservative)
Deputy Convener: Fergus Ewing (Scottish National Party); *Members*: Rhoda Grant, Richard Lochhead, Jamie McGrigor, Alasdair Morrison, John Farquhar Munro, Irene Oldfather, Mike Rumbles, Elaine Smith, Stewart Stevenson
Remit – to consider and report on matters relating to rural development, agriculture and fisheries and such other related matters as fall within the responsibility of the Minister for Rural Development.

Social Justice
Convener: Johann Lamont (Labour)

Deputy Convener: Kenneth Gibson (Scottish National Party); *Members*: Robert Brown, Cathie Craigie, Linda Fabiani, Lyndsay McIntosh, Karen Whitefield
Remit – to consider and report on matters relating to housing and the voluntary sector and such other related matters as fall within the responsibility of the Minister for Social Justice.

Standards
Convener: Mike Rumbles (Liberal Democrat)
Deputy Convener: Tricia Marwick (Scottish National Party); *Members*: Susan Deacon, Lord James Douglas-Hamilton, Frank McAveety, Kenneth Macintosh, Kay Ullrich
Remit – to consider and report on: whether a member's conduct is in accordance with the Standing Orders and any Code of Conduct for members, matters relating to member's interests, and any other matters relating to the conduct of members in carrying out their Parliamentary duties; the adoption, amendment and application of any Code of Conduct for members. Where the Committee considers it appropriate, it may by any motion recommend that a member's rights and privileges be withdrawn to such extent and for such period as are specified in the motion.

Subordinate Legislation
Convener: Margo MacDonald (Scottish National Party)
Deputy Convener: Ian Jenkins (Liberal Democrat); *Members*: Bill Butler, Colin Campbell, Murdo Fraser, Gordon Jackson, Bristow Muldoon
Remit – to consider and report on: a) (i) subordinate legislation which is laid before the Parliament; (ii) any Scottish Statutory Instrument not laid before the Parliament but classified as general according to its subject matter; and, in particular, to determine whether the attention of the Parliament should be drawn to any of the matters mentioned in Rule 10.3.1; b) proposed powers to make subordinate legislation in particular Bills or other proposed legislation; c) general questions relating to powers to make subordinate legislation; d) whether any proposed delegated powers in particular Bills or other legislation should be expressed as a power to make subordinate legislation.

Transport and Environment
Convener: Bristow Muldoon (Labour)
Deputy Convener: Nora Radcliffe (Liberal Democrat); *Members*: Robin Harper, Adam Ingram, Angus Mackay, Fiona McLeod, Maureen Macmillan, Des McNulty, John Scott
Remit – to consider and report on: matters relating to transport which fall within the responsibility of the Minister for Transport; matters relating to environment and natural heritage which fall within the responsibility of the Minister for Environment, Sport and Culture.

Profile of Local Authorities

Aberdeen City Council
Population: 217,200
Electorate: 169,203
Election 1995: poll 38.0%; Con 9; Lab 30; LD, 10; SNP 1
Election 1999: poll 52.6%; Con 6; Lab 22; LD 12; SNP 3
Referendum 1997: poll 53.0%; for parliament 71.8%; for tax power 60.3%
Council Tax (Band D): £934
Chief Executive: D Paterson
Lord Provost: Ms M Smith

Aberdeenshire Council
Population: 228,000
Electorate: 173,574
Election 1995: poll 39.7%; Con 4; Lab 0; LD 15; SNP 15; Ind 13
Election 1999: poll 57.3%; Con 7; Lab 0; LD 28; SNP 23; Ind 10
Referendum 1997: poll 57.0%; for parliament 63.9%; for tax power 52.3%
Council Tax (Band D): £855
Chief Executive: A G Campbell
Convenor: R Bisset, OBE

Angus Council
Population: 110,200
Electorate: 87,153
Election 1995: poll 43.7%; Con 2; Lab 0; LD 2; SNP 21; Ind 1
Election 1999: poll 56.7%; Con 2; Lab 1; LD 2; SNP 21; Ind 2
Referendum 1997: poll 60.2%; for parliament 64.7%; for tax power 53.4%
Council Tax (Band D): £821
Chief Executive: A B Watson
Provost: Mrs F M Duncan, OBE

Argyll and Bute Council
Population: 88,790
Electorate: 70,000
Election 1995: poll 51.2%; Con 3; Lab 2; LD 3; SNP 4; Ind 21
Election 1999: poll 63.1%; Con 3; Lab 1; LD 6; SNP 5; Ind 21
Referendum 1997: poll 65.0%; for parliament 67.3%; for tax power 57.0%
Council Tax (Band D): £984
Chief Executive: J A McLellan
Convenor: W Petrie

Clackmannanshire Council
Population: 48,500
Electorate: 36,870

Election 1995: poll 46.9%; Con 1; Lab 8; LD 0; SNP 3; Ind 0
Election 1999: poll 63.3%; Con 1; Lab 8; LD 0; SNP 9; Ind 0
Referendum 1997: poll 66.1%; for parliament 80.0%; for tax power 68.7%
Council Tax (Band D): £951
Chief Executive: K Bloomer
Provost: W McAdam

Dumfries and Galloway Council
Population: 148,000
Electorate: 117,430
Election 1995: poll 50.2%; Con 2; Lab 21; LD 10; SNP 9; Ind 28
Election 1999: poll 62.4%; Con 8; Lab 13; LD 6; SNP 5; Ind 14; Others 1
Referendum 1997: poll 63.4%; for parliament 60.7%; for tax power 48.8%
Council Tax (Band D): £857
Chief Executive: P N Jones
Provost: A Campbell, OBE

Dundee City Council
Population: 146,690
Electorate: 115,546
Election 1995: poll 43.8%; Con 4; Lab 28; SNP 3; Others 1
Election 1999: poll 53.7%; Con 0; Lab 14; SNP 10; Ind Lab 1
Referendum 1997: poll 55.7%; for parliament 76.0%; for tax power: 65.5%
Council Tax (Band D): £1,046
Chief Executive: A Stephen
Provost: John Letford

East Ayrshire Council
Population: 124,000
Electorate: 94,309
Election 1995: poll 53.2%; Con 0; Lab 22; LD 0; SNP 8
Election 1999: poll 62.8%; Con 1; Lab 17; LD 0; SNP 14
Referendum 1997: poll 64.8%; for parliament 81.1%; for tax power 70.5%
Council Tax (Band D): £828
Chief Executive: D Montgomery
Provost: J Boyd

East Dunbartonshire Council
Population: 110,000
Electorate: 85,388
Election 1995: poll 52.8%; Con 2; Lab 15; LD9; SNP 0
Election 1999: poll 67.1%; Con 3; Lab 11; LD 10; SNP 0; Ind 0
Referendum 1997: poll 62.7%; for parliament 69.8%; for tax power 59.1%
Council Tax (Band D): £872
Chief Executive: Dr V Nash
Provost: R McSkimming

East Lothian Council
Population: 85,600
Electorate: 71,103
Election 1995: Poll 48.4%; Con 3; Lab 15; LD 0; SNP 0
Election 1999: Poll 63.2%; Con 5; Lab 17; LD 0; SNP 1
Referendum 1997: Poll 65.0%; for parliament 74.2%; for tax power 62.7%
Council Tax (Band D):£909
Chief Executive: J Lindsay
Provost: J O'Brien

East Renfrewshire Council
Population: 89,280
Electorate: 68,122
Election 1995: Poll 49.2%; Con 9; Lab 8; LD 2; SNP 0; Others 1
Election 1999: Poll 67.8%; Con 8; Lab 9; LD 2; SNP 0; Others 1
Referendum 1997: Poll 68.2%; for parliament 61.7%; for tax power 51.6%
Council Tax (Band D): £859
Chief Executive: P Daniels
Provost: A Steele

City of Edinburgh Council
Population: 449,000
Electorate: 366,088
Election 1995: poll 44.5%; Con 14; Lab 33; LD 10; SNP 1
Election 1999: poll 61.0%; Con 13; Lab 31; LD 13; SNP 1
Referendum 1997: poll 60.1%; for parliament 71.9%; for tax power 62.0%
Council Tax (Band D): £960
Chief Executive: T N Aitchison
Lord Provost: Eric Milligan

Falkirk Council
Population: 144,688
Electorate: 112,129
Election 1995: poll 45.8%; Con 2; Lab 23; LD 0; SNP 8; Ind 3
Election 1999: poll 61.2%; Con 2; Lab 15; LD 0; SNP 9; Ind 6
Referendum 1997: poll 63.7%; for parliament 80.0%; for tax power 69.2%
Council Tax (Band D): £813
Chief Executive: Mrs M Pitcaithly
Provost: J Johnson

Fife Council
Population: 352,000
Electorate: 279,808
Election 1995: poll: 42.6%; Con 0; Lab 54; LD 25; SNP 9; Ind 3; Others 1
Election 1999: poll: 56.1%; Con 1; Lab 43; LD 21; SNP 9; Ind 2; Others 2
Referendum 1997: poll: 60.7%; for parliament 76.1%; for tax power 64.7%

Council Tax (Band D): £891
Chief Executive: D Sinclair
Convenor: J MacDougall

Glasgow City Council
Population: 611,500
Electorate: 493,033
Election 1995: poll 38.9%; Con 3; Lab 77; LD 1; SNP 1; Others 1
Election 1999: poll 47.0%; Con 1; Lab 74; LD 1; SNP 2; Others 1
Referendum 1997: poll 51.6%; for parliament 83.6%; for tax power 75.0%
Council Tax (Band D): £1,120
Chief Executive: J Andrews
Lord Provost: A Mosson

Highland Council
Population: 208,700
Electorate: 165,333
Election 1995: poll 46.4%; Con 1; Lab 7; LD 6; SNP 9; Ind 49
Election 1999: poll 62.4%; Con 0; Lab 10; LD 12; SNP 8; Ind 50
Referendum 1997: poll 60.3%; for parliament 72.6%; for tax power 62.1%
Council Tax (Band D): £889
Chief Executive: A D McCourt
Provost: D Green

Inverclyde Council
Population: 85,000
Electorate: 67,110
Election 1995: poll 47.0%; Con 1; Lab 14; LD 5; SNP 0
Election 1999: poll 58.6%; Con 1; Lab 11; LD 8; SNP 0
Referendum 1997: poll 60.4%; for parliament 78.0%; for tax power 67.2%
Council Tax (Band D): £894
Chief Executive: R Cleary
Provost: R Jackson

Midlothian Council
Population: 81,680
Electorate: 62,443
Election 1995: poll 44.9%; Con 0; Lab 13; LD 0; SNP 2
Election 1999: poll 62.0%; Con 0; Lab 17; LD 1; SNP 0
Referendum 1997: poll 65.1%; for parliament 79.9%; for tax power 67.7%
Council Tax (Band D): £1,001
Chief Executive: T Muir
Provost: S Campbell

Moray Council
Population: 86,000
Electorate: 65,352

Election 1995: poll 40.1%; Con 0; Lab 3; LD 0; SNP 13; Ind 2
Election 1999: poll 56%; Con 1; Lab 6; LD 2; SNP 2; Ind/Non Aligned 15
Referendum 1997: poll 57.8%; for parliament 67.2%; for tax power 52.7%
Council Tax (Band D): £825
Chief Executive: A Keddie
Convenor: E Aldridge

North Ayrshire Council
Population: 140,000
Electorate: 107,630
Election 1995: poll: 49.4%; Con 1; Lab 27; LD 0; SNP 1; Ind 1
Election 1999: poll 58.5%; Con 2; Lab 25; LD 0; SNP 2; Ind 1
Referendum 1997: poll 63.4%; for parliament 76.3%; for tax power 65.7%
Council Tax (Band D): £877
Chief Executive: B Devine
Convenor: S Taylor

North Lanarkshire Council
Population: 327,000
Electorate: 228,905
Election 1995: poll 48.1%; Con 0; Lab 60; LD 0; SNP 7; Ind 2
Election 1999: poll 57.3%; Con 0; Lab 56; LD 0; SNP 12; Ind 2
Referendum 1997: poll 60.8%; for parliament 82.6%; for tax power 72.2%
Council Tax (Band D): £844
Chief Executive: G Whitefield
Provost: B McCulloch

Orkney Islands Council
Population: 19,817
Electorate 15,468
No election in 1995; Con 0; Lab 0; LD 0; SNP 0; Ind 28
Election 1999: poll 59.6%; Con 0; Lab 0; LD 0; SNP 0; Ind 21
Referendum 1997: poll 53.4%; for parliament 57.3%; for tax power 47.4%
Council Tax (Band D): £754
Chief Executive: A Buchan
Convenor: A Halcro-Johnston

Perth and Kinross Council
Population: 134,000
Electorate: 105,653
Election 1995: poll 51.3%; Con 2; Lab 6; LD 5; SNP 18; Ind 1
Election 1999: poll 63.3%; Con 11; Lab 6; LD 6; SNP 16; Ind 2
Referendum 1997: poll 63.1%; for parliament 61.7%; for tax power 51.3%
Council Tax (Band D): £875
Chief Executive: H Robertson
Provost: M O'Malley

Renfrewshire Council
Population: 177,000
Electorate: 139,095
Election 1995: poll 47.4%; Con 2; Lab 22; LD 3; SNP 13
Election 1999: poll 58.7%; Con 1; Lab 22; LD 3; SNP 14
Referendum 1997: poll 62.8%; for parliament 79.0%; for tax power 63.6%
Council Tax (Band D): £896
Chief Executive: T Scholes
Provost: J McDowell

Scottish Borders Council
Population: 106,400
Electorate: 86,726
Election 1995: poll 40.3%; Con 3; Lab 2; LD 15; SNP 8; Ind 30
Election 1999: poll 60.6%; Con 1; Lab 1; LD 14; SNP 4; Ind 12
Referendum 1997: poll 64.8%; for parliament 62.8%; for tax power 50.7%
Council Tax (Band D): £785
Chief Executive: A M Croall
Convenor: A L Tulley

Shetland Islands Council
Population: 23,000
Electorate: 17,149
No election in 1995; Con 0; Lab 2; LD 2; SNP 0; Ind 15; Others 7
Election 1999: poll 62.1%; Con 0; Lab 0; LD 8; SNP 0; Ind 14
Referendum 1997: poll 51.5%; for parliament 62.4%; for tax power 51.6%
Council Tax (Band D): £747
Chief Executive: M Goodlad
Convenor: T Stove

South Ayrshire Council
Population: 114,440
Electorate: 91,349
Election 1995: poll 55.5%; Con 4; Lab 21; LD 0; SNP 0
Election 1999: poll 65.4%; Con 13; Lab 17; LD 0; SNP 0
Referendum 1997: poll 66.7%; for parliament 66.9%; for tax power 56.2%
Council Tax (Band D): £1,140
Chief Executive: G W F Thorley
Provost: Mrs E Foulkes

South Lanarkshire Council
Population: 301,000
Electorate: 237,934
Election 1995: poll 46.8%; Con 2; Lab 62; LD 2; SNP 8
Election 1999: poll 59.2%; Con 2; Lab 54; LD 1; SNP 10
Referendum 1997: poll 63.1%; for parliament 77.8%; for tax power 67.6%

Council Tax (Band D): £924
Chief Executive: M Docherty
Provost: A Dick

Stirling Council
Population: 85,200
Electorate: 66,068
Election 1995: poll 54.2%;Con 7; Lab 13; LD 0; SNP 2
Election 1999: poll 65.9%; Con 9; Lab 11; LD 0; SNP 2
Referendum 1997: poll 65.8%; for parliament 68.5%; for tax power 58.9%
Council Tax (Band D): £954
Chief Executive: K Yates
Provost: T Brookes

West Dunbartonshire Council
Population: 93,977
Electorate: 72,554
Election 1995: Poll: 49.7% Con 0; Lab 14; LD 0; SNP 7; Ind 1
Election 1999: Poll 59.8%; Con 0; Lab 14; LD 0; SNP 7; Ind 1
Referendum 1997: poll 63.7%; for parliament 84.7%; for tax power 74.7%
Council Tax (Band D): £1,024
Chief Executive: T Huntingford
Provost: A Macdonald

West Lothian Council
Population: 152,000
Electorate: 117,491
Election 1995: poll 46.7%; Con 1; Lab 15; LD 0; SNP 11
Election 1999: poll 59.9%; Con 1; Lab 20; LD 0; SNP 11
Referendum 1997: poll 62.6%; for parliament 79.6%; for tax power 67.3%
Council Tax (Band D): £919
Chief Executive: A M Linkston
Provost: J Thomas

Western Isles Council
Population: 27,560
Electorate: 22,626
No election in 1995; Con 0; Lab 5; LD 0; SNP 0; Ind 25
Election 1999: poll 64.2%; Con 0; Lab 6; LD 0; SNP 3; Ind 21
Referendum 1997: poll 55.8%; for parliament 79.4%; for tax power 68.4%
Council Tax (Band D): £765
Chief Executive: W Howat
Convenor: A A Macdonald

The UK Government

The Cabinet

Prime Minister, First Lord of the Treasury and Minister for the Civil Service
Rt Hon Tony Blair

Deputy Prime Minister and First Secretary of State
Rt Hon John Prescott

Chancellor of the Exchequer
Rt Hon Gordon Brown

President of the Council and Leader of the House of Commons
Rt Hon Robin Cook

Lord Chancellor
Rt Hon Lord Irvine of Lairg, QC

Secretary of State for Foreign and Commonwealth Affairs
Rt Hon Jack Straw

Secretary of State for the Home Department
Rt Hon David Blunkett

Secretary of State for Environment, Food and Rural Affairs
Rt Hon Margaret Beckett

Secretary of State for International Development
Rt Hon Clare Short

Secretary of State for Work and Pensions
Rt Hon Alistair Darling

Secretary of State for Transport, Local Government and the Regions
Rt Hon Stephen Byers

Secretary of State for Health
Rt Hon Alan Milburn

Secretary of State for Northern Ireland
Rt Hon Dr John Reid

Secretary of State for Wales
Rt Hon Paul Murphy

Secretary of State for Defence
Rt Hon Geoff Hoon

Chief Secretary to the Treasury
Rt Hon Andrew Smith

Secretary of State for Scotland
Rt Hon Helen Liddell

Lord Privy Seal and Leader of the House of Lords
Rt Hon Lord Williams of Mostyn, QC

Secretary of State for Trade and Industry
Rt Hon Patricia Hewitt

Secretary of State for Education and Skills
Rt Hon Estelle Morris

Secretary of State for Culture, Media and Sport
Rt Hon Tessa Jowell

Chief Whip
Rt Hon Hilary Armstrong

Minister Without Portfolio and Party Chair
Rt Hon Charles Clarke

The Scotland Office

London
Address: Dover House, Whitehall, London SW1A 2AU
Telephone: 020 7270 6754

Edinburgh
Address: 1 Melville Crescent, Edinburgh EH3 7HW
Telephone: 0131 244 9010

Glasgow
Address: 1st Floor, Meridian Court, Cadogan Street, Glasgow G2 6AT
Telephone: 0141-242 5958

Ministers
Secretary of State for Scotland: Helen Liddell, MP
Minister of State, Scotland Office: George Foulkes, MP
Advocate General: Dr Lynda Clark, QC, MP
Official Spokesperson, House of Lords: Lord McIntosh of Haringey

The role of the Secretary of State is to:
Represent Scottish interests within the UK government in matters that are reserved to the UK Parliament under the terms of the Scotland Act 1998;
Promote the devolution settlement by encouraging co-operation between Edinburgh and London (between both the Parliaments and the UK Government and Scottish Executive), or otherwise intervene as required by the Scotland Act;
Pay grant to the Scottish Consolidated Fund and manage other financial transactions;
Exercise certain residual functions in reserved matters (for example, the conduct and funding of elections and the making of private legislation at Westminster).
Reserved matters include: The constitution; foreign affairs; defence; international development; the civil service; financial and economic matters; national security; immigration and nationality; misuse of drugs; trade and industry; various aspects of energy regulation (e.g. electricity, coal, oil and gas, nuclear energy); various aspects of transport (e.g. regulation of air services, rail and international shipping; social security; employment; abortion, genetics, surrogacy, medicines; broadcasting; equal opportunities.

The UK Parliamentary Constituencies

June 2001
* denotes member of the previous parliament

ABERDEEN CENTRAL
Electorate 50,098 Poll 52.75%

*F Doran, Lab	12,025
W Gault, SNP	5,379
Ms E Anderson, LD	4,547
S Whyte, Con	3,761
Others	717
Lab majority	6,646

ABERDEEN NORTH
Electorate 52,746 Poll 57.55%

*M Savidge, Lab	13,157
Dr A Allan, SNP	8,708
J Donaldson, LD	4,991
R Cowling, Con	3,047
Others	454
Lab majority	4,449

ABERDEEN SOUTH
Electorate 58,907 Poll 62.62%

*Ms A Begg, Lab	14,696
I Yuill, LD	10,308
M Macdonald, Con	7,098
I Angus, SNP	4,293
Others	495
Lab majority	4,388

ABERDEENSHIRE WEST AND KINCARDINE
Electorate 61,180 Poll 61.97%

*Sir R Smith, LD	16,507
T Kerr, Con	11,686
K Hutchens, Lab	4,669
J Green, SNP	4,634
Others	418
LD majority	4,821

AIRDRIE AND SHOTTS
Electorate 58,349 Poll 54.39%

*Rt Hon Ms H Liddell, Lab	18,478
Ms A Lindsay, SNP	6,138
J Love, LD	2,376
G McIntosh, Con	1,960
Others	2,784
Lab majority	12,340

ANGUS
Electorate 59,004 Poll 59.34%

M Weir, SNP	12,347
M Booth, Con	8,736
I McFatridge, Lab	8,183

P Nield, LD	5,015
Others	732
SNP majority	3,611

ARGYLL AND BUTE
Electorate 49,175 Poll 62.95%

A Reid, LD	9,245
H Raven, Lab	7,592
D Petrie, Con	6,436
Ms A Samuel, SNP	6,433
Others	1,251
LD majority	1,653

AYR
Electorate 55,630 Poll 69.32%

*Mrs S Osborne, Lab	16,801
P Gallie, Con	14,256
J Mather, SNP	4,621
S Ritchie, LD	2,089
Others	793
Lab majority	2,545

BANFF AND BUCHAN
Electorate 56,496 Poll 54.53%

*A Salmond, SNP	16,710
A Wallace, Con	6,207
E Harris, Lab	4,363
D Herbison, LD	2,769
Others	757
SNP majority	10,503

CAITHNESS, SUTHERLAND AND EASTER ROSS
Electorate 41,225 Poll 60.32%

Viscount J Thurso, LD	9,041
M Meighan, Lab	6,297
J Macadam, SNP	5,273
R Rowantree, Con	3,513
Others	743
LD majority	2,744

CARRICK, CUMNOCK AND DOON VALLEY
Electorate 64,919 Poll 61.78%

*G Foulkes, Lab Co-op	22,174
G Miller, Con	7,318
T Wilson, SNP	6,258
Ms A Rogers, LD	2,932
Others	1,425
Lab Co-op majority	14,856

CLYDEBANK AND MILNGAVIE
Electorate 52,534 Poll 61.85%

*A Worthington, Lab	17,249
J Yuill, SNP	6,525
R Ackland, LD	3,909
Dr C Pickering, Con	3,514
Others	1,294
Lab majority	10,724

CLYDESDALE
Electorate 64,423 Poll 59.33%

*J Hood, Lab	17,822
J Wright, SNP	10,028
K Newton, Con	5,034
Ms M Craig, LD	4,111
Others	1,227
Lab majority	7,794

COATBRIDGE AND CHRYSTON
Electorate 52,178 Poll 58.09%

*Rt Hon T Clarke, Lab	19,807
P Kearney, SNP	4,493
A Tough, LD	2,293
P Ross-Taylor, Con	2,171
Others	1,547
Lab majority	15,314

CUMBERNAULD AND KILSYTH
Electorate 49,739 Poll 59.71%

*Mrs R McKenna, Lab	16,144
D McGlashan, SNP	8,624
J O'Donnell, LD	1,934
Ms A Ross, Con	1,460
Others	1,537
Lab majority	7,520

CUNNINGHAME NORTH
Electorate 54,993 Poll 61.49%

*B Wilson, Lab	15,571
C Martin, SNP	7,173
R Wilkinson, Con	6,666
R Chmiel, LD	3,060
Others	1,346
Lab majority	8,398

CUNNINGHAME SOUTH
Electorate 49,982 Poll 56.04%

*B Donohoe, Lab	16,424
B Kidd, SNP	5,194
Mrs P Paterson, Con	2,682
J Boyd, LD	2,094
Others	1,615
Lab majority	11,230

DUMBARTON
Electorate 56,267 Poll 60.42%

*J McFall, Lab Co-op	16,151
I Robertson, SNP	6,576
E Thompson, LD	5,265
P Ramsay, Con	4,648
Others	1,354
Lab Co-op majority	9,575

DUMFRIES
Electorate 62,931 Poll 67.67%

*R Brown, Lab	20,830
J Charteris, Con	11,996
J Ross Scott, LD	4,955
G Fisher, SNP	4,103
Others	702
Lab majority	8,834

DUNDEE EAST
Electorate 56,535 Poll 57.24%

I Luke, Lab	14,635
S Hosie, SNP	10,160
A Donnelly, Con	3,900
R Lawrie, LD	2,784
Others	879
Lab majority	4,475

DUNDEE WEST
Electorate 53,760 Poll 54.39%

*E Ross, Lab	14,787
G Archer, SNP	7,987
I Hail, Con	2,656
Ms E Dick, LD	2,620
Others	1,192
Lab majority	6,800

DUNFERMLINE EAST
Electorate 52,811 Poll 56.97%

*Rt Hon G Brown, Lab	19,487
J Mellon, SNP	4,424
S Randall, Con	2,838
J Mainland, LD	2,281
Others	1,056
Lab majority	15,063

DUNFERMLINE WEST
Electorate 54,293 Poll 57.05%

*Ms R Squire, Lab	16,370
B Goodall, SNP	5,390
R McPhate, LD	4,832
J Mackie, Con	3,166
Others	1,217
Lab majority	10,980

EAST KILBRIDE
Electorate 66,572 Poll 62.62%
*Rt Hon A Ingram, Lab	22,205
A Buchanan, SNP	9,450
E Hawthorn, LD	4,278
Mrs M McCulloch, Con	4,238
Others	1,519
Lab majority	12,755

EAST LOTHIAN
Electorate 58,987 Poll 62.51%
Mrs A Picking, Lab	17,407
H Mair, Con	6,577
Ms J Hayman, LD	6,506
Ms H Brown, SNP	5,381
Others	1,000
Lab majority	10,830

EASTWOOD
Electorate 68,378 Poll 70.74%
*J Murphy, Lab	23,036
R Robertson, Con	13,895
A Steele, LD	6,239
S Maxwell, SNP	4,137
Others	1,061
Lab majority	9,141

EDINBURGH CENTRAL
Electorate 66,089 Poll 52.04%
*Rt Hon A Darling, Lab	14,495
A Myles, LD	6,353
A Orr, Con	5,643
Dr I McKee, SNP	4,832
Others	3,067
Lab majority	8,142

EDINBURGH EAST AND MUSSELBURGH
Electorate 59,241 Poll 58.16%
*Rt Hon Dr G Strang, Lab	18,124
R Munn, SNP	5,956
G Peacock, LD	4,981
P Finnie, Con	3,906
Others	1,487
Lab majority	12,168

EDINBURGH NORTH AND LEITH
Electorate 62,475 Poll 53.20%
M Lazarowicz, Lab	15,271
S Tombs, LD	6,454
Ms K Stewart, SNP	5,290
I Mitchell, Con	4,626
Others	1,593
Lab majority	8,817

EDINBURGH PENTLANDS
Electorate 59,841 Poll 65.06%
*Dr L Clark, Lab	15,797
Sir M Rifkind, Con	14,055
D Walker, LD	4,210
S Gibb, SNP	4,210
Others	660
Lab majority	1,742

EDINBURGH SOUTH
Electorate 64,012 Poll 58.06%
*N Griffiths, Lab	15,671
Ms M MacLaren, LD	10,172
G Buchan, Con	6,172
Ms H Williams, SNP	3,683
Others	1,468
Lab majority	5,499

EDINBURGH WEST
Electorate 61,895 Poll 63.78%
J Barrett, LD	16,719
Ms E Alexandra, Lab	9,130
I Whyte, Con	8,894
A Smith, SNP	4,047
Others	688
LD majority	7,589

FALKIRK EAST
Electorate 57,633 Poll 58.48%
*M Connarty, Lab	18,536
Ms I Hutton, SNP	7,824
B Stevenson, Con	3,252
Ms K Utting, LD	2,992
Others	1,098
Lab majority	10,712

FALKIRK WEST
Electorate 53,583 Poll 57.65%
*E Joyce, Lab	16,022
D Kerr, SNP	7,490
S Murray, Con	2,321
H O'Donnell, LD	2,203
Others	2,855
Lab majority	8,532

FIFE CENTRAL
Electorate 59,597 Poll 54.55%
J MacDougall, Lab	18,310
D Alexander, SNP	8,235
Ms E Riches, LD	2,775
J Balfour, Con	2,351
Others	841
Lab majority	10,075

FIFE NORTH EAST
Electorate 61,900 Poll 56.05%

*Rt Hon M Campbell, LD	17,926
M Scott-Hayward, Con	8,190
Ms C Brennan, Lab	3,950
Ms K Murray-Browne, SNP	3,596
Others	1,030
LD majority	9,736

GALLOWAY AND UPPER NITHSDALE
Electorate 52,756 Poll 68.08%

P Duncan, Con	12,222
M Fleming, SNP	12,148
T Sloan, Lab	7,258
N Wallace, LD	3,698
Others	588
Con majority	74

GLASGOW ANNIESLAND
Electorate 53,290 Poll 50.14%

*J Robertson, Lab	15,102
G Thoms, SNP	4,048
C McGinty, LD	3,244
S Connell, Con	2,651
Others	1,677
Lab majority	11,054

GLASGOW BAILLIESTON
Electorate 49,268 Poll 47.21%

*J Wray, Lab	14,200
L McNeill, SNP	4,361
D Comrie, Con	1,580
J McVicar, SSP	1,569
Others	1,551
Lab majority	9,839

GLASGOW CATHCART
Electorate 52,094 Poll 52.57%

T Harris, Lab	14,902
Mrs J Docherty, SNP	4,086
R Cook, Con	3,662
T Henery, LD	3,006
Others	1,730
Lab majority	10,816

GLASGOW GOVAN
Electorate 54,068 Poll 46.76%

*M Sarwar, Lab	12,464
Ms K Neary, SNP	6,064
B Stewart, LD	2,815
M Menzies, Con	2,167
Others	1,774
Lab majority	6,400

GLASGOW KELVIN
Electorate 61,534 Poll 43.56%

*G Galloway, Lab	12,014
Ms T Mayberry, LD	4,754
F Rankin, SNP	4,513
Miss D Rankin, Con	2,388
Ms H Ritchie, SSP	1,847
Others	1,286
Lab majority	7,260

GLASGOW MARYHILL
Electorate 55,431 Poll 40.11%

Ms A McKechin, Lab	13,420
A Dingwall, SNP	3,532
S Callison, LD	2,372
G Scott, SSP	1,745
Others	1,162
Lab majority	9,888

GLASGOW POLLOK
Electorate 49,201 Poll 51.37%

*I Davidson, Lab Co-op	15,497
D Ritchie, SNP	4,229
K Baldassara, SSP	2,522
Ms I Nelson, LD	1,612
Others	1,417
Lab Co-op majority	11,268

GLASGOW RUTHERGLEN
Electorate 51,855 Poll 56.34%

*T McAvoy, Lab Co-op	16,760
Ms A McLaughlin, SNP	4,135
D Jackson, LD	3,689
M Macaskill, Con	3,301
Others	1,328
Lab Co-op majority	12,625

GLASGOW SHETTLESTON
Electorate 51,557 Poll 39.69%

*D Marshall, Lab	13,235
J Byrne, SNP	3,417
Ms R Kane, SSP	1,396
Others	2,417
Lab majority	9,818

GLASGOW SPRINGBURN
Electorate 55,192 Poll 43.67%

*Rt Hon M Martin, Speaker	16,053
S Bain, SNP	4,675
Ms C Leckie, SSP	1,879
Others	1,497
Speaker majority	11,378

GORDON
Electorate 59,996 Poll 58.34%

*M Bruce, LD	15,928
Mrs N Milne, Con	8,049
Mrs R Kemp, SNP	5,760
E Thorpe, Lab	4,730
Others	534
LD majority	7,879

GREENOCK AND INVERCLYDE
Electorate 47,884 Poll 59.35%

D Cairns, Lab	14,929
C Brodie, LD	5,039
A Murie, SNP	4,248
A Haw, Con	3,000
Others	1,203
Lab majority	9,890

HAMILTON NORTH AND BELLSHILL
Electorate 53,539 Poll 56.79%

*Rt Hon Dr J Reid, Lab	18,786
C Stephens, SNP	5,225
B Frain Bell, Con	2,649
K Legg, LD	2,360
Others	1,384
Lab majority	13,561

HAMILTON SOUTH
Electorate 46,665 Poll 57.32%

*B Tynan, Lab	15,965
J Wilson, SNP	5,190
J Oswald, LD	2,381
N Richardson, Con	1,876
Others	1,338
Lab majority	10,775

INVERNESS EAST, NAIRN AND LOCHABER
Electorate 67,139 Poll 63.24%

*D Stewart, Lab	15,605
A MacNeil, SNP	10,889
Ms P Kenton, LD	9,420
R Jenkins, Con	5,653
Others	894
Lab majority	4,716

KILMARNOCK AND LOUDOUN
Electorate 61,049 Poll 61.70%

*D Browne, Lab	19,926
J Brady, SNP	9,592
D Reece, Con	3,943
J Stewart, LD	3,177
Others	1,027
Lab majority	10,334

KIRKCALDY
Electorate 51,559 Poll 54.61%

*Dr L Moonie, Lab Co-op	15,227
Ms S-A Somerville, SNP	6,264
S Campbell, Con	3,013
A Weston, LD	2,849
Others	804
Lab Co-op majority	8,963

LINLITHGOW
Electorate 54,599 Poll 57.98%

*T Dalyell, Lab	17,207
J Sibbald, SNP	8,078
G Lindhurst, Con	2,836
M Oliver, LD	2,628
Others	906
Lab majority	9,129

LIVINGSTON
Electorate 64,850 Poll 55.56%

*Rt Hon R Cook, Lab	19,108
G Sutherland, SNP	8,492
G Mackenzie, LD	3,969
I Mowat, Con	2,995
Others	1,469
Lab majority	10,616

MIDLOTHIAN
Electorate 48,625 Poll 59.07%

D Hamilton, Lab	15,145
I Goldie, SNP	6,131
Ms J Bell, LD	3,686
R Traquair, Con	2,748
Others	1,014
Lab majority	9,014

MORAY
Electorate 58,008 Poll 57.27%

A Robertson, SNP	10,076
Mrs C Munro, Lab	8,332
F Spencer-Nairn, Con	7,677
Ms L Gorn, LD	5,224
Others	1,914
SNP majority	1,744

MOTHERWELL AND WISHAW
Electorate 52,418 Poll 56.61%

*F Roy, Lab	16,681
J McGuigan, SNP	5,725
M Nolan, Con	3,155
I Brown, LD	2,791
Others	1,321
Lab majority	10,956

OCHIL
Electorate 57,554 Poll 61.34%
*M O'Neill, Lab	16,004
K Brown, SNP	10,655
A Campbell, Con	4,235
P Edie, LD	3,253
Others	1,156
Lab majority	5,349

ORKNEY AND SHETLAND
Electorate 31,909 Poll 52.44%
A Carmichael, LD	6,919
R Mochrie, Lab	3,444
J Firth, Con	3,121
J Mowat, SNP	2,473
Others	776
LD majority	3,475

PAISLEY NORTH
Electorate 47,994 Poll 56.58%
*Mrs I Adams, Lab	15,058
G Adam, SNP	5,737
Ms J Hook, LD	2,709
C Stevenson, Con	2,404
Others	1,245
Lab majority	9,321

PAISLEY SOUTH
Electorate 53,351 Poll 57.24%
*D Alexander, Lab	17,830
B Lawson, SNP	5,920
B O'Malley, LD	3,178
A Cossar, Con	2,301
Others	1,307
Lab majority	11,910

PERTH
Electorate 61,497 Poll 61.49%
Ms A Ewing, SNP	11,237
Miss E Smith, Con	11,189
Ms M Dingwall, Lab	9,638
Ms V Harris, LD	4,853
Others	899
SNP majority	48

RENFREWSHIRE WEST
Electorate 52,889 Poll 63.33%
J Sheridan, Lab	15,720
Ms C Puthucheary, SNP	7,145

D Sharpe, Con	5,522
Ms C Hamblen, LD	4,185
Others	925
Lab majority	8,575

ROSS, SKYE AND INVERNESS WEST
Electorate 56,522 Poll 61.59%
*Rt Hon C Kennedy, LD	18,832
D Crichton, Lab	5,880
Ms J Urquhart, SNP	4,901
A Laing, Con	3,096
Others	2,103
LD majority	12,952

ROXBURGH AND BERWICKSHIRE
Electorate 47,059 Poll 61.19%
*A Kirkwood, LD	14,044
G Turnbull, Con	6,533
Ms C Maxwell-Stuart, Lab	4,498
R Campbell, SNP	2,806
Others	916
LD majority	7,511

STIRLING
Electorate 53,097 Poll 67.67%
*Mrs A McGuire, Lab	15,175
G Mawdsley, Con	8,901
Ms F Macaulay, SNP	5,877
C Freeman, LD	4,208
Others	1,769
Lab majority	6,274

STRATHKELVIN AND BEARSDEN
Electorate 62,729 Poll 66.14%
J Lyons, Lab	19,250
G Macdonald, LD	7,533
C Smith, SNP	6,675
M Roxburgh, Con	6,635
Others	1,393
Lab majority	11,717

TAYSIDE NORTH
Electorate 61,645 Poll 62.48%
P Wishart, SNP	15,441
M Fraser, Con	12,158
T Docherty, Lab	5,715
Ms J Robertson, LD	4,363
Others	840
SNP majority	3,283

TWEEDDALE, ETTRICK AND LAUDERDALE		WESTERN ISLES	
Electorate 51,966 Poll 63.92%		*Electorate 21,807 Poll 60.34%*	
*M Moore, LD	14,035	*C Macdonald, Lab	5,924
K Geddes, Lab	8,878	A Nicholson, SNP	4,850
A Brocklehurst, Con	5,118	D Taylor, Con	1,250
R Thomson, SNP	4,108	Others	1,135
Others	1,078	*Lab majority*	1,074
LD majority	5,157		

2001 General Election in Scotland

Party	Votes cast	Share of poll
Labour	1,001,173	43.27%
SNP	464,305	20.06%
Conservative	360,558	15.58%
Liberal Democrat	377,176	16.3%
Others	110,373	4.77%

In the last 10 general elections, the Scottish constituencies have been represented as follows:

Year	Lab	Con	Lib	SNP	Speaker	Party in power UK
1966	46	20	5	0	-	Labour
1970	44	23	3	1	-	Conservative
1974 Feb	40	21	3	7	-	Labour
1974 Oct	41	16	3	11	-	Labour
1979	44	22	3	2	-	Conservative
1983	41	21	8	2	-	Conservative
1987	50	10	9	3	-	Conservative
1992	49	11	9	3	-	Conservative
1997	56	0	10	6	-	Labour
2001	55	1	10	5	1	Labour

The European Parliament

June 1999

The result of the 1999 European election in Scotland was as follows:

Labour 283,490 (28.6%)
Scottish National Party 268,528 (27.1%)
Scottish Conservative 195,296 (19.7%)
Liberal Democrat 96,971 (9.8%)
Green 57,142 (5.8%)
Scottish Socialist Party 39,720 (4.0%)
Pro Euro Conservative 17,781 (1.7%)
UK Independence Party 12,549 (1.2%)
Socialist Labour Party 9,385 (0.9%)
British National Party 3,729 (0.3%)
Natural Law Party 2,087 (0.2%)
Charles F Y Lawson 1,632 (0.1%)

The allocation of seats was decided by proportional representation, resulting in the following allocation of seats: Labour, 3; Scottish National Party, 2; Conservative, 2; Liberal Democrats 1.

In the constituencies, the Conservatives polled the highest number of votes in 12 constituencies: Ayr; Dumfries; Eastwood; Edinburgh Pentlands; Edinburgh West; Galloway & Upper Nithsdale; North East Fife; Perth; Roxburgh & Berwickshire; Stirling; Tweeddale, Ettrick & Lauderdale; West Aberdeenshire & Kincardine. The SNP polled the highest number of votes in 15 constituencies: Aberdeen North; Aberdeen South; Angus; Argyll & Bute; Banff & Buchan; Caithness, Sutherland & Easter Ross; Dundee East; Dundee West; Gordon; Inverness East, Nairn & Lochaber; Moray; North Tayside; Ochil; Ross, Skye & Inverness West; Western Isles. The Liberal Democrats polled the highest number of votes in 1 constituency: Orkney & Shetland. Labour polled the highest number of votes in the remaining 44 constituencies.

The turnout in Scotland was 24.8%.

Members of the European Parliament for Scotland 1999-2004

Labour
David Martin, PO Box 27030, Edinburgh EH10 7YP
Bill Miller, 9 Chisholm Street, Glasgow G1 5HA
Catherine Taylor, 5a Alexandra Place, St Andrews KY16 9XD

Liberal Democrats
Elspeth Attwooll, Scottish Liberal Democrats, 4 Clifton Terrace, Edinburgh EH12 5DR

Conservative
Struan Stevenson, Scottish Conservative and Unionist Central Office, 14 Links Place, Edinburgh EH6 6EZ
John Purvis, CBE, Scottish Conservative and Unionist Central Office, 14 Links Place, Edinburgh EH6 6EZ

Scottish National Party
Ian Hudghton, 70 Rosemount Place, Aberdeen AB2 4XJ
Professor Neil MacCormick, Scottish National Party, 6 North Charlotte Street, Edinburgh EH2 4JH

Consulates and Cultural Institutes

CONSULATE OF AUSTRALIA 69 George Street, Edinburgh EH2 2JG
Tel: 0131 624 3333 Fax: 0131 624 3701
Consul: William Roxburgh

CONSULATE OF AUSTRIA Alderwood, 49 Craigcrook Road, Edinburgh EH4 3PH
Tel: 0131 332 3344 Fax: 0131 332 1777
Consul: James Miller

CONSULATE OF BELGIUM 2 West Street, Penicuik EH26 9DL
Tel: 01968 679969 Fax: 01968 677638
Consul: Yves Lemarchand

CONSULATE OF BRAZIL 126/10 High Street, Edinburgh EH1 1QS
Tel: 0131 247 7700
Consul: Robert Grant Baird

CONSULATE OF CANADA Standard Life House, 30 Lothian Road, Edinburgh EH1 2DH
Tel: 0131 245 6013 Fax: 0131 245 6010
Consul: A Scott Bell

CONSULATE OF CHINA Romano House, 43 Station Road, Edinburgh EH12 7AF
Tel: 0131 334 8501 Fax: 0131 334 6954
Consul General: Wang Weiyang

CONSULATE OF CZECH REPUBLIC 12a Riselaw Crescent, Edinburgh EH10 6HL
Tel: 0131 447 9509 Fax: 0131 447 9509
Consul: Paul Millar

CONSULATE OF DENMARK 215/221 Balgreen Road, Edinburgh EH11 2RZ
Tel: 0131 337 6352 Fax: 0131 346 8737
Consul: Norman Irons

CONSULATE OF FINLAND Carriden Sawmills, Bo'ness, West Lothian EH51 9SQ
Tel: 01506 823331 Fax: 01506 822590
Consul: Michael J Walker

CONSULATE OF FRANCE 11 Randolph Crescent, Edinburgh EH3 7TT
Tel: 0131 225 7954 Fax: 0131 225 8975
Consul General: Michel Roche

CONSULATE OF GERMANY 16 Eglinton Crescent, Edinburgh EH12 5DG
Tel: 0131 337 2323 Fax: 0131 346 1578
Consul General: Hans Mondorf

CONSULATE OF GREECE 1 Kirklee Quadrant, Glasgow G12 0TR
Tel: 0141 334 0360
Consul: Irene Cavoura

CONSULATE OF ICELAND 45 Queen Street, Edinburgh EH2 3NH
Tel: 0131 220 5775 Fax: 0131 225 6317
Honorary Consul: Cameron R M Buchanan

CONSULATE OF INDIA 17 Rutland Square, Edinburgh EH1 2BB
Tel: 0131 229 2144 Fax: 0131 229 2155
Consul General: S M Gavai

CONSULATE OF IRELAND 16 Randolph Crescent, Edinburgh EH3 7TT
Tel: 0131 226 7711 Fax: 0131 226 7704
Consul General: Conor O'Riordan

CONSULATE OF ITALY 32 Melville Street, Edinburgh EH3 7HA
Tel: 0131 226 3631 Fax: 0131 226 6260
Consul General: Giuseppe Zaccagnino

CONSULATE OF JAPAN 2 Melville Crescent, Edinburgh EH3 7HW
Tel: 0131 225 4777 Fax: 0131 225 4828
Consul General: Tsutomu Hiraoka

CONSULATE OF LATVIA 28 Cammo Road, Edinburgh EH4 8AP
Tel: 0131 339 3613
Acting Consul: R D Cairns

CONSULATE OF MALAWI 160a High Street, Irvine KA12 8AN
Tel: 01294 313100 Fax: 01294 312333
Consul: Colin Cameron

CONSULATE OF MALTA 1 Craiglockhart Crescent, Edinburgh EH14 1EZ
Tel: 0131 443 2533
Consul: Mr G A Hunter

CONSULATE OF MEXICO Balvarran, Enochdhu, Blairgowrie PH10 7PA
Tel: 01250 881248
Consul: Robin A Stormonth-Darling

CONSULATE OF MONACO 39 Castle Street, Edinburgh EH2 3BH
Tel: 0131 225 1200 Fax: 0131 225 4412
Consul: J K Scott Moncrieff

CONSULATE OF MONGOLIA Balhearty House, Coalsnaughton, Clackmann-
anshire FK13 6NA
Tel: 01259 752343 Fax: 01259 751670
Consul: Robyn M Murray

CONSULATE OF NETHERLANDS Thistle Court, 1-2 Thistle Street, Edinburgh EH2
1DD
Tel: 0131 220 3226 Fax: 0131 220 6446
Consul: Michael Hughes

CONSULATE OF NORWAY 86 George Street, Edinburgh EH2 3BU
Tel: 0131 226 5701 Fax: 0131 220 4976
Consul General: Arne Sivertesen

CONSULATE OF POLAND 2 Kinnear Road, Edinburgh EH3 5PE
Tel: 0131 552 0301 Fax: 0131 552 1086
Consul General: Wojciech Tycinski

CONSULATE OF RUSSIAN FEDERATION 58 Melville Street, Edinburgh EH3 7HL
Tel: 0131 225 7098 Fax: 0131 225 9587
Consul General: Anatoly Smimov

CONSULATE OF SPAIN 63 North Castle Street, Edinburgh EH2 3LJ
Tel: 0131 220 1843 Fax: 0131 226 4568
Consul General: vacant

CONSULATE OF SWEDEN Merchants' Hall, 22 Hanover Street, Edinburgh EH2 2EP
Tel: 0131 220 6050 Fax: 0131 220 6006
Consul General: Torvald Colliander

CONSULATE OF SWITZERLAND 66 Hanover Street, Edinburgh EH2 1HH
Tel: 0131 226 5660 Fax: 0131 226 5332
Consul: Alan G Stewart

CONSULATE OF THAILAND 4 Woodside Place, Charing Cross, Glasgow G3 7QF
Tel: 0141 353 5090 Fax: 0141 332 2928
Consul: A D Stewart

CONSULATE OF TURKEY 6 Coates Crescent, Edinburgh EH3 7AL
Tel: 0131 226 6222 Fax: 0131 226 5110
Consul: Ian Wittet

CONSULATE OF UNITED STATES 3 Regent Terrace, Edinburgh EH7 5BW
Tel: 0131 556 8315 Fax: 0131 557 6023
Principal Officer: Ms Liane Dorsey

DANISH CULTURAL INSTITUTE 3 Doune Terrace, Edinburgh EH3 6DY
Tel: 0131 225 7189 Fax: 0131 220 6162
Director: Mr Kim Caspersen

FRENCH INSTITUTE 13 Randolph Crescent, Edinburgh EH3 7TT
Tel: 0131 225 5366 Fax: 0131 220 0648
Director: Mr Ashok Adiceam

ITALIAN CULTURAL INSTITUTE 82 Nicholson Street, Edinburgh EH8 9EW
Tel: 0131 668 2232 Fax: 0131 668 2777
Director: Ewnio Drili

The Directory

A Classified Guide to Scottish Organisations

ADDICTION

ALCOHOL FOCUS SCOTLAND
2nd Floor, 166 Buchanan Street, Glasgow G1 2NH
Tel: 0141-572 6700
Fax: 0141 333 1606
e-mail: admin@alcohol-focus-scotland.org.uk
Chief Executive: Jack Law; *President:* Rt Hon Earl of Minto, OBE, DL, JP

ALCOHOLICS ANONYMOUS
Suite 442, Baltic Chambers 50 Wellington Street, Glasgow G2 6HJ
Tel: 0141-226 2214

SCOTTISH DRUGS FORUM
Shaftesbury House, 5 Waterloo Street, Glasgow G2 6AY
Tel: 0141-221 1175
e-mail: enquiries@sdf.org.uk
web: www.sdf.org.uk
Director: David Liddell; *Chairperson:* Anne Thomson
Founded in 1986 to provide a voice for those concerned about the effects of drug use in Scotland. A membership organisation funded by the government and by grants and donations, SDF arranges conferences and seminars; deals with inquiries from drug workers and users, the general public and the media; publishes material aimed at dispelling the myths surrounding drugs and their use; and supports local and regional initiatives. Its general aim has been to co-ordinate action on drug issues.

AGRICULTURE, FORESTRY AND LAND

ABERDEEN-ANGUS CATTLE SOCIETY
6 King's Place, Perth PH2 8AD
Tel: 01738 622477
Fax: 01738 636436
e-mail: info@aberdeen-angus.co.uk
web: www.aberdeen-angus.com
Chief Executive: Ronald McHattie; *President:* J Stobo
Maintains the pedigrees of Aberdeen-Angus cattle and preserves and publishes these along with other relevant information in the Herd Book. Promotes the breeding of Aberdeen-Angus cattle for the production of Aberdeen-Angus beef.

AYRSHIRE CATTLE SOCIETY OF GREAT BRITAIN AND IRELAND
1 Racecourse Road, Ayr KA7 2DE
Tel: 01292 267123
e-mail: society@ayrshires.org
web: www.ayrshires.org
General Manager: David Sayce; *President:* Jimmy Hunter
Breed society for Ayrshire dairy cows. Provides pedigrees, promotes the breed, tests progeny, and markets milk and dairy products under the "Ayrshires" brand.

CROFTERS COMMISSION
4/6 Castle Wynd, Inverness IV2 3EQ
Tel: 01463 663450
Fax: 01463 711820
e-mail: info@crofterscommission.org.uk
web: www.crofterscommission.org.uk
Chief Executive: Shane Rankin; *Chairman:* Iain MacAskill
Government-funded organisation responsible for the reorganisation, development and regulation of crofting. Works with communities towards improvement and stability in rural areas. The commission delivers the crofting counties' agricultural grants scheme.

DEER COMMISSION FOR SCOTLAND
Knowsley, 82 Fairfield Road, Inverness IV3 5LH
Tel: 01463 231751

Fax: 01463 712931
e-mail: deercom@aol.com
web: www.dcs.gov.uk
Director: Nick Reiter; *Chairman:* Andrew Raven
Established in 1959 to further the conservation and control of red deer and to keep under review all matters concerning them.

Its responsibilities were extended in 1982 to include sika deer and roe deer. As a result of legislation which came into effect in 1996, the commission's general functions were defined as the sustainable management of deer and their welfare, taking into account the impact on the natural heritage, the needs of agriculture and forestry, and the interests of owners and occupiers of land; and the protection of unenclosed woodlands and the natural heritage from damage by deer. Voluntary control agreements give the commission responsibility for co-ordinated deer control and management over wider areas than before. Under the new law, night shooting of any species of deer by any person must be authorised by the commission.

FORESTRY COMMISSION
231 Corstorphine Road, Edinburgh EH12 7AT
Tel: 0131-334 0303
Fax: 0131-334 3047
e-mail: enquiries@forestry.gsi.gov.uk
web: www.forestry.gov.uk
Director General: David Bills; *Chairman:* Lord Clark of Windermere
The Forestry Commission is the Government department responsible for forestry policy in Great Britain. It reports directly to forestry ministers to whom it is responsible for advice on forestry policy and for the implementation of that policy. Scottish ministers have responsibility for forestry in Scotland.

The commission's principal objectives are to protect Britain's forests and woodlands; expand Britain's forest area; enhance the economic value of the forest resources; conserve and improve the biodiversity, landscape and cultural heritage of forests and woodlands; develop opportunities for woodland recreation; and increase public understanding of, and community participation in, forestry.

GALLOWAY CATTLE SOCIETY OF GB AND IRELAND
15 New Market Street, Castle Douglas DG7 1HY
Tel: 01556 502753
Secretary: A J McDonald; *President:* Duke of Buccleuch and Queensberry, KT
Maintains pedigree herd book and promotes the breed of cattle known as Galloways, one of the oldest and purest breeds of cattle in the world.

HILL FARMING ADVISORY COMMITTEE FOR SCOTLAND
Room 347, Pentland House, 47 Robb's Loan, Edinburgh EH14 1TW
Tel: 0131-244 6422

INSTITUTE OF CHARTERED FORESTERS
7a St Colme Street, Edinburgh EH3 6AA
Tel: 0131-225 2705
Fax: 0131-220 6128
e-mail: icf@charteredforesters. org
web: www.charteredforesters.org
Executive Director: Mrs M W Dick, OBE; *President:* T J D Rollinson
Exists to maintain and improve the standards of professional practice. The representative body for the forestry profession throughout the UK.

NFU SCOTLAND
Rural Centre, Ingliston, Newbridge EH28 8LT
Tel: 0131-472 4000

Chief Executive: Ed Rainy Brown; *President:* Jim Walker
Provides an authoritative voice for the Scottish agricultural community in Edinburgh, Westminster and Europe. It speaks for farmers, growers and crofters as a united whole. In Scotland it has regular meetings with ministers. Its Brussels office gathers information, lobbies commissioners and MEPs, and maintains dialogue with other EU farming organisations.

A network of 80 branches and nine regional boards, backed by headquarters, enables the union to offer a locally based service to its 12,500 members – including, for example, help in obtaining compensation for the effects of major roadworks, support for co-operative ventures, the resolution of landlord-tenant problems, and advice on employment legislation. The NFU Mutual is Scotland's leading agricultural insurer.

QUALITY MEAT SCOTLAND LTD
Rural Centre, Ingliston, Newbridge EH28 8NZ
Tel: 0131-472 4040
Fax: 0131-472 4038
Managing Director: Alasdair Muir; *Chairman:* Neil Kilpatrick
Promotional and marketing body for specially selected Scotch beef, lamb and pork, set up to improve the competitive position of the Scottish meat and livestock industry at home and abroad and to provide co-ordination and leadership for the industry.

ROYAL HIGHLAND AND AGRICULTURAL SOCIETY OF SCOTLAND
Royal Highland Centre, Ingliston, Newbridge EH28 8NF
Tel: 0131-335 6200
Fax: 0131-333 5236
e-mail: info@rhass.org.uk
web: www.rhass.org.uk

Chief Executive: Ray Jones; *President:* A Salvesen
Established in 1784 as the Highland Society of Edinburgh, an association for the improvement of the Highlands, receiving its first royal charter in 1787 as the Highland Society of Scotland at Edinburgh. From its inception, the society promoted education and the arts in Scotland. In its first year a professor of Gaelic was elected and competitions in music were held.

The society's interest in agriculture dates from January 1785 when medals for essays on agricultural subjects were first offered. In 1790, the chair of agriculture at Edinburgh University was founded on the society's initiative, and in 1840 William Dick was installed as the first professor of veterinary studies at Edinburgh, under the society's auspices. These initiatives led to a change of title to the Highland and Agricultural Society of Scotland, and a second royal charter, in 1834. The final change of name came in 1948.

The present-day objectives of the society are the promotion of Scottish agriculture, allied industries and the rural economy. It has a membership of 14,000. Each June it organises the Royal Highland Show, which promotes all facets of the agricultural industry from livestock to crafts. It also awards medals and certificates for achievement and administers the Scottish woods and forest awards scheme.

ROYAL SCOTTISH AGRICULTURAL BENEVOLENT INSTITUTION
Ingliston, Edinburgh EH28 8NB
Tel: 0131-333 1023
Fax: 0131-333 1027
e-mail: rsabi@rsabi.org.uk
Director: Ian Purves-Hume; *President:* Duke of Buccleuch and Queensberry, KT

Exists to provide financial and/or in-kind help, welfare advice and support to anyone in need who is, or has been, in farming, forestry, fish farming, horticulture and rural estate work in Scotland, and their dependants.

ROYAL SCOTTISH FORESTRY SOCIETY
Hagg-on-Esk, Canonbie, Dumfries-shire DG14 0XE
Tel: 013873 71518
Fax: 013873 71418
e mail: rsfs@educt.co.uk
web: www.rsfs.org
Administrative Director: Andrew G Little; *President:* Peter J Fothergill
Has been promoting excellence in trees and forestry in Scotland since 1854.

SCOTTISH AGRICULTURAL SCIENCE AGENCY
82 Craigs Road, East Craigs, Edinburgh EH12 8NJ
Tel: 0131-244 8890
Fax: 0131-244 8940
e-mail: info@sasa.gov.uk
web: www.sasa.gov.uk
Director: Dr R K M Hay
Provides government with expert scientific information and advice on agricultural and horticultural crops and aspects of the environment. It also performs statutory and regulatory work in relation to national, EU and other international legislation and agreements on plant health, bee health, variety registration and crop improvement, genetically modified organisms, and the protection of crops, food and the environment.

SCOTTISH AGRICULTURAL WAGES BOARD
Pentland House, 47 Robb's Loan, Edinburgh EH14 1TY
Tel: 0131-244 6392
Secretary: Miss F H Anderson; *Chairperson:* Mrs C A M Davis, CBE

Exists to make Orders fixing minimum wage rates, holiday entitlement and other terms and conditions of service for workers employed in agriculture in Scotland.

SCOTTISH ASSOCIATION OF YOUNG FARMERS' CLUBS
Young Farmers' Centre, Ingliston, Newbridge EH28 8NE
Tel: 0131-333 2445
Fax: 0131-333 2488
web: www.sayfc.org
National Secretary: Fiona Bain

SCOTTISH CROFTERS UNION
Old Mill, Broadford, Isle of Skye IV49 9AQ
Tel: 01471 822529
Director: Rory Dutton; *President:* Donnie MacLennan
Promotes the interests of crofting and crofting communities.

SCOTTISH DAIRY ASSOCIATION
4a Torphichen Street, Edinburgh EH3 8JQ
Tel: 0131-221 0109

SCOTTISH LANDOWNERS' FEDERATION
Stuart House, Eskmills Business Park, Musselburgh EH21 7PB
Tel: 0131-653 5400
Fax: 0131-653 5401
e-mail: slfinfo@slf.org.uk
web: www.slf.org.uk
Director: Maurice S Hankey; *President:* W G Morrison
Membership organisation representing those who own and/or manage land in Scotland.

SCOTTISH MILK RECORDS ASSOCIATION
46 Underwood Road, Paisley PA3 1TJ
Tel: 0141-848 0404
Director: Duncan Todd; *Chairman:* Colin McKay
Provides milk recording service and information concerning dairy herds.

AMBULANCES

St Andrew's Ambulance Association

St Andrew's House, 48 Milton Street, Glasgow G4 0HR
Tel: 0141-332 4031
e-mail: firstaid@staaa.demon.co.uk
web: www.firstaid.co.uk
Chief Executive: Brendan Healy; *Chairman:* Dr E T Robinson
Provides first aid training and associated supplies.

Scottish Ambulance Service

Tipperlinn Road, Edinburgh EH10 5UU
Tel: 0131-446 7000
Chief Executive: Adrian Lucas
In 1775 two sedan chairs were acquired on behalf of doctors at Edinburgh Royal Infirmary for the "swift and commodious carriage of persons needful of medicinal enquiry yet unable to proceed thereto". This was the first organised ambulance service in Scotland. In 1882 the St Andrew's Ambulance Association was formed, starting with two horse-drawn wagons in Glasgow. The ambulance service was incorporated into the NHS in 1948, the name "St Andrew's" was dropped from the title in 1974. The service acquired trust status in 1995 and became a Special Health Board of the NHS in Scotland in 1999.

Scotland's is the only national ambulance service in the UK and the largest in Europe, employing over 3,000 people and an operational fleet of 1,000 vehicles. It operates the UK's only integrated air ambulance service, co-ordinating over 3,000 flights a year to ensure that even patients in the remotest parts of Scotland can have swift access to hospital and high-quality patient care on the way.

ANGLING

Scottish Anglers National Association

The Caledonian Club, 32 Abercromby Place, Edinburgh EH3 6QE
Tel: 0131-558 3644
Fax: 0131-557 6269
e-mail: admin@sana.org.uk
web: www.sana.org.uk
President: Jane Wright
Governing body for the sport of game fishing in Scotland.

Scottish Federation of Sea Anglers

Caledonia House, South Gyle, Edinburgh EH12 9DQ
Tel: 0131-317 7192
Secretary: Paula Lees
Governing body for the sport of sea fishing in Scotland.

ANIMALS AND WILDLIFE

Advocates for Animals

10 Queensferry Street, Edinburgh EH2 4PG
Tel: 0131-225 6039
e-mail: advocates.animals@virgin.net
web: www.advocatesforanimals.org.uk
Director: Les Ward, MBE; *President:* Jane Goodall, CBE
Animal protection organisation campaigning against animal abuse in Scotland, the UK, and across the world. Campaign areas include animal experiments, blood sports, factory farming, cruel slaughter, performing and captive animals, companion animals and marine life.

Animal Concern

PO Box 5178, Dumbarton G82 5YJ
Tel: 01389 841639
Campaigns Consultant: John Robins;

Chairperson: Agnes Lang
Promotes the abolition of animal exploitation.

FAIR ISLE BIRD OBSERVATORY TRUST
Fair Isle, Shetland ZE2 9JU
Tel: 01595 760258
e-mail: fairisle.birdobs@zetnet.co.uk
web: www.fairislebirdobs.co.uk
Administrator: Hollie Shaw

NATIONAL CANINE DEFENCE LEAGUE
Rehoming Centre, Dovecotwell, by Glencaple, Dumfries DG1 4RH
Tel: 01387 770346
Protects and defends dogs from abuse, cruelty, abandonment and any form of mistreatment.

PEOPLE'S DISPENSARY FOR SICK ANIMALS
1 Shamrock Street, Glasgow G4 9LA
Tel: 0141-353 1440

ROYAL ZOOLOGICAL SOCIETY OF SCOTLAND
Edinburgh Zoo, Corstorphine Road, Edinburgh EH12 6TS
Tel: 0131-334 9171
Fax: 0131-316 4050
e-mail: marketing@rzss.org.uk
web: www.edinburghzoo.org.uk
Director: Henry Elliot; *President:* John Grant of Rothiemurchus
Founded in 1909, a private society existing in the terms of its royal charter "to promote, facilitate and encourage the study of zoology and kindred subjects and to foster and develop among the people an interest in and a knowledge of animal life". The society promotes, through the presentation of its living collections, the conservation of animal species and wild places by captive breeding, environmental education and scientific research. The society maintains the Edinburgh Zoological Park and the Highland Wildlife Park.

RSPB (ROYAL SOCIETY FOR THE PROTECTION OF BIRDS)
Dunedin House, 25 Ravelston Terrace, Edinburgh EH4 3TP
Tel: 0131-311 6500
Fax: 0131-311 6569
e-mail: rspb.scotland@rspb.org.uk
web: www.rspb.org.uk/scotland
Director, Scotland: Stuart Housden
Has over one million members, making this the largest wildlife conservation organisation in Europe. RSPB Scotland (around 70,000 members) protects some of the UK's rarest species and habitats. Manages land, conducts research and education programmes, campaigns for better legal protection for wildlife, provides conservation advice, and works towards sustainable solutions to environmental problems.

SCOTTISH KENNEL CLUB
Eskmills Park, Station Road, Musselburgh EH21 7PQ
Tel: 0131-665 3920
e-mail: info@scottishkennelclub.org
web: www.scottishkennelclub.org
Secretary General: I A Sim; *Convener:* Robert Crawford
The prime source of canine information in Scotland, with responsible dog ownership at the core of its activities. Breeders' register provides comprehensive source of information on pedigree dogs. Licenses most dog shows and runs two in Edinburgh each year. Training, rescue and welfare information.

SCOTTISH SOCIETY FOR THE PREVENTION OF CRUELTY TO ANIMALS (SCOTTISH SPCA)
Braehead Mains, 603 Queensferry Road, Edinburgh EH4 6EA
Tel: 0131-339 0222
Fax: 0131-339 4777
e-mail: fundraising@scottishspca.org
web: www.scottishspca.org
Chief Executive: Ian Gardiner;

President: Rt Hon Lord Provost of Glasgow
Established in its present form from a merger of the Scottish and the Glasgow and West of Scotland societies and later mergers with the Glasgow Dog and Cat Home and the Aberdeen Association for the Prevention of Cruelty to Animals. Exists to prevent cruelty to animals and to promote kindness and humanity in their treatment.

Its inspectorate acts as the society's frontline in policing animal welfare legislation, rescuing animals in distress and providing advice and guidance to those in charge of animals. Animal welfare centres offer refuge to injured, abused and abandoned pets, farm animals and wildlife.

The society campaigns to improve animal welfare legislation both in the UK and the EU, provides an education programme in schools, and promotes improved animal husbandry systems.

SCOTTISH SOCIETY FOR THE PROTECTION OF WILD BIRDS
Foremount House, Kilbarchan PA10 2EZ
Tel: 01505 702419
Secretary: Dr J A Gibson

SCOTTISH WILDLIFE TRUST
Cramond House, Cramond Glebe Road, Edinburgh EH4 6NS
Tel: 0131-312 7765
e-mail: enquiries@swt.org.uk
web: www.swt.org.uk
Chief Executive: Steve Sankey
Works to protect wildlife in town and country. Through education, training and campaigning, surveying and managing wildlife habitats, looking after reserves, and partnerships with other organisations, it aims to safeguard the biodiversity of Scotland for the benefit of all. It is supported financially by its 17,000 members and by grants, donations and contracts from a variety of sources, including central and local government.

ARBITRATION

ADVISORY, CONCILIATION AND ARBITRATION SERVICE (ACAS) SCOTLAND
Franborough House, 123-157 Bothwell Street, Glasgow G2 7JR
Tel: 0141-248 1400
Tel: (Enquiries) 0141-204 2677
Fax: 0141-221 4697
web: www.acas.org.uk
Director Scotland: Frank Blair
Seeks to improve industrial relations and promote good employment practice, to minimise conflict and to encourage people at work to be included in, and committed to, the greater effectiveness and success of their organisations. Prevents and resolves collective disputes and aims to identify disputes at the earliest possible stage.

ACAS also has a statutory duty to promote settlement of claims arising on most issues within the jurisdiction of employment tribunals, such conciliation helping to avoid the cost of hearings. It also offers free, confidential and impartial information and advice on all aspects of employment relationships.

CHARTERED INSTITUTE OF ARBITRATORS (SCOTTISH BRANCH)
Whittinghame House, 1099 Great Western Road, Glasgow G12 0AA
Tel: 0141-334 7222
Honorary Secretary: Bruce L Smith;
Chairman: Sandra I Cassels
Exists to promote arbitration in Scotland and educate prospective and current arbitrators.

SCOTTISH COUNCIL FOR
INTERNATIONAL ARBITRATION
Excel House, 30 Semple Street,
Edinburgh EH3 8BL
Tel: 0131-229 5046
Director/Secretary: J M Arnott;
Chairman: Hon Lord Dervaird

ARCHAEOLOGY

COUNCIL FOR SCOTTISH
ARCHAEOLOGY
c/o National Museums of Scotland,
Chambers Street, Edinburgh EH1 1JF
Tel: 0131-247 4119
Fax: 0131-247 4126
Director: David Lynn; *President:* Dr
Alan Saville
Membership organisation which
works to advance the study and care
of Scotland's historic environment
and improve public awareness of its
past.

SOCIETY OF ANTIQUARIES OF
SCOTLAND
Royal Museum of Scotland,
Chambers Street, Edinburgh EH1 1JF
Tel: 0131-247 4115/4133
Fax: 0131-247 4163
Director: Fionna Ashmore
Founded in 1780 and incorporated by
royal charter in 1783, the second
oldest antiquarian society in Britain.
Its purpose, as set out in the first of its
laws, is the study of the antiquities
and history of Scotland, more
especially by means of archaeological
research. The society is concerned
with every aspect of the human past
in Scotland.
Members have, from the
beginning, been known as fellows.
There are now some 3,000 around the
world, as well as 21 honorary fellows
elected for their outstanding
scholarship. Membership is by
election, held annually on St
Andrew's Day, and is open to all with
an interest in Scottish history and
archaeology.
The society organises an annual
programme of meetings, including
monthly lectures in Edinburgh from
October to June, a conference, and
various seminars and excursions. All
fellows receive the *Proceedings of the
Society,* an annual record of research.
A major part of its programme is the
sponsorship of research, from survey
and excavation to finds analysis and
archival research.
In 1780 the society started to
collect antiquities, manuscripts and
books which formed the nucleus of
the National Museums of Scotland.
As the senior antiquarian body in
Scotland, it has an important role in
the cultural life and heritage of the
country and is often consulted on
heritage matters.

SUAT LTD (FORMERLY SCOTTISH
URBAN ARCHAEOLOGICAL TRUST)
55 South Methven Street, Perth PH1
5NX
Tel: 01738 622393
e-mail: director@suat.demon.co.uk
web: www.suat.demon.co.uk
Director: David Bowler; *Chairman:*
David R Penman
Concerned with archaeology in
Scottish towns and their hinterlands.

ARMED SERVICES AND
EX-SERVICES

ARMY HQ 2ND DIVISION
Craigiehall, South Queensferry EH30
9TN
Tel: 0131-310 2091/2
Fax: 0131-310 2058
*General Officer Commanding 2nd
Division:* Major General Robert
Gordon
In administrative charge of all regular
and reserve troops and cadets in
Scotland and Northern England.

EARL HAIG FUND SCOTLAND
New Haig House, Logie Green Road,
Edinburgh EH7 4HR
Tel: 0131-557 2782
Chief Executive: Major General J D
MacDonald, CB, CBE, DL; *President:*
Very Revd Dr James Harkness, CB,
OBE
Benevolent organisation concerned
with ex-Service men and women.
Funds raised from Scottish Poppy
Appeal.

OFFICERS' ASSOCIATION SCOTLAND
Haig House, 1 Fitzroy Place, Glasgow
G3 7RJ
Tel: 0141-221 8141
Secretary: Cmdr A C Herdman, RN
Provides financial assistance or
advice to ex-officers, their widows,
widowers and dependants, and
assists ex-officers to find suitable
employment.

ROYAL AIR FORCES ASSOCIATION
20 Queen Street, Edinburgh EH2 1JX
Tel: 0131-225 5221
Fax: 0131-220 0643
Director: G M Halloran; *President:* Air
Vice Marshal J Morris, CBE
Service charity providing welfare
assistance to former and serving RAF
members, their widows and
dependants. Offers nursing care,
convalescence, war pensions advice
and comradeship through its network
of branches and clubs.

ROYAL BRITISH LEGION SCOTLAND
New Haig House, Logie Green Road,
Edinburgh EH7 4HR
Tel: 0131-557 2782
General Secretary: Wing Cmdr Richard
Woodroffe, MBE; *President:* Very Revd
Dr James Harkness, CB, OBE
Set up to look after the social and
legislative needs of the ex-service
community.

SCOTTISH NATIONAL WAR MEMORIAL
The Castle, Edinburgh EH1 2YT
Tel: 0131-310 5130
Secretary to the Trustees: Lt-Col I
Shepherd; *Chairman of Trustees:* Major
General Sir John Swinton, KCVO,
OBE
Commemorates and keeps the rolls of
honour of Scottish war dead, 1914–18,
1939–45, and since 1945. Provides
information to relatives and amends
folls. The memorial is a basilica type
of building designed and built by
Scots.

**SCOTTISH SOCIETY FOR EMPLOYMENT
OF EX-REGULAR SAILORS, SOLDIERS &
AIRMEN**
New Haig House, Logie Green Road,
Edinburgh EH7 4HR
Tel: 0131-557 1747
Secretary/Treasurer: Frank McGuinness;
Chairman: Lt-Col (Retd) P J Rettie
Finds employment for regular ex-
Service personnel.

ARTS

*See also: Arts Centres; Dance; Museums
and Galleries; Music; Theatre; Theatres
and Concert Halls*

SCOTTISH ARTS COUNCIL
12 Manor Place, Edinburgh EH3 7DD
Tel: 0131-226 6051
Fax: 0131-225 9833
e-mail: help.desk@scottisharts.org.uk
web: www.sac.org.uk
Director: Graham Berry; *Chairman:*
James Boyle
One of the main funding sources for
arts organisations in Scotland, an
autonomous organisation operating
under a royal charter, responsible to
and financed by the Scottish
Executive. Its aim is to create a climate
in which arts of quality flourish and
are enjoyed throughout Scotland.
    The SAC's current priorities are
education; Scotland's indigenous arts;

encouraging international links and artistic innovation; creating greater access to the arts; and improving arts marketing. It distributes National Lottery money to the arts in Scotland.

The SAC funds 73 organisations on a continuing basis, including the four national companies – Scottish Opera, Royal Scottish National Orchestra, Scottish Chamber Orchestra and Scottish Ballet – art galleries, festivals, theatres, arts centres and touring companies. It also gives awards, bursaries and grants to writers and artists.

ARTS CENTRES
Listed is a selection of arts centres of special interest. A more comprehensive list can be obtained from the Scottish Arts Council.

CCA – CENTRE FOR CONTEMPORARY ARTS
350 Sauchiehall Street, Glasgow G2 3JD
Tel: 0141-332 7521
Fax: 0141-332 3226
e-mail: gen@cca-glasgow.com
web: www.cca-glasgow.com
Director: Graham McKenzie; *Chair:* Ruth Wishart
Hosts contemporary visual arts, performance, music and literary events. Has cafe/bar, bookshop and a number of cultural tenants.

CRAWFORD ARTS CENTRE
93 North Street, St. Andrews KY16 9AL
Tel: 01334 474610
Fax: 01334 479880
e-mail: crawfordarts@crawfordarts. free-online.co.uk
web: www.crawfordarts.free-online. co.uk
Gallery Director: Diana Sykes
Hosts temporary exhibitions of visual art and craft. Provides art classes for adults and children, artists' studio, and studio theatre.

DUNDEE CONTEMPORARY ARTS
152 Nethergate, Dundee DD1 4DY
Tel: 01382 909900
Director: Faith Liddell
Contains galleries, cinemas and extensive facilities for artists and designers.

AN LANNTAIR
Town Hall, South Beach, Stornoway, Isle of Lewis HS1 2BX
Tel: 01851 703307
Fax: 91851 703307
e-mail: lanntair@sol.co.uk
web: www.lanntair.com
Director: Roddy Murray; *Chairman:* Dr John Smith
The main public arts facility in the Western Isles. Its roles include the provision of a forum for local, national and international arts.

LEMON TREE
5 West North Street, Aberdeen AB24 5AT
Tel: 01224 647999
Director: Shona Powell; *Chair:* Councillor David Clyne
Arts centre, development agency, and community resource.

LYTH ARTS CENTRE
by Wick KW1 4UD
Tel: 01955 641270
Director: William Wilson
Provides exhibitions of contemporary fine art, plus live performances by professional touring theatre, dance and music companies.

MACROBERT ARTS CENTRE
University of Stirling, Stirling FK9 4LA
Tel: 01786 467155
Director: Liz Moran

PIER ARTS CENTRE
Victoria Street, Stromness, Orkney
KW16 3AA
Tel: 01856 850209
Director: Neil Firth
Permanent collection of 20th century British art, including works by Hepworth, Nicholson, Gabo, Frost, Heron, Paolozzi, Wallis. Programme of contemporary art exhibitions.

ATHLETICS

SCOTTISH ATHLETICS LIMITED
Caledonia House, South Gyle, Edinburgh EH12 9DQ
Tel: 0131-317 7320
Fax: 0131-317 7321
e-mail: admin@saf.org.uk
web: www.saf.org.uk
Chief Executive: David Joy; *President:* Joan Watt

BADMINTON

SCOTTISH BADMINTON UNION
Cockburn Centre, 40 Bogmoor Place, Glasgow G51 4TQ
Tel: 0141-445 1218
Fax: 0141-425 1218
e-mail: enquiries@scotbadminton. demon.co.uk
web: www.scotbadminton.demon. co.uk
Chief Executive: Anne Smillie; *President:* Morag McCulloch

BANKS
Listed are the Scottish head offices of non-Scottish banks as well as the major indigenous banks

ADAM & COMPANY GROUP PLC
22 Charlotte Square, Edinburgh EH2 4DF
Tel: 0131-225 8484
Fax: 0131-225 5136
web: www.adambank.com
Managing Director: Raymond Entwistle; *Chairman:* W M C Kennedy

BANK OF ENGLAND
Agency for Scotland, 19 St Vincent Place, Glasgow G1 2DT
Tel: 0141-221 7972
Agent for Scotland: Janet Bulloch
Reports to the monetary policy committee on business conditions in Scotland, as well as representing the Bank of England in Scotland.

BANK OF SCOTLAND
PO Box 5, The Mound, Edinburgh EH1 1YZ
Tel: 0131-442 7777
web: www.bankofscotland.co.uk
www.hbosplc.com
Chairman, HBOS plc: Dennis Stevenson, Lord Stevenson of Coddenham; *Executive Deputy Chairman, HBOS plc:* Peter A Burt; *Chief Executive, HBOS plc:* James Crosby
Established by an Act of the Parliament on 17 July 1695 "for the Carrying on and Managing of a Public Bank", the Bank of Scotland is the only bank ever to be founded by such an Act and the only commercial institution created by the Scots Parliament which is still in existence. It is also unique in being the oldest surviving UK clearing bank founded specifically to make a business of banking.

The bank was set up primarily to help develop Scotland's trade, mainly with England and the Low Countries. It was the first bank in Europe successfully to issue paper currency, redeemable for cash on demand. The right to issue banknotes has been maintained to the present day.

It was not until 1774 that the first branches were opened in Dumfries and Kelso.

In the last 30 years of the twentieth

century, a rapid expansion of its activities took place. It played a central role in financing the North Sea oil industry. In 1959 it became the first UK bank to instal a computer to process its accounts centrally.

Bank of Wales was established as a regional bank in 1986, and more recently it acquired Bank of Western Australia Ltd.

On 4 May 2001, the boards of Bank of Scotland and the Halifax group announced that they had agreed to merge to create the HBOS Group. The merger became effective four months later.

CITIBANK, NA
Capital House, 2 Festival Square, Edinburgh EH3 9SU
Tel: 0131-228 3000

CLYDESDALE BANK PLC
30 St Vincent Place, Glasgow G1 2HL
Tel: 0141-248 7070
Chief Executive: Stuart Grimshaw
Founded in 1838. Operates 267 branches in Scotland, England and the Isle of Man.

HBOS PLC
See Bank of Scotland

HSBC
76 Hanover Street, Edinburgh EH2 1HQ
Tel: 0131-456 3257
Area Manager: David Mackay

JP MORGAN PLC
91 George Street, Edinburgh EH2 3ES
Tel: 0131-225 7776
Managing Director (Scotland): Catherine Eardley

LLOYDS TSB SCOTLAND PLC
Henry Duncan House, 120 George Street, Edinburgh EH2 4TS
Tel: 0131-225 4555
web: www.lloydstsbscotland.co.uk

Chief Executive: Susan Rice; *Chairman:* Ewan Brown

NATWEST
8 George Street, Edinburgh EH2 2SB

THE ROYAL BANK OF SCOTLAND GROUP PLC
PO Box 31, 42 St Andrew Square, Edinburgh EH2 2YE
Tel: 0131-556 8555
Fax: 0131-557 6565
web: www.rbs.co.uk
Chairman: Sir George R Mathewson, CBE, LLD, FRSE, FCIBS; *Group Chief Executive:* Frederick A Goodwin, CA, FCIBS, DUniv
Founded 1727, following the expiry of the Bank of Scotland's monopoly 11 years earlier. It merged in 1969 with the National Commercial Bank of Scotland.

Now one of the UK's top 10 companies with share listings in London and New York, it provides banking, insurance and related financial services. Core market in the United Kingdom. Active in Europe to serve and develop its UK banking customer base, and in the north-east USA to diversify its earnings.

Through organic growth and acquisitions, it is one of the UK's fastest growing financial groups and is currently the second largest UK bank, and one of the largest in Europe.

UBS WARBURG
66 Hanover Street, Edinburgh EH2 1HH
Tel: 0131-225 9186

BASKETBALL

BASKETBALL SCOTLAND
Caledonia House, South Gyle, Edinburgh EH12 9DQ
Tel: 0131-317 7260
Chief Executive: Rodger Thompson

BEREAVEMENT

**CRUSE BEREAVEMENT CARE
SCOTLAND**
Riverview House, Friarton Road,
Perth PH2 8DF
Tel: 01738 444178
Director: Stewart Wilson; *Chairman:*
John Birrell
Helps people who have been
bereaved to go on with their lives in a
positive way through counselling.
Also trains those who work with
death and dying.

BLOOD TRANSFUSION

**SCOTTISH NATIONAL BLOOD
TRANSFUSION ASSOCIATION**
2 Otterburn Park, Edinburgh EH14
1JX
Tel: 0131-443 7636
Secretary and Treasurer: William Mack;
Chairman: Peter C Taylor
Promotes, encourages and maintains
the principles of voluntary, non-
remunerated blood donation, and
safeguards and protects the interests
of the voluntary donor.

**SCOTTISH NATIONAL BLOOD
TRANSFUSION SERVICE**
Ellen's Glen Road, Edinburgh EH17
7QT
Tel: 0131-536 5700
General Manager: Angus Macmillan
Douglas
Provides a comprehensive range of
blood components, blood products,
clinical services and human tissue for
patient care throughout Scotland. A
thousand blood donors are needed
every day in Scotland to supply
hospitals throughout the country.
Blood donor sessions – about 4,000 a
year – take place in community
centres, five regional blood donor
centres, workplaces, and universities,
colleges and schools.

BOOK PUBLISHERS

*Listed is a selection of the larger
publishers and a few others of special
interest. A more comprehensive list is
obtainable from the Scottish Publishers
Association.*

ACAIR LTD
7 James Street, Stornoway, Isle of
Lewis HS1 2QN
Tel: 01851 703020
Fax: 01851 703294
e-mail: enquiries@acairbooks.com
web: www.acairbooks.com
Chairman: Donald John MacSween
Publishes a wide range of Gaelic,
English and bilingual books for
children and adults.

B&W PUBLISHING LTD
99 Giles Street, Edinburgh EH6 6BZ
Tel: 0131-625 4500

BUTTERWORTHS SCOTLAND
4 Hill Street, Edinburgh EH2 3JZ
Tel: 0131-225 7828
e-mail: order.line@butterworths.com
web: www.butterworthsscotland.com
Legal publishers.

CANONGATE BOOKS
14 High Street, Edinburgh EH1 1TE
Tel: 0131-557 5111
e-mail: info@canongate.co.uk
web: www.canongate.net

CHAMBERS HARRAP PUBLISHERS LTD
7 Hopetoun Crescent, Edinburgh EH7
4AY
Tel: 0131-556 5929
Fax: 0131-556 5313
e-mail: admin@chambersharrap.
co.uk
web: www.chambersharrap.com
Managing Director: Maurice Shepherd;
Chairman: Anne Tavard
Publishers of the *Chambers Dictionary*,
Chambers offers a full range of
English dictionaries and thesauruses,

ELT dictionaries and study aids, English usage guides, subject dictionaries, crossword and official Scrabble publications. Harrap offers French, Spanish, German, Italian and Portuguese bilingual dictionaries and study aids, plus a range of specialist French business dictionaries.

EDINBURGH UNIVERSITY PRESS
22 George Square, Edinburgh EH8 9LF
Tel: 0131-650 4218
Fax: 0131-662 0053
e-mail: marketing@eup.ed.ac.uk
web: www.eup.ed.ac.uk
Publishers of academic and Scottish interest books and journals.

W GREEN
21 Alva Street, Edinburgh EH2 4PS
Tel: 0131-225 4879
Fax: 0131-225 2104
e-mail: enquiries@wgreen.co.uk
web: www.wgreen.co.uk
Director: Gilly Michie
Scots law publishers.

HARCOURT PUBLISHERS
Robert Stevenson House, 1-3 Baxter's Place, Edinburgh EH1 3AF
Tel: 0131-556 2424

HARPERCOLLINS PUBLISHERS/HARPERCOLLINS CARTOGRAPHIC
Westerhill Road, Bishopbriggs, Glasgow G64 2QT
Tel: 0141-772 3200

LOMOND BOOKS
36 West Shore Road, Granton, Edinburgh EI I5 1QD
Tel: 0131-551 2261

MAINSTREAM PUBLISHING
7 Albany Street, Edinburgh EH1 3UG
Tel: 0131-557 2959

MERCAT PRESS
James Thin Ltd, 53-59 South Bridge, Edinburgh EH1 1YS
Tel: 0131-622 8222
web: www.mercatpress.com
Publishes non-fiction books of Scottish interest.

NEIL WILSON PUBLISHING LTD
Suite 303a, The Pentagon Centre, 36 Washington Street, Glasgow G3 8AZ
Tel: 0141-221 1117
Fax: 0141-221 5363
e-mail: info@nwp.sol.co.uk
web: www.nwp.co.uk
Managing Director: Neil Wilson
Publishers of Scottish books.

POLYGON
22 George Square, Edinburgh EH8 9LF
Tel: 0131-650 4218

RAMSAY HEAD PRESS
9 Glenisla Gardens, Edinburgh EH9 2HR
Tel: 0131-662 1915

SAINT ANDREW PRESS
121 George Street, Edinburgh EH2 4YN
Tel: 0131-225 5722
Fax: 0131-220 3113
Publishing arm of Church of Scotland.

SCOTTISH CULTURAL PRESS AND SCOTTISH CHILDREN'S PRESS
Unit 13D, Newbattle Abbey Business Annexe, Newbattle Road, Dalkeith EH22 3LJ
Tel: 0131-660 4757/6366
Fax: 0131-660 6414
e-mail: info@scottishbooks.com
web: www.scottishbooks.com
Publishers of Scottish interest books.

BOWLING

SCOTTISH BOWLING ASSOCIATION
50 Wellington Street, Glasgow G2 6EF
Tel: 0141-221 8999/2004
e-mail: scottishbowling@aol.com
Secretary: Roger Black; *President:*
William Kerr

SCOTTISH WOMEN'S BOWLING
ASSOCIATION
Kingston House, 3 Jamaica Street,
Greenock PA15 1XX
Tel: 01475 724676
Secretary: Mrs Eleanor Allan

BUILDING SOCIETIES

DUNFERMLINE BUILDING SOCIETY
Caledonia House, Carnegie Avenue,
Dunfermline KY11 8PJ
Tel: 01383 627727
Chief Executive: Graeme D Dalziel;
Chairman: John Herd

SCOTTISH BUILDING SOCIETY
23 Manor Place, Edinburgh EH3 7XE
Tel: 0131-220 1111
Chief Executive: Roderick Matheson;
Chairman: Peter C Brown

BUSINESS ORGANISATIONS

CBI SCOTLAND (CONFEDERATION OF
BRITISH INDUSTRY)
16 Robertson Street, Glasgow G2 8DS
Tel: 0141-222 2184
Director: Iain M McMillan; *Chairman:*
Jack Perry
Aims "to help create and sustain the
conditions in which business in
Scotland and the UK can compete and
prosper". Represents its members'
views to the government and to other
national and international
administrations. Supplies advice,
information and research services to
members and provides a forum for
the exchange and encouragement of
best practice. CBI Scotland claims to
bring "business reality" to political
debate, reacting to government
proposals which it regards as
unwelcome or ill-considered.

INSTITUTE OF DIRECTORS SCOTLAND
29 Abercromby Place, Edinburgh EH3
6QE
Tel: 0131-557 5488
Director: Tom Sunter

QUALITY SCOTLAND FOUNDATION
13 Abercromby Place, Edinburgh EH3
6LB
Tel: 0131-556 2333
Fax: 0131-566 7111
e-mail: info@qualityscotland.co.uk
web: www.qualityscotland.co.uk
Chief Executive: David B Justice, MBE;
Chairman: Andrew Cubie
Fourteen prominent Scottish-based
organisations came together in 1991
with the mission of making
commitment to quality "a recognised
national characteristic". Non-profit-
making and non-political, it aims to
promote business excellence. It is the
official national partner in Scotland
for the European Foundation for
Quality Management (EFQM).
    Quality Scotland supports its
members in implementing their
improvement plans, and in the
application of the European
Excellence Model, which forms a
framework for sustained competitive
advantage.
    Launched in 1994, the Scottish
Awards for Business Excellence
recognise those organisations, in the
four categories of manufacturing,
service, small enterprise, and public
sector, which have achieved
excellence. The awards are presented
at the annual Scottish Forum for
Business Excellence.

SCOTTISH COUNCIL FOR DEVELOPMENT AND INDUSTRY
Campsie House, 17 Park Circus Place, Glasgow G3 6AH
Tel: 0141-332 9119
Fax: 0141-333 0039
e-mail: glasgow@scdi.org.uk
web: www.scdi.org.uk
Chief Executive: Alan Wilson;
Chairman: Donald Turner
Established in 1946, an independent, broadly-based membership organisation (current membership: 2,200) which aims to influence and strengthen Scotland's economy through the formulation and promotion of innovative, non-partisan public policies and the delivery of market-driven services for members.

The Scottish Council Foundation is an independent think tank committed to developing longer-term public policy research.

SCOTTISH FINANCIAL ENTERPRISE
91 George Street, Edinburgh EH2 3ES
Tel: 0131-247 7700
Fax: 0131-247 7709
e-mail: info@sfe.org.uk
web: www.sfe.org.uk
Chief Executive: Ray Perman;
Chairman: Mike Ross
Private sector initiative, established in 1986 to represent and promote the Scottish financial industry, SFE serves a membership of some 200 companies and individuals who are its principal funders, and operates in partnership with Scottish Enterprise and Highlands and Islands Enterprise. Its general aims are to strengthen Scotland's global financial role and to maintain the independence and cohesion of the industry.

SFE publishes a wide range of publications about facts, trends and issues, backed up by an intensive programme of briefings, seminars and conferences. It conducts regular surveys of its members, prepares research papers, represents the interests of its members to the government, regulatory bodies and the EC, arranges missions to or from countries which offer an actual or potential market, and helps with bids to attract new business to Scotland. It works with Scottish Enterprise to improve access to finance for small and medium-sized enterprises, aiming to develop a financial infrastructure not only for Scottish companies but for entrepreneurs from other parts of the EU interested in doing business in Scotland.

SFE was instrumental in founding the advanced management programme in Scotland, which aims to enhance the provision of business and management education.

BUSINESS ORGANISATIONS (YOUTH AND COMMUNITY)

CBS NETWORK (FORMERLY COMMUNITY BUSINESS SCOTLAND)
Society Place, West Calder EH55 8EA
Tel: 01506 871370
Company Secretary John Pearce

PRINCE'S SCOTTISH YOUTH BUSINESS TRUST
6th Floor, Mercantile Chambers, 53 Bothwell Street, Glasgow G2 6TS
Tel: 0141-248 4999
Fax: 0141-248 4836
e-mail: team@psybt.org.uk
Chief Executive: Mark Strudwick, CBE;
Chairman: William Y Hughes, CBE
Provides seedcorn finance and professional support to young people in Scotland aged 18-25 to enable them to set up and run their own businesses. It has particular concern

for the disadvantaged. The trust will identify and arrange training, help with the business plan, and suggest additional sources of support and finance. All recipients benefit from a structured business support service for a minimum of two years.

RATHBONE SCOTLAND
CI Building, Scott Street, Motherwell ML1 1PN
Tel: 01698 252326
Fax: 01698 256700
web: www.rathbone–ci.co.uk
e-mail: johndick@connectfree.co
Director for Scotland: John Dick; *Chair:* Diana Brittan
Rathbone is a charity which aims to ensure that people who have special educational or training needs realise their full potential and participate fully in the social and economic life of the community.

SCOTTISH BUSINESS IN THE COMMUNITY (SBC)
PO Box 408, Bankhead Avenue, Edinburgh EH11 4HE
Tel: 0131-442 2020
Fax: 0131-442 3555
e-mail: info@sbcscot.com
web: www.sbcscot.com
Chief Executive: Samantha Barber; *Chairman:* George Borthwick, CBE
SBC's aim is to involve businesses in supporting the economic and social regeneration of communities across Scotland. This is achieved through: business support groups – channelling private sector support through community-focused business groupings; professional firms group – administering a pool of *pro bono* services offered by participating companies; development assignment programme – arranging employee secondments into community initiatives; partners in leadership – linking senior managers with head teachers for mutual exchange of

management and leadership skills; senior executive programme – co-ordinating the provision of in-kind professional support by retired managers.

YOUNG ENTERPRISE SCOTLAND
Graham Hills Building, 50 George Street, Glasgow G1 1BA
Tel: 0141-548 4930
Chief Executive: Lynn Hendry
Scheme to encourage and develop enterprise and skills in older school students. Teams form companies which trade for about eight months.

CAMPING AND CARAVANNING

CAMPING AND CARAVANNING CLUB (SCOTTISH REGION)
20 The Oval, Clarkston, Glasgow G76 8LY
Tel: 01360 870236
Secretary: Mrs P McIlraith; *Chairman:* D Batty

CARERS

CARERS NATIONAL ASSOCIATION
91 Mitchell Street, Glasgow G1 3LN
Tel: 0141-221 9141
Fax: 0141-221 9140
e-mail: info@carerscotland.org
Provides information and advocacy and campaigns on behalf of carers.

CROSSROADS (SCOTLAND)
24 George Square, Glasgow G2 1EG
Tel: 0141-226 3793
e-mail: enquiries@crossroads-scot.k-web.co.uk
web: www.crossroads-scotland.co.uk
Chief Executive: Jack Ryan; *Chairman:* W Douglas Allan
Provides respite care to carers in Scotland.

CHAMBERS OF COMMERCE

SCOTTISH CHAMBERS OF COMMERCE
12 Broughton Place, Edinburgh EH1 3RX
Tel: 0131-557 9500
Fax: 0131-558 3257
e-mail: mail@scottishchambers.org.uk
web: www.scottishchambers.org.uk
Director: Lex Gold; *Chairman:* Vernon Murphy
Collectively chambers in Scotland have a turnover of about £9m, with members ranging from the country's largest companies to the smallest retail and professional operations. Together they provide more than half the private sector jobs in Scotland. They vary in size from the chambers of Aberdeen, Dundee, Edinburgh and Glasgow, all with full-time professional staff, to small rural and island chambers serviced voluntarily.

Scottish Chambers of Commerce is the national body which promotes co-operation between chambers in the provision of services and represents their common interests. Policy is determined by a council on which all chambers have equal representation.

JUNIOR CHAMBER SCOTLAND
24 Portland Road, Kilmarnock KA1 2BS
Tel: 01563 572255
President: Shona Frame
A worldwide organisation for people aged 18 to 40, offering opportunities in business and social networking, personal development and community activities.

Local chambers:

ABERDEEN AND GRAMPIAN CHAMBER OF COMMERCE
213 George Street, Aberdeen AB25 1XA.
Tel: 01224 620621
Fax: 01224 213221
Chief Executive: Amanda Harvie

ALLANDER CHAMBER OF COMMERCE
2 Stewart Street, Milngavie, Glasgow G62 6BW
Tel: 0141-956 4454
Secretary: Anne O'Hagan

ARBROATH & DISTRICT CHAMBER OF COMMERCE
c/o Small Business Gateway Angus, 61 Marketgate, Arbroath DD11 1AT
Tel: 01241 870563
Fax: 01241 434300
Secretary: Jennifer MacLellan

AYRSHIRE CHAMBER OF COMMERCE & INDUSTRY
Suite 1005, Glasgow Prestwick International Airport, Prestwick KA9 2PL
Tel: 01292 678666
Chief Executive: Pamela Anderson

CAIRNGORMS CHAMBER OF COMMERCE
Old School House, Inverdruie, by Aviemore PH22 1QH
Tel: 01479 812373
Chairman: Philippa Grant

CAITHNESS & SUTHERLAND CHAMBER OF COMMERCE
Bryn Tirion, Castlegreen Road, Thurso KW134 7DN
Tel: 01847 892552
Secretary: George Bruce, OBE

CENTRAL SCOTLAND CHAMBER OF COMMERCE
Haypark Business Centre, Marchmont Avenue, Polmont FK2 0NZ
Tel: 01324 716868
Chief Executive: David Blues

CLYDE VALE CHAMBER OF COMMERCE
30 Hope Street, Lanark ML11 7NE
Tel: 01555 665064
Chairman: Tom Mitchell

CUMBERNAULD & DISTRICT CHAMBER OF COMMERCE
c/o GIST, Orchardton Road, Westfield, Cumbernauld G68 9HD
Tel: 01236 730030
President: Deirdre Duncan

DRUMNADROCHIT CHAMBER OF COMMERCE AND TOURIST ASSOCIATION
PO Box 8, Drumnadrochit IV63 6TX
Tel: 01456 450170
Chairman: Ian Urquhart

DUMFRIES & GALLOWAY CHAMBER OF COMMERCE
Galloway House, The Crichton, Bankend Road, Dumfries DG1 4ZZ
Tel: 01387 702380
Secretary: Sue Taylor

DUNDEE & TAYSIDE CHAMBER OF COMMERCE
Chamber of Commerce Buildings, Panmure Street, Dundee DD1 1ED
Tel: 0845 4589499
e-mail: admin@dundeechamber.co.uk
Chief Executive: Merv Rolfe, CBE

EAST KILBRIDE CHAMBER OF COMMERCE
Platthorn New Ventures, 4 Platthorn Road, East Kilbride G74 1NW
Tel: 01355 238456
Secretary: Ronnie Simpson

EAST RENFREWSHIRE CHAMBER OF TRADE AND COMMERCE
46 Ayr Road, Whitecraigs, Glasgow G46 6SA
Tel: 0141-571 0150
President: Keith Roberts

EDINBURGH CHAMBER OF COMMERCE
27 Melville Street, Edinburgh EH3 7JF
Tel: 0131-477 7000
e-mail: info@ecce.org
Chief Executive: Bill Furness

FIFE CHAMBER OF COMMERCE AND ENTERPRISE
Wemyssfield House, Wemyssfield, Kirkcaldy KY1 1XN
Tel: 01592 201932
Chief Executive: Ian McLaren

FORT WILLIAM & DISTRICT CHAMBER OF COMMERCE
151 High Street, Fort William PH33 6EA
Tel: 01397 703581
Chairman: John Steel

GLASGOW CHAMBER OF COMMERCE
30 George Square, Glasgow G2 1EQ
Tel: 0141-572 2121
Fax: 0141-221 2336
e-mail: chamber@glasgowchamber.org
Chief Executive: Duncan Tannahill

GREENOCK CHAMBER OF COMMERCE
The Business Store, 75–81 Cathcart Street, Greenock PA15 1DE
Tel: 01475 715555
Executive Administrator: Hugh Bunten

HAMILTON & CLYDESDALE CHAMBER OF COMMERCE
Barncluith Business Centre, Townhead Street, Hamilton ML3 7DP
Tel: 01698 426882
Secretary: Cathy Miller

HELENSBURGH & LOMOND CHAMBER OF COMMERCE
Helensburgh Enterprise Centre, 1 East Princes Street, Helensburgh G84 7QG
Tel: 01436 670001
President: Anne Mitchell

INVERNESS & DISTRICT CHAMBER OF COMMERCE
PO Box 5512, Inverness IV2 3ZE
Tel: 01463 718131
Director: Simon Cole-Hamilton

LEITH CHAMBER OF COMMERCE
c/o Edinburgh Chamber of
Commerce, 27 Melville Street,
Edinburgh EH3 7JF
Tel: 0131-477 7000
Secretary: John Kennedy

MID ARGYLL CHAMBER OF COMMERCE
Kilmory   Industrial   Estate,
Lochgilphead, Argyll PA31 8RR
Tel: 01546 606666
Secretary: Jane MacLeod

MIDLOTHIAN CHAMBER OF COMMERCE AND ENTERPRISE
25 Eskbank Road, Dalkeith EH22 1HJ
Tel: 0131-654 1234
Chief Executive: Gregor Murray

MONTROSE CHAMBER OF COMMERCE
55 High Street, Montrose DD10 8LR
Tel: 01674 671199
Secretary: Hamish Watt

MORAY CHAMBER OF COMMERCE
12–14 Greyfriars Street, Elgin IV30 1LF
Tel: 01343 563540
Director: James Johnston

MOTHERWELL AND DISTRICT CHAMBER OF COMMERCE
Dalziel Workspace, Mason Street,
Motherwell ML1 1YE
Tel: 01698 230200
President: Robert Westwood

MULL AND IONA CHAMBER OF COMMERCE
The Ferry Shop, Fionnphort, Isle of
Mull PA66 6BL
Tel: 01681 700470
e-mail: bruntonmull@cs.com
President: Sandy Brunton

OBAN AND LORN CHAMBER OF COMMERCE
2 Queen's Park Place, Oban PA34 5RS
Tel: 01631 562071
Secretary: Alan Cathro

ORKNEY CHAMBER OF COMMERCE
PO Box 6202, Kirkwall, Orkney KW15 1YG
Tel: 01856 873251
Chairman: Duncan McLean

PERTHSHIRE CHAMBER OF COMMERCE
The Atrium, 137 Glover Street, Perth
PH2 0JB
Tel: 01738 637626
Business Manager: Marilyn Wallace

RENFREWSHIRE CHAMBER OF COMMERCE
Bute Court, St Andrews Drive,
Glasgow Airport, Paisley PA3 2SW
Tel: 0141-847 5450
e-mail: info@renfrewshirechamber.com
Chief Executive: Elizabeth K Cameron

STRANRAER AND DISTRICT CHAMBER OF COMMERCE
The Millennium Centre, 75 George
Street, Stranraer DG9 7RJ
Tel: 01776 700000
Chairman: Ronnie Bowie

STRATHKELVIN CHAMBER OF COMMERCE AND TRADE
37 Eastside, Kirkintilloch G66 1QA
Tel: 0141-777 8081
President: Robert Wilson

WEST DUNBARTONSHIRE CHAMBER OF COMMERCE
Tell House, Bankend Road,
Dumbarton G82 2RT
Tel: 01389 768222
Chief Executive: Bill Whiland

WEST LOTHIAN CHAMBER OF COMMERCE
The Business Centre, Almondvale
Boulevard, Livingston EH54 6QP
Tel: 01506 777937
Executive Director: Stuart Duffin

WESTERN ISLES CHAMBER OF COMMERCE
MacKinnon Plant Hire, 18 Inaclete Road, Stornoway, Isle of Lewis HS1 2RB
Tel: 01851 702984
Chairman: Alastair MacKinnon

CHARITABLE TRUSTS

CARNEGIE HERO FUND TRUST
Abbey Park House, Abbey Park Place, Dunfermline KY12 7PB
Tel: 01383 723638
Fax: 01383 721862
Secretary: William C Runciman;
Chairman: George R Atkinson
Gives aid to a rescuer or to a rescuer's family where a heroic act has brought misfortune (concerned with cases which have resulted in death or serious injury only).

CARNEGIE UNITED KINGDOM TRUST
Comely Park House, Dunfermline KY12 7EJ
Tel: 01383 721445
web: www.carnegieuktrust.org.uk
Secretary and Treasurer: John Naylor, OBE
Grant-making trust whose current priorities are in rural community development, creativity and imagination, young people's active participation in society.

SCOTTISH COMMUNITY FOUNDATION
27 Palmerston Place, Edinburgh EH12 5AP
Tel: 0131-225 9804
Fax: 0131-225 9818
e-mail: mail@scottishcommunity
 foundation.com
web: www.scottishcommunity
 foundation.com
Chief Executive: Alan Hobbett;
Chairman: Alastair Dempster
Working with individuals, companies and others, the foundation matches donor interests with community needs, supporting charities and community groups throughout Scotland.

CHILDREN

BARNARDO'S SCOTLAND
235 Corstorphine Road, Edinburgh EH12 7AR
Tel: 0131-334 9893
Fax: 0131-316 4008
e-mail: hugh.mackintosh@
 barnardos.org.uk
web: www.barnardos.org.uk
Director: Hugh Mackintosh, OBE
Provides 49 services for children and young people in greatest need; demonstrates effective good practice and promotes developments in practice widely; influences social policy for the benefit of children; promotes good childhood experiences for all children.

THE BOYS' BRIGADE
Scottish HQ, Carronvale House, Carronvale Road, Larbert FK5 3LH
Tel: 01324 562008
Fax: 01324 552323
e-mail: carronvale@boys-brigade.
 org.uk
web: www.boys-brigade.org.uk
Director Scotland: Tom Boyle
National voluntary youth organisation committed to the personal and social development of children and young people in Scotland. As part of the community education provision, promoting the concept of life-long learning, it seeks to serve local churches in most communities by offering a range of informal educational programmes which are led by voluntary youth workers.

BOYS AND GIRLS CLUBS OF SCOTLAND
88 Giles Street, Edinburgh EH6 6BZ
Tel: 0131-555 1729
Fax: 0131-555 5921
e-mail: bgcs@freezone.co.uk
web: www.freezone.co.uk/
bgcscotland
Chief Adviser: Tom Leishman

BRITISH AGENCIES FOR ADOPTION AND FOSTERING
40 Shandwick Place, Edinburgh EH2 4RT
Tel: 0131-225 9285
Scottish Director: Barbara J Hudson
Concerned with supporting people working to provide a high standard of care for children.

CHILDLINE SCOTLAND
18 Albion Street, Glasgow G1 1LH
Tel: 0141-552 1123
e-mail: scotland@childline.org.uk
web: www.childline.org.uk
Director: Anne Houston
Provides free, confidential telephone counselling for any child or young person with any problem. The organisation "speaks with the voice of children" to influence policy and practice in childcare services.

CHILDREN 1ST
41 Polwarth Terrace, Edinburgh EH11 1NU
Tel: 0131-337 8539
Fax: 0131-346 8284
web: www.children1st@org.uk
Chief Executive: Margaret McKay;
Chairman: Rev William Brown
For over 100 years Children 1st, the Royal Scottish Society for Prevention of Cruelty to Children, has been working to give every child in Scotland a safe and secure childhood. Today it supports families under stress, protects children from harm and neglect, helps them recover from abuse and promotes children's rights and interests.

CHILDREN IN SCOTLAND
Princes House, 5 Shandwick Place, Edinburgh EH2 4RG
Tel: 0131-228 8484
Fax: 0131-228 8585
e-mail: info@childreninscotland.
org.uk
web: www.childreninscotland.org.uk
Chief Executive: Bronwen Cohen;
Convener: Kenneth Munro
The central independent Scottish agency for over 300 voluntary, statutory and professional organisations and individuals working with children and families throughout Scotland. It aims to promote the exchange of information and the development of policies to improve children's quality of life, and services the Scottish All Party Parliamentary Group for Children. It publishes a monthly subscription magazine, *Children in Scotland,* and a six-monthly magazine, *Children in Europe,* with partners across the EU.

CHILDREN'S HOSPICE ASSOCIATION SCOTLAND (CHAS)
18 Hanover Street, Edinburgh EH2 2EN
Tel: 0131-226 4933
Fax: 0131-220 1626
e-mail: morag@chasedinburgh.sol.
co.uk
web: www.chas.org
Chief Executive: Agnes Malone; *Chair:* Barbara Duffner
Provides a hospice service to children and their families.

FAMILY MEDIATION SCOTLAND
18 York Place, Edinburgh EH1 3EP
Tel: 0131-558 9898
Fax: 0131-558 9831
e-mail: info@familymediation
scotland.org.uk
web: www.familymediationscotland.
org.uk
Director: Elizabeth Foster; *Chair:* Hugh Donald, OBE
Supports 12 local mediation services

throughout Scotland working to meet the needs of children of separating or divorced parents.

THE FOSTERING NETWORK
2nd Floor, Ingram House, 227 Ingram Street, Glasgow G1 1DA
Tel: 0141-204 1400
Executive Director: Gerri McAndrew
Aims to ensure the highest standards of care for all children and young people who are fostered, by providing training, advice, support, information and consultancy.

GIRLS' BRIGADE IN SCOTLAND
Boys' Brigade House, 168 Bath Street, Glasgow G2 4TQ
Tel: 0141-332 1765
Fax: 0141-331 2681
e-mail: hq@girls-brigade-scotland. org.uk
web: www.girls-brigade-scotland
National Director: Ann Webster; *National President:* Susan A MacKenzie
Part of an international, interdenominational, Christian, uniformed organisation for girls. Four specific areas are covered in its programme: spiritual, physical, education and service.

GUIDE ASSOCIATION SCOTLAND
16 Coates Crescent, Edinburgh EH3 7AH
Tel: 0131-226 4511
Executive Director: Sally Pitches; *Scottish Chief Commissioner:* Mrs Sally McMath
Provides self-development opportunities to girls and young women through a programme of activities delivered by trained volunteer leaders.

ONE PARENT FAMILIES SCOTLAND
13 Gayfield Square, Edinburgh EH1 3NX
Tel: 0131-556 3899

Director: Sue Robertson; *Convener:* Ruth Lockwood
Helps lone parents achieve their full potential as individuals and as parents.

QUARRIERS
Quarriers Village, Bridge of Weir PA11 3SX
Tel: 01505 612224
Fax: 01505 613906
e-mail: enquiries@quarriers.org.uk
web: www.quarriers.org.uk
Chief Executive: Phil Robinson; *Chairman:* Robin Wilson
Quarriers is a long-established Scottish charity which works in close partnerships with local authorities and other agencies to provide a range of services for children, families and young people, and people with a disability.

SAILORS' ORPHAN SOCIETY OF SCOTLAND
18 Woodside Crescent, Glasgow G3 7UL
Tel: 0141-353 2090
Fax: 0141-353 2190
Secretary: Michael J Beveridge
Provides financial support to orphans of sea-faring men throughout Scotland.

ST ANDREW'S CHILDREN'S SOCIETY
Gillis Centre, 113 Whitehouse Loan, Edinburgh EH9 1BB
Tel: 0131-452 8248
e-mail: info@standrews-children. org.uk
Chairperson: Maureen McEvoy; *President:* Archbishop Keith O'Brien
Recruits, trains and approves adopting parents and foster carers. Works with everyone involved in adoption.

ST MARGARET'S CHILDREN AND FAMILY CARE SOCIETY
274 Bath Street, Glasgow G2 4JR

Tel: 0141-332 8371
Director: Margaret Campbell
Voluntary adoption agency operating in the West of Scotland. Provides a range of pre- and post-adoption services.

SAVE THE CHILDREN FUND, SCOTLAND PROGRAMME OFFICE

2nd Floor, Haymarket House, 8 Clifton Terrace, Edinburgh EH12 5DR
Tel: 0131-527 8200
Director: Alison Davies
The organisation's work, based on the UN Convention on the Rights of the Child, has three aims: building a movement for children's rights in Scotland; promoting the interests of the most marginalised children; developing the role of children and young people as community activists. Aims to give children and young people the opportunity to take part in society by encouraging them to express their views, and to take part in research and in the development and running of initiatives addressing issues that concern them.

SCOTTISH ADOPTION ASSOCIATION

2 Commercial Street, Leith, Edinburgh EH6 6JA
Tel: 0131-553 5060
Director: Ann Sutton
Aims to offer as comprehensive an adoption service as possible to all affected by adoption.

SCOTTISH CHILDMINDING ASSOCIATION

Suite 3, 7 Melville Terrace, Stirling FK8 2ND
Tel: 01786 445377
Director: Anne McNellan, MBE; *Convener:* Margaret Williams
Aims to raise the profile and quality of registered childminding by offering support, information and training.

SCOTTISH CHILDREN'S REPORTER ADMINISTRATION

Ochil House, Springkerse Business Park, Stirling FK7 7XE
Tel: 01786 459500
e-mail: scra@dial.pipex.com
Principal Reporter: Alan D Miller; *Chairman:* Sally Kuenssberg
As part of local government reorganisation in 1996, Children's Reporters and their support staff were united in one national organisation with a new professional framework and the status of a non-departmental public body funded directly by grant-in-aid. It is responsible for facilitating the work of reporters, deploying and managing staff to carry out that work, and providing suitable accommodation for children's hearings.

A referral is a notification of concern about a child to the reporter, as long as that concern can be related to one or more of the statutory grounds for intervention. For every referral received, the reporter must make an appropriate investigation and reach a decision – a process which normally involves obtaining reports from agencies in contact with the child and family. Eight out of 10 children referred to children's hearings become subject to a supervision requirement.

SCOUT ASSOCIATION (SCOTTISH COUNCIL)

Fordell Firs, Hillend, Dunfermline KY11 7HQ
Tel: 01383 419073
Fax: 01383 414892
e-mail: shq@scouts-scotland.org.uk
web: www.scouts-scotland.org.uk
Chief Executive: James A Duffy; *Honorary President:* Rt Hon Earl of Airlie, KT, GCVO, PC, DL
Aims to promote the development of young people in achieving their full physical, intellectual, social and spiritual potential as individuals, as

responsible citizens, and as members of their local, national and international communities.

STEPPING STONES FOR FAMILIES
55 Renfrew Street, Glasgow G2 3BD
Tel: 0141-331 2828
Fax: 0141-331 1991
e-mail: steppingstones@lineone.net
Director: Isobel Lawson; *Chairperson:* Jennie Hynd
National voluntary organisation working to empower families affected by disadvantage so that they can effectively seek to improve their own lives and the communities in which they live.

CHURCHES

ASSOCIATED PRESBYTERIAN CHURCHES
Fernhill, Polvinster Road, Oban PA34 5TN
Tel: 01631 567076
Clerk: Rev Archie McPhail

BAPTIST UNION OF SCOTLAND
14 Aytoun Road, Glasgow G41 5RT
Tel: 0141-423 6169
General Secretary: Rev William Slack; *President:* Rev John Greenshields
Among Oliver Cromwell's troops arriving in Scotland in the 17th century were many Baptist soldiers who used their influence to establish small churches in Leith, Perth, Cupar, Ayr and Aberdeen. When the army withdrew, these churches disappeared and for the next 100 years Baptist life in Scotland ceased to exist. It was revived in 1750 when a congregation was established in the village of Keiss, Caithness.

The present Baptist Union of Scotland came into being in 1869. Strict practice gave way to greater freedom of worship and the introduction of hymns, choirs and organs. Rich Christian industrialists, including Coats of Paisley, Pullar of Perth and Quarrier of Bridge of Weir, gave financial support. Today, there are 170 churches in membership of the Baptist Union of Scotland, representing 15,000 members.

Baptists believe in the truths expressed in the historic creeds of the church, stressing the importance of personal faith in Christ as saviour and the importance of the Bible in guiding the conduct of individuals. A distinctive feature is their practice of Christian baptism – normally by total immersion in water – following the New Testament pattern of baptising those who have come to personal faith in Christ. Historically, Baptists have stood for the separation of church and state.

CHURCH OF SCOTLAND
121 George Street, Edinburgh EH2 4YN
Tel: 0131-225 5722
e-mail: cofsmedia@dial.pipex.com
web: www.churchofscotland.org.uk
Principal Clerk: Rev Dr F A J Macdonald
Regards itself as a "national church" rather than an "established church". The third of the articles declaratory of the constitution in matters spiritual declares: "As a national church representative of the Christian faith of the Scottish people, (the church) acknowledges its distinctive call and duty to bring the ordinances of religion to the people in every parish in Scotland through a territorial ministry." The church enjoys spiritual freedom in that the state recognises "the separate and independent government and jurisdiction of the church in matters spiritual".

Since 1690, the settled government of the church has been presbyterian, the essential features of which are that ministers, elders and deacons participate on equal terms, that there is parity of ministers, and that there is a hierarchy of courts rather than of individuals. There are three courts: the kirk session (congregational); the presbytery (district or regional); and the General Assembly (national). The Assembly, which meets annually in May, does much of its business through standing committees. Its moderator serves for one year and is styled Right Reverend.

Only 17% of Scotland's adult population are now members of the national church compared with an estimated 38% in 1960, when it celebrated the 400th anniversary of the Reformation.

FREE CHURCH OF SCOTLAND
The Mound, Edinburgh EH1 2LS
Tel: 0131-226 4978/5286
Principal Clerk: Rev James Maciver
In its worship and doctrine, the Free Church claims to adhere to the position adopted by the Church of Scotland at the Reformation. Its divergence dates from the disruption of 1843 when, under the leadership of Dr Thomas Chalmers, the evangelical party broke away from the Church of Scotland.

In the late 19th century, a movement to unite the splintered presbyterian churches was begun. A minority within the Free Church took the view that doctrines vital to the faith were being treated as open questions, and when the great majority entered the union of 1900 to form the United Free Church of Scotland (and, in 1929, to re-unite with the Church of Scotland), this minority elected to continue the Free Church of Scotland. The adherents of this "constitutionalist" party, as it was termed, were to be found mainly, though not exclusively, in the Highlands and islands.

Today the Free Church has 4,500 members in 100 congregations. Though much reduced in size, it maintains in continuity with the church of 1843 the post-Reformation system of doctrine and form of worship. The singing of the Scottish metrical psalms unaccompanied by instrumental music is a distinctive feature of its liturgy, but the chief emphasis of its worship is to be found in the centrality of the pulpit and the proclamation of a free and sovereign salvation.

The Free Church of Scotland College, which operates under the oversight of the General Assembly, prepares men for the ministry.

FREE CHURCH OF SCOTLAND (CONTINUING)
Free Church Manse, Portmahomack, Tain IV20 1YL
Tel: 01862 871467
Clerk to the General Assembly: Rev John MacLeod
Established 2000, following a split within the Free Church of Scotland. Claims historical and theological succession to the Church of the Scottish Reformation and the Free Church of Scotland of 1843. Has 38 ministers, 32 active congregations, and around 2000 members/adherents.

FREE PRESBYTERIAN CHURCH OF SCOTLAND
133 Woodlands Road, Glasgow G3 6LE
Tel: 0141-332 9283
Fax: 0141-332 4271
e-mail: fpcofsoffice@cs.com
web: www.fpchurch.org.uk
Principal Clerk: Rev John MacLeod
Pre-1900 breakaway from the Free Church. It has 3,000 adult members. There are 27 congregations in mainland Scotland, mainly in the Highlands, six on Lewis, four on Harris, one on North Uist, seven on

Skye and Raasay, one in Northern Ireland and three in England. The church maintains a whole-hearted allegiance to the Westminster Confession of Faith. It holds that Christ is the sole head of the church; is opposed to the doctrine of universal redemption, believing that Christ died for the elect only; maintains that the Bible is the word of God from beginning to end; opposes the use of instrumental music (and hymns) in public worship; and exercises firm scriptural discipline.

ROMAN CATHOLIC CHURCH

General Secretariat, Bishops' Conference of Scotland, 64 Aitken Street, Airdrie ML6 6LT
Tel: 01236 764061
Fax: 01236 762489
e-mail: GenSec@BpsConfScot.com
General Secretary: Very Rev Mgr Henry Docherty; *Acting President:* Most Rev Keith O'Brien
By the end of the 12th century, there were clearly defined dioceses with territorial bishops in the (Roman Catholic) Church of Scotland. In 1560, following the purging of the Scottish church by John Knox, the ancient order collapsed, some RC bishops joining the reformed church.

The hierarchy formally ended with the death of James Beaton, Archbishop of Glasgow, in 1603, but long before then it was virtually impossible in many parts of the country to obtain a priest to carry out pastoral duties. An apostolic letter in March 1878 restored the hierarchy and divided Scotland into the province of St Andrews and Edinburgh with a metropolitan see and four suffragan sees of Aberdeen, Argyll and the Isles, Dunkeld, and Galloway; and the archdiocese of Glasgow directly subject to the Holy see. Apostolic constitutions in 1947 erected the archdiocese of Glasgow

into a province, with a metropolitan see and two suffragan sees of Motherwell and Paisley.

By 1960, 400 years after the Reformation, the Roman Catholic Church had become the second most important church in Scotland with 530,000 adult members, 15% of the adult population, its revival having been brought about largely by the influx during the Industrial Revolution of Irish emigrants working in the new industries of the west of Scotland. Today, there is an estimated Catholic population of 725,000, which places its membership slightly ahead of that of the Church of Scotland.

SALVATION ARMY

30 Rutland Square, Edinburgh EH1 2BW
Tel: 0131-221 9699
Fax: 0131-221 1482
e-mail: scotland@salvationarmy. org.uk
Scotland Secretary: Colonel John Flett
Part of the universal Christian Church. Its purpose is to proclaim the Christian Gospel and serve the practical needs of humanity.

SCOTTISH EPISCOPAL CHURCH

21 Grosvenor Crescent, Edinburgh EH12 5EE
Tel: 0131-225 6357
Fax: 0131-346 7247
e-mail: office@scotland.anglican.org
web: www.scotland.anglican.org
Secretary-General: John F Stuart; *Primus:* Most Rev Bruce Cameron
Called "Scottish" because it traces its history back to the earliest known Christian communities in Scotland; called "Episcopal" (from the word for bishops) because it has maintained that form of church order, of bishops, priests and deacons, which was in use from those early years until the late 1600s. Supported the Jacobite cause. A

province of the worldwide Anglican communion, but financially self-supporting.

The church does not have archbishops. Instead one of its bishops is chosen as the primus (first among equals), thereby picking up a practice of the Scottish church prior to the 15th century. Describes its relationship with the Church of Scotland as cordial and is committed to unity.

The church is grouped into seven dioceses with a total membership of 50,000, more than half of whom live in Edinburgh and Glasgow.

SYNOD OF METHODIST CHURCH IN SCOTLAND
Central Hall, 2 West Tollcross, Edinburgh EH3 9BP
Tel: 0131-221 9029
Secretary: Rev David Cooper;
Chairman: Rev James W Jones

UNITED FREE CHURCH OF SCOTLAND
11 Newton Place, Glasgow G3 7PR
Tel: 0141-332 3435
Fax: 0141-333 1973
e-mail: ufcos@charis.co.uk
web: www.ufcos.org.uk
Principal Clerk: Rev Joseph G McPhee;
General Secretary: Rev John O Fulton
Founded in 1900 as a result of a union between the United Presbyterian Church and the Free Church (though those members of the Free Church who would not unite continued under that name). In 1929, a majority re-united with the Church of Scotland, leaving what constitutes today the United Free Church of Scotland.

The church is opposed to state establishment of religion and believes that any special state-church relationship is an implicit threat to spiritual autonomy. It further believes that the special recognition by the state of one denomination in Scotland

places the churches on an unequal footing and is not in the best interests of inter-church relations.

UNITED REFORMED CHURCH SYNOD OF SCOTLAND
PO Box 189, Glasgow G1 2BX
Tel: 0141-332 7667
Fax: 0141-332 8463
e-mail: scotland@urc.org.uk
web: www.urc.org.uk
Moderator: Rev John Arthur

CLANS

STANDING COUNCIL OF SCOTTISH CHIEFS
Hope Chambers, 52 Leith Walk, Edinburgh EH6 5HW
Tel: 0131-554 6321
Fax: 0131-553 5319
General Secretary: G A Way of Plean, SSC; *Lord Convener:* Rt Hon Earl of Elgin, KT
Represents major clan chiefs. Answers clansmen's queries on heraldry, ancestry, etc.

COLLEGES OF FURTHER/HIGHER EDUCATION

ABERDEEN COLLEGE
Gallowgate, Aberdeen AB25 1BN
Tel: 01224 612000
Principal: Rae Angus

ANGUS COLLEGE
Keptie Road, Arbroath DD11 3EA
Tel: 01241 432600
Principal: John Burt

ANNIESLAND COLLEGE
Hatfield Drive, Glasgow G12 0YE
Tel: 0141-357 3969
Principal: Linda McTavish

AYR COLLEGE
Dam Park, Ayr KA8 0EU
Tel: 01292 265184
Principal: Frank Burns

BANFF AND BUCHAN COLLEGE OF FURTHER EDUCATION
Henderson Road, Fraserburgh AB43 9GA
Tel: 01346 515777
Principal: Robert Sinclair

BARONY COLLEGE
Parkgate, Dumfries DG1 3NE
Tel: 01387 860251
Principal: Russell Marchant

BELL COLLEGE
Almada Street, Hamilton ML3 0JB
Tel: 01698 283100
Dumfries Campus, Dudgeon House, Crichton University Campus, Bankend Road, Dumfries DG1 4ZN
Principal: Dr Ken MacCallum

BORDERS COLLEGE
Thorniedean House, Melrose Road, Galashiels TD1 2AF
Tel: 08700 505152
Principal: Dr Robert Murray

CARDONALD COLLEGE
690 Mosspark Drive, Glasgow G52 3AY
Tel: 0141-272 3333
Principal: Ros Micklem

CENTRAL COLLEGE OF COMMERCE
300 Cathedral Street, Glasgow G1 2TA
Tel: 0141-552 3941
Principal: Peter Duncan

CLACKMANNAN COLLEGE OF FURTHER EDUCATION
Branshill Road, Alloa FK10 3BT
Tel: 01259 215121
Principal: John Taylor

CLYDEBANK COLLEGE
Kilbowie Road, Clydebank G81 2AA
Tel: 0141-952 7771
Acting Principal: Matt Mochar

COATBRIDGE COLLEGE
Kildonan Street, Coatbridge ML5 3LS
Tel: 01236 422316
Principal: Norman Williamson

CUMBERNAULD COLLEGE
Town Centre, Cumbernauld G67 1HU
Tel: 01236 731811
Principal: Brian Lister

DUMFRIES AND GALLOWAY COLLEGE
Heathhall, Dumfries DG1 3QZ
Tel: 01387 261261
Principal: Tony Jakimciw

DUNDEE COLLEGE
Kingsway Campus, Old Glamis Road, Dundee DD3 8LE
Tel: 01382 834834
Principal: Iain Ovens

EDINBURGH COLLEGE OF ART
Lauriston Place, Edinburgh EH3 9DF
Tel: 0131-221 6000
web: www.eca.ac.uk
Principal: Professor Ian Howard

EDINBURGH'S TELFORD COLLEGE
Crewe Toll, Edinburgh EH4 2NZ
Tel: 0131-332 2491
Principal and Chief Executive: Fiona M Baikie

ELMWOOD COLLEGE
Carslogie Road, Cupar KY15 4JB
Tel: 01334 658800
Principal: Christina Potter

FALKIRK COLLEGE OF FURTHER AND HIGHER EDUCATION
Grangemouth Road, Falkirk FK2 9AD
Tel: 01324 403000
Principal: Linda Mackay

FIFE COLLEGE OF FURTHER AND HIGHER EDUCATION
St Brycedale Avenue, Kirkcaldy KY1 1EX
Tel: 01592 268591
Principal: Joyce Johnston

GLASGOW COLLEGE OF BUILDING AND PRINTING
60 North Hanover Street, Glasgow G1 2BP
Tel: 0141-332 9969
Principal: Thomas Wilson

GLASGOW COLLEGE OF FOOD TECHNOLOGY
230 Cathedral Street, Glasgow G1 2TG
Tel: 0141-552 3751
Principal and Chief Executive: Donald H Leitch

GLASGOW COLLEGE OF NAUTICAL STUDIES
21 Thistle Street, Glasgow G5 9XB
Tel: 0141-565 2500
Principal: Christopher Hunter

GLASGOW SCHOOL OF ART
167 Renfrew Street, Glasgow G3 6RQ
Tel: 0141-353 4500
Fax: 0141-353 4528
e-mail: s.reid@gsa.ac.uk
web: www.gsa.ac.uk
Director: Professor Seona Reid

GLENROTHES COLLEGE
Stenton Road, Glenrothes KY6 2RA
Tel: 01592 772233
Principal: Dr Craig Thomson

INVERNESS COLLEGE
Longman Road, Inverness IV1 1SA
Tel: 01463 273000
Principal and Chief Executive: Dr Graham Clark

JAMES WATT COLLEGE OF FURTHER AND HIGHER EDUCATION
Finnart Street, Greenock PA16 8HF
Tel: 01475 724433
Principal: Terry Davies

JEWEL AND ESK VALLEY COLLEGE
24 Milton Road East, Edinburgh EH15 2PP
Tel: 0131-660 1010
Principal: Howard McKenzie

JOHN WHEATLEY COLLEGE
1346 Shettleston Road, Glasgow G32 9AT
Tel: 0141-778 2426
Principal: Ian Graham

KILMARNOCK COLLEGE
Holehouse Road, Kilmarnock KA3 7AT
Tel: 01563 523501
Principal: Michael Roebuck

LANGSIDE COLLEGE
50 Prospecthill Road, Glasgow G42 9LB
Tel: 0141-649 4991
Principal: A Graeme Hyslop

LAUDER COLLEGE
Halbeath, Dunfermline KY11 8DY
Tel: 01383 845000
Principal: Janet Lowe

LEWS CASTLE COLLEGE
Stornoway, Isle of Lewis HS2 0XR
Tel: 01851 770000
Principal: David Green

MORAY COLLEGE
Moray Street, Elgin IV30 1JJ
Tel: 01343 576000
Principal: Dr James G Logan

MOTHERWELL COLLEGE
Dalzell Drive, Motherwell ML1 2DD
Tel: 01698 232323
Principal and Chief Executive: Richard Millham

NEWBATTLE ABBEY COLLEGE
Dalkeith EH22 3LL
Tel: 0131-663 1921
Principal: Ann Southwood

NORTH GLASGOW COLLEGE
110 Flemington Street, Springburn, Glasgow G21 4BX
Tel: 0141-558 9001
Principal: Ian Miller

NORTH HIGHLAND COLLEGE
Ormlie Road, Thurso KW14 7EE
Tel: 01847 889000
Principal: Hugh Logan

OATRIDGE AGRICULTURAL COLLEGE
Ecclesmachan, Broxburn EH52 6NH
Tel: 01506 854387
Principal: Angus Allan

ORKNEY COLLEGE
Kirkwall, Orkney KW15 1LX
Tel: 01856 569000
Principal: Peter Scott

PERTH COLLEGE
Crieff Road, Perth PH1 2NX
Tel: 01738 877000
Principal: Michael Webster

QUEEN MARGARET UNIVERSITY COLLEGE
Clerwood Terrace, Edinburgh EH12 8TS
Tel: 0131-317 3000
Fax: 0131-317 3256
e-mail: marketing@qmuc.ac.uk
web: www.qmuc.ac.uk
Principal: Professor Joan Stringer, CBE

REID KERR COLLEGE
Renfrew Road, Paisley PA3 4DR
Tel: 0141-581 2222
Principal: Joe Mooney

ROYAL SCOTTISH ACADEMY OF MUSIC AND DRAMA
100 Renfrew Street, Glasgow G2 3DB
Tel: 0141-332 4101

Fax: 0141-332 8901
e-mail: registry@rsamd.ac.uk
web: www.rsamd.ac.uk
Principal: John Wallace; *Chairman:* Lord Gill

SABHAL MÒR OSTAIG
Teangue, Sleat, Isle of Skye IV44 8RQ
Tel: 01471 888000
Director: Norman N Gillies

SAC (SCOTTISH AGRICULTURAL COLLEGE)
West Mains Road, Edinburgh EH9 3JG
Tel: 0131-535 4000
web: www.sac.ac.uk
Principal and Chief Executive: Professor Karl A Linklater; *Chairman:* Dr M M Mackie

SHETLAND COLLEGE OF FURTHER EDUCATION
Gremista, Lerwick, Shetland ZE1 0PX
Tel: 01595 695514
Principal: Gordon Dargie

SOUTH LANARKSHIRE COLLEGE
Hamilton Road, Glasgow G72 7NY
Tel: 0141-641 6600
Principal: Susan Moore

STEVENSON COLLEGE
Bankhead Avenue, Edinburgh EH11 4DE
Tel: 0131-535 4600
Principal: Dr Ray Harris

STOW COLLEGE
43 Shamrock Street, Glasgow G4 9LD
Tel: 0141-332 1786
Principal: Robert G McGrory

WEST LOTHIAN COLLEGE
Almondvale Crescent, Livingston EH54 7DN
Tel: 01506 418181
Principal: Sue Pinder

COMMUNITY

ASSOCIATION OF SCOTTISH COMMUNITY COUNCILS
21 Grosvenor Street, Edinburgh EH12 5ED
Tel: 0131-225 4033
Secretary: Douglas Murray; *Chairperson:* Ian Jarvie
Aims to promote the role, effectiveness and status of community councils in Scotland; to encourage the exchange of information; and to ascertain, co-ordinate and express the views of community councils.

SCOTTISH COMMUNITY DEVELOPMENT CENTRE
329 Baltic Chambers, 50 Wellington Street, Glasgow G2 6HJ
Tel: 0141-248 1924
Directors: Stuart Hashagen/Alan Barr; *Committee Chairman:* Colin Williams, OBE
Partnership between the University of Glasgow and the Community Development Foundation which aims to promote best practice in community development.

CONSERVATION

ANCIENT MONUMENTS BOARD FOR SCOTLAND
Longmore House, Salisbury Place, Edinburgh EH9 1SH
Tel: 0131-668 8764
Fax: 0131-668 8765
e-mail: ancient.monuments@scotland. gov.uk
Secretary: R A J Dalziel; *Chairman:* Professor M Lynch
Advises Scottish ministers on the protection and preservation of monuments of national importance and the maintenance and preservation of monuments in their care. Protection may be provided by including a monument in a statutory list of protected monuments by acquisition or by guardianship. Encourages a close working relationship with other bodies and individuals concerned with Scotland's built heritage.

ARCHITECTURAL HERITAGE SOCIETY OF SCOTLAND
The Glasite Meeting House, 33 Barony Street, Edinburgh EH3 6NX
Tel: 0131-557 0019
Director: Dr Seán O'Reilly; *Chair:* Adam Swan

ASSOCIATION FOR THE PROTECTION OF RURAL SCOTLAND
Gladstone's Land (3rd Floor), 483 Lawnmarket, Edinburgh EH1 2NT
Tel: 0131-225 7012
Fax: 0131-225 6592
e-mail: aprs@aprs.org.uk
Director: Joan Geddes; *Chairman:* Sue Hamilton
Charity, founded in 1926, which seeks to protect Scotland's countryside and to promote ideas for its care and improvement by means of constructive proposals, careful research and active involvement in the maintenance of landscape features. Its core work is involvement in land use matters, submitting comments on policies for structure and local plans, presenting precognitions at public inquiries and commenting on draft consultation papers.

CHARLES RENNIE MACKINTOSH SOCIETY
Queen's Cross, 870 Garscube Road, Glasgow G20 7EL
Tel: 0141-946 6600
Fax: 0141-945 2321
web: www.crmsociety.com

COCKBURN ASSOCIATION (EDINBURGH CIVIC TRUST)
Trunk's Close, 55 High Street, Edinburgh EH1 1SR
Tel: 0131-557 8686
Director: Martin Hulse; *Chairman:* Hon Lord Macfadyen
Maintains and enhances the amenity of the city of Edinburgh and its neighbourhood; protects and conserves its architectural, historical, and landscape heritage.

EDINBURGH WORLD HERITAGE TRUST
5 Charlotte Square, Edinburgh EH2 4DR
Tel: 0131-220 7720
Fax: 0131-220 7730
e-mail: info@ewht.org.uk
web: www.ewht.org.uk
Director: Richard Griffith
Established in 1999 (replacing Edinburgh New Town Conservation Committee and Edinburgh Old Town Renewal Trust). Awards grants for appropriate external repairs, advises central and local government as a formal consultee on major policy and development issues, and monitors and promotes the World Heritage Site. Funded by the Scottish Executive and City of Edinburgh Council.

HISTORIC BUILDINGS COUNCIL FOR SCOTLAND
Longmore House, Salisbury Place, Edinburgh EH9 1SH
Tel: 0131-668 8817
Secretary: Susan Williamson; *Chairman:* Sir Raymond Johnstone
Encourages the conservation and revitalisation of buildings of outstanding historic or architectural interest and promotes the preservation and enhancement of the character or appearance of outstanding conservation areas.
Established in 1953 under the Historic Buildings and Ancient Monuments Act, the council supports the government's policy that "no worthwhile building of architectural or historic merit is lost to our environment unless it is demonstrated beyond reasonable doubt that every effort has been exerted by all concerned to find practical ways of keeping it". Advises Scottish ministers on applications for grants and loans towards repair or maintenance and co-operates closely with bodies and individuals who share its objective of keeping Scotland's built heritage alive and in use.

HISTORIC SCOTLAND
Longmore House, Salisbury Place, Edinburgh EH9 1SH
Tel: 0131-668 8600
web: www.historic-scotland.gov.uk
Chief Executive: Graeme Munro
Established as an executive agency in 1991 by the Secretary of State of Scotland. The agency is headed by the Director and Chief Executive, who is accountable to Scottish ministers.
Historic Scotland's principal activities are to protect, present and promote Scotland's built heritage, which includes ancient monuments and archaeological sites, historic buildings, parks and gardens, and designed landscapes.
Historic Scotland is the largest operator of paid visitor attractions in Scotland. It safeguards the nation's built heritage by scheduling monuments of national importance, listing buildings of special architectural or historic interest and helping owners with maintenance and repair.

KEEP SCOTLAND BEAUTIFUL
7 Melville Terrace, Stirling FK8 2ND
Tel: 01786 471333
Director: John P Summers

NATIONAL TRUST FOR SCOTLAND
Wemyss House, 28 Charlotte Square,
Edinburgh EH2 4ET
Tel: 0131-243 9300
Fax: 0131-243 9301
e-mail: information@nts.org.uk
web: www.nts.org.uk
Chief Executive: Dr Robin Pellew;
President: Earl of Airlie, KT
Exists "for the purposes of promoting
the permanent preservation for the
benefit of the nation of lands and
buildings in Scotland of historic or
national interest or natural beauty". It
encourages the public to enjoy its 120
properties, which include castles and
mansions, gardens, historic sites,
islands, countryside, waterfalls,
coastline and "little houses"
(examples of Scotland's distinctive
vernacular architecture).

Every year it welcomes two
million visitors to those of its
properties where numbers can be
counted. It is estimated that as many
again visit the countryside and open
areas.

An independent charity founded
in 1931, the trust is the largest
voluntary conservation body in
Scotland, dependent for its support
on donations and legacies and the
subscriptions of 228,000 members.

ROYAL COMMISSION ON THE ANCIENT
AND HISTORICAL MONUMENTS OF
SCOTLAND
16 Bernard Terrace, Edinburgh EH8
9NX
Tel: 0131-662 1456
Fax: 0131-662 1477
e-mail: postmaster@rcahms.gov.uk
web: www.rcahms.gov.uk
*Secretary and Curator, National
Monuments Record of Scotland:* R J
Mercer; *Chairman:* Mrs Kathleen
Dalyell
Independent non-departmental
government body, established in
1908, financed by Parliament under

the sponsorship of Historic Scotland.
Its main objectives are to record and
interpret the sites, monuments and
buildings of Scotland's past,
promoting a greater appreciation of
their value through the maintenance
of the National Monuments Record of
Scotland (NMRS), and presenting
them more directly by selective
publications and exhibitions.

The birth of the commission
reflected increasing concern about the
destruction of the country's historical
monuments and appreciation of the
need for a nationwide assessment of
surviving sites and structures. Every
year the commission undertakes
about 500 surveys of threatened
buildings.

The National Archaeological
Survey identifies and maps sites and
monuments of all periods. The
Thematic Architectural Survey deals
strategically with classes of buildings
of particular architectural or historical
interest which are vulnerable to
redundancy or other long-term threat.
The National Monuments Record of
Scotland, with its 179,000 site records,
is the country's largest repository of
information on ancient monuments
and historic buildings.

SCOTTISH CHURCH ARCHITECTURAL
HERITAGE TRUST
15 North Bank Street, Edinburgh EH1
2LP
Tel: 0131-225 8644
Director: Florence MacKenzie, MBE;
Chairman: Rt Hon Lord Penrose
Awards grants for fabric repairs to
Scottish churches of all
denominations.

SCOTTISH CIVIC TRUST
Tobacco Merchant's House, 42 Miller
Street, Glasgow G1 1DT
Tel: 0141-221 1466
Fax: 0141-248 6952
e-mail: sct@scotnet.co.uk

web: www.scotnet.co.uk/sct
Director: John N P Ford; *Chairman:* Sir James Dunbar-Nasmith, CBE
Sees itself as both catalyst and guardian, aiming to encourage: well-informed public concern for the environment of both town and country; high quality in planning and in new architecture; the conservation and, where necessary, adaptation for re-use of older buildings of distinction or historic interest; knowledgeable and therefore effective comment in planning matters; and the elimination of ugliness, whether resulting from social deprivation, bad design or neglect.

Founded in 1967, the trust is financed by donations, covenants and subscriptions, with help from local and central government.

SCOTTISH HISTORIC BUILDINGS TRUST

33 High Street, Cockenzie, East Lothian EH32 0HP
Tel: 01875 813608
Fax: 01875 813608
e-mail: shbt@btinternet.com
Chairman: George McNeill
Acquires, repairs, and identifies new uses for historic buildings which are at risk.

SCOTTISH INLAND WATERWAYS ASSOCIATION

1 Craiglockhart Crescent, Edinburgh WEH14 1EZ
Tel: 0131-443 2533
Secretary: George A Hunter, OBE; *Chairman:* Donald MacKinnon
Membership consists of all canal societies in Scotland. Concerned with the protection of Scottish canals.

SCOTTISH NATURAL HERITAGE

12 Hope Terrace, Edinburgh EH9 2AS
Tel: 0131-447 4784
Fax: 0131-446 2277
e-mail: george.anderson@snh.gov.uk

web: www.snh.org.uk
Chief Executive: Roger Crofts, CBE; *Chairman:* John Markland
Established in 1992 from a merger of the Nature Conservancy Council for Scotland and the Countryside Commission for Scotland. A government agency which receives its funding of £51.1 million from the Scottish Executive.

It has two roles: to advise government and others about the management and use of natural heritage, and to carry out executive tasks on behalf of government. SNH's mission is "to work with Scotland's people to care for our natural heritage". Much of its conservation effort for species, habitats and landscapes focuses on parts of Scotland designated as SSSIs (Sites of Special Scientific Interest), including Special Areas of Conservation, Special Protection Areas and National Nature Reserves, and National Scenic Areas.

SNH provides financial assistance to, and establishes special projects with, a wide range of bodies to replenish depleted areas in remote areas of the countryside and in and around towns and cities. It works through environmental education to increase the awareness and understanding of the natural heritage and encourages people to enjoy it by providing such facilities as footpaths and signposts, as well as grant-aiding the Scottish Countryside Ranger service.

The first UK government organisation to have a formal statutory responsibility for sustainability, SNH encourages the development of strategies and financial assistance schemes which recognise the importance of the natural heritage. Its priorities in the medium term are: to promote biodiversity; to manage special natural heritage sites, particularly the government's Natura 2000 programme to implement the EU's directives on habitats and birds; to facilitate the integrated management of the Cairngorms, and Loch Lomond and the Trossachs; to improve environmental education in Scotland; and to help land managers to care for the natural heritage and manage the public's enjoyment of it.

SCOTTISH RIGHTS OF WAY AND ACCESS SOCIETY (SCOTWAYS)
24 Annandale Street, Edinburgh EH7 4AN
Tel: 0131-558 1222
Fax: 0131-558 1222
e-mail: info@scotways.com
web: www.scotways.com
Secretary: Alexander C H Valentine
Chairman: Bruce Logan
Safeguards public access throughout Scotland. Activities include putting up signposts and maintaining the National Catalogue of Rights of Way.

SCOTTISH SOCIETY FOR CONSERVATION & RESTORATION
The Glasite Meeting House, Chantstoun, Tartraven, Bathgate Hills, West Lothian EH48 4NP
Tel: 01506 811777
Administrator: Kim Dalland; *Chair:* Ylva Player-Dhansjo
Independent organisation promoting the conservation and restoration of Scotland's historic, scientific and artistic materials. Provides a forum for people concerned with this, working in the public or independent sectors, or primarily interested in the conservation and restoration of objects and buildings.

SCRAN (SCOTTISH CULTURAL RESOURCES ACCESS NETWORK)
Abden House, 1 Marchhall Crescent, Edinburgh EH16 6HP
Tel: 0131-662 1211
Fax: 0131-662 1511

web: www.scran.ac.uk
Chief Executive: Bruce Royan
A fully searchable resource base of Scottish material culture and human history. Works with project partners such as museums, galleries, archives and universities to digitise selected parts of their collections. Gives access to hundreds of thousands of images and film clips, copyright cleared for educational use.

WWF
8 The Square, Aberfeldy PH15 2DD
Tel: 01887 820449
Fax: 01887 829453
e-mail: wwfscotland@wwfscotland. org.uk
web: www.wwf.org.uk
Director (Scotland): Simon Pepper, OBE
Global environment network working to conserve endangered species, protect endangered species, and address global threats to nature by seeking long-term solutions.

CONSUMER ADVICE AND PROTECTION

CITIZENS ADVICE SCOTLAND
26 George Square, Edinburgh EH8 9LD
Tel: 0131-667 0156
web: www.cas.org.uk
Chief Executive Officer: Kaliani Lyle; *Chair:* Bob Brodie
Member bureaux of Citizens Advice Scotland (the Scottish Association of Citizens Advice Bureaux) give advice and information on problems brought by the public. There are 58 Citizens Advice Bureaux and 150 CAB service points in Scotland. The association's work is funded by the Department of Trade of Industry and from other sources. In addition to its information and advisory services, it lobbies policy-makers on social matters.

COMMISSIONER FOR LOCAL ADMINISTRATION IN SCOTLAND (LOCAL GOVERNMENT OMBUDSMAN)
23 Walker Street, Edinburgh EH3 7HX
Tel: 0131-225 5300
web: www.ombudslg.scot.org.uk
Commissioner: Ian Smith
Free independent service for members of the public who have complaints of injustice arising from maladministration on the part of local government and related bodies. In addition to the 32 local authorities and their joint committees and boards, the ombudsman has jurisdiction over licensing boards, Scottish Homes (as landlord) and the Strathclyde Passenger Transport Authority.

Any individual or body can make a complaint, which requires to be in writing. A complaint form is available, but is not obligatory. Complaints must usually be made within 12 months of the problem arising and should first have been raised with the authority concerned. Emphasis is placed on facilitating the resolution of complaints. Of those taken up, about a third are satisfactorily resolved.

In cases where the ombudsman conducts a formal investigation, his findings are issued in a public report. He has no power to enforce his findings but, in practice, authorities generally comply with his recommendations which can include taking corrective action and paying financial compensation.

ENERGY ACTION SCOTLAND
Suite 4a, Ingram House, 227 Ingram Street, Glasgow G1 1DA
Tel: 0141-226 3064
Fax: 0141-221 2788
e-mail: eas@eas.org.uk
Director: Ann Loughrey; *President:* David Marshall, MP
National charity which aims to eliminate fuel poverty by: raising awareness of fuel poverty, particularly as it affects low income households, and working towards affordable warmth for all; identifying effective solutions which can transform cold, damp houses into warm, dry homes; securing public and private investment in domestic energy efficiency initiatives.

ENERGYWATCH
2nd Floor, Delta House, West Nile Street, Glasgow G1 2NP
Tel: 0845 906 0708
e-mail: enquiry@energywatch.org.uk
web: www.energywatch.org.uk
Director: Audrey Gallacher; *Scottish Chair:* John Hanlon
Brand name for the Gas and Electricity Consumer Council. Independent consumer watchdog serving all Scottish domestic and industrial gas and electricity consumers. Energywatch handles customer complaints and campaigns on energy related issues. It replaced the Gas Consumers Council and the Electricity Consumers Committees.

HEALTH SERVICE OMBUDSMAN FOR SCOTLAND
28 Thistle Street, Edinburgh EH2 1EN
Tel: 0845 601 0456
Fax: 0131-226 4447
e-mail:
    SHSC.Enquiries@ombudsman.
    gsi.gov.uk
web: www.ombudsman.org.uk/hse/
    index.html
Ombudsman: Michael Buckley; *Deputy Ombudsman:* Hilary Scott
Investigates complaints about the National Health Service. The ombudsman may investigate complaints about hospitals or community health services which concern (a) poor service; (b) failure to purchase or provide a service which people are entitled to receive; (c)

maladministration, such as avoidable delay, not following proper procedures, rudeness, etc. The ombudsman may also investigate complaints about the care and treatment provided by a doctor, nurse or other trained professional.

Before asking the ombudsman to look into a complaint, a patient must first take it up locally with his or her local hospital, clinic or surgery. If a complaint is found to be justified, the ombudsman will seek an apology or other remedy for the complainant. The ombudsman is completely independent of the NHS and the government. There is no charge for the service.

LOCAL GOVERNMENT OMBUDSMAN
See Commissioner for Local Administration

OFFICE OF GAS AND ELECTRICITY MARKETS (OFGEM)
70 West Regent Street, Glasgow G2 2QZ
Tel: 0141-331 2678
Fax: 0141-331 2777
Managing Director: Charles Coulthard
Ofgem is the office of the regulator for the gas and electricity markets, which was formed in June 1999 to protect the interests of consumers, ensuring they obtain genuine value and choice, by promoting effective competition in both gas and electricity markets and regulating monopolies. It does this by issuing licences, encouraging competition, and where no competition exists, by imposing price controls and efficiency standards as a substitute for competition.

RAIL PASSENGERS COMMITTEE SCOTLAND
Corunna House, 29 Cadogan Street, Glasgow G2 7AB
Tel: 0141-221 7760
Fax: 0141-221 3393
e-mail: scottishrailusersasupanet.com
Secretary: Bill Ure; *Convener:* Mike Lunan
Statutory watchdog protecting and promoting the interests of rail passengers. Formerly known as the Rail Users Consultative Committees (eight cover the UK), set up under the Railways Act 1993 and funded by the Rail Regulator. The train operating companies serving Scotland are: Great North Eastern Railway, ScotRail, and Virgin Trains; the committee for Scotland also has responsibility for dealing with matters concerning Caledonian MacBrayne shipping services.

The committee actively seeks the views of passengers, including those with special needs, and represents passengers' interests to the industry and to those who regulate or influence it. Locally it keeps watch on such matters as the punctuality and reliability of train services, timetable changes, safety and security, overcrowding, cleanliness, fares, the quality and design of trains, station facilities, provision of information at stations as well as on trains, and whether operators are meeting their franchise specifications.

Customers should first contact the company operating the service. If they are not satisfied with the response to their complaint, they should then contact the committee.

SCOTTISH ADVISORY COMMITTEE ON TELECOMMUNICATIONS
28 Thistle Street, Edinburgh EH1 2EN
Tel: 0131-226 7275
Established in 1984 to advise the Director General of the Office of Telecommunications (OFTEL) on regulatory policy and its effects on customers. Companies operating public telecommunications sytems are required by their licences to consider the committee's

representations. Its secretariat handles customer complaints, but people who wish to complain should first give the supplier an opportunity to put things right.

SCOTTISH CONSUMER COUNCIL

Royal Exchange House, 100 Queen Street, Glasgow G1 3DN
Tel: 0141-226 5261
Fax: 0141-221 0731
e-mail: scc@scotconsumer.org.uk
web: www.scotconsumer.org.uk
Director: Martyn Evans; *Chairman:* Graeme Millar
Represents, promotes and safeguards the interests of consumers by providing advice, information and redress, identifying issues and problems, monitoring and reporting on services, influencing decision-making, responding to proposals and encouraging consumer representation in the public services and privatised utilities. It has a particular remit for those who face disadvantage in society.

The SCC does not deal with individual complaints or test consumer products. Established by the government in 1975, it is funded mainly through a grant from the Department of Trade and Industry.

SCOTTISH LEGAL SERVICES OMBUDSMAN

17 Waterloo Place, Edinburgh EH1 3DL
Tel: 0131-244 3055
Fax: 0131-244 3065
e-mail: Ombudsman@slso.org.uk
web: www.slso.org.uk
Ombudsman: Linda Costelloe Baker
The ombudsman is appointed by Scottish ministers and cannot be a lawyer. He or she looks into complaints about the way a professional body (the Law Society of Scotland, the Faculty of Advocates or the Scottish Conveyancing and Executry Services Board) has handled a complaint against a legal practitioner. The ombudsman's job is to decide if the professional body has given each complaint proper attention, if it has taken appropriate action on the basis of a fair and thorough examination of all the evidence, and if it has acted reasonably, impartially and effectively.

If the ombudsman finds that a professional body has mismanaged the investigation or failed to investigate the complaint properly, he or she can recommend that it: provides more information to the complainant; investigates the complaint further; re-considers the complaint; exercises its powers in relation to the practitioner; pays compensation for inconvenience or distress caused by the way the investigation was handled; re-imburses part or all of the costs of the complainant making the complaint to the ombudsman.

The ombudsman may report a case to the Scottish Solicitors' Discipline Tribunal where it appears that a solicitor may have been guilty of professional misconduct.

The professional body has three months to decide if it will accept the ombudsman's recommendations. If it does not accept, the ombudsman can publish an announcement, giving his or her views and the professional body's views. Neither the complainant nor the legal practitioner are identified. The professional body pays the costs of the publicity.

The ombudsman does not investigate complaints about legal practitioners.

WATER INDUSTRY COMMISSIONER FOR SCOTLAND

Ochil House, Springkerse Business Park, Stirling FK7 7XE

Tel: 01786 430200
Fax: 01786 462018
e-mail: enquiries@water
    commissioner.co.uk
web: www.watercommissioner.co.uk
Water Industry Commissioner for Scotland: Alan Sutherland
Professional regulator of the Scottish water authorities, responsible for regulating all aspects of their economic and customer service performance.

COUNSELLING

COSCA (CONFEDERATION OF SCOTTISH COUNSELLING AGENCIES)
18 Viewfield Street, Stirling FK8 1UA
Tel: 01786 475140
Executive Director: Stewart Wilson; *Convenor:* Colin Kirkwood
Aims to support and develop all forms of counselling in Scotland.

COURTS AND TRIBUNALS

APPEAL SERVICE
Scottish Regional Office, Wellington House, 134-136 Wellington Street, Glasgow G2 2XL
Tel: 0141-354 8400
Acting Regional Chairman: David Lang
Independent, statutory body responsible for the running of Social Security, Medical, Vaccine Damage, Disability and Child Support appeal tribunals.

CHILD SUPPORT COMMISSIONERS
23 Melville Street, Edinburgh EH3 7PW
Tel: 0131-225 2201
Secretary: Miss S M Niven
Commissioners are independent members of the judiciary. They exercise appellate jurisdiction on questions of law arising from child support appeals.

COUNCIL ON TRIBUNALS, SCOTTISH COMMITTEE
44 Palmerston Place, Edinburgh EH12 5BJ
Tel: 0131-220 1236
e-mail: sccot@gtnet.gov.uk
Secretary: Marjorie MacRae; *Chairman:* R John Elliot, WS
The Scottish Committee exercises supervision of the operation of most tribunals and inquiries in Scotland. Established in 1958 by Act of Parliament. Keeps under review the working of some 40 tribunals in such fields as social security, education, taxation, employment and child care. The council regards openness, fairness and impartiality as the elements essential to the proper functioning of the tribunal and inquiry system. Its greatest concern is that lay men and women involved in any hearing system receive fair treatment and can obtain an unbiased decision on their case whatever the outcome.

The council has a statutory right to visit tribunals to observe their conduct at first hand. Visiting members take a close interest in such matters as the suitability of the premises, the working of the tribunal and its staffing, and the quality of any guidance literature. Shortcomings, if sufficiently serious, may be brought to the attention of the body responsible for the administration of the tribunal or inquiry concerned.

COURT OF THE LORD LYON
HM New Register House, Edinburgh EH1 3YT
Tel: 0131-556 7255
Fax: 0131-557 2148
Lord Lyon King of Arms: Robin O Blair, LVO
In Scotland, the use of armorial

bearings is strictly controlled by statute and they may only be lawfully used and displayed if they have been granted by the Lord Lyon King of Arms and recorded in the Public Register of All Arms and Bearings in Scotland, a register established by Act of Parliament in 1672.

Armorial bearings are granted by the Lord Lyon King of Arms to private individuals, corporate bodies, schools, charities, etc, and once arms are granted they become the property and visual identity of the individual or organisation concerned. The Lord Lyon also considers petitions in a judicial capacity from those who wish to re-record the arms of an ancestor in the Public Register. Arms descend to the heir in each generation of the original grantee.

The Lord Lyon King of Arms, accompanied by three Heralds and three Pursuivants, appears on ceremonial occasions such as installation services of the Order of the Thistle and the opening of the General Assembly of the Church of Scotland. The Lord Lyon is appointed by the Crown, as is the Lyon Clerk and Keeper of the Records.

EMPLOYMENT TRIBUNALS IN SCOTLAND
Eagle Building, 215 Bothwell Street, Glasgow G2 7TS
Tel: 0141-204 0730
Secretary: D Easton
Independent judicial bodies with jurisdiction to hear cases which relate to people's rights in the field of employment law. The issues it deals with include unfair dismissal, redundancy payments, and sex, race and disability discrimination, together with some health and safety matters.

The tribunal will always have a legally qualified chairman, who is appointed in Scotland by the Court of Session. Most cases are heard at permanent industrial tribunal offices. The tribunal will always send a written decision – and its reason for making that decision – to the parties or their representatives. Either party may apply for a review of the decision, or lodge an appeal against it within set time limits.

LANDS TRIBUNAL FOR SCOTLAND
1 Grosvenor Crescent, Edinburgh EH12 5ER
Tel: 0131-225 7996
Fax: 0131-226 4812
Clerk: Neil M Tainsh; President: Hon Lord McGhie
Judicial body established in 1971 to determine a wide range of questions relating to valuation of land, the discharge or variation of restrictive land obligations and disputed compensation (for example, on compulsory purchase of land). Its members have recognised expertise in the fields of law and surveying.

Numerous Acts of Parliament have conferred additional areas of jurisdiction, including appeals against the Keeper of the Registers of Scotland under the Land Registration (Scotland) Act 1979 and disputes concerning council house purchase under various tenants' rights legislation. Valuation Appeal Committees can refer complaints to the Tribunal over non-domestic rating assessments under the valuation acts and regulations. The Tribunal can also act as arbiter where a reference is brought jointly by disputing parties.

PENSIONS APPEAL TRIBUNALS FOR SCOTLAND
20 Walker Street, Edinburgh EH3 7HS
Tel: 0131-220 1404
Fax: 0131-225 2596
Secretary: Bill Barclay; President: Colin N McEachran, QC

Hears and decides on appeals against the rejection by the Department of Social Security of War Pension claims.

RENT ASSESSMENT PANEL FOR SCOTLAND

48 Manor Place, Edinburgh EH3 7EH
Tel: 0131-226 1123
Secretary: Mrs N Eagle; *President:* John H Barton, WS
Provides chairmen and members for rent assessment committees. These committees determine rents for private sector housing.

SCOTTISH COURT SERVICE

Hayweight House, 23 Lauriston Street, Edinburgh EH3 9DQ
Tel: 0131-229 9200
Chief Executive: John Ewing
Provides and maintains court houses and supplies trained staff to meet the needs of the judiciary and court users.

SCOTTISH LAND COURT

1 Grosvenor Crescent, Edinburgh EH12 5ER
Tel: 0131-225 3595
Principal Clerk: K H R Graham; *Chairman:* Hon Lord McGhie
Constituted by the Small Landholders (Scotland) Act 1911 and brought into being in 1912. The chairman was required to be an advocate of not fewer than 10 years' standing with the same rank and tenure as a judge of the Court of Session. The other members were to be appointed on the basis of their expert and practical knowledge of agriculture and the statute. One of the members had to be able to speak Gaelic.

The Act conferred on the court the jurisdictions which had been exercised by the original Crofters Commission in the seven crofting counties and extended the jurisdiction to landholders' holdings and statutory small tenancies throughout Scotland.

SCOTTISH SOLICITORS' DISCIPLINE TRIBUNAL

22 Rutland Square, Edinburgh EH1 2BB
Tel: 0131-229 5860

SOCIAL SECURITY COMMISSIONERS

23 Melville Street, Edinburgh EH3 7PW
Tel: 0131-225 2201
Secretary: Miss S M Niven
Commissioners are independent members of the judiciary. They exercise appellate jurisdication on questions of law arising from appeal tribunals on matters under the governance of the Department of Social Security and on child support appeals.

CRICKET

SCOTTISH CRICKET UNION

National Cricket Academy, MES Sports Centre, Ravelston, Edinburgh EH4 3NT
Tel: 0131-313 7420
General Manager: David Hays; *Chairman:* Alun Davies

CRIME

CRIMINAL INJURIES COMPENSATION AUTHORITY

Tay House, 300 Bath Street, Glasgow G2 4LN
Tel: 0141-331 2726
web: www.cica.gov.uk
Chief Executive: Howard Webber
Administers the government-funded scheme to provide compensation for innocent victims of violent crime.

CROWN OFFICE

25 Chambers Street, Edinburgh EH1 1LA
Tel: 0131-226 2626
web: www.crownoffice.gov.uk

Crown Agent: Andrew Normand Sole public prosecuting authority in Scotland. Has the duty to investigate all sudden, suspicious or unexplained deaths. Headquarters of the Procurator Fiscal Service.

VICTIM SUPPORT SCOTLAND
15/23 Hardwell Close, Edinburgh EH8 9RX
Tel: 0131-668 4486
Fax: 0131-662 5400
e-mail: info@victimsupportsco. demon.co.uk
web: www.victimsupport.org
Chief Executive: David McKenna; *Honorary President:* Sheriff Gordon Nicholson, QC; *Chairperson:* James Brodie
National charity for crime victims. Volunteers provide practical help and emotional support to people affected by crime. The service is free and confidential.

CULTURE (SCOTTISH)

INSTITUTE OF CONTEMPORARY SCOTLAND
2nd Floor, House 6, 94 Elmbank Street, Glasgow G2 4PF
Tel: 0141-204 2848
Fax: 0141-204 2849
e-mail: icsadmin@ contemporaryscotland.com
Director: Kenneth Roy; *President:* Rose Galt
Established in 2000 with the aim of stimulating ideas and debate more widely by the promotion of lectures, conferences and other events. It is strongly committed to social inclusion.

ROYAL CELTIC SOCIETY
23 Rutland Street, Edinburgh EH1 2RN
Tel: 0131-228 6449

Secretary: J Gordon Cameron; *Chairman:* A C Macpherson
Founded in 1820. Primary aims are to maintain and promote interest in the history, traditions, language and arts of the Highlands and Western Isles. Annual donations are made to cultural bodies and events.

SALTIRE SOCIETY
9 Fountain Close, 22 High Street, Edinburgh EH1 1TF
Tel: 0131-556 1836
Fax: 0131-557 1675
e-mail: saltire@saltire.org.uk
web: www.saltire-society.demon. co.uk
Administrator: Kathleen Munro; *President:* Paul H Scott
Founded in 1936 by a group of people who were anxious to see Scotland restored to its proper position as a cultural entity. The society aims to foster and enrich the cultural heritage of Scotland in all its aspects. It looks to the future as well as to the past, encouraging creativity as a living element of European civilisation. It encourages the study and appreciation of arts and sciences and presents annual awards for excellence in civil engineering, planning, literature, housing design, and science.

CURLING

ROYAL CALEDONIAN CURLING CLUB
Cairnie House, Ingliston Showground, Newbridge EH28 8NB
Tel: 0131-333 3003
Fax: 0131-333 3323
e-mail: secretaryandoffice@ rccc1.fsbusiness.co.uk
web: www.rccc.org.uk
Secretary: W J Duthie Thomson; *President:* Andrew Hepburn

CYCLING

CTC SCOTLAND
3 Canning Street, Dundee DD3 7RZ
Tel: 01382 884540
Secretary: Peter Hawkins; *Chairman:* Ron Harrow
Voluntary national cycling association. Represents cycling interests on national bodies, campaigns for better cycling facilities, produces an annual calendar of events, and organises events nationally and locally.

SCOTTISH CYCLISTS' UNION
The Velodrome, Meadowbank Sports Centre, London Road, Edinburgh EH7 6AD
Tel: 0131-652 0187
Fax: 0131-661 0474
e-mail: scottish.cycling@btinternet. com
web: www.scuweb.com
Executive Officer: Gordon Walker

SUSTRANS SCOTLAND
162 Fountainbridge, Edinburgh EH3 9RX
Tel: 0131-624 7660
e-mail: scotland@sustrans.org.uk
Manager in Scotland: Tony Grant
"Sustrans" stands for sustainable transport. It works through practical projects to design and build routes for cyclists, walkers and wheelchair users.

DANCE

DANCE SCOTLAND
c/o 100 Beith Street, Partick, Glasgow G11 6BR
Tel: 0141-334 2000
Supports all aspects of dance throughout Scotland. Publishes *Dance Network Directory* and *Dance News Scotland*.

ROYAL SCOTTISH COUNTRY DANCE SOCIETY
12 Coates Crescent, Edinburgh EH3 7AF
Tel: 0131-225 3854
Fax: 0131-225 7783
e-mail: info@rscdshq.freeserve.co.uk
web: www.rscds.org
Secretary/Administrator: Elspeth Gray; *Chairman:* Alan Mair
Aims to promote Scottish country dancing and preserve its traditions by providing opportunities for members to learn dances and steps.

SCOTTISH BALLET
261 West Princes Street, Glasgow G4 9EE
Tel: 0141-331 2931
Fax: 0141-331 2629
e-mail: scottishballet.co.uk
web: www.scottishballet.co.uk
Artistic Director: Robert North; *Executive Director:* Norman L Quirk; *Chairman:* Duncan McGhie
Scotland's leading national and international touring ballet company. Formed by Peter Darrell as the Western Theatre Ballet in Bristol in 1957, it transferred to Glasgow in 1969 to become Scotland's national dance company.
In an average year the company gives 125 performances to a total audience of 115,000. Its work ranges from traditional classics using up to 50 dancers and an orchestra of 70 musicians to performances involving six dancers and a pianist.
The company has performed in a variety of spaces from the Edinburgh Festival Theatre to village halls across Scotland. Its programme of education and outreach has included a summer school for young people in Easterhouse, Glasgow, and work with visually and hearing-impaired adults.

SCOTTISH TRADITIONS OF DANCE TRUST
54 Blackfriars Street, Edinburgh EH1

1NE
Tel: 0131-558 8737
e-mail: edinburgh.stdt@virgin.net
Co-ordinator: Liam Paterson
The national organisation which exists to research, conserve, foster and promote all of Scotland's dance traditions.

DEMOCRACY

SCOTTISH CIVIC FORUM
21 Queen Street, Edinburgh EH2 1JX
Tel: 0131-225 6789
Fax: 0870 051 1192
e-mail: enquiries@civicforum.org.uk
web: www.civicforum.org.uk
Convener, Management Board: Campbell Christie; *Director:* Donald Reid
Exists to build links between the people of Scotland and the Scottish Parliament and between different parts of civic society. Supports the move to a participative democracy, believing that there is more to democracy than casting a vote every four or five years. It aims to increase participation, find new ways to open up dialogue, raise awareness and stimulate debate on the challenges facing Scotland.
    Full membership of the forum is open to any organisation which is non-statutory, non-commercial and non-political.

DISABLED

BRITISH DEAF ASSOCIATION (SCOTLAND)
3rd Floor, Princes House, 5 Shandwick Place, Edinburgh EH2 4RG
Tel: 0131-221 1137
Chief Executive: Jeff McWhinney; *Chairperson:* Austin Reeves

Supplies information to the deaf community about health issues, education, access to services, and the use of British sign language. Also supports young deaf people.

CAPABILITY SCOTLAND
Central Office, 22 Corstorphine Road, Edinburgh EH12 6HP
Tel: 0131-337 9876
Fax: 0131-346 7864
e-mail: capability@capability-scotland.org.uk
web: www.capability-scotland.org.uk
Chief Executive: Alan Dickson
Services for disabled children and adults.

DISABLEMENT INCOME GROUP – SCOTLAND
5 Quayside Street, Edinburgh EH6 6EJ
Tel: 0131-555 2811
Chairman: Mike Coveney
Free information, advice and advocacy on welfare benefits to disabled people all over Scotland.

ENABLE
6th Floor, 7 Buchanan Street, Glasgow G1 3HL
Tel: 0141-226 4541
Fax: 0141-204 4398
e-mail: enable@enable.org.uk
Director: Norman Dunning; *Chairperson:* David Barraclough; *President:* John Spence
Supports people with learning disabilities and their carers.

ERSKINE HOSPITAL
Bishopton, Renfrewshire PA7 5PU
Tel: 0141-812 1100
Chief Executive: Colonel Martin Gibson, OBE; *Chairman:* Mark Sherriff, CBE, DL
Provides appropriate care (for example, nursing, residential, housing, supported employment, respite) to ex-Service men and women across Scotland.

GUIDE DOGS FOR THE BLIND ASSOCIATION
Princess Alexandra House, Dundee Road, Forfar DD8 1JA
Tel: 01307 463531

PHAB SCOTLAND
Norton Park, 57 Albion Road, Edinburgh EH7 5QY
Tel: 0131-475 2313
Fax: 0131-475 2685
Chief Executive: Fiona Hird

REHAB SCOTLAND
1650 London Road, Glasgow G31 4QF
Tel: 0141-554 8822
web: www.rehab-scotland.co.uk
Chief Executive: Ian Welsh; *Chairman:* Eric R Taylor, OBE
Voluntary organisation providing vocational training and rehabilitation services to enable people with disabilities and those who are socially and economically excluded to gain greater independence, skills and access to employment.

RNIB SCOTLAND (ROYAL NATIONAL INSTITUTE FOR THE BLIND, SCOTLAND)
Dunedin House, 25 Ravelston Terrace, Edinburgh EH4 3TP
Tel: 0131-311 8500
Director: Mike Cairns

ROYAL NATIONAL INSTITUTE FOR DEAF PEOPLE
Crowngate Business Centre, 117 Brook Street, Glasgow G40 3AP
Tel: 0141-554 0053
Fax: 0141-554 5837
web: www.rnid.org.uk
Director: Stuart Smith
Aims to achieve a radically better quality of life for deaf and hard of hearing people. Campaigns, lobbies and raises awareness of deafness and hearing loss; provides services; carries out social, medical and technical research.

SCOTTISH DISABILITY SPORT
Fife Sports Institute, Viewfield Road, Glenrothes KY6 2RB
Tel: 01592 415700
Fax: 01592 415710
e-mail: ssadsds@aol.com
Administrator: Norma Buchanan

SCOTTISH DISABLED SPORTS TRUST
7 Westerton of Mugdock, Milngavie G62 8LQ
Tel: 0141-956 6415
Chairman of Trustees: A Mills
Charitable trust giving grants to appropriate sports organisations for disabled people.

SCOTTISH EMPLOYMENT OPPORTUNITIES
Unit 26, Adelphi Centre, 12 Commercial Road, Glasgow G5 0PQ
Tel: 0141 429 8429
Director (Scotland): Graham Young
Helps people with disabilities to find employment.

SCOTTISH NATIONAL FEDERATION FOR THE WELFARE OF THE BLIND
5 Balmashanner Rise, Forfar, Angus DD8 1PD
Tel: 01307 460359
Fax: 01307 460359
Honorary Secretary: John Duncan; *President:* Richard Mazur
Charitable organisation concerned with promoting the interests of blind and partially-sighted people in Scotland.

SCOTTISH NATIONAL INSTITUTION FOR THE WAR BLINDED
PO Box 500, Gillespie Crescent, Edinburgh EH10 4HZ
Tel: 0131-229 1456
Fax: 0131-229 4060
e-mail: enquiries@rbas.org.uk
Secretary and Treasurer: Mr J B M Munro; *President:* Duke of Buccleuch

and Queensberry, KT
Provides training, employment and aftercare to Scottish ex-Service, visually impaired men and women.

SCOTTISH SOCIETY FOR AUTISM
Hilton House, Alloa Business Park, Whins Road, Alloa FK10 3SA
Tel: 01259 720044
Fax: 01259 720055
e-mail: autism@autism-in-scotland. org.uk
web: www.autism-in-scotland.org.uk
Chief Executive: Donald J Liddell
Provides care, support, education and opportunities for people with autism in Scotland.

SENSE SCOTLAND
45 Finnieston Street, Clydeway Centre, Glasgow G3 8JU
Tel: 0141-564 2444
Fax: 0141-564 2443
e-mail: info@sensescotland.org.uk
web: www.sensescotland.org.uk
Director: Gillian Morbey, OBE; *Chairperson:* Roy Cox
Charitable company representing deafblind and multisensory impaired people. Provides a range of services including respite, residential and day care.

THISTLE FOUNDATION
Niddrie Mains Road, Edinburgh EH16 4EA
Tel: 0131-661 9287
Director: Jayne Fisher
Promotes independence for disabled people by providing accommodation and support.

DISADVANTAGED

POVERTY ALLIANCE
162 Buchanan Street, Glasgow G1 2LL
Tel: 0141-353 0440
Director: Damian Killeen

SCOTTISH LOW PAY UNIT
24 Sandyford Place, Glasgow G3 7NG
Tel: 0141-221 4491
Fax: 0141-221 6318
e-mail: unit@scotlpu.org.uk
web: www.scotlpu.org.uk
Director: vacant; *Chairperson:* Angus Graham
Delivers a range of information, advice and research services designed to advance the economic position of low-paid workers.

WISE GROUP
72 Charlotte Street, Glasgow G1 5DW
Tel: 0141-303 3131
e-mail: feedback@thewisegroup.co.uk
Chief Executive: Alan Sinclair, CBE
Charitable organisation helping people into work.

DYSLEXIA

DYSLEXIA INSTITUTE SCOTLAND
74 Victoria Crescent Road, Dowanhill, Glasgow G12 9JN
Tel: 0141-334 4549
Administrator: Elizabeth Robin; *Principal:* Elizabeth Mackenzie
Assesses and teaches dyslexic adults and children. Provides teacher training and short courses for parents and teachers.

SCOTTISH DYSLEXIA ASSOCIATION
Stirling Business Centre, Wellgreen, Stirling FK8 2DZ
Tel: 01786 446650
e-mail: dyslexia.scotland@dial. pipex.com
web: www.dyslexia.scotland.dial. pipex.com
Chairman: Elizabeth J Reilly; *President:* Gill Thomson, MBE
Aims to raise public awareness of dyslexia and its related difficulties. Provides information, advice and support, workshops and speakers and acts as a resource centre.

EDUCATION

ASSOCIATION OF SCOTTISH COLLEGES
Argyll Court, The Castle Business Park, Stirling FK9 4TY
Tel: 01786 892100
Fax: 01786 892109
e-mail: enquiries@ascol.org.uk
Chief Executive: Tom Kelly
Represents FE colleges throughout Scotland.

ASSOCIATION OF UNIVERSITY TEACHERS (SCOTLAND)
6 Castle Street, Edinburgh EH2 3AT
Tel: 0131-226 6694
Fax: 0131-226 2066
e-mail: scotland&ne@aut.org.uk
web: www.aut.org.uk/scotland
Regional Assistant General Secretary: David Bleiman; *President:* Bill Stewart
Trade union and professional association for academic and related staff in Scottish higher education.

BRITISH COUNCIL SCOTLAND
3 Bruntsfield Crescent, Edinburgh EH10 4HD
Tel: 0131-446 3000
Fax: 0131-446 3045
web: www.britishcouncil.org/scotland
Director Scotland: Michael Bird, OBE
The British Council is the UK's international organisation for educational and cultural relations, with offices in over 100 countries worldwide. The British Council in Scotland aims to make a valued contribution to building an international, outward-looking Scotland by promoting Scottish education and training as part of the overall UK education brand, enhancing the quality of education in Scotland through international contact, showcasing the international excellence of Scotland's arts, scientific research and innovation, providing access to Scottish experience and expertise in governance, law and human rights, and creating and linking national and international networks of young professionals as a resource for Scotland.

CARNEGIE TRUST FOR THE UNIVERSITIES OF SCOTLAND
Cameron House, Abbey Park Place, Dunfermline KY12 7PZ
Tel: 01383 622148
Secretary: Sir John Arbuthnott; *Chairman:* Sir Lewis Robertson, CBE
Assists the Scottish universities, facilitating research by their staff and graduates, and assists students of Scottish birth or extraction with the payment of fees for first degrees at Scottish universities.

COMMITTEE OF SCOTTISH HIGHER EDUCATION PRINCIPALS
53 Hanover Street, Edinburgh EH2 2PJ
Tel: 0131-226 1111
Fax: 0131-226 1100
e-mail: info@universities-scotland.ac.uk
web: www.universities-scotland.ac.uk
Director: David Caldwell; *Convener:* Professor Sir Stewart Sutherland
Representative body for higher education in Scotland.

COMMUNITY LEARNING SCOTLAND
Rosebery House, 9 Haymarket Terrace, Edinburgh EH12 5EZ
Tel: 0131-313 2488
Fax: 0131-313 6800
e-mail: info@cls.dircon.co.uk
web: www.communitylearning.org
Chief Executive: Charlie McConnell; *Chair:* Linda McTavish
Non-departmental public body which works to open up access to learning opportunities and overcome the barriers to learning. Recognising that many adults and young people are not attracted by the thought of

returning to educational institutions, which are seen as neither relevant nor accessible, the council helps to enable them to develop their talents and skills in less formal settings.

Participation in community-based learning has doubled in the last 20 years, with a far higher proportion now coming from disadvantaged areas and groups. More than a million young people and adults across Scotland now regularly participate every week in subjects of their choice – acquiring job-seeking skills, setting up a business, engaging in the arts, taking part in health education groups, running a housing co-operative, improving numeracy and literacy, organising an environmental campaign or a youth group.

EDUCATIONAL BROADCASTING COUNCIL FOR SCOTLAND

Broadcasting House, Queen Margaret Drive, Glasgow G12 8DG
Tel: 0141-338 3422
Secretary: John S. Russell; *Chairman*: Ann Auchterlonie
Provides strategic policy and programming advice to BBC Scotland for schools programming and offers advice to BBC Network for schools and adult programming.

EDUCATIONAL INSTITUTE OF SCOTLAND

46 Moray Place, Edinburgh EH3 6BH
Tel: 0131-225 6244
Fax: 0131-220 3151
web: www.eis.org.uk
General Secretary: Ronald A Smith; *President*: Sandy Fowler
Founded in 1847 by royal charter, the EIS is the oldest teaching union in the world. The stated aim of the founding members was the "promotion of sound learning".

In addition to its professional role, the institute has developed through the years its function of seeking to improve and protect the pay and conditions of service of teachers and lecturers in Scotland. In recent years it has also played an important role in the campaign to protect the distinctive nature of Scottish education and the quality of education. The EIS has 52,671 members, representing 80% of teachers in Scotland.

GENERAL TEACHING COUNCIL FOR SCOTLAND

Clerwood House, 96 Clermiston Road, Edinburgh EH12 6UT
Tel: 0131-314 6000
Fax: 0131-314 6001
e-mail: gtcs@gtcs.org.uk
web: www.gtcs.org.uk
Registrar: Matthew MacIver; *Council Convener*: Mrs Norma Anne Watson
Established in 1955 in response to professional and public dissatisfaction with standards in Scottish schools in the 1950s and early 1960s, arising largely from the employment of unqualified people as "uncertificated teachers". The government set up a committee of enquiry under the chairmanship of Lord Wheatley, which recommended the establishment of a General Teaching Council for Scotland "in which, subject to appropriate safeguards, control of entry to the teaching profession would be vested".

The council has 49 members widely representative of the educational community. Every teacher registered to teach in Scotland is required to pay an annual registration fee; the council is therefore self-financing and independent.

The council seeks to protect professional standards by maintaining a register of qualified teachers, advising on the supply of teachers, overseeing standards of entry to the profession, accrediting and reviewing the operation of all courses of initial teacher education, and exercising disciplinary powers. In a case of gross professional misconduct, the council has the power to remove the teacher's name from the register. It is illegal for an education authority to employ an unregistered teacher.

HEADTEACHERS' ASSOCIATION OF SCOTLAND
University of Strathclyde, Jordanhill Campus, Southbrae Drive, Glasgow G13 1PP
Tel: 0141-950 3298
Fax: 0141-950 3434
e-mail: head.teachers@strath.ac.uk
General Secretary: George Ross; *President*: Gordon Mackenzie
Promotes the highest standards of education in Scottish secondary schools and provides for the needs and interests of members (headteachers, depute and assistant headteachers).

LEAD SCOTLAND (LINKING EDUCATION AND DISABILITY)
Queen Margaret University College, Clerwood Terrace, Edinburgh EH12 8TS
Tel: 0131-317 3439
Director: Rona Connolly
Provides guidance to physically disabled and/or sensory impaired adults enabling access to education, training and lifelong learning opportunities.

LEARNING AND TEACHING SCOTLAND (LT SCOTLAND)
Gardyne Road, Dundee DD5 1NY
Tel: 01382 443600
Fax: 01382 443645/6
Dowanhill, 74 Victoria Crescent Road, Glasgow G12 9JN
Tel: 0141-337 5000
Fax: 0141-337 5050
e-mail: enquiries@LTScotland.com
web: www.LTScotland.com

Chief Executive: Mike Baughan; *Chairman*: Professor Tom Wilson
A national public body sponsored by the Scottish Executive Education Department. Its remit is to provide advice, support, resources and staff development which enhance the quality of educational experiences in Scotland with a view to improving attainment and achievement and promoting lifelong learning. It combines expertise on the school and pre-school curriculum and on the use of information and communications technology in education and lifelong learning. Actively involved in software and internet development and multimedia production of educational resources.

NAS/UWT (SCOTLAND)
6 Waterloo Place, Edinburgh EH1 3BG
Tel: 0131-523 1110
Acting Scottish Regional Official: Pat O'Donnell

NATIONAL UNION OF STUDENTS SCOTLAND
29 Forth Street, Edinburgh EH1 3LE
Tel: 0131556 6598
Fax: 0131-5575679
e-mail: nus-scot@dircon.co.uk
Director: Liam Jarnecki; *President*: Amanda Telford
Federation of student associations representing 80% of students in Scotland. Also provides welfare, training, developmental and commercial services to constituent members.

PROFESSIONAL ASSOCIATION OF TEACHERS IN SCOTLAND
4/6 Oak Lane, Edinburgh EH12 6XH
Tel: 0131-317 8282

SCOTTISH COUNCIL OF INDEPENDENT SCHOOLS
21 Melville Streeet, Edinburgh EH3 7PE

Tel: 0131-220 2106
Director: Judith Sischy; *Chairman*: Professor B J McGettrick
Communicates with government departments and other bodies on behalf of the independent sector, advises member schools on educational developments, develops in-service training, and provides information for parents and the media. 75 member schools with 31,000 pupils.

SCOTTISH COUNCIL FOR RESEARCH IN EDUCATION
15 St John Street, Edinburgh EH8 8JR
Tel: 0131-557 2944
Fax: 0131-556 9454
e-mail: scre@scre.ac.uk
web: www.scre.ac.uk
Director: Dr Valerie Wilson; *Chair*: Bill Furness
Independent body, established in 1928 by a partnership of teaching unions, local authorities, universities and colleges. The council conducts research for the benefit of education and training in Scotland (and elsewhere) and is funded by contracts for specific projects, as well as by grants from local authorities and teacher unions. SCRE's work covers all phases of education, formal and informal, from pre-five to higher education, and includes overseas consultancies and collaborative projects with other institutions.

SCOTTISH FURTHER EDUCATION FUNDING COUNCIL
Donaldson House, 97 Haymarket Terrace, Edinburgh EH12 5HD
Tel: 0131-313 6500
Fax: 0131-313 6501
e-mail: info@sfc.ac.uk
web: www.sfefc.ac.uk
Chief Executive: Professor John Sizer, CBE; *Chairman*: Robert Beattie, MBE
Established in 1999, SFEFC is responsible for discharging the First Minister's duty to secure adequate and efficient provision of further education in Scotland. Functions include: funding Scotland's FE colleges; promoting innovation and collaboration; offering guidance to colleges; monitoring the financial health of the sector; advising the First Minister on funding matters; securing efficient provision of FE in Scotland.

SCOTTISH HIGHER EDUCATION FUNDING COUNCIL
Donaldson House, 97 Haymarket Terrace, Edinburgh EH12 5HD
Tel: 0131-313 6500
Fax: 0131-313 6501
e-mail: info@sfc.ac.uk
web: www.shefc.ac.uk
Chief Executive: Professor John Sizer, CBE; *Chairman*: Dr Chris Masters
Provides financial support for Scottish higher education institutions. It distributes funds to support teaching and research; assesses the quality of higher education supported by the council; and provides the government with information and advice. Distributes more than £600 million each year, most of which is allocated through formula grants.

SCOTTISH JOINT COMMITTEE ON RELIGIOUS AND MORAL EDUCATION
6 Claremont Gardens, Glasgow G3 7LW
Tel: 0141-353 3595
Secretary: Lachlan Bradley; *Convener*: Mrs Pamela Paterson
Concerned with an overview of religious and moral education in Scottish schools.

SCOTTISH OUT OF SCHOOL CARE NETWORK
Floor 6, Fleming House, 134 Renfrew Street, Glasgow G3 6ST
Tel: 0141-331 1301
Director: Irene Audain; *Chair*: Sue

Robertson
Scotland's lead representative body for school-aged childcare. Provides information, advice and membership services to individuals, organisations, local networks, local government and childcare partnerships.

SCOTTISH PARENT TEACHER COUNCIL
63-65 Shandwick Place, Edinburgh EH2 4SD
Tel: 0131-228 5320/1.
Convenor: Eleanor Coner
National organisation for PAs/PTAs. Publishes a newsletter, gives advice to callers, responds to consultations, and operates an insurance scheme for members.

SCOTTISH PRE-SCHOOL PLAY ASSOCIATION
SPPA Centre, 14 Elliot Place, Glasgow G3 8EP
Tel: 0141-221 4148
Chief Executive: Ian McLaughlan; *Chairperson*: Irene Mackay

SCOTTISH QUALIFICATIONS AUTHORITY
Hanover House, 24 Douglas Street, Glasgow G2 7NQ
Tel: 0141-248 7900
web: www.sqa.org.uk
Chief Executive: David Fraser; *Interim Chairman:* Professor John Ward
Scotland's national body for qualifications, since 1996 the successor to SCOTVEC and the Scottish Examination Board and now the only organisation responsible for the qualifications on offer in schools, colleges, training centres and workplaces.
The SQA, though self-financing, answers to government for the credibility, reliability and value of its qualifications. It upholds the quality of established qualifications and develops new ones.
Rationalising and unifying the qualifications system in Scotland was one of the aims behind the establishment of the new body. It is responsible for most types of qualification in Scotland except university degrees. These range from the standard grade, higher grade and national certificate modules taken by almost all school pupils to higher national certificates, higher national diplomas and Scottish vocational qualifications.

SCOTTISH SCHOOLS EQUIPMENT RESEARCH CENTRE (SSERC)
2nd Floor, St Mary's Building, 23 Holyrood Road, Edinburgh EH8 8AE
Tel: 0131-558 8180
Fax: 0131-558 8191
e-mail: sts@sserc.org.uk
web: www.sserc.org.uk
Director: J Richardson; *Chairperson*: Councillor David L. McGrouther, JP
Information, advisory and training service for Scottish science and technology education.

SCOTTISH SECONDARY TEACHERS' ASSOCIATION
15 Dundas Street, Edinburgh EH3 6QG
Tel: 0131-556 5919
web: ssta.org.uk
General Secretary: David Eaglesham

SCOTTISH UNIVERSITY FOR INDUSTRY
Europa Building, 450 Argyle Street, Glasgow G2 8LG
Tel: 0141-285 6000
Fax: 0141-285 6001
e-mail: info@scottishufi.com
web: www.scottishufi.com
Chief Executive: Frank Pignatelli; *Chairman:* Christine Lenihan
Organisation concerned with lifelong learning. Aims to stimulate demand for learning among individuals and within businesses.

**SEAD (SCOTTISH EDUCATION &
ACTION FOR DEVELOPMENT)**
167-171 Dundee Street, Edinburgh
EH11 1BY
Tel: 0131-477 2780
Fax: 0131-477 2781
e-mail: sead@gn.apc.org
Director: Martin Coyle
Membership organisation which
challenges poverty and social
injustice, working for development
that puts communities at the heart of
decision-making.

**STUDENT AWARDS AGENCY FOR
SCOTLAND**
Gyleview House, 3 Redheughs Rigg,
Edinburgh EH12 9HH
Tel: 0131-476 8212
Fax: 0131-244 5887
Chief Executive: David Stephen
An agency of the Scottish Executive
Enterprise and Lifelong Learning
Department. Administers the
provision of assistance for eligible
Scottish-domiciled students
undertaking higher education courses
throughout the UK. Also has related
functions in connection with student
loans, hardship funds and
educational endowments.

WORKERS' EDUCATIONAL ASSOCIATION
Riddles Court, 322 Lawnmarket,
Edinburgh EH1 2PG
Scottish Secretary: Joyce Connon;
Convenor: Esther Quinn
National democratic voluntary
organisation providing adults with
access to organised learning. Priority
given to the most disadvantaged and
excluded groups.

ELDERLY

ABBEYFIELD SOCIETY FOR SCOTLAND
15 West Maitland Street, Edinburgh
EH12 5EA
Tel: 0131-225 7801

Fax: 0131-225 7606
e-mail: abbeyfieldscotland@quista.net
web: www.scotland.abbeyfield.com
General Secretary: Sue Jones; *Chairman*:
Rev Dr J W S Clark
Provides lonely older people with
their own home within family-sized
homes run by groups of local
volunteers.

AGE CONCERN SCOTLAND
113 Rose Street, Edinburgh EH2 3DT
Tel: 0131-220 3345
Director: Maureen O'Neill
National voluntary organisation with
the primary aim of improving the
quality of life for older people in
Scotland. Committed to working
throughout Scotland to ensure that all
older people have their rights upheld
and their voices heard, and enjoy
choice and control over all aspects of
their lives. Provides a comprehensive
information service on all issues
affecting older people, including a
factsheet helpline on 0800 009966. Has
more than 250 local groups providing
practical services including day care,
lunch clubs and information and
advice, as well as social activities.

DISCOVERY AWARD
Ancrum Centre for the Environment,
10 Ancrum Road, Dundee DD2 2HZ
Tel: 01382 641800
Director: Laurie M Young, MBE;
Chairperson: Margaret Hutton
Achievement award offering
challenges to individuals over the age
of 50. Enables and encourages people
to make choices about their own lives
and to increase their contribution to
life around them.

HELP THE AGED
Heriot House, Heriothill Terrace,
Edinburgh EH7 4DY
Tel: 0131-556 4666
Scottish Executive: Elizabeth Duncan

SCOTTISH PRE-RETIREMENT COUNCIL
Alexandra House, 204 Bath Street,
Glasgow G2 4HL
Tel: 0141-332 9427
Director: Angela Fowlis; *Chairman*:
James Henshelwood
Promotes preparation and education
for retirement.

ENERGY SUPPLIERS

BRITISH ENERGY PLC
3 Redwood Crescent, Peel Park, East
Kilbride G74 5PR
Tel: 01355 262000
Fax: 01355 262626
web: www.british-energy-com
Chief Executive: Peter Hollins;
Chairman: Dr Robin Jeffrey
Operates eight nuclear stations and
one coalfired power station and has a
market share of around 21% in the UK
and 50% in Scotland.

SCOTTISH AND SOUTHERN ENERGY PLC
200 Dunkeld Road, Perth PH1 3AQ
Tel: 01738 456000
Fax: 01738 456005
web: www.scottish-southern.co.uk
Chief Executive: Jim Forbes
Formerly Scottish Hydro-Electric
PLC. Supplies energy throughout the
UK.

SCOTTISHPOWER PLC
1 Atlantic Quay, Glasgow G2 8SP
Tel: 0141-248 8200
Fax: 0141-248 8300
web: www.scottishpower.com
Chief Executive: Ian Russell; *Chairman*:
Charles Miller Smith
Serves around 7 million homes. The
company's activities span electricity,
gas, water, telecommunications and
retail. ScottishPower is one of the
biggest industrial groups in the UK
with a market capitalisation of almost
£9bn.

ENTERPRISE COMPANIES

SCOTTISH ENTERPRISE
150 Broomielaw, Atlantic Quay,
Glasgow G2 8LU
Tel: 0141-248 2700
Fax: 0141-221 3217
e-mail: network.helpline@scotent.
co.uk
web: www.scottish-enterprise.com
Chief Executive: Dr Robert M
Crawford; *Chairman*: Sir Ian Robinson
Set up in 1991 under the Enterprise
and New Towns Scotland Act.
Scottish Enterprise is the main
economic development agency for
Scotland, covering 93 per cent of the
population from Grampian to the
Borders. The Scottish Enterprise
Network consists of Scottish
Enterprise and 12 local enterprise
companies. Working in partnership
with the private and public sectors,
the network aims to build more and
better businesses, to develop the skills
and knowledge of Scottish people,
and to encourage innovation to make
Scottish business internationally
competitive. Reports to the Scottish
Executive.

HIGHLANDS AND ISLANDS ENTERPRISE
Cowan House, Inverness Retail and
Business Park, Inverness IV2 7GF
Tel: 01463 234171
Fax: 01463 244469
e-mail: hie.general@hient.co.uk
web: www.hie.co.uk
Chief Executive: Sandy Cumming;
Chairman: Dr James Hunter, CBE
Created by Parliament and came into
being in 1991. Its task is to design and
deliver economic and community
development, training and
environmental renewal, in an area
stretching from Shetland in the north
to the Mull of Kintyre in the south,
and from Moray in the east to the
Western Isles – an area on the edge of

Europe.

The HIE network has substantial powers and resources to achieve economic and social development results. Powers include finance for business; provision of factories and offices; training programmes; assistance for community and cultural projects; and also measures for environmental renewal.

Ten local enterprise companies, locally-based and private sector-led, provide frontline delivery of assistance and advice. They are backed up by the network's strategic core body in the Highland capital of Inverness.

Local enterprise companies:

ARGYLL AND THE ISLANDS ENTERPRISE
The Enterprise Centre, Kilmory Industrial Estate, Lochgilphead PA31 8SH
Tel: 0845 7794285
Chief Executive: Ken Abernethy

CAITHNESS AND SUTHERLAND ENTERPRISE
Tollemache House, High Street, Thurso KW14 8AZ
Tel: 01847 896115
Fax: 01847 893383
web: www.case-lec.co.uk
Acting Chief Executive: Carroll Buxton

INVERNESS AND NAIRN ENTERPRISE
The Greenhouse, Beechwood Business Park North, Inverness IV2 3BL
Tel: 01463 713504
Chief Executive: Bill Sylvester

LOCHABER ENTERPRISE
St Mary's House, Gordon Square, Fort William PH33 6DY
Tel: 01397 704326
Chief Executive: Jackie Wright

MORAY BADENOCH AND STRATHSPEY ENTERPRISE
Elgin Business Centre, Maisondieu Road, Elgin IV30 1RH
Tel: 01343 550567
Fax: 01343 550678
e-mail: mbse@hient.co.uk
Chief Executive: Dick Ruane; *Chairman:* James Lochhead

ORKNEY ENTERPRISE
14 Queen Street, Kirkwall, Orkney KW15 1JE
Tel: 01856 874638
Chief Executive: Ken Grant

ROSS AND CROMARTY ENTERPRISE
69-71 High Street, Invergordon IV18 0AA
Tel: 01349 853666
Chief Executive: Gordon Cox

SCOTTISH ENTERPRISE AYRSHIRE
17-19 Hill Street, Kilmarnock KA3 1HA
Tel: 01563 526623
Fax: 01563 543636
Chief Executive: Evelyn McCann; *Chairman:* Bill Kerr

SCOTTISH ENTERPRISE BORDERS
Bridge Street, Galashiels TD1 1SW
Tel: 01896 758991
Fax: 01896 758625
Chief Executive: David Gass; *Chairman:* Hugh Tasker

SCOTTISH ENTERPRISE DUMFRIES AND GALLOWAY
Solway House, Dumfries Enterprise Park, Tinwald Downs Road, Heathhall, Dumfries DG1 3SJ
Tel: 01387 245000
Fax: 01387 246224
Chief Executive: Irene Walker; *Chairman:* Tom Gillespie

SCOTTISH ENTERPRISE DUNBARTONSHIRE
2nd Floor, Spectrum House, Clydebank Business Park, Clydebank,

Glasgow G81 2DR
Tel: 0141-951 2121
Fax: 0141-951 1907
Chief Executive: Dave Anderson;
Chairman: Jim Duncan

SCOTTISH ENTERPRISE EDINBURGH AND LOTHIAN
Apex House, 99 Haymarket Terrace, Edinburgh EH12 5HD
Tel: 0131-313 4000
Fax: 0131-313 4231
Chief Executive: David Crichton;
Chairman: Dr Ian Sword

SCOTTISH ENTERPRISE FIFE
Kingdom House, Saltire Centre, Glenrothes KY6 2AQ
Tel: 01592 623000
Fax: 01592 623149
Chief Executive: Joe Noble; *Chairman:* Allan Burns

SCOTTISH ENTERPRISE FORTH VALLEY
Laurel House, Laurelhill Business Park, Stirling FK7 9JQ
Tel: 01786 451919
Fax: 01786 478123
Chief Executive: Lorna Jack; *Chairman:* Michael Cantlay

SCOTTISH ENTERPRISE GLASGOW
Atrium Court, 50 Waterloo Street, Glasgow G2 6HQ
Tel: 0141-204 1111
Fax: 0141-248 1600
Chief Executive: Ron Culley; *Chairman:* Tom O'Neil

SCOTTISH ENTERPRISE GRAMPIAN
27 Albyn Place, Aberdeen AB10 1DB
Tel: 01224 252000
Fax: 01224 213417
Chief Executive: Ed Gillespie; *Chairman:* Moir Lockhead, OBE

SCOTTISH ENTERPRISE LANARKSHIRE
New Lanarkshire House, Strathclyde Business Park, Bellshill ML4 3AD
Tel: 01698 745454

Fax: 01698 842211
Chief Executive: Liz Connolly;
Chairman: David Ennis, OBE

SCOTTISH ENTERPRISE RENFREWSHIRE
27 Causeyside Street, Paisley PA1 1UL
Tel: 0141-848 0101
Chief Executive: Lorraine MacMillan;
Chairman: Bob Beaty

SCOTTISH ENTERPRISE TAYSIDE
45 North Lindsay Street, Dundee DD1 1HT
Tel: 01382 223100
Fax: 01382 201319
Chief Executive: Graham McKee;
Chairman: Ian McMillan

SHETLAND ENTERPRISE
Toll Clock Shopping Centre, 26 North Road, Lerwick, Shetland ZE1 0DE
Tel: 01595 693177
Chief Executive: David Finch

SKYE & LOCHALSH ENTERPRISE
King's House, The Green, Portree, Isle of Skye IV51 9BS
Tel: 01478 612841
Chief Executive: Robert D. Muir

WESTERN ISLES ENTERPRISE (IOMAIRT NAN EILEAN SIAR)
James Square, 9 James Street, Stornoway, Isle of Lewis HS1 2QN
Tel: 01851 703703
Chief Executive: Donnie Macaulay

ENTERPRISE TRUSTS

BUSINESS ENTERPRISE SCOTLAND
18 Forth Street, Edinburgh EH1 3LH
Tel: 0131-550 3839
Fax: 031-550 3840
e-mail: bes@bes.org.uk
web: www.bes.org.uk
Chief Executive: Robin Miller;
Chairman: David Chalmers
Founded in 1996 by the Scottish enterprise trusts to answer the

requirement for a lead body to guide, shape, promote and represent their network. BES represents the trusts to the Scottish Executive, Scottish Enterprise, local authorities and others.

It provides training, organises members' meetings and runs a service quality programme. Individual enterprise trusts provide start-up advice to people wishing to go into business for themselves, as well as marketing and business planning advice to existing businesses.

*Local enterprise trusts (*denotes membership of Business Enterprise Scotland):*

*ABERDEEN ENTERPRISE TRUST
6 Albyn Grove, Aberdeen AB10 6SQ
Tel: 01224 252168
Fax: 01224 584488
Chief Executive: Bill Ferguson

AYRSHIRE MARKETING EXECUTIVE
Freeport, Shawfarm Road, Prestwick KA9 2TR
Tel: 01292 678920
Fax: 01292 678921

BARRAS ENTERPRISE TRUST
Unit 1, 54 Carlton Entry, Glasgow G40 2SB
Tel: 0141-552 7258
Fax: 0141-552 4164

CAMPBELTOWN & KINTYRE ENTERPRISE TRUST
51 Kirk Street, Campbeltown A28 6BW
Tel: 01586 552372
Fax: 01586 553486

CLACKMANNANSHIRE ENTERPRISE
Alba Business Centre, Alloa FK10 2HU
Tel: 01259 721454
Fax: 01259 217303

*CLYDESDALE DEVELOPMENT COMPANY LIMITED
30 Hope Street, Lanark ML11 7NE
Tel: 01555 665064
Fax: 01555 665733
General Manager: Chris Parkin

COWAL ENTERPRISE TRUST
Unit 16, Sandbank Business Park, Highland Avenue, Sandbank, Dunoon PA23 8PB
Tel: 01369 705624
Fax: 01369 707751

*CUMBERNAULD AREA ENTERPRISE
Business Development Centre, Suite 402, 4th Floor, Fleming House, Cumbernauld G67 1JW
Tel: 01236 611600
Fax: 01236 611610
Director: Jim Telford

*DEVELOPING NORTH AYRSHIRE
Sovereign House, Academy Road, Irvine KA12 8RL
Tel: 01294 315120
Fax: 01294 315123
Acting Operational Manager: Bill Anderson

DEVELOPING STRATHCLYDE
Unit 37, Ladywell Business Centre, 94 Duke Street, Glasgow G4 0UW
Tel: 0141-572 5551
Fax: 0141-572 5553

DUNDEE INDUSTRIAL ASSOCIATION
Meadow Mill, Blackness Trading Precinct, West Henderson Wynd, Dundee DD1 5BY
Tel: 01382 226001
Fax: 01382 203085

*EAST DUNBARTONSHIRE ENTERPRISE TRUST
Enterprise House, Southbank Business Park, Kirkintilloch G66 1XQ
Tel: 0141-777 7171
Fax: 0141-775 3636
Chief Executive: Susan Steggles

*EAST KILBRIDE BUSINESS CENTRE
PO Box 1, Scottish Enterprise Technology Park, East Kilbride G75 0NS
Tel: 01355 238456
Fax: 01355 260300
Chief Executive: Ronnie Simpson

*EDINBURGH BUSINESS DEVELOPMENT
Edinburgh Chamber of Commerce, 27 Melville Street, Edinburgh EH3 7JF
Tel: 0131-477 7000
Fax: 0131-477 7002
Director: Grahame Cunningham

EDINBURGH OLD TOWN RENEWAL TRUST
343 High Street, Edinburgh EH1 1PW
Tel: 0131-225 8818
Fax: 0131-225 8636

*ENTERPRISE NORTH EAST LIMITED
Business Centre, Glebefield, 21 Links Terrace, Peterhead AB42 2XA
Tel: 01779 472224
Fax: 01779 478897
Chief Executive: Bill Emslie

*FALKIRK ENTERPRISE ACTION TRUST
Newhouse Business Park, Newhouse Road, Grangemouth FK3 8LL
Tel: 01324 665500
Fax: 01324 474418
Director: Sandy Riddell

GLASGOW NORTH
St Rollox House, 130 Springburn Road, Glasgow G21 1YL
Tel: 0141-552 5413
Fax: 0141-552 0886

GLASGOW OPPORTUNITIES
36 North Hanover Street, Glasgow G1 2AD
Tel: 0141-572 8300
Fax: 0141-572 8400
Executive Director: Agnes Samuel

*GORDON ENTERPRISE TRUST
Thainstone Business Centre, Thainstone, Inverurie AB51 5TB

Tel: 01467 621166
Fax: 01467 621919
Chief Executive: Ken Sturgeon

GREATER EASTERHOUSE DEVELOPMENT Co.
Westwood Business Centre, 69 Aberdalgie Road, Easterhouse, Glasgow G34 9HJ
Tel: 0141-781 2000
Fax: 0141-781 2010

*HAMILTON ENTERPRISE DEVELOPMENT COMPANY
Barncluith Business Centre, Townhead Street, Hamilton ML3 7DP
Tel: 01698 429425
Fax: 01698 891916
Director: Ronnie Smith

*HIGHLAND OPPORTUNITY LIMITED
Highland Council, Glenurquhart Road, Inverness IV3 5NX
Tel: 01463 702557
Fax: 01463 702298
Company Manager: David Owen

*KINCARDINE AND DEESIDE ENTERPRISE TRUST
Aboyne Business Centre, Unit 1, Huntly Road, Aboyne AB34 5HE
Tel: 01339 887222
Fax: 01339 885271
Chief Executive: Chris Travis

*LENNOX PARTNERSHIP
Strathleven House, Vale of Leven Industrial Estate, Dumbarton G82 3PD
Tel: 01389 750005
Fax: 01389 755424
Chief Executive: Graham Keith

*MIDLOTHIAN ENTERPRISE TRUST
Midlothian Chamber of Commerce and Enterprise, 29A Eskbank Road, Dalkeith EH22 1HJ
Tel: 0131-654 1234
Fax: 0131-660 4057
Executive Director: Gregor Murray

*MONKLANDS ENTERPRISE DEVELOPMENT COMPANY
Atrium Business Centre, North Caldeen Road, Coatbridge ML5 4EF
Tel: 01236 702020
Fax: 01236 702021
Chief Executive: Marian Gardiner

*MOTHERWELL AREA ENTERPRISE
Dalziel Workspace, Mason Street, Motherwell ML1 1YE
Tel: 01698 328328
Fax: 01698 260750
Chief Executive: Bill Duncan

PAISLEY & RENFREW ENTERPRISE TRUST
Bute Court, St. Andrews Drive, Glasgow Airport PA3 2SW
Tel: 0141-847 5450
Fax: 0141-847 5499

*SMALL BUSINESS GATEWAY RUTHERGLEN AND CAMBUSLANG
238 Main Street, Rutherglen G73 2HP
Tel: 0141-613 4800
Fax: 0141-613 4801
Manager: Margaret Donaldson

*STIRLING ENTERPRISE
John Player Building, Stirling FK7 7RP
Tel: 01783 463416
Fax: 01786 479611
Executive Director: Derek Gavin

*WELLPARK ENTERPRISE CENTRE
120 Sydney Street, Glasgow G31 1JF
Tel: 0141-550 4994
Fax: 0141-550 4443

*WEST LOTHIAN ECONOMIC DEVELOPMENT
The Business Centre, Almondvale Boulevard, Livingtson EH54 6QP
Tel: 01506 777400
Fax: 01506 777919
Economic Development Manager: Alistair Shaw

*WIGTOWN RURAL DEVELOPMENT COMPANY
Galloway Business Centre, Cree House, 20-22 Victoria Street, Newton Stewart DG8 6BT
Tel: 01671 404500
Fax: 01671 404502
Business Development Executive: Elaine Marr

ENVIRONMENT

FRIENDS OF THE EARTH SCOTLAND (FOE SCOTLAND)
72 Newhaven Road, Edinburgh EH6 5QG
Tel: 0131-554 9977
e-mail: info@foe-scotland.org.uk
web: www.foe-scotland.org.uk
Director: Kevin Dunion, OBE; Chairman: Dr Mark Huxham
Campaigns for environmental justice, our right to live in a better environment, and our responsibility to share the world's resources fairly.

HABITAT SCOTLAND
Hazelmount, Heron Place, Portree, Isle of Skye IV51 9EU
Tel: 01478 612898
Fax: 01478 613254
e-mail: graeme@islandstudies.org
web: www.islandstudies.org
Director: Graeme Robertson; Chairman: William McGhee
Independent environmental research charity.

JOHN MUIR TRUST
41 Commercial Street, Leith EH6 6JD
Tel: 0131-554 0114
web: www.jmt.org
Director: Nigel Hawkins; Chairman: Andrew Thin
Owns areas of wild land and manages them for conservation benefits, taking into account the needs of the local community.

LIVING WATER
5 Holyrood Road, Edinburgh EH8 8AE
Tel: 0131-558 3313
Fax: 0131-558 1550
e-mail: hello@livingwater.org.uk
web: www.livingwater.org.uk
Partners: Jane Shields; David Shields
Environmental education; community outreach; ecological water and waste management and treatment.

SCOTTISH ENVIRONMENT PROTECTION AGENCY
Erskine Court, Castle Business Park, Stirling FK9 4TR
Tel: 01786 457700
Fax: 01786 446885
e-mail: publicrelations@sepa.org.uk
web: www.sepa.org.uk
Chief Executive: M Patricia Henton;
Chairman: Ken Collins
Established under the Environment Act 1995 as a non-departmental public body. SEPA took on the responsibilities of HM Industrial Pollution Inspectorate, seven river purification boards and their counterparts in the three islands councils, as well as the functions of 56 district and islands councils, thus creating for the first time a single agency responsible for the control of pollution of the air, land, sea and water.

SEPA's mission is "to provide an efficient and integrated environmental protection system for Scotland which will both improve the environment and contribute to the government's goal of sustainable development".

Accountable to the Scottish Parliament, SEPA is responsible for preserving and improving the quality of rivers and lochs, estuaries and coastal waters, dealing with 40,000 consents a year relating to the discharge of materials. It also regulates 1,200 of Scotland's most complex industrial processes, including oil refineries, paper and chemical works, the disposal and treatment of 13 million tonnes of controlled waste, involving 800 managed sites and 6,500 carriers, and oversees programmes to restore land damaged by contamination.

SEPA registers organisations handling radioactive materials, controls the discharges of radioactive waste from Scottish nuclear installations (which supply about 50% of our electricity requirements) and monitors radioactivity in Scotland.

SCOTTISH FIELD STUDIES ASSOCIATION
Kindrogan Field Centre, Enochdhu, Blairgowrie, PH10 7PG
Tel: 01250 881286
Fax: 01250 881433
e-mail: kindrogan@btinternet.com
web: www.kindrogan.com
Chairman: Robin Noble
Assists in the popularisation of field studies in Scotland, provides facilities for every kind of field study, and provides a means of contact among societies engaged in field study.

SCOTTISH WILD LAND GROUP
8 Hartington Place, Edinburgh EH10 4LE
Tel: 0131-229 2094
web: www.swlg.org.uk
Co-ordinator: Alistair Cant
Campaigns to conserve and enhance wild land in Scotland and protects it against intrusive developments. Supports local communities in conserving wild land.

EQUAL OPPORTUNITIES

EQUAL OPPORTUNITIES COMMISSION SCOTLAND
St Stephen's House, 279 Bath Street, Glasgow G2 4JL

Tel: 0141-248 5833
Fax: 0141-248 5834
e-mail: scotland@ecc.org.uk
web: www.eoc.org.uk
Director Scotland: John Wilks;
Commissioner for Scotland: Rowena Arshad
Public body set up under the Sex Discrimination Act 1975, working to remove unlawful discrimination on grounds of sex or marriage, and to promote equal opportunities for women and men. These commitments often involve the commission in legal cases to uphold the basic principle of equal rights. Sometimes the desired end can be achieved by giving information and advice, but in situations where people refuse to act in accordance with the sex discrimination laws, the EOC, as a law enforcement body, has powers to take legal action.

The Scottish office delivers the commission's services throughout Scotland. It runs training sessions for lay advisers and lawyers, publishes guides to good practice for a specifically Scottish readership, and offers free advice based on practical experience.

EUROPE

EUROPEAN COMMISSION REPRESENTATION IN SCOTLAND
9 Alva Street, Edinburgh EH2 4PH
Tel: 0131-225 2058
Head of Representation: Elizabeth Holt

EXHIBITION AND CONFERENCE CENTRES

EDINBURGH INTERNATIONAL CONFERENCE CENTRE
The Exchange, Edinburgh EH3 8EE

Tel: 0131-300 3000
Fax: 0131-300 3030
e-mail: sales@eicc.co.uk
web: www.eicc.co.uk
Chief Executive: Hans Rissmann;
Chairman: Lezley Cameron O'Brien

SCOTTISH EXHIBITION + CONFERENCE CENTRE
Exhibition Way, Glasgow G3 8YW
Tel: 0141-248 3000
e-mail: info@secc.co.uk
web: www.secc.co.uk
Chief Executive: Michael Closier

FAMILY PLANNING

fpa SCOTLAND
Unit 10, Firhill Business Centre, 76 Firhill Road, Glasgow G20 7BA
Tel: 0141-576 5088
Scottish Director: Susan Stewart
Works to advance the sexual health and reproductive rights and choices of all people throughout the country.

FENCING

SCOTTISH FENCING
The Cockburn Centre, 40 Bogmoor Place, Glasgow G51 4TQ
Tel: 0141-445 1602

FESTIVALS

Listed is a selection of festivals of special interest. A more comprehensive list can be obtained from the Scottish Arts Council.

CELTIC CONNECTIONS
Glasgow Royal Concert Hall, 2 Sauchiehall Street, Glasgow G2 3NY
Tel: 0141-353 8000
e-mail: colinhynd@grch.demon.co.uk
web: www.grch.com
Festival Director: Colin Hynd

CELTIC FILM AND TELEVISION FESTIVAL
249 West George Street, Glasgow G2
4QE
Tel: 0141-302 1737
e-mail: mail@celtic.film.co.uk
web: www.celticfilm.co.uk
Chief Executive: Frances Hendron
Annual four-day industry festival
celebrating the best film, TV, radio
and new media from the Celtic
countries.

DUMFRIES AND GALLOWAY ARTS
FESTIVAL
Gracefield Arts Centre, 28 Edinburgh
Road, Dumfries DG1 1NW
Tel: 01387 260447
Fax: 01387 260447
e-mail: dgartsfestival@ukgateway.net
Hon Secretary: Ruth Bell; *Chairman:* Jill
Hardy

EDINBURGH FESTIVAL FRINGE
180 High Street, Edinburgh EH1 1QS
Tel: 0131-226 5257
Director: Paul Gudgin; *Chairperson:*
Baroness Smith of Gilmorehill
Cited by the Guinness Book of
Records as the largest arts festival in
the world, playing host every August
to 10,000 performers of every art form
and entertainment imaginable.

The Fringe originated informally
at the first Edinburgh International
Festival in 1947, when six Scottish
companies and two English decided
to turn up uninvited. They were
referred to originally as "festival
adjuncts", but this name was quickly
dropped and the phrase "fringe" came
into being in August 1948 when
Robert Kemp wrote describing a
production in Dunfermline Abbey as
being "on the fringes of the festival".

The Festival Fringe Society was
formed in 1958 to publish a
comprehensive programme, sell
tickets centrally, and offer advice to
future performers. It was agreed that

there would never be any form of
artistic vetting – a policy maintained
to the present day.

EDINBURGH INTERNATIONAL FESTIVAL
The Hub, Castlehill, Edinburgh EH1
2NE
Tel: 0131-473 2099
Fax: 0131-473 2002
e-mail: eif@eif.co.uk
web: www.eif.co.uk
Festival Director and Chief Executive:
Brian McMaster, CBE
Lasts for three weeks from the middle
of August to early September. Its
founders in 1947 believed that the
programme should be of the highest
possible artistic standard; that the
festival should enliven and enrich the
cultural life of Europe, Britain and
Scotland; and that it should provide a
period of flowering of the human
spirit.

Using all the major concert and
theatre venues in the city, the festival
brings to Edinburgh some of the best
in international theatre, music, dance
and opera. The audience is 60%
Scottish-based, but the festival also
attracts many visitors to the city, with
25% coming from the rest of the UK
and 15% from overseas.

EDINBURGH MILITARY TATTOO
Tattoo Office, 32 Market Street,
Edinburgh EH1 1QB
Tel: 0131-225 1188
Fax: 0131-225 8627
e-mail: edintattoo@edintattoo.co.uk
web: www.edintattoo.co.uk
Chief Executive and Producer: Brigadier
Melville Jameson

HIGHLAND FESTIVAL
The Castle, Inverness IV2 3EG
Tel: 01463 719000

IMAGINATE
45a George Street, Edinburgh EH2
2HT
Tel: 0131-225 8050

e-mail: info@imaginate.org.uk
web: www.imaginate.org.uk
Director: Tony Reekie; *Chair*: Esther Roberton
Originally the Scottish International Children's Festival, Imaginate is a year-round organisation, with a portfolio of initiatives and events aimed at promoting and developing performing arts for children in Scotland. Its vision is that all children in Scotland, by the age of 12, will have had a positive experience of performing arts. Its mission is to act as an advocate for the provision of high-quality performing arts for children in Scotland.

ST MAGNUS FESTIVAL
60 Victoria Street, Kirkwall KW15 1DN
Tel: 01856 871445
Fax: 01856 871170
web: www.stmagnusfestival.com
Director: Glenys Hughes
Midsummer arts festival – music, drama, dance, literature, and the visual arts.

SCOTTISH INTERNATIONAL STORYTELLING FESTIVAL
The Netherbow: Scottish Storytelling Centre, 43-45 High Street, Edinburgh EH1 1SR
Tel: 0131-557 5724
Director: Joanna Bremner

FILM

BAFTA SCOTLAND (BRITISH ACADEMY OF FILM AND TELEVISION ARTS)
249 West George Street, Glasgow G2 4QE
Tel: 0141-302 1770
Fax: 0141-302 1771
e-mail: info@baftascotland.co.uk
web: www.baftascotland.co.uk
Director: Alison Forsyth; *Committee Chair*: Blair Jenkins

Rewards Scottish industry and talent in film and television.

SCOTTISH SCREEN
249 West George Street, Glasgow G2 4QE
Tel: 0141-302 1700
Fax: 0141-302 1711
e-mail: info@scottishscreen.com
web: www.scottishscreen.com
Chief Executive: Steve McIntyre; *Chairman*: James Lee
Unified organisation which came into existence in 1997 from the merger of the Scottish Film Council, Scottish Film Production Fund, Scottish Broadcast and Film Training, and Scottish Screen Locations.
A film and television agency funded by the government, charged with promoting film both as an industry and as a moving image culture, it brings together education, training, script development, production finance, locations, marketing, exhibitions and archives in a one-stop shop. It is part of Scottish Screen's role to stimulate debate on film and television matters and to represent the interests of the industry to government.
The agency's locations department aims to attract production companies to film in Scotland. Scottish Screen Training provides courses and events to encourage technical and creative talent. Scottish Screen Development considers 350 film projects a year, of which about 20 will be given development finance. Scottish Screen Production advises on production finance available from the Glasgow Film Fund and administers four short film schemes. The Scottish National Film and Video Archive, established in 1976, locates and preserves the indigenous film heritage. Scottish Screen Exhibition promotes public screenings. The agency also acts as a distributor.

FISHING

FISHERIES RESEARCH SERVICES
PO Box 101, Victoria Road, Aberdeen
AB11 9DB
Tel: 01224 876544
Fax: 01224 295511
web: www.marlab.ac.uk
Chief Executive: Professor A D Hawkins
Marine Laboratory provides expert scientific and technical advice on marine and freshwater fisheries, aquaculture, and the protection of the aquatic environment and its wildlife. The laboratory monitors the state of the fish and shellfish stocks exploited by Scottish fishermen, investigates fishing methods and ways of promoting the conservation of fish stocks through technical measures, monitors the state of the seas, and carries out the statutory inspection of fish and shellfish farms. **Freshwater Fisheries Laboratory** is the only government research laboratory in Britain wholly devoted to freshwater fisheries. Monitors the reported annual catches of salmon and sea trout, and provides scientific advice to government.

SCOTTISH FISHERIES PROTECTION AGENCY
Pentland House, 47 Robb's Loan, Edinburgh EH14 1TY
Tel: 0131-244 6059
Chief Executive: P E Du Vivier
Britain's sea fisheries have been protected and controlled by authority of parliament for nearly 200 years. The 19th-century "Commissioners of the British White Herring Fishery" used naval vessels to superintend the fisheries. In 1882 responsibility for protecting sea fisheries in Scottish waters was given to the Fishery Board for Scotland, and in 1939 its functions were transferred to the Secretary of State for Scotland. The present agency is responsible to the Scottish Executive Environment and Rural Affairs Department.
It enforces fisheries legislation and regulations in the 140,000 square miles of sea around Scotland and in Scottish ports, with the aim of conserving fish stocks. Aims to deter and detect illegal fishing. Among its resources are two surveillance aircraft based at Prestwick, four offshore patrol vessels based at Leith and Greenock, one inshore patrol vessel, and fishery offices at 18 of the main fishing ports in Scotland.

SCOTTISH FISHERMEN'S FEDERATION
14 Regent Quay, Aberdeen AB11 5AE
Tel: 01224 582583
Chief Executive: Hamish Morrison, OBE; *President*: Alexander Smith
Represents the political interests of Scotland's seven main fishing associations to the UK government and European institutions.

SCOTTISH FISHERMEN'S ORGANISATION
Braehead, 601 Queensferry Road, Edinburgh EH4 6EA
Tel: 0131-339 7972
Fax: 0131-339 6662
e-mail: info@scottishfishermen.co.uk
web: www.scottishfishermen.co.uk
Chief Executive: I M MacSween

SCOTTISH QUALITY SALMON
Durn, Isla Road, Perth PH2 7HG
Tel: 01738 587000
Fax: 01738 621454
e-mail: enquiries@scottishsalmon. co.uk
web: www.scottishsalmon.co.uk
Chief Executive: Brian Simpson; *Chairman:* Earl of Lindsay
Membership organisation enhancing and promoting the value of all sectors of the salmon farming industry in Scotland.

SCOTTISH WHITE FISH PRODUCERS'
ASSOCIATION LTD
40 Broad Street, Fraserburgh AB43
9AH
Tel: 01346 514545
Fax: 01346 518069
Secretary: George MacRae; *Chairman*:
Michael Park
Develops the interests of commercial
seagoing fishermen.

SEA FISH INDUSTRY AUTHORITY
18 Logie Mill, Logie Green Road,
Edinburgh EH7 4HG
Tel: 0131-558 3331
Fax: 0131-558 1442
e-mail: seafish@seafish.co.uk
web: www.seafish.co.uk
Chief Executive: Alasdair C Fairbairn;
Chairman: Eric Davey
Replaced the White Fish Authority
and the Herring Industry Board in
1981. Works with the industry to meet
consumer demands, raise standards,
improve efficiency, and secure a
prosperous future. Undertakes
research and development; provides
or helps with training; promotes the
marketing and consumption of
seafood; gives financial assistance to
co-operatives.

FITNESS

FITNESS SCOTLAND
Caledonia House, South Gyle,
Edinburgh EH12 9DQ
Tel: 0131-317 7243
Fax: 0131-317 1998

FOOD

FOOD STANDARDS AGENCY SCOTLAND
St Magnus House, 25 Guild Street,
Aberdeen AB11 6NJ
Tel: 01224 285100

e-mail: scotland@foodstandards.
gsi.gov.uk
web: www.food.gov.uk/scotland/
Director Scotland: George Paterson
New organisation which has taken on
the food safety work and functions
previously carried out by the Food
Standards and Safety Division of the
Scottish Executive. Handles issues
involving: food standards, nutrition
and diet; general food hygiene, fish,
shellfish and milk hygiene; hygiene
controls on meat and meat products;
regulation of animal feeding stuffs;
novel foods, radiological safety and
emergencies. Operates within the UK
Food Standards Agency.

TASTE OF SCOTLAND
33 Melville Street, Edinburgh EH3 7JF
Tel: 0131-220 1900
e-mail: tastescotland@sol.co.uk
web: www.taste-of-scotland.com
Chief Executive: Amanda Clark
Publishes annual guide to good
eating places in Scotland through a
stringent quality assurance
programme.

FOOTBALL

SCOTTISH FOOTBALL ASSOCIATION
Hampden Park, Glasgow G42 9AY
Tel: 0141-616 6000
Chief Executive: David Taylor;
President: Jack McGinn
Governing body for football in
Scotland.

SCOTTISH FOOTBALL LEAGUE
Hampden Park, Glasgow G42 9EB
Tel: 0141-620 4160
Fax: 0141-620 4161
e-mail: info@sfl.scottishfootball.com
web: www.scottishfootball.com
Secretary: Peter Donald
Promotes and extends association
football and provides League

Championship and League Cup competitions for the clubs. Concludes commercial contracts on their behalf.

SCOTTISH PREMIER LEAGUE
Hampden Park, Glasgow G42 9DE
Tel: 0141-620 4140
Company Secretary: Iain Blair

FREEMASONRY

GRAND LODGE OF ANTIENT FREE AND ACCEPTED MASONS OF SCOTLAND
Freemasons' Hall, 96 George Street, Edinburgh EH2 3DH
Tel: 0131-225 5304
web: www.grandlodgesscotland.com
Grand Secretary: C Martin McGibbon;
Curator: Robert L D Cooper
Governing body for freemasonry in Scotland.

GAELIC

COMHAIRLE NAN LEABHRAICHEAN THE GAELIC BOOKS COUNCIL
22 Mansfield Street, Glasgow G11 5QP
Tel: 0141-337 6211
Fax: 0141-341 0515
e-mail: fios@gaelicbooks.net
web: www.gaelicbooks.net
Director: Ian MacDonald; *Chairperson:* Donalda MacKinnon
Assists publishers with grants for books, commissions authors, provides an editorial service. It has its own bookshop and publishes a catalogue of all Gaelic and Gaelic-related books in print.

COMHAIRLE NAN SGOILTEAN ARAICH
53 Church Street, Inverness IV1 1DR
Tel: 01463 225469
Provides Gaelic pre-school education.

AN COMUNN GAIDHEALACH
109 Church Street, Inverness IV1 1EY
Tel: 01463 231226
Fax: 01463 715557
Chief Executive: Donald John MacSween; *President:* Peter MacIntyre
Works for the preservation and development of the Gaelic language. Organises and stages the annual National Mod and produces the Gaelic newspaper *An Gaidheal Ur*. There are branches of the association throughout the world and thousands of members, many of whom work voluntarily on behalf of the language.

COMUNN NA GAIDHLIG
5 Mitchell's Lane, Inverness IV2 3HQ
Tel: 01463 234138
Acting Chief Executive: Donald Martin;
Chairperson: Mairi Bremner
Gaelic language development agency, established in 1984 to co-ordinate the revival of Gaelic at all levels and sectors in Scotland.

FEISEAN NAN GAIDHEAL
Meall House, Portree, Isle of Skye IV51 9BZ
Tel: 01478 613355
Secretary: Rita Hunter; *Chairman:* John Macdonald
Independent umbrella organisation promoting and supporting the tuition of traditional Gaelic music, song and dance.

GARDENS

SCOTLAND'S GARDENS SCHEME
22 Rutland Square, Edinburgh EH1 2BB
Tel: 0131-229 1870
Director: R St Clair-Ford
Opens mainly private gardens all over Scotland for charity.

GAY RIGHTS

OUTRIGHT SCOTLAND
PO Box 23253, Edinburgh EH1 3XD
Tel: 0131-558 9216
web: www.outright-scotland.org
National membership-based organisation promoting the interests and rights of lesbian, gay, bisexual and transgendered people.

GENEALOGY

SCOTS ANCESTRY RESEARCH SOCIETY
8 York Road, Edinburgh EH5 3EH
Tel: 0131-552 2028
Fax: 0131-552 2028
e-mail: scotsanc@aol.com
web: www.royalmile.com/
 scotsancestry/
Hon Secretary: Jean Brodie
Undertakes genealogical research in Scottish records for people of Scottish descent all over the world.

SCOTTISH GENEALOGY SOCIETY
15 Victoria Terrace, Edinburgh EH1 2JL
Tel: 0131-220 3677
Fax: 0131-220 3677
e-mail: info@scotsgenealogy.com
web: www.scotsgenealogy.com
Hon Secretary: Miss J P S Ferguson
Promotes research into Scottish family history; collects, exchanges and publishes information and material relating to Scottish genealogy by means of meetings, lectures, etc.

GOLF

LADIES GOLF UNION
The Scores, St Andrews KY16 9AT
Tel: 01334 475811
Fax: 01334 472818

e-mail: info@lgu.org
web: www.lgu.org
President: Mrs S Johnson
Governing body of ladies' amateur golf.

THE ROYAL AND ANCIENT GOLF CLUB
The Links, St Andrews KY16 9JD
Tel: 01334 460000
Fax: 01334 460001
Secretary: Peter Dawson
Governing body for rules of golf for all countries of the world (except USA). Organisers of Open Golf Championship.

SCOTTISH GOLF UNION
Scottish National Golf Centre, Drumoig, Leuchars, St Andrews KY16 0DW
Tel: 01382 549500
Secretary: Hamish Grey
Governing body for amateur golf in Scotland.

SCOTTISH LADIES GOLFING ASSOCIATION
Scottish National Golf Centre, Drumoig, Leuchars, St Andrews KY16 0DW
Tel: 01382 549502
Fax: 01382 549512
e-mail: slga@scottishgolf.com
web: www.scottishgolf.com
Secretary: Susan Simpson

GOVERNMENT

See pages 22 to 28 for detailed information about The Scottish Executive. Some public bodies are listed under subject category.

AUDITOR GENERAL FOR SCOTLAND
ACCOUNTS COMMISSION FOR SCOTLAND
AUDIT SCOTLAND
110 George Street, Edinburgh EH2 4LH

Tel: 0131-477 1234
Fax: 0131-477 4567
web: www.audit-scotland.gov.uk
Auditor General: Robert W Black;
Secretary to the Accounts Commission:
William F Magee
The Auditor General holds the Scottish Executive and other public spending bodies (except local authorities) to account for the proper, efficient and effective use of public funds.

The Accounts Commission ensures that local authorities, fire and police boards, spend £9 billion of public money properly and wisely.

Audit Scotland provides services to the Auditor General and Accounts Commission.

BENEFITS AGENCY
Central Support Unit Scotland, Argyle House, 3 Lady Lawson Street, Edinburgh EH3 9SH
Tel: 0131-229 9191
Area Director: Douglas Kerr

BOUNDARY COMMISSION FOR SCOTLAND
3 Drumsheugh Gardens, Edinburgh EH3 7QJ
Tel: 0131-538 7200
Secretary: Bob Smith; *Deputy Chairman:* Hon Lady Cosgrove
Keeps under review the boundaries of the Parliamentary constituencies in Scotland.

COMMON SERVICES AGENCY FOR NHSSCOTLAND
Trinity Park House, South Trinity Road, Edinburgh EH5 3SE
Tel: 0131-552 6255
Acting Chief Executive: Eric Harper-Gow; *Chairman:* Graeme Millar
Provides and co-ordinates for NHSScotland: national data processing and information services, health surveillance, blood transfusion and laboratory requests, specialist legal, technical, and purchasing services, commissioning specialist care.

COMPANIES HOUSE
37 Castle Terrace, Edinburgh EH12 7PP
Tel: 0870 3333636
Fax: 0131-535 5820
e-mail: jhenderson@companieshouse.gov.uk
web: www.companieshouse.gov.uk
Registrar of Companies: James Henderson; *Chief Executive:* John Holden
Reponsible for the incorporation, re-registration and striking off of companies and the registration of documents required to be filed under the companies, insolvency and related legislation. Also provides company information to the public.

THE CROWN ESTATE
10 Charlotte Square, Edinburgh EH2 4DR
Tel: 0131-226 7241
Fax: 0131-220 1366
e-mail: cescotland@crownestate.co.uk
web: www.crownestate.co.uk
Head of Scottish Estates: Michael Cunliffe; *Scottish Commissioner:* Ian Grant
Manages property held "in right of the Crown". In Scotland, this includes commercial property, agricultural land, about half the foreshore, and almost all the seabed. All profit is paid to the Treasury.

EMPLOYMENT SERVICE – OFFICE FOR SCOTLAND
Argyle House, 3 Lady Lawson Street, Edinburgh EH3 9SD
Tel: 0131-221 4000
Fax: 0131-221 4004
Director: Alan R Brown
Responsible for managing the JobCentre network and delivering New Deal.

HEALTH AND SAFETY EXECUTIVE
Belford House, 59 Belford Road, Edinburgh EH4 3UE
0131-247 2000
Director for Scotland: Allan Sefton
Responsible for the control of risks to people's health and safety from work activities and the enforcement of health and safety legislation.

HM CUSTOMS AND EXCISE SCOTLAND
44 York Place, Edinburgh EH1 3JW
Tel: 0131-469 2000
Head: Ian Mackay
Regional unit within the Customs and Excise department. It collects and manages VAT, insurance premium tax, landfill tax, excise duties (including air passenger duty); collects EU duties and levies; enforces import and export prohibitions.

INLAND REVENUE SCOTLAND
Clarendon House, 114-116 George Street, Edinburgh EH2 4LH
Tel: 0131-473 4000
Director: David Hinstridge

LOCAL GOVERNMENT BOUNDARY COMMISSION FOR SCOTLAND
3 Drumsheugh Gardens, Edinburgh EH3 7QJ
Tel: 0131-538 7510
Secretary: R Smith; *Chairman:* J Marjoribanks
Permanent body appointed under the Local Government (Scotland) Act 1973 to keep under review local government boundaries and electoral areas.

SCOTTISH INDUSTRIAL DEVELOPMENT ADVISORY BOARD
Meridian Court, 5 Cadogan Street, Glasgow G2 6AT
Tel: 0141-242 5676
Chairman: J J G Good, CBE

SCOTTISH PARLIAMENTARY COMMISSIONER FOR ADMINISTRATION
28 Thistle Street, Edinburgh EH2 1EN
Tel: 0845 601 0456
Fax: 0131-226 4447
web: www.ombudsman.org.uk
Ombudsman: Michael Buckley; *Deputy Ombudsman:* Alan Watson
Investigation of complaints made to him by members of the Scottish Parliament about injustice resulting from maladministration by the Scottish Executive, the Parliamentary Corporation and a range of bodies involved in devolved Scottish affairs.

SCOTTISH TRAFFIC AREA OFFICE
J Floor, Argyle House, 3 Lady Lawson Street, Edinburgh EH3 9SE
Tel: 0131-200 4955
Fax: 0131-529 8501
Administrative Director: Cathy Drury
Responsible for HGV and PSV operator licensing.

VALUATION OFFICE AGENCY
50 Frederick Street, Edinburgh EH2 1NG
Tel: 0131-465 0700
Chief Valuer (Scotland): Allan Ainslie
Provides valuation and property-related advice for all classes of property to the public sector, including government departments, local authorities, the NHS and non-departmental public bodies.

HEALTH BOARDS

ARGYLL AND CLYDE NHS BOARD
Ross House, Hawkhead Road, Paisley PA2 7BN
Tel: 0141-842 7200
Fax: 0141-848 1414
Chief Executive: N A McConachie; *Chairman:* John Mullin

AYRSHIRE AND ARRAN NHS BOARD
Boswell House, 10 Arthur Street, Ayr
KA7 1QJ
Tel: 01292 611040
Fax: 01292 286762
General Manager: Mrs Wia-yin Hatton;
Chairman: Mr George L Irving

BORDERS NHS BOARD
Newstead, Melrose TD6 9DB
Tel: 01896 825500
General Manager: Dr Lindsay Burley;
Chairman: David A G Kilshaw

NHS DUMFRIES AND GALLOWAY
Grierson House, The Crichton,
Bankend Road, Dumfries DG1 4ZH
Tel: 01387 272700
Fax: 01387 252375
Chief Executive: Malcolm Wright;
Interim Chairman: Dr R H Mack

FIFE NHS BOARD
Springfield House, Cupar KY15 5UP
Tel: 01334 656200
Chief Executive: Tony Ranzetta;
Chairman: Esther Roberton

FORTH VALLEY NHS BOARD
33 Spittal Street, Stirling FK8 1DX
Tel: 01786 463031
Chief Executive: Fiona Mackenzie;
Chairman: Professor Frank Clark, CBE

GRAMPIAN NHS BOARD
Summerfield House, 2 Eday Road,
Aberdeen AB15 6RE
Tel: 01224 663456
Chief Executive: Neil Campbell; *Chair:*
Jim Royan

NHS GREATER GLASGOW
Dalian House, 350 St Vincent Street,
Glasgow G3 8YZ
Tel: 0141-201 4444
Fax: 0141-201 4401
Chief Executive: Tom Divers; *Chairman:*
Professor David L Hamblen

HIGHLAND NHS BOARD
Assynt House, Beechwood Park,
Inverness IV2 3HG
Tel: 01463 717123
General Manager: Dr Roger Gibbins;
Chairman: Caroline Thomson

NHS LANARKSHIRE
14 Beckford Street, Hamilton ML3
0TA
Tel: 01698 281313
Chief Executive: T A Divers; *Chairman:*
Ian Livingstone

LOTHIAN NHS BOARD
Deaconess House, 148 Pleasance,
Edinburgh EH8 9RS
Tel: 0131-536 9000
Fax: 0131-536 9009
Chief Executive: James Barbour; *Acting
Chairman:* Richard Findlay

NHS ORKNEY
Garden House, New Scapa Road,
Kirkwall KW15 1BH
Tel: 01856 885400
Fax: 01856 885411
Chief Executive: Judi Wellden;
Chairman: Eoin Leslie

NHS SHETLAND
Brevik House, South Road, Lerwick
ZE1 0TG
Tel: 01595 696767
Fax: 01595 696727
Chief Executive: Sandra Laurenson;
Chairman: John Telford

NHS TAYSIDE
Gateway House, Luna Place
Technology Park, Dundee DD2 1TP
Tel: 01382 561818
Fax: 01382 424003
Chief Executive: Tim Brett; *Chairman:*
Peter Bates

WESTERN ISLES NHS BOARD
37 South Beach Street, Stornoway, Isle of Lewis HS1 2BN
Tel: 01851 702997
Chief Executive: Murdo MacLennan; Chair: Alexander Matheson

HEALTH ORGANISATIONS

ASH SCOTLAND (ACTION ON SMOKING AND HEALTH)
8 Frederick Street, Edinburgh EH2 2HB
Tel: 0131-225 4725
e-mail: ashscotland@aschscotland.org.uk
web: www.ashscotland.org.uk
Director: Maureen Moore; *Chair*: Professor Keith Fox
Campaigns for effective tobacco control policies and for effective support services for those who wish to stop smoking.

ESSENTIA GROUP
Lower Ground, Sky Park, 72 Finnieston Square, Glasgow G3 8ET
Tel: 0141-568 4000
Managing Director: Joe Costello
Health and public sector telephone information service.

HEALTH EDUCATION BOARD FOR SCOTLAND
Woodburn House, Canaan Lane, Edinburgh EH10 4SG
Tel: 0131-536 5500
Fax: 0131-536 5501
Acting Chief Executive: Graham Robertson; *Chairman*: Lesley Hinds
Public body established in 1991 and funded by the Scottish Executive which aims to promote good health by the empowerment of individuals, groups and communities. HEBS is committed to the development, implementation and support of effective, efficient and ethical health education, responsive to the needs and priorities of the population and its sub-groups. As well as providing programmes of health education nationally, the Board facilitates the development and co-ordination of complementary initiatives sub-nationally across Scotland. It contributes to the education and training of relevant professionals and others; reviews, undertakes and commissions relevant research; and gives advice on policies which affect health.

SCOTTISH ASSOCIATION OF HEALTH COUNCILS
24a Palmerston Place, Edinburgh EH12 5AL
Tel: 0131-220 4101
Fax: 0131-220 4108
e-mail: admin1@sahc.sol.co.uk
web: www.show.scot.nhs.uk/sahc
Convener: George S Harvie
Seeks to be the national voice of the public in health matters.

HIGHLAND DANCING

SCOTTISH OFFICIAL BOARD OF HIGHLAND DANCING
32 Grange Loan, Edinburgh EH9 2NR
Tel: 0131-668 3965
Administrator: Marjory Rowan; *Chairman*: Miss S Russell
Governing body for Highland dancing.

HIGHLAND GAMES

SCOTTISH GAMES ASSOCIATION
24 Florence Place, Perth PH1 5BH
Tel: 01738 627782
Fax: 01738 639622
Secretary: Andrew Rettie; *President*: Alan Sim

HISTORY

GENERAL REGISTER OFFICE FOR SCOTLAND

New Register House, Edinburgh EH1 3YT
Tel: 0131-334 0380
Fax: 0131-314 4400
e-mail: records@gro-scotland.gov.uk
web: www.gro-scotland.gov.uk
Registrar General: John Randall;
Deputy Registrar General: Brian Philp
Government department established by Act of Parliament in 1854 and headed by the Registrar General for Scotland, who is appointed by Scottish ministers. The office administers civil registration of "vital events" – births, deaths, marriages, divorces and adoptions – and the statutes relating to the formalities of marriage. It arranges periodic censuses of Scotland's population and maintains the NHS central register of patients. New Register House, one of the most advanced ancestral research facilities in the world, is the prime source of genealogical records in Scotland, giving the serious searcher access to unique records and a source of reference books.

Before the introduction of compulsory civil registration in 1855, the registers of births, deaths, marriages, etc, were kept by parish ministers or session clerks. These old parish registers, numbering 3,500, are far from complete and for some parishes there are no registers at all. Even where pre-1855 records do exist, they may contain relatively little information.

The branch of the department based at Ladywell House publishes a wide range of reports and tables on vital statistics, population statistics and census statistics.

Every year, the department oversees the local registration of 170,000 "vital events"; undertakes up to 25,000 searches on behalf of personal callers and postal customers; issues up to 30,000 copies of entries in statutory registers; maintains 100 search places for members of the public themselves to access the open records, allowing 450,000 such accesses each year; deals with 7,000 requests for statistical information; processes 500,000 changes to the NHS central register; and handles up to 50,000 transactions in connection with medical research projects.

It has introduced central electronic recording of all births, deaths and marriages from information obtained by local registration offices.

NATIONAL ARCHIVES OF SCOTLAND

HM General Register House, 2 Princes Street, Edinburgh EH1 3YY
Tel.: 0131-535 1314
Fax: 0131-535 1360
e-mail: enquiries@nas.gov.uk
web: www.nas.gov.uk
Keeper of the Records of Scotland: George P Mackenzie
As the repository for the public and legal records of Scotland, the National Archives of Scotland (formerly known as the Scottish Record Office) is responsible for maintaining the national archives. In addition, it accepts many local and private archives.

The records cover the period from the 12th century to the present day, ranging from medieval parchments to modern microfiche, from the formal records of government and the law courts to personal letters and diaries. The holdings include family papers and estate records, thousands of hand-drawn and engraved maps and plans which illustrate the changing face of urban and rural Scotland, the Scottish railway archives, and the records of a number of firms, charities and public bodies.

The office provides personal access to the records through its search rooms and answers postal inquiries from all over the world.

REGISTERS OF SCOTLAND
Meadowbank House, 153 London Road, Edinburgh EH8 7AU
Tel: 0131-659 6111
Fax: 0131-479 3688
e-mail: keeper@ros.gov.uk
web: www.ros.gov.uk
Customer Service Centres:
Erskine House, 68 Queen Street, Edinburgh EH2 4NF
Tel: 0845 6070161
Fax: 0131-200 3932
9 George Square, Glasgow G2 1DY
Tel: 0845 6070164
Fax: 0141-306 4424
e-mail: customer.services@ros.gov.uk
Keeper of the Registers: Alan Ramage
Information about property and property transactions is available to the general public at either the Registers of Scotland or the Scottish Record Office, and can be obtained by paying a fee. The main registers are the Sasine Register, established in 1617, and the Land Register, introduced into Scotland by the 1979 Land Registration Scotland Act. Both deal with the registration of property and interests in property. Unlike the Sasine Register (which is being replaced), the Land Register does not provide historical information on past owners of properties. It is an up to date statement of the ownership and details of each registered title, which can be easily found by reference to the Ordnance Survey map.

Land registration is a modern system allowing for the simple transfer of registered property. By dispensing with the need to examine legal documents spanning a long period to ensure that the title to a property is sound, it helps make conveyancing transactions simpler. Staff deal with half a million transactions every year.

SCOTTISH HISTORY SOCIETY
Department of Scottish History, University of Edinburgh, 17 Buccleuch Place, Edinburgh EH8 9LN
Tel: 0131-650 4030
Hon Secretary: Dr S Boardman

SCOTTISH RECORDS ASSOCIATION
National Archives of Scotland, HM General Register House, 2 Princes Street, Edinburgh EH1 3YY
Tel: 0131-535 1314
Honorary Secretary: Mr R Cullen; *Chairman*: Professor Iain Levitt
For all those interested in the preservation and use of Scotland's historical records. Publishes journal, *Scottish Archives*.

1745 ASSOCIATION
Ferry Cottage, Corran, Ardgour, Fort William PH33 7AA
Tel: 01855 841306
Secretary: Miss C Aikman; *President*: David Lumsden of Cushnie
Studies the period of Jacobite history (1688-1788), marks sites of Jacobite interest, publishes a journal three times a year, organises annual gathering, visits to houses and annual dinner.

HOCKEY

SCOTTISH HOCKEY UNION
589 Lanark Road, Edinburgh EH14 5DA
Tel: 0131-453 9070
Fax: 0131-453 9079
e-mail: info@scottish-hockey.org.uk
General Manager: Colin Grahamslaw; *President*: Gerry Ralph

HORSES

SCOTTISH EQUESTRIAN ASSOCIATION
Grange Cottage, Station Road, Langbank PA14 6YB
Tel: 01475 540687
Fax: 01475 540348
Secretary: Muriel Colquhoun; *Chairperson:* Lorna Clarke
New governing body in Scotland for all equestrian activities.

TREKKING AND RIDING SOCIETY OF SCOTLAND
Bruach-na-h'Abhainne, Maragowan, Killin FK21 8TN
Tel: 01567 820909
Secretary: Susan Howard; *Chairman:* Lt Col Howard C Paterson.

HORTICULTURE

ROYAL CALEDONIAN HORTICULTURAL SOCIETY
6 Kirkliston Road, South Queensferry EH30 9LT
Tel: 0131-331 1011
Secretary: Tom Mabbott; *President:* Professor F T Last, OBE
Instituted in 1809 with the intention of "promoting and improving the cultivation of the best kinds of fruit, of the most choice sorts of flowers and of those vegetables which are most useful in the kitchen".

HOUSING

COMMUNITIES SCOTLAND
Thistle House, 91 Haymarket Terrace, Edinburgh EH12 5HE
Tel: 0131-313 0044
Fax: 0131-313 2680
web: www.communitiesscotland. gov.uk
Chief Executive: Bob Millar; *Chairman:* John Ward

Formerly known as Scottish Homes. Plays an important role in delivering Scottish ministers' policies to promote social justice through neighbourhood renewal, community empowerment and housing investment. As an executive agency, it reports directly to ministers.

A residuary body, retaining the name Scottish Homes, manages the 4,000 houses which have not yet transferred from Scottish Homes to community ownership. These houses are expected to transfer as tenants vote in local ballots over the next few years.

SCOTTISH COUNCIL FOR SINGLE HOMELESS
5th Floor, Wellgate House, 200 Cowgate, Edinburgh EH1 1NQ
Tel: 0131-226 4382
Director: Robert Aldridge; *Convener:* Alice Ann Jackson
National charity promoting the interests of single homeless people.

SCOTTISH FEDERATION OF HOUSING ASSOCIATIONS
38 York Place, Edinburgh EH1 3HU
Tel: 0131-556 5777
Fax: 0131-557 6028
e-mail: sfha@sfha.co.uk
web: www.sfha.co.uk
Director: David Alexander
Voice of housing associations and co-operatives, representing them in negotiations on housing policy with government and other bodies, as well as campaigning on their behalf. A membership organisation, it promotes, encourages and assists the formation of housing associations and provides training, advice and support to help them operate. Housing associations and co-operatives are collectively responsible for managing over 140,000 homes.

SHELTER – SCOTTISH CAMPAIGN FOR HOMELESS PEOPLE
4th Floor, Scotiabank House, 6 South Charlotte Street, Edinburgh EH2 4AW
Tel: 0131-473 7170
Director: Liz Nicholson; *Chair*: Peter Robson

McIlwhan; *Chair*: John Scott
Aims to promote human rights in Scotland through: public education and advice; research; scrutiny of legislation; monitoring the application of international human rights treaties within Scotland.

TENANT PARTICIPATION ADVISORY SERVICE
74-78 Saltmarket, Glasgow G1 5LD
Tel: 0141-552 3633
Director: Lesley Baird

ICE HOCKEY

SCOTTISH ICE HOCKEY ASSOCIATION
230 Paisley Road West, Glasgow G51 1BU
e-mail: secretary@siha.net

HUMAN RELATIONS

SCOTTISH INSTITUTE OF HUMAN RELATIONS
18 Young Street, Edinburgh EH2 4JB
Tel.: 0131-226 9610
Fax: 0131-226 9611

ICE SKATING

SCOTTISH ICE SKATING ASSOCIATION
Ice Sports Centre, Riversdale Crescent, Edinburgh EH12 5XN
Tel: 0131-337 3976
Fax: 0131-337 9239

HUMAN RIGHTS

AMNESTY INTERNATIONAL
6 Castle Street, Edinburgh EH1 1DR
Tel: 0131-466 6200
Fax: 0131-466 6201
Scottish Development Manager: Rosemary Burnett; *Chair*: Andrew McEntee
Works worldwide for the release of prisoners of conscience, fair trials for political prisoners, and an end to torture, extra-judicial killings, "disappearances", and the death penalty.

SCOTTISH HUMAN RIGHTS CENTRE
146 Holland Street, Glasgow G2 4NG
Tel: 0141-332 5960
Fax: 0141-332 5309
e-mail: shrc@dial.pipex.com
web: www.shrc.pipex.com
Principal Officer: Rosemarie

IMMIGRATION

IMMIGRATION APPELLATE AUTHORITY
5th Floor, The Eagle Building, 215 Bothwell Street, Glasgow G2 7EZ
Tel: 0141-242 7553
Fax: 0141-242 7555
Regional Adjudicator: Mungo E Deans
Hears appeals against decisions relating to immigration or asylum made by the Secretary of State, by immigration officers, or by officers in Embassies or High Commissions overseas.

SCOTTISH REFUGEE COUNCIL
First Floor, Wellgate House, 200 Cowgate, Edinburgh EH1 1NQ
Tel: 0131-225 9994
Chief Executive: Sally Daghlian; *Chair*: Jane Ryder
Provides advice, information, legal representation and practical

assistance to asylum seekers and refugees in Scotland and campaigns on issues which affect them.

INSURANCE COMPANIES AND PERSONAL FINANCE

SCOTTISH EQUITABLE PLC
Edinburgh Park, Edinburgh EH12 9SE
Tel: 0131-339 9191
Managing Director: Graham Dumble;
Chairman: David Henderson

SCOTTISH LIFE
19 St Andrew Square, Edinburgh EH2 1YE
Tel: 0131-456 7777
Chief Executive: Brian Duffin

SCOTTISH MUTUAL ASSURANCE PLC
Abbey National House, 301 St Vincent Street, Glasgow G2 5HN
Tel: 0141-248 6321
Fax: 0141-275 9230
web: www.scottishmutual.co.uk
Chief Executive: Graham Pottinger

SCOTTISH WIDOWS PLC
69 Morrison Street, Edinburgh EH3 8YF
Tel: 0131-655 6000
web: www.scottishwidows.co.uk
Group Chief Executive: M D Ross;
Chairman: Lawrence M Urquhart

STANDARD LIFE ASSURANCE CO
Standard Life House, 30 Lothian Road, Edinburgh EH1 2DH
Tel: 0131-225 2552
Managing Director: Scott Bell

INTERNATIONAL

BRITISH RED CROSS – HEAD OFFICE (SCOTLAND)
Alexandra House, 204 Bath Street,
Glasgow G2 4HL
Tel: 0141-332 9591
Director: Gerald McLaughlin;
Chairman, Scottish Council: Rosalind Birchall
Gives skilled and impartial care to people in crisis everywhere, meeting the needs of vulnerable people in times of emergency. Twelve Scottish branches.

CONCERN
40 St. Enoch Square, Glasgow G1 4DH
Tel: 0141-221 3610
Development Officer: Mhairi Owens

FEED THE MINDS
41 George IV Bridge, Edinburgh EH1 1EL
Tel: 0131-226 5254
Scottish Secretary: Stanley Bonthron
Works inter-denominationally to help Christian literature and communication projects around the world.

INTERNATIONAL VOLUNTARY SERVICE
7 Upper Bow, Edinburgh EH1 2JN
Tel: 0131-226 6722
Director: Neil Harrower

MERCY CORPS SCOTLAND
10 Beaverhall Road, Edinburgh EH7 4JE
Tel: 0131-477 3677
Fax: 0131-477 3678
web: www.mercycorps.org
Executive Director: Jane Salmonson
Largest international aid agency in Scotland. Linked with the Worldwide Mercy Corps operation based in the USA.

OXFAM SCOTLAND
Floor 5, Fleming House, 134 Renfrew Street, Glasgow G3 6ST
Tel: 0141-331 1455

Fax: 0141-331 2264
web: www.oxfam.org.uk
Head of Scotland: Marie Hearle

SCOTTISH CAMPAIGN FOR NUCLEAR DISARMAMENT (CND)
15 Barrland Street, Glasgow G41
Tel: 0141-423 1222
Administrator: John Ainslie; *Chair:* Neil Cruickshank
Campaigns for the elimination of nuclear weapons.

JUDO

SCOTTISH JUDO FEDERATION
Caledonia House, South Gyle, Edinburgh EH12 9DQ
Chief Executive: Colin McIver; *Chairperson:* Richard Kenney

LACROSSE

SCOTTISH LACROSSE ASSOCIATION
St Leonards, St Andrews
Tel: 01334 472126
e-mail: pat@scottishlacrosse. freeserve. co.uk
web: www.scottish-lacrosse.org.uk
President: John Wolfenden

LANGUAGE

ENGLISH SPEAKING UNION – SCOTLAND
23 Atholl Crescent, Edinburgh EH3 8HQ
Tel: 0131-229 1528
Fax: 0131-229 1533
e-mail: esuscotland@ukonline.co.uk
web: www.esuscotland.org.uk
Secretary: Richard Wilkins; *Chairman:* J Grant Carson

SCOTS LANGUAGE SOCIETY
Scots Language Resource Centre, AK Bell Library, York Place, Perth PH2

8EP
01738 440199
Preses: Irene McGugan, MSP
Tae forder an uphaud the Scots leid in leiterature, poetrie, drama, sang an ballant.

SCOTTISH ESPERANTO ASSOCIATION
47 Airbles Crescent, Motherwell ML1 3AP
Tel: 01698 263199
e-mail: david@bissetioo.freeserve. co.uk
web: www.scottishesperanto. gothere.uk.com
Hon Secretary: David W Bisset; *President:* Dr Chris Gledhill
Promotion of Esperanto: improving proficiency in the language; encouraging dissemination of Scottish culture by means of Esperanto.

SCOTTISH GAELIC TEXTS SOCIETY
McLeish Carswell, 29 St Vincent Place, Glasgow G1 2DT
Hon Secretary: Miss A F Wilson; *President:* Rev Dr R MacLeod
Promotes the publication of texts in the Scottish Gaelic language.

LAW
See also: Courts and Tribunals

ABERDEEN BAR ASSOCIATION
889 Bon Accord Crescent, Aberdeen AB11 6DN
Tel: 01224 589700
Secretary: Lynn Bentley; *President:* Stuart Beveridge

EDINBURGH BAR ASSOCIATION
Wilson McLeod, 57 Jeffrey Street, Edinburgh EH1 1DH
Tel: 0131-556 0055
President: Eddie Wilson

FACULTY OF ADVOCATES
Advocates' Library, Parliament Square, Edinburgh EH1 1RF

Tel: 0131-226 5071
Dean of Faculty: Colin M. Campbell, QC
Part of the College of Justice, which was founded in 1532. A self-governing organisation consisting of those admitted to practise before the Court of Session, the faculty is located within its own library in Parliament House, where the Supreme Courts are also to be found. The library, founded in 1682, is the only copyright law library in Scotland and is open 24 hours a day, 365 days a year.

The faculty is headed by an elected dean and has 424 practising members, of whom 91 are women. Candidates for admission to the office of advocate are called intrants. There are no restrictions to entry provided an intrant satisfies the relevant standards in law and experience and has undertaken a period of pupillage.

FAMILY LAW ASSOCIATION
c/o Balfour and Manson, 54–56 Frederick Street, Edinburgh
Secretary: Angela Alexander; **Chair:** Shona Smith
Brings together solicitors with an interest predominantly in family law. Represents family law interests relating to new legislation, court practice, legal aid, etc.

GLASGOW BAR ASSOCIATION
Room 1.51, 1st Floor, Glasgow Sheriff Court, 1 Carlton Place, Glasgow G5 9DA
Tel: 0141-420 6142
President: Vincent Smith

LAW SOCIETY OF SCOTLAND
26 Drumsheugh Gardens, Edinburgh EH3 7YR
Tel: 0131-226 7411
Fax: 0131-225 2934
e-mail: lawscot@lawscot.org.uk
web: www.lawscot.org.uk
Chief Executive: Douglas R Mill;

President: Martin McAllister
Membership body of the Scottish legal profession. Promotes the interests of both practising solicitors and the public. Regulates its members and provides services which include: continuing legal education; advice on professional practice, European law, mediation, changes in the law, and marketing; a solicitor referral service for the public; and Dial-A-Law, a telephone information service for the public. It also promotes law reforms and undertakes legal research.

There are around 8,600 practising solicitors in Scotland, most in private practice, although 20% work in central and local government, industry and commerce. The society has a council of 50 members of the profession.

LEGAL DEFENCE UNION
HLB Kidsons, 274 Sauchiehall Street, Glasgow G2 3EH
Tel: 0141-307 5000

ROYAL FACULTY OF PROCURATORS IN GLASGOW
12 Nelson Mandela Place, Glasgow G2 1BT
Tel: 0141-331 0533
General Manager: Iain C Pearson;
Dean: Raymond M Williamson
Seeks to provide a centre for the legal profession in Glasgow, including library services, auditing, and education and training. The Faculty Hall is also available to other organisations as a conference venue.

SCOTTISH ASSOCIATION OF LAW CENTRES
Unit 28, 42 Dalsetter Avenue, Glasgow G15 8TE
Tel: 0141-944 0507
Fax: 0141-944 7605
e-mail: law@dlmac.fsnet.co.uk

Secretary: Amanda Pringle; *Chair*: Pat Bonar
Promotes and supports Scottish law centres.

SCOTTISH CHARITIES OFFICE

Crown Office, 25 Chambers Street, Edinburgh EH1 1LA
Tel: 0131-226 2626
Division of the Crown Office operating under the authority of the Lord Advocate. The law gives to the Lord Advocate the power to investigate misconduct or mismanagement in the administration of charitable organisations. The investigations are carried out by the Scottish Charities Office, which has a multi-disciplinary legal, accountancy and investigative staff.

SCOTTISH CHILD LAW CENTRE

54 East Crosscauseway, Edinburgh EH8 9HD
Tel: 0131-667 6333
Fax: 0131-662 1713
Convenor: Alison Cleland
Charitable legal advice line for Scots law as it applies to under 18s.

SCOTTISH COUNCIL OF LAW REPORTING

Law Society's Hall, 26 Drumsheugh Gardens, Edinburgh EH3 7YR
Tel: 0131-226 7411
Deputy Secretary: David Cullen; *Chairman*: Angus Stewart, QC
Publisher of Session Cases and the Faculty Digest.

SCOTTISH LAW AGENTS SOCIETY

11 Parliament Square, Edinburgh EH1 1RF
Tel: 0131-225 5061
Secretary: Janice H Webster, WS; *President*: Andrew D Anderson
Voluntary organisation of Scottish solicitors, founded in 1884. Operates specialist committees; publishes *Scottish Law Gazette* and *Memorandum Book*; represents the interests of its members; administers a Benevolent Fund.

SCOTTISH LAW COMMISSION

140 Causewayside, Edinburgh EH9 1PR
Tel: 0131-668 2131
Secretary: Miss J L McLeod; *Chairman*: Hon Lord Gill
Established in 1965 under the Law Commissions Act for the purpose of promoting the reform of the law of Scotland.

SCOTTISH LEGAL AID BOARD

44 Drumsheugh Gardens, Edinburgh EH3 7SW
Tel: 0131-226 7061
e-mail: general@slab.org.uk
web: www.slab.org.uk
Chief Executive: Lindsay Montgomery; *Chairman*: Jean Couper
Responsible for the administration of civil and criminal legal aid, as well as advice and assistance. In Scotland it determines eligibility for legal aid (other than for solemn criminal cases, where it is determined by the courts) and controls payments from the Legal Aid Fund in respect of legal aid and advice and assistance.

Non-departmental public body sponsored by the Scottish Executive Justice Department, established in 1987, which manages legal aid in Scotland. It derives its general powers and functions from the Legal Aid (Scotland) Act 1986. The board's main tasks are: to assess and where appropriate grant applications for legal aid; to scrutinise and pay legal aid accounts submitted by solicitors and advocates; and to advise the Scottish ministers on legal aid matters.

SHERIFFS' ASSOCIATION

PO Box 23, 1 Carlton Place, Glasgow G5 9DA
Tel: 0141-429 8888

Hon Secretary: Sheriff Brian A Lockhart; *President*: Sheriff J Douglas Allan
Promotion of the interests of the sheriffs of Scotland. Considers all subjects connected with the law and administration of justice.

SIGNET OFFICE
Court of Session, Parliament House, 2 Parliament Square, Edinburgh EH1 1RQ
Tel: 0131-225 2595

SOCIETY OF ADVOCATES IN ABERDEEN
Advocates' Hall, Concert Court, Aberdeen AB10 1BS
Tel: 01224 640079

SOCIETY OF PROCURATORS AND SOLICITORS IN THE CITY AND COUNTY OF PERTH
8 Atholl Crescent, Perth PH1 5NG
Tel: 01738 451616

SOCIETY OF WRITERS TO HM SIGNET
Signet Library, Parliament Square, Edinburgh EH1 1RF
Tel: 0131-225 4923
General Manager: M R McVittie; *Deputy Keeper of the Signet*: R John Elliot
Body of solicitors based primarily in Edinburgh. Maintains and improves the standards of professional knowledge, practice and competence of its members through the provision of library, educational and other facilities. Provides a forum for discussion of legislation and other matters affecting the law and its practice in Scotland. Promotes social activity. Acts as guardian of the Signet Library and of the works of scholarly and historical importance contained within it.

SSC SOCIETY
SSC Library, 11 Parliament Square, Edinburgh EH1 1RF
Tel: 0131-225 6268

Fax: 0131-225 2270
e-mail: ssc.library@dial.pipex.com
Keeper of the Library: C A Wilcox; *Secretary*: Dr Ian L S Balfour; *President*: John Loudon
Legal society formed in 1784 by royal charter to maintain standards in the solicitor profession, to uphold Scots law, and to encourage solicitors in public service.

STAIR SOCIETY
Saltire Court, 20 Castle Terrace, Edinburgh EH1 2ET
Tel: 0131-228 9900
Secretary and Treasurer: Thomas H Drysdale; *President*: Rt Hon Lord Hope of Craighead
Encourages and advances the knowledge of the history of Scots law.

LIBRARIES

NATIONAL LIBRARY OF SCOTLAND
George IV Bridge, Edinburgh EH1 1EW
Tel: 0131-226 4531
Fax: 0131-622 4803
e-mail: enquiries@nls.uk
web: www.nls.uk
Librarian and Secretary to Board of Trustees: Ian D McGowan
Scotland's largest library, serving both as a general research library of international importance and as the world's leading repository for the written record of Scotland's history and culture.

Direct descendant of the Advocates' Library (the library of the Scottish Bar), which was founded in 1689, the National Library since 1710 has had the privilege of legal deposit (the right to claim a copy of every book published in the UK and Ireland), and is currently one of five libraries in the UK to enjoy this privilege and the only one north of Cambridge. Created by Act of Parliament in 1925, when the Advocates' Library (by then a national library in all but name) gifted all but its legal collections to the nation.

The library holds Scotland's largest collection of books and manuscripts: 7 million printed items and pamphlets, 100,000 volumes of manuscripts, 20,000 current newspapers and periodicals, on 85 miles of shelves. Among the library's treasures are the last letter of Mary Queen of Scots, the Gutenberg Bible, Earl Haig's war diaries, and the world's most significant collection of Sir Walter Scott's manuscripts.

Access is restricted to those carrying out research or reference work requiring material not easily available in other libraries.

SCOTTISH LIBRARY ASSOCIATION
Scottish Centre for Information and Library Services, 1 John Street, Hamilton ML3 7EU
Tel: 01698 458888
Fax: 01698 458899
e-mail: sla@slainte.org.uk
web: www.slainte.org.uk
Director: Robert Craig

SCOTTISH LIBRARY AND INFORMATION COUNCIL
Scottish Centre for Information and Library Services, 1 John Street, Hamilton ML3 7EU
Tel: 01698 458888
e-mail: slic@slainte.org.uk
web: www.slainte.org.uk/slic/
slichome.htm
Director: Robert Craig
Advises government on library and information matters, promotes and monitors standards, provides grant-aid for projects.

LIGHTHOUSES

NORTHERN LIGHTHOUSE BOARD (COMMISSIONERS OF NORTHERN LIGHTHOUSES)
84 George Street, Edinburgh EH2 3DA
Tel: 0131-473 3100
Fax: 0131-220 2093
e-mail: enquiries@nlb.org.uk
web: www.nlb.org.uk
Chief Executive: James Taylor; *Chairman:* Lord Maclay, DL
Created by Act of Parliament in 1786, authorising the construction of four lighthouses in Scotland and the establishment of a commission for their administration. Responsible now for a network of 200 lights, 119 lit buoys, 42 unlit beacons, 27 racons and three DGPS stations. For the delivery of stores and supplies, the board has two ships, MV Pharos based at Oban and MV Polestar based at Stromness.

The area covered reaches from Muckle Flugga in Shetland to Chicken Rock off the Isle of Man. From Edinburgh headquarters, 75 automated lighthouses are monitored by landline and radio link and by satellite, night and day throughout the year. Running costs are met from a general lighthouse fund, financed by the collection of light dues paid by ships loading or discharging cargoes at British and Irish ports and by fishing vessels over 10 metres in length. A programme to automate all major lighthouses was completed in March 1998. The Board's motto is "In Salutem Omnium" (For the Safety of All).

LITERATURE

ASSOCIATION FOR SCOTTISH LITERARY STUDIES
Department of Scottish History, 9 University Gardens, University of

Glasgow, Glasgow G12 8QH
Tel: 0141-330 5309
e-mail: d.jones@scothist.arts.gla.ac.uk
web: www.asls.org.uk
Secretary: Jim Alison; *President*:
Dorothy McMillan
Educational charity promoting and
publishing the languages and
literature of Scotland.

EDINBURGH BIBLIOGRAPHICAL SOCIETY
c/o National Library of Scotland,
George IV Bridge, Edinburgh EH1
1EW
Tel: 0131-226 4531
Honorary Secretary: Dr W McDougall;
President: Dr M C T Simpson
Promotion and study of bibliography
and the history of the book.

EDINBURGH INTERNATIONAL BOOK FESTIVAL
Scottish Book Centre, 137 Dundee
Street, Foutainbridge, Edinburgh
EH11 1BG
Tel: 0131-228 5444
Director: Catherine Lockerbie;
Chairman: Susan Rice
Celebrates and promotes books and
the written word.

SCOTTISH BOOK TRUST
Scottish Book Centre, 137 Dundee
Street, Edinburgh EH11 1BG
Tel: 0131-229 3663
Fax: 0131-228 4293
e-mail: info@scottishbooktrust.com
web: www.scottishbooktrust.com
Executive Director: Lindsey Fraser;
Chairman: Richard Holloway
Promotes the role of books and
literature in the enrichment and
enjoyment of life.

SCOTTISH PEN
126 West Princes Street, Glasgow G4
9DB
Tel: 0141-564 1958
President: Simon Berry
Writers' association with centres

worldwide, which aims to foster
friendly co-operation between writers
and to defend freedom of expression.

SCOTTISH PUBLISHERS ASSOCIATION
Scottish Book Centre, 137 Dundee
Street, Edinburgh EH11 1BG
Tel: 0131-228 6866
Director: Lorraine Fannin; *Chairman*:
Peter Mackenzie
Aims to help publishing concerns in
Scotland to conduct their book
publishing businesses in a
professional manner, and to market
their output to the widest possible
readership. Encourages the
development of a literary culture in
Scotland.

SCOTTISH TEXT SOCIETY
27 George Square, Edinburgh EH8
9LD
Editorial Secretary: Nicola Royan;
President: Dr S Mapstone
Furthers the study and teaching of
Scottish literature, its language and
history, in particular by publishing
editions of original texts.

LOCAL GOVERNMENT

COSLA
Rosebery House, 9 Haymarket
Terrace, Edinburgh EH12 5XZ
Tel: 0131-474 9200
Fax: 0131-474 9292
e-mail: enquiries@cosla.gov.uk
web: www.cosla.gov.uk
Chief Executive: Oonagh Aitken;
President: Norman Murray
Representative voice of Scottish local
government. Aims to provide
national leadership to help councils
strengthen local democracy and
community support for local
goverment; to increase the role and
influence of local government; to
increase the control which local

government has over its affairs; to establish effective relationships with government, European institutions and partner organisations.

COSLA acts as the employers' association on behalf of its member councils, negotiating salaries, wages and conditions of service for local government employees in Scotland. It also has a responsibility to develop, encourage and promote best practice for local government in partnership with its member councils.

Local authorities:

ABERDEEN CITY COUNCIL
Town House, Broad Street, Aberdeen AB10 1FY
Tel: 01224 522000
Chief Executive: Douglas Paterson

ABERDEENSHIRE COUNCIL
Woodhill House, Westburn Road, Aberdeen AB16 5GB
Tel: 01467 620981
Chief Executive: A G Campbell

ANGUS COUNCIL
7 The Cross, Forfar DD8 1BX
Tel: 01307 461460
Chief Executive: A B Watson

ARGYLL AND BUTE COUNCIL
Kilmory, Lochgilphead PA31 8RT
Tel: 01546 602127
Chief Executive: J McLellan

CLACKMANNANSHIRE COUNCIL
Greenfield, Alloa FK10 2AD
Tel: 01259 450000
Chief Executive: Keir Bloomer

DUMFRIES AND GALLOWAY COUNCIL
Council Offices, English Street, Dumfries DG1 2DD
Tel: 01387 260000
Chief Executive: P N Jones

DUNDEE CITY COUNCIL
City Chambers, 21 City Square, Dundee DD1 3BY
Tel: 01382 434000
Chief Executive: A Stephen

EAST AYRSHIRE COUNCIL
Council Headquarters, London Road, Kilmarnock KA3 7BU
Tel: 01563 576000
Chief Executive: D Montgomery

EAST DUNBARTONSHIRE COUNCIL
Tom Johnston House, Civic Way, Kirkintilloch G66 4TJ
0141-578 8000
Chief Executive: Vicki Nash

EAST LOTHIAN COUNCIL
John Muir House, Haddington EH41 3HA
Tel: 01620 827827
Chief Executive: J Lindsay

EAST RENFREWSHIRE COUNCIL
Council Headquarters, Eastwood Park, Rouken Glen Road, Giffnock, East Renfrewshire G46 6UG
Tel: 0141-577 3000
Chief Executive: P Daniels

CITY OF EDINBURGH COUNCIL
Wellington Court, 10 Waterloo Place, Edinburgh EH1 3EG
Tel: 0131-469 3002
Chief Executive: T N Aitchison

FALKIRK COUNCIL
Municipal Buildings, Falkirk FK1 5RS
Tel: 01324 506070
Chief Executive: Mary Pitcaithly

FIFE COUNCIL
Fife House, North Street, Glenrothes KY7 5LT
Tel: 01592 414141
Chief Executive: Douglas Sinclair

GLASGOW CITY COUNCIL
City Chambers, George Square, Glasgow G2 1DU
Tel: 0141-287 2000
Chief Executive: J Andrew

HIGHLAND COUNCIL
Council Buildings, Glenurquhart Road, Inverness IV3 5NX
Tel: 01463 702000
Chief Executive: A D McCourt

INVERCLYDE COUNCIL
Municipal Buildings, Clyde Square, Greenock PA15 1LY
Tel: 01475 717171
Chief Executive: R Cleary

MIDLOTHIAN COUNCIL
Midlothian House, Buccleuch Street, Dalkeith EH22 1DJ
Tel: 0131-270 7500
Chief Executive: T Muir

MORAY COUNCIL
Council Offices, High Street, Elgin IV30 1BX
Tel: 01343 563001
Chief Executive: Alastair Keddie

NORTH AYRSHIRE COUNCIL
Cunninghame House, Irvine KA12 8EE
Tel: 01294 324100
Chief Executive: Bernard Devine

NORTH LANARKSHIRE COUNCIL
PO Box 14, Civic Centre, Motherwell ML1 1TW
Tel: 01698 302222
Chief Executive: Gavin Whitefield

ORKNEY ISLANDS COUNCIL
Council Offices, Kirkwall KW15 1NY
Tel: 01856 873535
Chief Executive: A Buchan

PERTH AND KINROSS COUNCIL
2 High Street, Perth PH1 5PH
Tel: 01738 475000
Chief Executive: H Robertson

RENFREWSHIRE COUNCIL
North Building, Cotton Street, Paisley PA1 1WB
Tel: 0141-842 5000
Chief Executive: T Scholes

SCOTTISH BORDERS COUNCIL
Newtown St Boswells, Melrose TD6 0SA
Tel: 01835 824000
Chief Executive: A M Croall

SHETLAND ISLANDS COUNCIL
Town Hall, Lerwick ZE1 0HB
Tel: 01595 693535
Chief Executive: Morgan Goodlad

SOUTH AYRSHIRE COUNCIL
County Buildings, Wellington Square, Ayr KA7 1DR
Tel: 01292 612000
Chief Executive: G W F Thorley

SOUTH LANARKSHIRE COUNCIL
Council Offices, Almada Street, Hamilton ML3 0AA
Tel: 01698 454444
Chief Executive: M Docherty

STIRLING COUNCIL
Viewforth, Stirling FK8 2ET
Tel: 01786 443322
Chief Executive: K Yates

WEST DUNBARTONSHIRE COUNCIL
Garshake Road, Dumbarton G82 3PU
Tel: 01389 737000
Chief Executive: T Huntingford

WEST LOTHIAN COUNCIL
West Lothian House, Almondvale Boulevard, Livingston EH54 6QG
Tel: 01506 777000
Chief Executive: A M Linkston

WESTERN ISLES COUNCIL (COMHAIRLE NAN EILEAN SIAR)
Council Offices, Sandwick Road, Stornoway HS1 2BW
Tel: 01851 703773
Chief Executive: Bill Howat

MAGAZINES

CA MAGAZINE
1a St Bernards Row, Stockbridge, Edinburgh EH4 9HW
Tel: 0131-343 7500
Editor: Robert Outram

CHAPMAN
4 Broughton Place, Edinburgh EH1 3RX
Tel: 0131-557 2207
Editor: Joy Hendry
Literary magazine.

LIFE AND WORK
121 George Street, Edinburgh EH2 4YN
Tel: 0131-225 5722
Editor: Rosemary Goring
Magazine of Church of Scotland.

THE LIST
14 High Street, Edinburgh EH1 1TE
Tel: 0131-558 1191
Fax: 0131-557 8500
e-mail: editor@list.co.uk
Editor: Mark Fisher
Fortnightly arts and entertainments guide.

SCOTS LAW TIMES
W Green & Son Ltd, 21 Alva Street, Edinburgh EH2 4PS
Tel: 0131-225 4879
Fax: 0131-225 2104
e-mail: peter.nicholson@wgreen.co.uk
web: www.wgreen.co.uk
Editor: Peter Nicholson
Law reporting, including full text decisions from all Scottish courts, as well as news and articles on current legal matters.

THE SCOTS MAGAZINE
2 Albert Square, Dundee DD1 9QJ
Tel: 01382 223131
Fax: 01382 322214
e-mail: scotsmagazine@dcthomson.co.uk
web: www.scotsmagazine.com
Editor: John Methven
Articles of Scottish interest.

SCOTTISH BANKER
7 Castle Street, Edinburgh EH2 3AH
Tel: 0131-535 5555
Fax: 0131-535 5527
e-mail: abird@insider.co.uk
Editor: Alison Bird

SCOTTISH BUSINESS INSIDER
7 Castle Street, Edinburgh EH2 3AH
Tel: 0131-535 5555
Editor: Alasdair Northrop

SCOTTISH CATHOLIC OBSERVER
19 Waterloo Street, Glasgow G2 6BT
Tel: 0141-221 4956
e-mail: info@scottishcatholicobserver.com
Editor: Harry Conroy

SCOTTISH EDUCATIONAL JOURNAL
46 Moray Place, Edinburgh EH3 6BH
Tel: 0131-225 6244
Editor: Simon Macaulay
Magazine of the Educational Institute of Scotland.

THE SCOTTISH FARMER
200 Renfield Street, Glasgow G2 3PR
Tel: 0141-302 7700
Editor: Alasdair Fletcher

SCOTTISH FIELD
Royston House, Caroline Park, Edinburgh EH5 1QJ
Tel: 0131-551 2942
Editor: Archie Mackenzie

SCOTTISH REVIEW
Institute of Contemporary Scotland, 2nd Floor, House 6, 94 Elmbank Street, Glasgow G2 4PF
Tel: 0141-204 2848
Fax: 0141-204 2849
e-mail: icsadmin@contemporaryscotland.com
Editor: Kenneth Roy

Quarterly magazine of Scottish current affairs. Official journal of the Institute of Contemporary Scotland.

TIMES EDUCATIONAL SUPPLEMENT SCOTLAND
Scott House, 10 South St Andrew Street, Edinburgh EH2 2AZ
Tel: 0131-557 1133
Fax: 0131-558 1155
e-mail: scoted@tes.co.uk
web: www.tes.co.uk/scotland
Editor: Neil Munro
Weekly newspaper of educational news and articles.

MARRIAGE AND RELATIONSHIPS

COUPLE COUNSELLING SCOTLAND
40 N Castle Street, Edinburgh EH2 3BN
Tel: 0131-225 5006
e-mail: enquiries@couplecounselling. org
web: www.couplecounselling.org
Director: Frances Love; *Chairperson*: Lady Caplan
Exists to promote, co-ordinate and develop a confidential counselling service to those in marriage and other intimate personal relationships throughout Scotland.

SCOTTISH MARRIAGE CARE
72 Waterloo Street (1st Floor Suite), Glasgow G2 7DA
Tel: 0141-222 2166
Fax: 0141-222 2144
e-mail: chiefexecutive@scottish marriagecare.co.uk
web: www.scottishmarriagecare. co.uk
Chief Executive: Mary Toner; *Executive Chair*: Paul Biagi
Supports marriage and relationships with counselling, preparation for marriage courses, and training.

MEDICAL CHARITIES

Listed is a selection of the larger charities and some others of special interest. A more comprehensive list can be obtained from the Scottish Council for Voluntary Organisations.

ALZHEIMER SCOTLAND – ACTION ON DEMENTIA
22 Drumsheugh Gardens, Edinburgh EH3 7RN
Tel: 0131-243 1453
24-hour helpline: 0808 808 3000
Fax: 0131-243 1450
e-mail: alzheimer@alzscot.org
web: www.alzscot.org
Chief Executive: Jim Jackson; *Convener*: Dr Alan Jacques
Helps people with dementia and their carers and families, providing services and campaigning to improve public policies.

ARTHRITIS RESEARCH CAMPAIGN
140 High Street, Lochee, Dundee DD2 3BZ
Tel: 01382 400911
Fax: 01382 400933
e-mail: scotland@arc.org.uk
web: www.arc.org.uk
Chief Executive: Fergus Logan; *President*: Professor Roger Sturrock
Funding of research for finding the cause, treatment and cure of arthritis. Education of medical students, doctors and allied healthcare professionals about arthritis. Information for people affected by arthritis and for the general public.

BRITISH HEART FOUNDATION
4 Shore Place, Edinburgh EH6 6UU
Tel: 0131-555 5891
Director: Iain Lowis

CANCER BACUP SCOTLAND
30 Bell Street, Glasgow G1 1LG
Tel: 0141-553 1553
Chief Executive: Joanne Rule; *Chairman*: Maurice Slevin

CANCER RESEARCH CAMPAIGN
SCOTLAND
222 Queensferry Road, Edinburgh
EH4 2BN
Tel: 0131-343 1344
Regional Director: W McKinlay

CHEST, HEART AND STROKE SCOTLAND
65 North Castle Street, Edinburgh
EH2 3LT
Tel: 0131-225 6963
Fax: 0131-220 6313
e-mail: admin@chss.org.uk
web: www.chss.org.uk
Chief Executive: David Clark
Aims to improve the quality of life for people in Scotland affected by chest, heart and stroke illness, through medical research, advice and information, and support in the community.

DIABETES UK SCOTLAND
Savoy House, 140 Sauchiehall Street, Glasgow G2 3DH
Tel: 0141-332 2700
Fax: 0141-332 4880
e-mail: scotland@diabetes.org.uk
web: www.diabetes.org.uk
National Manager: Delia Henry
Diabetes UK is the new name of the British Diabetic Association.

EPILEPSY ACTION SCOTLAND
48 Govan Road, Glasgow G51 1JL
Tel: 0141-427 4911
Helpline: 0141-427 5225
Fax: 0141-419 1709
e-mail: enquiries@epilepsyscotland.org.uk
web: www.epilepsyscotland.org.uk
Chief Executive: Hilary Mounfield; *Chairman*: Chris Ritchie
Works to enable people with epilepsy in Scotland to maximise their choices in life.

MACMILLAN CANCER RELIEF
9 Castle Terrace, Edinburgh EH1 2DP
Tel: 0131-229 3276
Director for Scotland: Ian Gibson

MARIE CURIE CANCER CARE
29a Albany Street, Edinburgh EH1 3QN
Tel: 0131-456 3700
Secretary (Scotland): Sarah Grotrian

ME FOUNDATION (SCOTLAND)
8 Inverleith Gardens, Edinburgh EH3 5PU
Tel: 0131-478 7879
Secretary: George Smart; *Chairperson*: Helen Armstrong

MS SOCIETY, SCOTLAND
Rural Centre, Hallyards Road, Ingliston, Edinburgh EH28 8NZ
Tel: 0131-472 4106
Fax: 0131-472 4099
Director: Mark Hazelwood

MUSCULAR DYSTROPHY CAMPAIGN
PO Box 28618, Edinburgh EH13 0QL
Tel: 0131-441 3558
Fax: 0131-441 3558
e-mail: kenb@muscular-dystrophy.org
web: www.muscular-dystrophy.org
Director: Ken Brown

NATIONAL ASTHMA CAMPAIGN
SCOTLAND
2A North Charlotte Street, Edinburgh
EH2 4HR
Tel: 0131-226 2544
Fax: 0131-226 2401
e-mail: enquiries@asthma5.demon.co.uk
web: www.asthma.org.uk
Director: Marjory O'Donnell
Independent UK charity working to conquer asthma through a combination of research, education and support.

PAIN ASSOCIATION SCOTLAND
Cramond House, Cramond Glebe Road, Edinburgh EH4 6NS
Tel: 0131-312 7955
National Organiser: David Falconer

SARGENT CANCER CARE FOR CHILDREN
SCOTLAND
5th Floor, Mercantile Chambers, 53
Bothwell Street, Glasgow G2 6TS
Tel: 0141-572 5700
Fax: 0141-572 5701
e-mail: Sargent@Glasgow.org
web: www.sargent.org
Operations Manager (Scotland): May
Martindale

SCOTTISH COT DEATH TRUST
Royal Hospital for Sick Children,
Yorkhill, Glasgow G3 8SJ
Tel: 0141-357 3946
Director: Hazel Brooke, MBE;
Chairman: Dr Angus Gibson

SCOTTISH DOWN'S SYNDROME
ASSOCIATION
158 Balgreen Road, Edinburgh EH11
3AU
Tel: 0131-313 4225
Fax: 0131-313 4285
e-mail: info@sdsa.org.uk
web: www.sdsa.org.uk
Director: Karen Watchman;
Chairperson: Sam Campbell

SCOTTISH HEART AND ARTERIAL RISK
PREVENTION
University Department of Medicine,
Ninewells Hospital and Medical
School, Dundee DD1 9SY
Tel: 01382 660111, Ext. 33124
Fax: 01382 660675
*Honorary Secretary and Medical
Administrator:* Dr Shirley R. McEwan

SCOTTISH SPINA BIFIDA ASSOCIATION
190 Queensferry Road, Edinburgh
EH4 2BW
Tel: 0131-332 0743
Fax: 0131-343 3651
e-mail: mail@ssba.org.uk
web: www.ssba.org.uk
Chief Executive: Andrew H D Wynd;
President: Professor D G Young
Charity for people with spina bifida,
hydrocephalus and related disorders.

TENOVUS - SCOTLAND
234 St Vincent Street, Glasgow G2 5RJ
Tel: 0141-221 6268
Fax: 01292 311433
e-mail: gen.sec@talk21.com
web: www.tenovus-scotland.org.uk
General Secretary: E R Read; *Chairman:*
Sir Malcolm Macnaughton
Supports medical/dental research
projects across the full spectrum of
the sciences in Scotland. Has regional
committees based in Aberdeen,
Dundee, Edinburgh and Glasgow and
a district committee in Paisley.

MENTAL HEALTH

MENTAL HEALTH FOUNDATION
5th Floor, Merchants House, 30
George Square, Glasgow G2 1EG
Tel: 0141-572 0125
Fax: 0141-572 0246
e-mail: scotland@mhf.org.uk
web: www.mhf.org.uk
Director Scotland: Maddy Halliday

MENTAL WELFARE COMMISSION FOR
SCOTLAND
Argyle House, K Floor, 3 Lady
Lawson Street, Edinburgh EH3 9SH
Tel: 0131-222 6111
web: www.mwcscot.org.uk
Director: Dr James A T Dyer; *Chair:* Ian
Miller, OBE
A Crown-appointed statutory body
with a remit to protect the welfare and
rights of people vulnerable through
mental disorder. Independent body,
separate from the government and
the medical, legal and social work
professions, which safeguards the
welfare and rights of people with
mental illness or learning disability
whether they are in hospital, living in
their own homes, or in other
accommodation.
    The commission has existed in
various forms since 1859. Those who

serve on it are appointed by the Queen. It reports and can make enquiries on individual situations, and requests for discharge from people who are detained in hospital, liable to detention or on guardianship under the Mental Health (Scotland) Act 1984. The Mental Health (Patients in the Community) Act 1995 introduced community care orders in Scotland.

NATIONAL SCHIZOPHRENIA FELLOWSHIP (SCOTLAND)
Claremont House, 130 East Claremont Street, Edinburgh EH7 4LB
Tel: 0131-557 8969
e-mail: info@nsfscot.org.uk
web: www.nsfscot.org.uk
Chief Executive: Mary Weir; *Chairman*: Susan Kirkwood

THE RICHMOND FELLOWSHIP SCOTLAND
26 Park Circus, Glasgow G3 6AP
Tel: 0141-353 4050
Director: Peter Millar
Supported living, day services, community advocacy, and counselling.

SCOTTISH ASSOCIATION FOR MENTAL HEALTH
Cumbrae House, 15 Carlton Court, Glasgow G5 9JP
Tel: 0141-568 7000
Chief Executive: Ms S M Barcus; *Chair*: Professor Kevin Woods
Campaigns on mental health issues, providing an information service; 66 projects across Scotland.

STATE HOSPITALS BOARD FOR SCOTLAND
The State Hospital, Carstairs, by Lanark ML11 8RP
Tel: 01555 840293
Chief Executive: Gordon Melrose; *Chairman*: Gordon Craig

Responsible for providing high-quality high-security mental health services to patients from Scotland and Northern Ireland whose behaviour may lead them to pose a significant threat to others.

MOTOR SPORT

ROYAL SCOTTISH AUTOMOBILE CLUB (MOTOR SPORT) LTD
11 Blythswood Square, Glasgow G2 4AG
Tel: 0141-204 4999
Secretary: Jonathan C Lord; *Chairman*: I B M Lyle
Promotion and development of motor sport in Scotland.

MOUNTAINEERING AND HILL-WALKING

MOUNTAINEERING COUNCIL OF SCOTLAND
Ground Floor, The Old Granary, West Mill Street, Perth PH1 5QP
Tel: 01738 638227
Fax: 01738 442095
web: www.mountaineering-scotland.org.uk
Honorary Secretary: Nick Halls; *President:* John Donohoe
Representative body for mountaineers, including those on ski, climbers and hill-walkers. Aims to protect the mountain environment, safeguard and secure access to hill and crag, and initiate and encourage safe practice in the mountains.

RAMBLERS' ASSOCIATION SCOTLAND
Kingfisher House, Auld Mart Business Park, Milnathort, Kinross KY13 9DA
Tel: 01577 861222
Director: Dave Morris; *Chairman,*

Scottish Council: John Holms Promotes health benefits of walking, campaigns for more freedom of access to countryside and on other environmental issues.

SCOTTISH MOUNTAIN LEADER TRAINING BOARD
Glenmore, Aviemore PH22 1QU
Tel: 01479 861248
Fax: 01479 861 249
e-mail: smltb@aol.com
Secretary: Allen Fyffe; *Chair:* Ally Morgan
Develops and operates schemes for training and assessing those engaged in leading others on the mountains and moorlands of the UK.

MUSEUMS AND GALLERIES
Listed is a selection of the larger museums and galleries and visual arts organisations.

DEAN GALLERY
Belford Road, Edinburgh EH4 3DS
Tel: 0131-624 6200
Fax: 0131-343 3250
e-mail: pressinfo@natgalscot.ac.uk
web: www.natgalscot.ac.uk
Director-General: Sir Timothy Clifford; *Chairman, Board of Trustees:* Brian Ivory
Opened on 27 March 1999, the gallery provides a home for the Eduardo Paolozzi gift of sculpture and graphic art, the Gallery of Modern Art's Dada and Surrealist collections, a major library and archive centre, along with temporary exhibition space for modern and contemporary art.

EDINBURGH CITY MUSEUMS AND ART GALLERIES
City Art Centre, 2 Market Street, Edinburgh EH1 1DE
Tel: 0131-529 3993

Fax: 0131-529 3977
web: www.cac.org.uk
Acting Head of Heritage and Arts: Derek Janes
Consists of: The Museum of Edinburgh, Museum of Childhood, Writers' Museum, City Art Centre, Brass Rubbing Centre, The People's Story Museum, Scott Monument, Nelson Monument, Lauriston Castle, Queensferry Museum, Newhaven Heritage Museum.

GLASGOW MUSEUMS AND GALLERIES
Kelvingrove, Glasgow G3 8AG
Tel: 0141-287 2699
Fax: 0141-287 2690
Head of Service: Mark O'Neill
The oldest of the city's galleries, Kelvingrove, was opened in 1893 on a surplus of income from the 1888 Exhibition. It is now part of a group of civic-controlled galleries including the People's Palace, St Mungo Museum of Religious Life and Art and Provand's Lordship, which together house collections ranging from armour and ancient artefacts to religious art and displays of working-class Glaswegian life.

The Burrell Collection, housed in a purpose-built gallery, contains the collection of a Glasgow entrepreneur, Sir William Burrell, who travelled the world collecting treasures. In 1996 Glasgow opened a Gallery of Modern Art in the city centre, which features paintings and sculptures by living artists.

Other museums/galleries within the group are: Fossil Grove, Martyrs School/Open Museum, McLellan Galleries, Museum of Transport, Pollok House, and Scotland Street School Museum.

NATIONAL GALLERY OF SCOTLAND
The Mound, Edinburgh EH2 2EL
Tel: 0131-624 6200
Fax: 0131-343 3250
e-mail: pressinfo@natgalscot.ac.uk

web: www.natgalscot.ac.uk
Director-General: Sir Timothy Clifford; *Chairman, Board of Trustees:* Brian Ivory
Founded in 1859, one of the finest smaller galleries in the world. Includes an outstanding collection of paintings, drawings and prints by the greatest artists from the Renaissance to Post-Impressionism, including Velazquez, El Greco, Rembrandt, Vermeer, Turner, Constable, Monet and Van Gogh, shown alongside the national collection of Scottish art.

NATIONAL MUSEUMS OF SCOTLAND
Chambers Street, Edinburgh EH1 1JF
Tel: 0131-225 7534
Fax: 0131-247 4308
web: www.nms.ac.uk
Acting Director: Dale Idiens; *Chairman:* Sir Robert Smith
Sets out to provide Scotland with a national museum service of international standing which preserves and enhances the collections in its care and promotes research on them so that they can be used to communicate and increase knowledge, understanding and enjoyment of human and natural history.
The **Museum of Scotland** opened in 1998 is a striking new landmark in Edinburgh's historic Old Town. The Museum presents, for the first time, the history of Scotland – its land, its people and their achievements. The series of galleries, displaying the national collections, takes the visitor on a journey from Scotland's geological beginnings through to the twentieth century.
The **Royal Museum** (adjacent to the Museum of Scotland) houses international collections reflecting the diversity of life and the ingenuity of humankind. The collections are housed in a magnificent Victorian building, distinguished by its soaring

glass-topped roof.
The **National War Museum of Scotland** (formerly the Scottish United Services Museum) opened in 2000 and explores the Scottish experience of war and military service over the last 400 years.
The **Museum of Flight** at East Fortune Airfield, East Lothian, comprises two massive hangars, part of a World War II airfield, packed with aeroplanes, rockets, models and memorabilia.
Shambellie House Museum of Costume is a beautiful Victorian country house, located seven miles south of Dumfries. Shambellie offers visitors the opportunity to see period clothes from the 1850s to the 1950s, in appropriate room settings, with accessories, furniture and decorative art.
The new **Museum of Scottish Country Life**, the result of a unique partnership between the National Trust for Scotland and the National Museums of Scotland, opened in July 2001 and shows how country people lived and worked in Scotland in the past, and how this has shaped the countryside of today.
The **Granton Centre** is the major storehouse for the National Museums of Scotland. Important conservation work is carried on there, preparing thousands of objects for display. The Granton Centre is open to the public on Tuesdays.

ROYAL GLASGOW INSTITUTE OF THE FINE ARTS
Second Floor, 5 Oswald Street, Glasgow G1 4QR
Tel: 0141-248 7411
Fax: 0141-221 0417
Secretary: Gordon C McAllister; *President:* Dr Kenneth G Chrystie
Promotes art by open exhibitions and lectures and with a small gallery to encourage solo or group exhibitions.

ROYAL SCOTTISH ACADEMY

17 Waterloo Place, Edinburgh EH1 3BG
Tel: 0131-558 7097
Fax: 0131-557 6417
web: www.royalscottishacademy.org
Administrative Secretary: Bruce Laidlaw; *President:* Dr Ian McKenzie Smith, OBE

Founded in 1826 when 11 artists met in Edinburgh with the object of improving conditions for artists and art exhibitions in Scotland. Based loosely on the Royal Academy in London, it consisted of academicians and associates in the fields of painting, sculpture and architecture.

The first annual exhibition was held in premises in Waterloo Place, Edinburgh, in 1827 and has continued without a break (the 175th in 2001), although the venue has changed.

Designed in 1822 by William Henry Playfair, who also designed the National Gallery, the Royal Scottish Academy building was first occupied by the Royal Institution for the Encouragement of the Fine Arts in Scotland and was known then as "The Royal Institution". The building is owned by the government and administered by the National Galleries of Scotland. There are on average 40 full members of the academy and 50 associate members, elected from the disciplines of painting, sculpture, architecture and printmaking.

ROYAL SCOTTISH SOCIETY OF PAINTERS IN WATERCOLOUR

Second Floor, 5 Oswald Street, Glasgow G1 4QR
Tel: 0141-248 7411
Fax: 0141-221 0417
Secretary: Gordon C McAllister; *President:* Philip Reeves

The declared aim of the founders in 1878 was "to do for Scotland what has been done for England and to give the watercolour art the position it deserves and which is at present not the case". Offers encouragement to artists of all ages by financial awards. Its annual exhibition in January is held at the McManus Galleries, Albert Square, Dundee.

SCOTTISH MUSEUMS COUNCIL

County House, 20-22 Torphichen Street, Edinburgh EH3 8JB
Tel: 0131-229 7465
Fax: 0131-229 2728
e-mail: inform@scottishmuseums.org.uk
web: www.scottishmuseums.org.uk
Director: Jane Ryder; *Chair:* Professor Malcolm McLeod

National agency for central government support to Scotland's local museums. Founded in 1964, SMC is an independent company with charitable status. The 200-strong membership cares for some 330 museums and galleries.

The Council aims to improve the quality of museums and gallery provision in Scotland by providing a range of advice, services and financial support to its membership and by working to promote recognition of the essential role played by museums in the country's cultural, social and economic life.

SCOTTISH NATIONAL GALLERY OF MODERN ART

Belford Road, Edinburgh EH4 3DR
Tel: 0131-624 6200
Fax: 0131-343 3250
e-mail: pressinfo@natgalscot.ac.uk
web: www.natgalscot.ac.uk
Director-General: Sir Timothy Clifford; *Chairman, Board of Trustees:* Brian Ivory

An outstanding collection of 20th-century painting, sculpture and graphic art. Includes major works by artists such as Bacon, Baselitz, Bonnard, Kirchner, Leger,

Lichtenstein, Matisse, Moore and Picasso and important Scottish paintings by artists such as Bellany, Gillies, Peploe, Davie and Redpath.

SCOTTISH NATIONAL PORTRAIT GALLERY
1 Queen Street, Edinburgh EH2 1JD
Tel: 0131-624 6200
Fax: 0131-558 3691
e-mail: pressinfo@natgalscot.ac.uk
web: www.natgalscot.ac.uk
Director: James Holloway; *Chairman, Board of Trustees:* Brian Ivory
Unique visual history of Scotland told through the portraits of those who shaped it: royals and rebels, poets and philosophers, heroes and villains. The collection includes work not only by Scottish artists but by great English, European and American masters such as Van Dyck, Gainsborough, Rodin and Kokoschka. In addition to paintings, the gallery displays sculptures, miniatures, coins, medallions, drawings and watercolours. The National Photography Collection is also based there.

MUSIC

ASSEMBLY DIRECT
89 Giles Street, Edinburgh EH6 6BZ
Tel: 0131-553 4000
Directors: Fiona Alexander/Roger Spence

BBC SCOTTISH SYMPHONY ORCHESTRA
BBC Scotland, Queen Margaret Drive, Glasgow G12 8DG
Tel: 0141-338 2606
Fax: 0141-307 4312
e-mail: bbcsso@bbc.co.uk
web: www.bbc.co.uk/bbcsso
Director: Hugh Macdonald
Founded in 1935 with Ian Whyte as its conductor, the SSO worked initially as a studio orchestra. After the Second World War, it was invited to participate in the Edinburgh Festival and thus began its policy of giving public concerts. Since then it has established an international reputation with concert tours throughout Europe, Canada, the USA and China. Contemporary music, especially by Scottish composers, has always been central to its work. In addition to regular series of concerts in Glasgow, Aberdeen, Stirling, Inverness and Ayr, it makes appearances at the BBC Proms and at other major UK festivals. Most of its concerts and studio recordings are broadcast on BBC Radio 3.

BT SCOTTISH ENSEMBLE
Centre for Contemporary Arts, 350 Sauchiehall Street, Glasgow G2 3JD
Tel: 0141-332 4747
Fax: 0141-332 3555
e-mail: office@btscottishensemble.co.uk
Artistic Director: Clio Gould; *General Manager:* Heather Duncan
Young professional string ensemble.

CAPPELLA NOVA
1/R, 172 Hyndland Road, Glasgow G12 9HZ
Tel: 0141-552 0634
Fax: 0141-552 4053
e-mail: rebecca@cappella-nova.com
web: www.cappella-nova.com
Manager and Co-Artistic Director: Rebecca Tavener; *Chairperson:* Lord Balfour of Burleigh
Professional vocal ensemble, prominent in Scottish early and contemporary vocal music.

COUNCIL FOR MUSIC IN HOSPITALS
10 Forth Street, Edinburgh EH1 3LD
Tel: 0131-556 5848
Director: Alison Frazer; *Convenor:* Dr William Boyd
Provides concerts by professional

musicians for people in hospitals, hospices, nursing and residential homes, and day centres for people with disabilities.

LIVE MUSIC NOW! (SCOTLAND)
14 Lennox Street, Edinburgh EH4 1QA
Tel: 0131-332 6356
e-mail: scotland@livemusicnow.org
Director: Carol Main; *Chairman*: Hon Mrs Elizabeth Fairbairn, MBE
Aims to bring live music of high standard to all in the community, especially those who are disadvantaged, while giving outstanding young musicians performance opportunities.

NATIONAL YOUTH ORCHESTRAS OF SCOTLAND
13 Somerset Place, Glasgow G3 7JT
Tel: 0141-332 8311
Director: Richard Chester; *Chairman*: Alan Simpson
Provides orchestral and jazz training for young musicians resident in Scotland.

PARAGON ENSEMBLE LTD
1 Bowmont Gardens, Glasgow G12 9LR
Tel: 0141-342 4242
Fax: 0141-342 4442
e-mail: mail@paragon.sol.co.uk
web: www.paragonensemble.org.uk
Artistic Director: John Harris

PIOBAIREACHD SOCIETY
16-24 Otago Street, Glasgow G12 8JH
Tel: 0141-334 3587
Secretary: Dugald MacNeil; *President*: Andrew Wright
Encourages the study and playing of piobaireachd on the Highland bagpipe.

ROYAL SCOTTISH NATIONAL ORCHESTRA
73 Claremont Street, Glasgow G3 7JB
Tel: 0141-226 3868

Fax: 0141-221 4317
e-mail: admin@rsno.org.uk
web: www.rsno.org.uk
Chief Executive: Simon Crookall; *Chairman*: James Miller, CBE
Founded in 1891. An 89-member orchestra, it is a major provider of symphonic music, gives about 100 concerts each year in Edinburgh, Aberdeen, Dundee, Perth and other venues, and makes regular tours overseas. Its work also includes recordings and performances for radio and television and an extensive programme of education and community work.

ROYAL SCOTTISH PIPE BAND ASSOCIATION
45 Washington Street, Glasgow G3 8AZ
Tel: 0141-221 5414
Chairman: G Ussher
Promotes and encourages the culture and advancement of pipe band music internationally. Organises and operates the World, European, British, Scottish and Cowal Championships.

SCOTTISH AMATEUR MUSIC ASSOCIATION
18 Craigton Crescent, Alva FK12 5DS
Tel: 01259 760249
e-mail: secretary@sama.org.uk
web: www.sama.org.uk
Hon Secretary: Margaret W Simpson; *Chairperson, Executive Committee*: E J B Catto
Encourages and stimulates amateur music-making throughout Scotland by organising and running residential courses.

SCOTTISH CHAMBER ORCHESTRA
4 Royal Terrace, Edinburgh EH7 5AB
Tel: 0131-557 6800
Fax: 0131-557 6933
e-mail: info@sco.org.uk
web: www.sco.org.uk
Managing Director: Roy McEwan;

Chairman: Donald MacDonald, CBE Promotion of orchestral music throughout Scotland and abroad. Since it was formed in 1974, the SCO has visited the USA four times and tours regularly throughout Europe. It has commissioned more than 50 new works and enjoys close relationships with several leading composers. The orchestra has an extensive programme of education and community projects.

The SCO Chorus was formed in 1991 to provide a resident choir.

SCOTTISH MUSIC INFORMATION CENTRE

1 Bowmont Gardens, Glasgow G12 9LR
Tel: 0141-334 6393
Fax: 0141-337 1161
e-mail: info@smic.org.uk
web: www.smic.org.uk
Director: Andrew Logan; *Chairperson*: Roderick Wylie
Independent organisation which documents, preserves and promotes Scottish music of all types and of all periods.

SCOTTISH NATIONAL JAZZ ORCHESTRA

Smythe Music, PO Box 3743, Lanark ML11 9WD
Tel: 07710 585231
Director: Tommy Smith

SCOTTISH OPERA

39 Elmbank Crescent, Glasgow G2 4PT
Tel: 0141-248 4567
Fax: 0141-221 8812
web: www.scotopera.org.uk
Chief Executive: Christopher Barron; *Chairman:* Duncan McGhie
Scotland's national opera company and the largest performing arts organisation in Scotland. Founded in 1962 by Sir Alexander Gibson, it staged its first production, *Madama Butterfly*, at the King's Theatre,

Glasgow, and set up a permanent home at the Theatre Royal, Glasgow, in 1974. In its early years, under the guidance of Sir Alexander Gibson, it established a considerable reputation with such productions as *The Trojans*, *The Ring Cycle*, *Der Rosenkavalier*, *Turn of the Screw* and *Die Meistersinger*.

Scottish Opera is committed to bringing the widest range of opera, performed to the highest standard, to the maximum audience throughout Scotland. As owners of the Theatre Royal, it is also responsible for the administration and development of one of Scotland's principal theatres. It employs 200 people, including a full-time chorus and full-size orchestra.

In a typical season it gives some 90 main-scale performances. In addition, Scottish Opera Go Round and Essential Scottish Opera visit smaller venues not always served by other professional opera companies. The company's educational unit, Scottish Opera For All, works extensively in the community.

SCOTTISH SOCIETY OF COMPOSERS

4 Glen Road, Lennoxtown G65 7JX
Tel: 01360 313217
Secretary: Derek Ball; *Chairperson*: Neil Butterworth
Promotes wider knowledge of contemporary music in Scotland through international and local liaison, annual awards to musicians, distribution of catalogues, sponsorship of new music recording.

TRADITIONAL MUSIC AND SONG ASSOCIATION OF SCOTLAND

95-97 St Leonards Street, Edinburgh EH8 9QY
Tel: 0131-667 5587
Fax: 0131-662 9153
e-mail: tmsa@tmsa.demon.co.uk
Promotes, preserves and presents traditional music and song of Scotland.

NETBALL

NETBALL SCOTLAND
24 Ainslie Road, Hillington Business Park, Glasgow G52 4RU
Tel: 0141-570 4016
Administrator: Margaret Martin; *Chairperson*: Dr Irene O'Brien

NEWSPAPERS

BUSINESS AM
40 Torphichen Street, Edinburgh EH3 8JB
Tel: 0131-330 0000
Editor: John Penman

DAILY RECORD
One Central Quay, Glasgow G3 8DA
Tel: 0141-248 7000
Editor: Peter Cox

DUNDEE COURIER
80 Kingsway East, Dundee DD4 8SL
Tel: 01382 223131
Editor: Adrian Arthur

EDINBURGH EVENING NEWS
108 Holyrood Road, Edinburgh EH8 8AS
Tel: 0131-620 8702
Editor: John McLellan

EVENING EXPRESS
Lang Stracht, Mastrick, Aberdeen AB15 6DF
Tel: 01224 690222
Editor: Donald Martin

EVENING TELEGRAPH
80 Kingsway East, Dundee DD4 8SL
Tel: 01382 223131
Editor: Alan Proctor

EVENING TIMES
200 Renfield Street, Glasgow G2 3PR
Tel: 0141-302 7000
Editor: Charles McGhee

GREENOCK TELEGRAPH
2 Crawfurd Street, Greenock PA15 1LH
Tel: 01475 726511
Editor: Stewart N Peterson

THE HERALD
200 Renfield Street, Glasgow G2 3PR
Tel: 0141-302 7000
Editor: Mark Douglas-Home

PRESS AND JOURNAL
Lang Stracht, Mastrick, Aberdeen AB15 6DF
Tel: 01224 690222
Editor: Derek Tucker

SCOTLAND ON SUNDAY
108 Holyrood Road, Edinburgh EH8 8AS
Tel: 0131-620 8620
web: www.scotlandonsunday.com
Editor: Margot Wilson

THE SCOTSMAN
108 Holyrood Road, Edinburgh EH8 8AS
Tel: 0131-620 8620
Fax: 0131-620 8615
web: www.scotsman.com
Editor: Iain Martin

SUNDAY HERALD
200 Renfield Street, Glasgow G2 3PR
Tel: 0141-302 7800
Editor: Andrew Jaspan

SUNDAY MAIL
One Central Quay, Glasgow G3 8DA
Tel: 0141-248 7000
Editor: Allan Rennie

SUNDAY POST
2 Albert Square, Courier Buildings, Dundee DD1 9QJ
Tel: 01382 223131
Editor: David Pollington

PLANNING AND DESIGN

PLANNING AID FOR SCOTLAND
Bonnington Mill, 72 Newhaven Road,
Edinburgh EH6 5QG
Tel: 0131-555 1565
Director: Alan Pollock

PLANNING EXCHANGE
Tontine House, 8 Gordon Street,
Glasgow G1 3PL
Tel: 0141-248 8541
web: www.planex.co.uk
Managing Director: Anthony Burton,
OBE; *Chairman*: Edward
Cunningham, CB
Provides information and expertise in
the fields of economic, environmental
and social development.

ROYAL FINE ART COMMISSION FOR
SCOTLAND
Bakehouse Close, 146 Canongate,
Edinburgh EH8 8DD
Tel: 0131-556 6699
Fax: 0131-556 6633
e-mail: plan@RoyfinartcomforSco.
  gov.uk
web: www.RoyfinartcomforSco.
  gov.uk
Secretary: Charles Prosser; *Chairman*:
Rt Hon Lord Cameron of Lochbroom
Advisory body operating outside the
machinery of government, whose
terms of reference are set by royal
warrant. Established to provide an
independent view on matters of
general environmental, planning and
design criteria.
  In considering whether to call in
planning applications for new
developments, the Scottish ministers
take particular account of the
commission's views. Planning
authorities are advised to seek its
advice on a development proposal
which is likely to have a strong visual
impact or to be of exceptional
environmental significance, such as a
prominent proposal within a
conservation area.

POETRY

ROBERT BURNS WORLD FEDERATION
Dean Castle Country Park, Dower
House, Kilmarnock KA3 1XB
Tel: 01563 572469
Fax: 01563 572469
e-mail: robertburnsfederation@
  kilmarnock26.freeserve.co.uk
web: www.robertburnsfederation.net
Chief Executive: Shirley Bell; *President*:
James Gibson
Stimulates the development of
Scottish literature, art, and music and
encourages and arranges
competitions for school children.
Helps and encourages Burns Clubs
and kindred societies.

SCOTTISH POETRY LIBRARY
5 Crichton's Close, Edinburgh EH8
8DT
Tel: 0131-557 2876
e-mail: inquiries@spl.org.uk
web: www.spl.org.uk
Director: Robyn Marsack
Stocks Scottish and international
poetry for free browsing and
borrowing. Travelling van service,
postal lendings, branches, on-line
catalogue, indexes, children's events,
schools' workshops. Newsletter and
reading room for members.

POLICE FORCES

CENTRAL SCOTLAND POLICE
Randolphfield, Stirling FK8 2HD
Tel: 01786 456000
Chief Constable: Andrew Cameron

DUMFRIES AND GALLOWAY
CONSTABULARY
Cornwall Mount, Dumfries DG1 1PZ
Tel: 01387 252112
Chief Constable: David Strang

FIFE CONSTABULARY
Detroit Road, Glenrothes KY6 2RJ
Tel: 01592 418888
Chief Constable: Peter Wilson, QPM

GRAMPIAN POLICE
Queen Street, Aberdeen AB10 1ZA
Tel: 01224 386000
Chief Constable: Andrew Brown

LOTHIAN AND BORDERS POLICE
Fettes Avenue, Edinburgh EH4 1RB
Tel: 0131-311 3131
Chief Constable: Sir Roy Cameron

NORTHERN CONSTABULARY
Perth Road, Inverness IV2 3SY
Tel: 01463 715555
Chief Constable: W A Robertson

STRATHCLYDE POLICE
173 Pitt Street, Glasgow G2 4JS
Tel: 0141-532 2000
Chief Constable: William Rae, QPM

TAYSIDE POLICE
PO Box 59, West Bell Street, Dundee
DD1 9JU
Tel: 01382 223200
Chief Constable: John Vine

POLICE
ORGANISATIONS

SCOTTISH POLICE COLLEGE
Tulliallan Castle, Kincardine, Alloa
FK10 4BE
Tel: 01259 732000
Director: D Garbutt, QPM
Provision of central police training for
the Scottish police service.

SCOTTISH POLICE FEDERATION
5 Woodside Place, Glasgow G3 7QF
Tel: 0141-332 5234
e-mail: spf@scottishpolicefederation.
org.uk
web: www.spf.org.uk
General Secretary: Douglas J Keil,
QPM; *Chairman*: Norrie Flowers
Representative body of constables,
sergeants, inspectors and chief
inspectors in the Scottish police
service. Considers and brings to the
notice of the authorities and Scottish
ministers matters affecting welfare
and efficiency.

POLITICAL PARTIES AND
ORGANISATIONS

SCOTTISH CONSERVATIVE AND
UNIONIST PARTY
83 Princes Street, Edinburgh EH2 2ER
Tel: 0131-247 6890
Fax: 0131-247 6891
e-mail: central.office@scottishtories.
org.uk
web: www.scottishtories.org.uk
Chairman: David W Mitchell, CBE
Has operated in various forms and
under various formal titles since the
late 17th century. In 1955 the party
polled just over 50% of the Scottish
votes in the general election and won
36 of the 71 seats compared with
Labour's 34. Since this high point the
party's fortunes have declined
steadily. In the 1997 general election
its share of the poll fell to 17.5%, and
the party lost all 11 of its seats. In the
2001 general election it regained one
seat.

SCOTTISH GREEN PARTY
PO Box 14080, Edinburgh EH10 6YG
Tel: 0141-478 7896
e-mail: office@scottishgreens.org.uk

web: www.scottishgreens.org.uk
Council Convenor: Mark Ballard;
Executive Convenor: Gavin Corbett

SCOTTISH LABOUR PARTY
John Smith House, 145 West Regent
Street, Glasgow G2 4RE
Tel: 0141-572 6900
Fax: 0141-572 2566
e-mail: scotland@new.labour.org.uk
web: www.scottishlabour.org.uk
General Secretary: Lesley Quinn
The Scottish Labour Party describes
itself as a democratic socialist party. It
believes that more is achieved by the
strength of common endeavour than
is achieved alone. It is the party most
widely supported by the electorate
since the Second World War. In the
general election of 2001, it received
43% of the votes cast, and won 55 of
the 72 seats. The party is governed by
an executive committee which brings
together representatives of local party
organisations, trade unions, and
specific sections including women's,
socialist societies, the Scottish Co-
operative Party, youth and local
government.

SCOTTISH LIBERAL DEMOCRATS
4 Clifton Terrace, Edinburgh EH12
5DR
Tel: 0131-337 2314
Fax: 0131-337 3566
e-mail: scotlibdem@cix.co.uk
web: www.scotlibdems.org.uk
Chief Executive: Kilvert Croft;
President: Malcolm Bruce, MP

SCOTTISH NATIONAL PARTY
107 McDonald Road, Edinburgh EH7
4NW
Tel: 0131-525 8900
e-mail: snp.hq@snp.org
web: www.snp.org
National Secretary: Stewart Hosie
A democratic left-of-centre political
party committed to Scottish

independence. Aims to create a just,
caring and enterprising society by
releasing Scotland's full potential as
an independent nation in the
mainstream of modern Europe.

Founded in 1934, the party scored
its first Parliamentary success at
Westminster when Dr Robert
McIntyre won the Motherwell by-
election in 1945, and has had
continuous representation at
Westminster since 1967 when Winnie
Ewing won the Hamilton by-election.
At the 2001 Westminster elections the
SNP retained its position as the
second party in Scotland and is
represented by five MPs.

At the first Scottish Parliament
elections in 1999, the party returned a
total of 35 MSPs and is now the
official opposition.

The SNP has two members of the
European Parliament and at local
authority level more than 200 SNP
councillors representing almost 30%
of the national vote.

PORT AUTHORITIES

ABERDEEN HARBOUR BOARD
Harbour Office, 16 Regent Quay,
Aberdeen AB11 5SS
Tel: 01224 597000
General Manager: R B Braithwaite;
Chairman: D R Paton

CLYDEPORT
16 Robertson Street, Glasgow G2 8DS
Tel: 0141-221 8733
Fax: 0141-248 3167
e-mail: tom.allison@clydeport.co.uk
web: www.clydeport.co.uk
Chief Executive: Tom Allison

FORTH PORTS
Tower Place, Leith, Edinburgh EH6
7DB
Tel: 0131-555 8750
Chief Executive: Charles Hammond

POSTAL SERVICES

CONSIGNIA ADVISORY BOARD FOR SCOTLAND
102 West Port, Edinburgh EH3 9HS
Tel: 0131-228 7300
Fax: 0131-228 7218
Service Delivery Director: Alexander Gibb; *Chairman:* John M Ward, CBE
Represents Consignia (formerly The Post Office) in Scotland and advises the main board in London on Scottish opinions of Consignia policy as well as on a wide range of social, economic and political issues. Consignia is a wholly-government-owned plc required by government to operate its services commercially. It also has a long tradition of strong social commitment, particularly to rural areas.

PRISONS AND PRISONERS

APEX SCOTLAND
9 Great Stuart Street, Edinburgh EH3 7TP
Tel: 0131-220 0130
Fax: 0131-220 6796
e-mail: admin@apexscotland.org.uk
Director: Janice Hewitt; *Chairman:* John Carruthers, MBE
Aims to create equality of access to employment and employment opportunities for individuals with a criminal record.

HOWARD LEAGUE SCOTLAND
17 Warriston Crescent, Edinburgh EH3 5LB
Tel: 0131-556 1687

PAROLE BOARD FOR SCOTLAND
Saughton House, Broomhouse Drive, Edinburgh EH11 3XD
Tel: 0131-244 8755
Secretary: H P Boyle; *Chairman:* Dr J McManus
Directs and advises Scottish ministers on the release on licence and recall from licence of persons serving sentences of imprisonment or detection whose cases have been referred to the board, and the conditions of such licences. Under a law introduced in 1993, prisoners serving a determinate sentence of less than four years are released automatically after serving half of their sentence. All life prisoners and those prisoners serving four years or more and who have served half their sentences are now eligible for consideration by the board.

SACRO
1 Broughton Market, Edinburgh EH3 6NU
Tel: 0131-624 7270
Fax: 0131-624 7269
e-mail: info@national.sacro.org.uk
web: www.sacro.org.uk
Chief Executive: Susan Matheson; *Chair:* Dr David Colvin, CBE
Increases community safety by reducing conflict and offending by providing high quality services and influencing government policies and legislation in criminal justice and social policy.

SCOTTISH PRISONS COMPLAINTS COMMISSION
Government Buildings, Broomhouse Drive, Edinburgh EH11 3XD
Tel: 0131-244 8423
Prisoners' Line: 0845 702 3402
e-mail: joan.aitken@scotland.
gsi.gov.uk
Commissioner: Joan Aitken
Investigation of complaints from prisoners who have not obtained satisfaction from the prison internal complaints system.

SCOTTISH PRISON SERVICE
Calton House, 5 Redheughs Rigg,
Edinburgh EH12 9HW
Tel: 0131-244 8745
Fax: 0131-244 8774
e-mail: gaolinfo@sps.gov.uk
web: www.sps.gov.uk
Chief Executive: Tony Cameron
Established in 1993, the Service is an executive agency of the Scottish Executive. Manages the following establishments: Aberdeen Prison; Barlinnie Prison, Glasgow; Castle Huntly Prison, near Dundee; Cornton Vale Prison and Young Offenders Institution, Stirling; Dumfries Prison and Young Offenders Institution; Edinburgh Prison; Glenochil Prison and Young Offenders Institution, Tullibody; Greenock Prison; Inverness Prison; Low Moss Prison, Bishopbriggs; Noranside Prison, near Forfar; Perth Prison; Peterhead Prison; Polmont Young Offenders Institution, near Falkirk; Shotts Prison; Camp Zeist.

The Scottish Prison Service keeps in custody those committed by the courts; and aims to: maintain good order in each prison, care for prisoners with humanity, and provide prisoners with a range of opportunities to exercise personal responsibility and to prepare for release.

PROFESSIONAL BODIES AND LEARNED SOCIETIES

ASSOCIATION OF CHARTERED
CERTIFIED ACCOUNTANTS
1 Woodside Place, Glasgow G3 7QF
Tel: 0141-309 4109
Head of ACCA Scotland: Stuart Riddell

BRITISH ASSOCIATION OF SOCIAL
WORKERS – SCOTLAND
28 North Bridge, Edinburgh EH1 1QG
Tel: 0131-225 4549
Professional Officer: Ruth Stark;
Scottish Convener: Ronnie Barnes

BRITISH MEDICAL ASSOCIATION
14 Queen Street, Edinburgh EH2 1LL
Tel: 0131-247 3000
Fax: 0131-247 3001
Scottish Secretary: Dr Bill O'Neill;
Chairman: Dr John A Garner, MB, ChB, DObst, FRCGP
Regarded as the voice of the medical profession. A voluntary professional association, independent trade union, scientific and educational body and publishing house, it represents doctors from all branches of medicine in the UK. Founded in 1832, it has a UK membership of 120,000, of whom 12,000 are in Scotland.

CHARTERED INSTITUTE OF BANKERS IN
SCOTLAND
38B Drumsheugh Gardens,
Edinburgh EH3 7SW
Tel: 0131-473 7777
Fax: 0131-473 7788
e-mail: info@ciobs.org.uk
web: www.ciobs.org.uk
Chief Executive: Charles Munn;
President: Tom Abraham
Oldest professional body of its kind in the world, founded in 1875, the institute offers a platform for the exchange and development of ideas about financial services, helps its 12,500 members to improve their knowledge and expertise, and provides a framework for lifelong learning.

ACIBS (for students who pass the associateship programme), MCIBS (primarily a management programme) and FCIBS (the highest level, attained by many years' experience and by nomination) are the letters denoting membership. The institute is committed to continuing professional development of its members through education programmes.

CHARTERED INSTITUTE OF PUBLIC FINANCE AND ACCOUNTANCY
8 North West Circus Place, Edinburgh EH3 6ST
Tel: 0131-220 4316
Fax: 0131-220 4305
e-mail: cipfa.scotland@cipfa.org
web: www.cipfascotland.org.uk
Director, CIPFA in Scotland: Ian Doig

COMMITTEE OF SCOTTISH CLEARING BANKERS
38 Drumsheugh Gardens, Edinburgh EH3 7SW
Tel: 0131-473 7770
Secretary: Gordon P Fenton
"Trade association" for the four Scottish clearing banks.

DAVID HUME INSTITUTE
21 George Square, Edinburgh EH8 9LD
Tel: 0131-650 4633
Director: Brian Main
Promotes discourse and research on economic and legal aspects of public policy questions by arranging seminars, lectures and conferences and by publication of papers.

FACULTY OF ACTUARIES
Maclaurin House, 18 Dublin Street, Edinburgh EH1 3PP
Tel: 0131-240 1300
Secretary: W W Mair; *President:* T David Kingston
Professional body in Scotland for actuaries, with members throughout the UK and abroad. One of its main purposes is to develop the role and maintain the standing of the actuarial profession.

HARVEIAN SOCIETY OF EDINBURGH
The Sleep Centre, Ward 48, Royal Infirmary, Lauriston Place, Edinburgh EH3 9YW
Joint Secretaries: A B MacGregor, Professor N J Douglas
Promotes the scientific and medical discoveries of William Harvey through an annual festival.

INSTITUTE OF CHARTERED ACCOUNTANTS OF SCOTLAND
CA House, 21 Haymarket Yards, Edinburgh EH12 5BH
Tel: 0131-347 0100
Fax: 0131-347 0105
e-mail: icas@icas.org.uk
web: www.icas.org.uk
Chief Executive: David Brew; *President:* Andrew Christie
Oldest accountancy body in the world with a membership of 14,651 in around 100 countries. The institute educates its students as well as examining them. The professional designatory letters CA are exclusive in the British Isles to members of the institute.

NATIONAL BOARD FOR NURSING, MIDWIFERY AND HEALTH VISITING FOR SCOTLAND
22 Queen Street, Edinburgh EH2 1NT
Tel: 0131-226 7371
web: www.nbs.org.uk
Chief Executive: David Benton; *Chairman:* Margaret Alexander
Ensuring standards of professional education for nurses, midwives and health visitors in Scotland.

QUEEN'S NURSING INSTITUTE SCOTLAND
31 Castle Terrace, Edinburgh EH1 2EL
Tel: 0131-229 2333
Fax: 0131-229 0443
e-mail: qnis@aol.com

web: www@qnis.co.uk
Director: Lis Cook; *Chairman of Council:* Lady Prosser
Promotion of community nursing via projects, innovations, multi-professional education and development, and national representation. Welfare of retired Queen's nurses.

ROYAL COLLEGE OF GENERAL PRACTITIONERS (SCOTLAND)
25 Queen Street, Edinburgh EH2 1JX
Tel: 0131-260 6800
Honorary Secretary: Dr Jenny Bennison; *Chairman, Scottish Council:* Dr Bill Reith
Academic professional body for general practitioners.

ROYAL COLLEGE OF MIDWIVES, SCOTTISH BOARD
37 Frederick Street, Edinburgh EH2 1EP
Tel: 0131-225 1633
Director: Patricia Purton
Exists to promote the art and science of midwifery and to protect and advance the interests of midwives and the midwifery profession. The Scottish Board acts as a forum for discussion and to promote continuing education for midwives.

ROYAL COLLEGE OF NURSING, SCOTTISH BOARD
42 South Oswald Road, Edinburgh EH9 2HH
Tel: 0131-662 1010
Scottish Board Secretary: James Kennedy

ROYAL COLLEGE OF PHYSICIANS OF EDINBURGH
9 Queen Street, Edinburgh EH2 1JQ
Tel: 0131-225 7324
Fax: 0131-220 3939

e-mail: rcpe.ac.uk
web: www.rcpe.ac.uk
Secretary: Dr R Smith; *President:* Dr Niall D C Finlayson
Founded in 1681. Concerned with promoting and maintaining specialist standards among physicians. It has 2,000 fellows in the UK and about the same number overseas. The college disseminates knowledge by meetings and publications.

ROYAL COLLEGE OF PHYSICIANS AND SURGEONS OF GLASGOW
232-242 St Vincent Street, Glasgow G2 5RJ
Tel: 0141-221 6072
Registrar: Robert K Littlejohn; *President:* Professor A Ross Lorimer
Founded in 1599. The college has 4,500 members and fellows in many countries. It sets examinations and provides education to maintain standards of practice in all medical and dental specialties.

ROYAL COLLEGE OF SURGEONS OF EDINBURGH
Nicolson Street, Edinburgh EH8 9DW
Tel: 0131-527 1600
Fax: 0131-557 6406
web: www.rcsed.ac.uk
Chief Executive: J R C Foster; *President:* Professor J G Temple
Founded in 1505. Concerned with education and training for medical and surgical practice and for the maintenance of high standards of professional competence and conduct. It is the college's policy to invest in education and training for surgeons at all stages.

ROYAL ENVIRONMENTAL HEALTH INSTITUTE OF SCOTLAND
3 Manor Place, Edinburgh EH3 7DH
Tel: 0131-225 6999
Chief Executive: John Frater

ROYAL INCORPORATION OF
ARCHITECTS IN SCOTLAND
15 Rutland Square, Edinburgh EH1
2BE
Tel: 0131-229 7545
Fax: 0131-228 2188
e-mail: info@rias.org.uk
web: www.rias.org.uk
Secretary and Treasurer: Sebastian
Tombs; *President:* Gordon Davies
Professional body for chartered
architects in Scotland, founded in
1840, with a current membership of
3,000. It publishes books and journals,
organises exhibitions and events,
helps to co-ordinate architectural
competitions, and keeps members up
to date with the latest developments
in the profession.

Potential clients can obtain help in
finding an architect for their project,
as well as general guidance on design,
from the RIAS client advisory service.
Its bookshops stock specialist
architecture and design titles,
including books published by the
RIAS's own Rutland Press.

ROYAL INSTITUTION OF CHARTERED
SURVEYORS IN SCOTLAND
9 Manor Place, Edinburgh EH3 7DN
Tel: 0131-225 7078
Fax: 0131-226 3599
web: www.rics-scotland.org.uk
Director: Eileen Masterman; *Chairman:*
Alex Baird
Established in 1868, it is now one of
the largest professional institutions in
the world with a current membership
in Scotland of 9,000. The RICS defines
and maintains the educational
standards and competence required
for qualification as a chartered
surveyor, lays down standards of
professional conduct, and is active in
advising government on measures
needed for the proper planning,
development and management of
property.

ROYAL PHILOSOPHICAL SOCIETY OF
GLASGOW
Hutchesons' Trust Office, 21 Beaton
Road, Glasgow G41 4NW
Tel: 0141-433 4452
Fax: 0141-424 1731
e-mail: info@royalphil.org
web: www.royalphil.org
Honorary Secretary: Jeremy Hall;
President: Ephraim Borowski
Organises public lectures on topics of
general interest in the arts and
sciences.

ROYAL SCOTTISH GEOGRAPHICAL
SOCIETY
Graham Hills Building, 40 George
Street, Glasgow G1 1QE
Tel: 0141-552 3330
Fax: 0141-552 3331
e-mail: rsgs@strath.ac.uk
web: www.geo.ed.ac.uk/esgs/
Director: Dr David M Munro;
Chairman of Council: Professor George
Gordon
Founded as an educational trust in
1884. Foremost independent
geographical body in Scotland
promoting the understanding of the
relationships between people, places
and the environment through
geographical research, education,
debate, travel and exploration.
Stimulates research into the nature
and causes of change in human and
physical environments on earth,
disseminates knowledge of these
changes and their possible
consequences, and evaluates current
environmental issues.

Each year from September to
March, the RSGS presents more than
100 illustrated talks at its centres
throughout the country. The society
helps with the funding of Scottish-
based expeditions to many parts of
the world, many of the expeditions
returning with new scientific
discoveries. Its medals and

fellowships are among the world's most prestigious awards for outstanding contributions to geography and exploration.

ROYAL SOCIETY OF EDINBURGH
22-26 George Street, Edinburgh EH2 2PQ
Tel: 0131-240 5000
Fax: 0131-240 5024
e-mail: rse@royalsoced.org.uk
web: www.royalsoced.org.uk
Executive Secretary: Dr William Duncan; *President*: Sir William Stewart
An independent, non-party-political body with charitable status. Organises conferences and lectures both for the specialist and the general public, a forum for informed debate on issues of national and international importance. Drawing on the expertise of its multi-disciplinary fellowship, the society provides expert advice to decision-making bodies, including government and parliament. Its research awards programme annually awards £500,000 to young academics and potential entrepreneurs.

Born out of the intellectual ferment of the Scottish Enlightenment, the RSE was founded in 1783 by royal charter for the "advancement of learning and useful knowledge". It is committed to Scotland's social, economic and cultural well-being.

ROYAL TOWN PLANNING INSTITUTE IN SCOTLAND
57 Melville Street, Edinburgh EH3 7HL
Tel: 0131-226 1959
Fax: 0131-226 1909
e-mail: scotland@rtpi.org.uk
web: www.rtpi.org.uk
Director: W Graham U'ren; *Convener, Scottish Executive Committee*: Anne McCall
Charitable organisation with a royal

charter, advancing the art and science of town planning. The Edinburgh office acts as a first point of contact in Scotland for all RTPI services, including professional standards, public affairs and conferences.

RELIGIOUS ORGANISATIONS
See also: Churches

ACTION OF CHURCHES TOGETHER IN SCOTLAND
Scottish Churches House, Dunblane FK15 0AJ
Tel: 01786 823588
Fax: 01786 825844
e-mail: acts.ecum@dial.pipex.com
General Secretary: Rev Dr Kevin Franz
Official ecumenical body in Scotland, expressing the Scottish churches' commitment to unity.

APOSTLESHIP OF THE SEA (SCOTLAND)
937 Dumbarton Road, Glasgow G14 9UF
Tel: 0141-339 6657
National Director: Leo Gilbert
Welfare and provision of facilities for seafarers – including Stella Maris Club and accommodation.

CHRISTIAN AID SCOTLAND
41 George IV Bridge, Edinburgh EH1 1EL
Tel: 0131-220 1254
National Secretary: Rev John N Wylie; *Chairperson*: Margaret Macintosh
Aid and development in more than 60 countries worldwide, as well as education and campaigning in the UK on the causes of poverty.

IONA COMMUNITY
4th Floor, Savoy House, 140 Sauchiehall Street, Glasgow G2 3DH
Tel: 0141-332 6343
Fax: 0141-332 1090

e-mail: ionacomm@gla.iona.org.uk
web: www.iona.org.uk
Leader: Rev Norman Shanks
Ecumenical Christian community founded in 1938 by the late George MacLeod (Lord MacLeod of Fuinary). Gathered around the rebuilding of the ancient monastic buildings of Iona Abbey, the community has sought ever since the "rebuilding of the common life", bringing together work and worship, prayer and politics, the sacred and the secular.

The members – from many backgrounds, countries and denominations – are committed to a rule of daily prayer and Bible study, sharing and accounting for their use of time and money, to regular meeting, and to action for justice and peace. The community maintains three centres on Iona and Mull, and a base in Glasgow. In 1997 many people travelled to Iona to commemorate the 1400th anniversary of the death of St Columba.

THE LEPROSY MISSION SCOTLAND
89 Barnton Street, Stirling FK8 1HJ
Tel: 01786 449266
Fax: 01786 449766
e-mail: lindatodd@compuserve.com
web: www.biggar-net.co.uk/
    tlmscotland
Executive Director: Linda Todd

SCIAF (SCOTTISH CATHOLIC INTERNATIONAL AID FUND)
19 Park Circus, Glasgow G3 6BE
Tel: 0141-354 5555
Director: Paul Chitnis; *President:* Rt Rev John Mone

SCOTTISH BIBLE SOCIETY
7 Hampton Terrace, Edinburgh EH12 5XU
Tel: 0131-337 9701
Fax: 0131-337 0641
e-mail: info@scottishbiblesociety.org
web: www.scottishbiblesociety.org

Executive Director: Rev Douglas Campbell; *Chairperson:* Neil McTaggart
Aims to provide God's word to all people in a language they can understand, in a format they can use, and at a price they can afford.

SCOTTISH CATHOLIC ARCHIVES
Columba House, 16 Drummond Place, Edinburgh EH3 6PL
Tel: 0131-556 3661
Keeper of the Archives: Dr Christine Johnson

SCOTTISH CHURCH HISTORY SOCIETY
39 Southside Road, Inverness IV2 4XA
Tel: 01463 231140
Fax: 01463 230537
Hon Secretary: Rev Dr P H Donald; *President:* Professor D E Meek
Encourages the study of all aspects of Scottish church history.

SCOTTISH CHURCHES WORLD EXCHANGE
23 Inverleith Terrace, Edinburgh EH3 5NS
Tel: 0131-315 4444
e-mail: we@stcolms.org
web: www.worldexchange.org.uk
Chief Executive: Rev Robert S Anderson
Draws on the churches' extensive network of international contacts to provide opportunities for people of all ages and skills to live and work overseas for a year.

SCOTTISH COUNCIL OF JEWISH COMMUNITIES
222 Fenwick Road, Glasgow G46 6UE
Tel: 0141-577 8208
Fax: 0141-577 8202
e-mail: j-scot@j-scot.org
Honorary Secretary: Ephraim Borowski; *Chair:* Dr Kenneth Collins
Represents the Jewish community of Scotland in its relations with government and others.

SCOTTISH CRUSADERS
Challenge House, 29 Canal Street, Glasgow G4 0AD
Tel: 0141-331 2400
Fax: 0141-564 1211
e-mail:scottishcrusaders@ compuserve.com
web: www.charitynet.org/~ScotCrus
Director: Rob Rawson; *Chairman*: Kenneth White
Christian-based youth organisation working with young people aged 8-18 years.

SCOTTISH NATIONAL TRIBUNAL
22 Woodrow Road, Glasgow G41 5PN
Tel: 0141-427 3036
President: Rev Gerard Tartaglia
First instance court of the Catholic Church in Scotland, competent for all Canonical matters, including nullity of marriage, separation of spouses, and privileges of the faith.

SCOTTISH REFORMATION SOCIETY
The Society, The Magdalen Chapel, 41 Cowgate, Edinburgh EH1 1JR
Tel: 0131-220 1450
Fax: 0131-220 1450
e-mail: horne.a@blueyonder.co.uk
Secretary: Rev. Sinclair Horne;
Chairman: Rev E H Sawer
Religious organisation founded in 1851 to promote a witness to the heritage of the Reformation – its history, theology and principles, and their application to the present day.

SCOTTISH SUNDAY SCHOOL UNION FOR CHRISTIAN EDUCATION
2 Fraser Avenue, Newton Mearns, Glasgow G77 6HW
Tel: 0141-571 7359
e-mail: sssu@dcollingham.fsnet.co.uk
Secretary/Treasurer: Lynne Collingham;
Chairperson of Trustees: Rev Jan Mathieson
Promotes Christian education among and for the benefit of children in Scotland.

SCRIPTURE UNION SCOTLAND
9 Canal Street, Glasgow G4 0AB
Tel: 0141-332 1162
e-mail: info@scriptureunionscotland. org.uk
web: www.scriptureunionscotland. org.uk
General Director: Andy Bathgate; *Chairperson*: Rev Neil Dougall
Seeks first to encourage young people in Scotland to consider embracing the Christian faith and second to encourage Bible reading among those of all ages.

SOCIETY FOR THE PROTECTION OF UNBORN CHILDREN
5 St Vincent Place, Glasgow G1 2DH
Tel: 0141-221 2094
Director: Ian Murray; *Chairperson*: Mary Grant
Seeks to protect with love all human life from the moment of conception until natural death.

SOCIETY OF ST VINCENT DE PAUL
546 Sauchiehall Street, Glasgow G2 3NG
Tel: 0141-332 7752
National Secretary: K Gorman; *National President*: Ian J McTurk
Aims to relieve all forms of poverty by person to person contact, regardless of race or creed.

SOCIETY IN SCOTLAND FOR PROPAGATING CHRISTIAN KNOWLEDGE
Tods, Murray WS, 66 Queen Street, Edinburgh EH2 4NE
Tel: 0131-226 4771

RESCUE ORGANISATIONS

MOUNTAIN RESCUE COMMITTEE OF SCOTLAND
31 Craigfern Drive, Blanefield, Glasgow G63 9DP

Tel: 01360 770431
e-mail: lomondbob@Talk21.com
Secretary: Dr Bob Sharp; *Chairman:*
Willie Marshall

ROYAL NATIONAL LIFEBOAT
INSTITUTION
Unit 3, Ruthvenfield Grove,
Inveralmond Industrial Estate, Perth
PH1 3GL.
Tel: 01738 642999
e-mail: scotland@rnli.org.uk
web: www.rnli.org.uk
National Organiser Scotland: Maren
Caldwell

RUGBY

SCOTTISH RUGBY UNION
Murrayfield, Edinburgh EH12 5PJ
Tel: 0131-346 5000
Fax: 0131-346 5001
e-mail: feedback@sru.org.uk
web: www.sru.org.uk
Chief Executive: W.S. Watson

SAFETY

MARITIME AND COASTGUARD AGENCY
Scotland and Northern Ireland
Region, Marine House, Blaikies Quay,
Aberdeen AB11 5EZ
Tel: 01224 574122
Regional Manager: Michael Comerford

RoSPA (ROYAL SOCIETY FOR THE
PREVENTION OF ACCIDENTS)
Slateford House, 53 Lanark Road,
Edinburgh EH14 1TL
Tel: 0131-455 7457
Head, Training Division: Dr Karen
McDonnell; *Heads, Safety Policy
Division:* Elizabeth Lumsden, Michael
A McDonnell

SCOTTISH ACCIDENT PREVENTION
COUNCIL
Slateford House, 53 Lanark Road,
Edinburgh EH14 1TL
Tel: 0131-455 7457
Secretary: Michael A McDonnell

SCOTTISH ROAD SAFETY CAMPAIGN
(SRSC)
Heriot Watt Resrearch Park (North),
Riccarton, Currie, Edinburgh EH14
4AP
Tel: 0131-472 9200
Fax: 0131-472 9201
e-mail: enquiries@srsc.org.uk
web: www.srsc.org.uk
Director: Fiona Murray
Scotland's central organisation for the
promotion and development of key
Scottish road safety publicity
messages and educational materials.
Funded by the Scottish Executive.

SAILING

ROYAL YACHTING ASSOCIATION,
SCOTLAND
Caledonia House, South Gyle,
Edinburgh EH12 9DQ
Tel: 0131-317 7388
Fax: 0131-317 8566
Honorary Secretary: Stewart Boyd

SCIENCE

BOTANICAL SOCIETY OF SCOTLAND
Royal Botanic Garden, Inverleith
Row, Edinburgh EH3 5LR
Tel: 0131-552 7171
Hon Secretary: Robert Galt; *President:*
Dr George Argent
Founded in 1836 as the Botanical
Society of Edinburgh, the society
exists to promote the study of plants
and to exchange botanical

information among members. The activities of the Society include lectures on current botanical topics, field meetings, and the publication of a scientific journal.

EDINBURGH INTERNATIONAL SCIENCE FESTIVAL
Roxburgh's Court, off 323 High Street, Edinburgh EH1 1PW.
Tel: 0131-530 2001
Director: Dr Simon Gage; *Chairman*: Donald Wilson
World's first and largest public celebration of science and technology.

HANNAH RESEARCH INSTITUTE
Ayr KA6 5HL
Tel: 01292 674000
Director: Professor Malcolm Peaker
International centre for biological research in lactation, reproduction and metabolism, ranging from the whole animal through organs, tissues and cells to molecular biology, milk and the science and technology of dairy foods.

MACAULAY LAND USE RESEARCH INSTITUTE
Craigiebuckler, Aberdeen AB15 8QH
Tel: 01224 498200
Fax: 01224 311556
e-mail: enq@mluri.sari.ac.uk
web: www.mluri.sari.ac.uk
Director: Professor Margaret Gill
Established by the Scottish Office in 1987 from the merger of the Macaulay Institute for Soil Research and the Hill Farming Research Organisation, in response to the need for agriculture to take account of other land uses and the developing environmental policy objectives of the EC and UK.

An international leader in research on the use of rural land resources for the benefit of people and the environment. Concerned with assessing opportunities for integrating new land uses with traditional land use, and developing understanding of the impact of land use on the soils and waters of river catchments and of the ecology of soils, trees, plants and grazing animals and their inter-relationships.

MOREDUN RESEARCH INSTITUTE
Pentlands Science Park, Bush Loan, Penicuik EH26 0PZ
EH17 7JH
Tel: 0131-445 5111
web: www.mri.sari.ac.uk
Chief Executive: Professor Q A McKellar; *Chairman*: John Izat
Promotes multidisciplinary study of selected animal pathogens, the diseases they cause and the response to the infected host. Its activities contribute new knowledge to biological science, comparative medicine, environmental protection and public health.

ROSLIN INSTITUTE
Roslin Bio Centre, Roslin, Midlothian EH25 9PS
Tel: 0131-527 4200
Fax: 0131-440 0434
web: www.roslin.ac.uk
Director: Professor Grahame Bulfield
Works to understand and improve the productivity, breeding and welfare of farm animals. Created in 1993 from the Edinburgh Research Station of the Insitute of Animal Physiology and Genetics Research, which in turn was the result of the amalgamation in 1986 of the Poultry Research Centre and the Animal Breeding Research Organisation.

The institute is the UK's major centre for research on molecular and quantitative genetics of farm animals and poultry science and has important programmes of research on transgenic technology, development, growth, reproduction and animal welfare. In 1997 it succeeded in producing live lambs by nuclear transfer from a variety of differentiated cultured cells. One, "Dolly", was created from an adult mammary cell – a breakthrough which attracted intense interest internationally.

ROWETT RESEARCH INSTITUTE
Greenburn Road, Bucksburn, Aberdeen AB21 9SB
Tel: 01224 712751
Fax: 01224 715349
e-mail: enquiries@rri.sari.ac.uk
web: www.rri.sari.ac.uk
Director: Professor Peter J Morgan; Chairman: Dr James Stewart
Founded in 1913 under the direction of Dr John Boyd Orr to carry out research on nutrition related to farm animals, the institute swiftly expanded its remit to cover humans also. Boyd Orr was the first to demonstrate the link between poverty, a poor diet and ill-health and was recognised as the father of modern food and health policies. The institute boasts three Nobel Laureates, including Boyd Orr, among the scientists it has employed.

In recent years, as consumers have become more aware of the positive value of good nutrition and more demanding in their choice of food, the insitute has emphasised its lead role in highlighting the importance of diet. Human and animal studies are undertaken together to improve the welfare and health of humans, to enhance food quality and safety, and to improve animal welfare through the efficient husbandry of milk- and meat-producing animals.

ROYAL BOTANIC GARDEN EDINBURGH
20A Inverleith Row, Edinburgh EH3 5LR
Tel: 0131-552 7171
Fax: 0131-248 2900
web: www.rbge.org.uk
Regius Keeper: Professor Stephen Blackmore; Chairman, Board of Trustees: Dr Paul A Nicholson
Began in 1670 with its founding as a physic garden to grow medicinal plants in the vicinity of Holyrood Palace. Throughout the 18th and 19th centuries it expanded as a centre of learning and the study of plants. In the 20th century the Garden increased both its scientific research base with the establishment of dedicated laboratories, and its national outreach with the acquisition of three additional gardens. Its Living Collections are now distributed across four sites: Inverleith in Edinburgh, Benmore Botanic Garden near Dunoon, Logan Botanic Garden near Stranraer, and Dawyck Botanic Garden near Peebles. These four gardens, under the umbrella term, the National Botanic Gardens of Scotland, each with their different climate and landscape, enable the cultivation of a much wider range of species than would be possible in any single location. Each of the four gardens is also a major visitor attraction, offering the visitor an experience that is enjoyable and educational in surroundings of exceptional beauty.

The Garden's Living Plant Collection, representing more than 16,500 species, is one of the largest and most diverse collections in the world. These collections are essential for both classification research and precise identifications. Together, the four gardens cultivate some 1,400 threatened plant species – more than any other botanic garden in the world.

Housed in the herbarium at

Inverleith, the Preserved Plant Collections, totalling 2,500,000 specimens, comprise a physical record of plant diversity through the last three centuries. The oldest specimen was collected at the Cape of Good Hope in 1697. The Garden also houses one of Britain's finest botanical libraries with 80,000 books, 130,000 journals and 100,000 archival items.

Since 1986, the RBGE has been administered by a board of trustees established under the National Heritage (Scotland) Act 1985. It receives an annual grant from the Rural Affairs Department of the Scottish Executive.

SCOTTISH ASSOCIATION FOR MARINE SCIENCE
Dunstaffnage Marine Laboratory, Oban PA34 4AD
Tel: 01631 559000
Fax: 01631 559001
e-mail: mail@dml.ac.uk
web: www.sams.ac.uk
Director: Professor Graham B Shimmield; *President:* Dr Ian Graham-Bryce
Marine scientific research and education.

SCOTTISH CROP RESEARCH INSTITUTE
Invergowrie, Dundee DD2 5DA
Tel: 01382 562731
web: www.scri.sari.ac.uk/
Director: Professor J R Hillman
Aims to increase knowledge in the basic biological sciences; to improve crop quality and utilisation by the application of conventional and molecular genetical techniques and novel agronomic practices; and to develop environmentally benign methods of protecting crops from depredations by pests, pathogens and weeds. A non-departmental public body, it was formed in 1981 from the merger of the Scottish Plant Breeding Station and the Scottish Horticultural Research Institute.

Varieties bred by SCRI (and its predecessor organisations) are widely released throughout the world. A broad, yet full integrated programme of fundamental and strategic research of the highest quality is a special strength of the Institute. The range of skills available, from fundamental studies on genetics and physiology, through agronomy and pathology, to glasshouse and field trials, is unique within the UK research service. SCRI is the UK's lead centre for research on potatoes and barley, and carries out additional research on a range of temperate, sub-tropical and tropical crops.

SCOTTISH SCIENCE TRUST
12 Queen Street, Edinburgh EH2 1JE
Tel: 0131-226 3481
Fax: 0131-226 3482
e-mail: trust@sst.org.uk
web: www.sst.org.uk
Executive Director: Chris Brittain
Aims to engage the public in issues relating to science, engineering, technology and medicine in Scotland. It facilitates the development of exisiting science centres, the creation of new ones, and the integration of outreach projects to form a coherent network throughout the country.

UK ASTRONOMY TECHNOLOGY CENTRE
Royal Observatory Edinburgh, Blackford Hill, Edinburgh EH9 3HJ
Tel: 0131-668 8100
Director: Dr Adrian Russell
The observatory was granted the title Royal Observatory by George IV in 1822, having begun its existence in 1811 as the Astronomical Institution

of Edinburgh. The original observatory was opened in 1818 on Calton Hill, on the site of an earlier observatory which had been run primarily as a scientific novelty. ROE moved away from the smoke of the town centre to its present site on Blackford Hill in 1896.

From 1957 to 1997, the Royal Observatory built up a capability to develop new instrumentation and telescopes which have played a major part in putting the UK into a leading position in world astronomy. Key projects were the UK Schmidt Telescope in 1973 which did a series of deep surveys of the southern sky, the UK Infrared Telescope in Hawaii in 1978 (the first telescope dedicated to infrared observations), the COSMOS and SuperCOSMOS measuring machines, the world's first facility class infrared camera (IRCAM) in 1986, the world's most sensitive infrared spectrometer in 1990, and SCUBA, the most sensitive submillimetre camera in the world. SCUBA was at least five years ahead of the competition when installed on the James Clerk Maxwell Telescope in 1996.

In 1998, the UK Astronomy Technology Centre was set up at the Royal Observatory Edinburgh, following a merger with the technology division of the Royal Greenwich Observatory in Cambridge. The UK ATC exists to help keep the UK at the forefront of world astronomy by providing a focus for the design, production and promotion of state of the art astronomical technology. It does this by building instruments and systems working across the spectrum from visible through near and mid-infrared to the submillimetre, often in collaboration with UK universities and establishments, industry and worldwide partners, and by

managing major projects such as the VISTA telescope in Chile. A team of astronomers works closely with the engineers to help ensure the new instruments significantly enhance the ability to answer fundamental questions ranging from how planets form to the question of when the first galaxies were made.

The UK ATC promotes new technology developments to enhance future projects, and to improve the UK's competitiveness through partnerships with industry, such as the Smart Optics Faraday Partnership.

SHINTY

CAMANACHD ASSOCIATION
Algarve, Badabrie, Banavie, Fort William PH33 7LX
Tel: 01397 772772
Fax: 01397 772255
e-mail: executive@camanachd.
freeserve.co.uk
web: www.shinty.com
Executive Officer: Alastair MacIntyre

SHOOTING

BRITISH ASSOCIATION FOR SHOOTING AND CONSERVATION
Scottish Centre, Trochry, Dunkeld PH8 0DY
Tel: 01350 723226
Fax: 01350 723227
e-mail: scotland@basc.demon.co.uk
Director: Dr Colin Shedden; *Chairman, Scotland:* Professor Geoff Moore
Represents and safeguards the interests of all those who enjoy shooting sports.

SKIING

SNOWSPORT SCOTLAND
Hillend Park, Biggar Road, Midlothian EH10 7EF
Tel: 0131-445 4151
Chief Executive: Bruce Crawford
Fosters and develops skiing and snowboarding in Scotland from beginner to world cup racing standard through a network of clubs across Scotland.

SPORT AND RECREATION

See also entries for individual sports' governing bodies under the name of the sport

NATIONAL PLAYING FIELDS ASSOCIATION (SCOTLAND)
20 Queen Street, Edinburgh EH2 1JX
Tel: 0131-225 4307
Fax: 0131-225 5763
Administrator: Ken Hamer; *Chairman*: David Reynolds
Preserves and protects recreational space and aims to create as much recreational space as possible. NPFA Scotland is the originator of Millennium Fields and Parks, a scheme preserving fields in perpetuity. Responsible for all King George Vth Memorial Fields.

SPORTSCOTLAND
Caledonia House, South Gyle, Edinburgh EH12 9DQ
Tel: 0131-317 7200
e-mail: library@sportscotland.org.uk
web: www.sportscotland.org.uk
Chief Executive: Ian Robson; *Chairman*: Alastair Dempster
Established in 1972, the council leads the development of sport and physical recreation in Scotland, with the aim of increasing participation and improving standards of performance. Focuses its resources on investing in high quality sporting opportunities for young people, and a comprehensive programme for aspiring and top performers which will improve standards of performance. Distributes more than £20 million a year to develop the infrastructure of Scottish sport through the Lottery sports fund.
The council's national sports centres develop the skills of instructors, coaches and leaders, and provide a training ground for Scotland's national squads. The centres also offer courses and tuition for individuals, clubs and schools.

Glenmore Lodge All-year-round outdoor activities, including skiing, rock climbing, mountaineering, kayaking and open Canadian canoeing. Concerned with mountain safety. Offers accommodation and amenities. *web: www.glenmorelodge. org.uk*

Cumbrae Coaching at every level in a range of water sports, including dinghy sailing, cruising, board sailing, canoeing, sub aqua driving. Works with colleges to develop vocational training in sport. *web: www.nationalcentrecumbrae.org.uk*

Inverclyde Facilities for 30 team and individual indoor and outdoor sports. 24 governing bodies of sport use the facilities to train national squads and the centre is a regular venue for national and international championships. Runs a sports sciences programme. *web: www.nationalcentreinverclyde.org.uk*

SQUASH

SCOTTISH SQUASH
Caledonia House, South Gyle, Edinburgh EH12 9DQ

Tel: 0131-317 7343
Administration Manager: Derek Welch

STOCK EXCHANGE

LONDON STOCK EXCHANGE
69 Buchanan Street, Glasgow G1 3HL
Tel: 0141-221 7060
Senior Manager: Julie Boyle

SURVEYS

BRITISH GEOLOGICAL SURVEY
Murchison House, West Mains Road,
Edinburgh EH9 3LA
Tel: 0131-667 1000
Head of Station: Dr Chris Browitt
Provides nation-wide surveys and monitoring and develops and disseminates expertise and information in the earth sciences for government, industry and the public. Covers geology, environmental geochemistry, groundwater, earthquakes, offshore oil.

ORDNANCE SURVEY
Grayfield House, 5 Bankhead
Avenue, Edinburgh EH11 4AE
Tel: 0131-442 2590
Customer Information Helpline: 08456 050505
web: www.ordnancesurvey.co.uk
Britain's national mapping agency. Produces paper maps and computer data products for business, leisure, educational and administrative use.

SWIMMING

SCOTTISH AMATEUR SWIMMING ASSOCIATION
National Swimming Academy, University of Stirling, Stirling FK9 4LA

Tel: 01786 466520
Fax: 01786 466521
e-mail: info@scottishswimming.com
web: www.scottishswimming.com
Chief Executive: Paul Bush;
Chairperson: Ian Mason

TARTANS

SCOTTISH TARTANS SOCIETY
The Hall of Records, Cockenzie Business Centre, Edinburgh Road, Cockenzie EH32 0HL
Tel: 01875 819900
Fax: 01875 819911
e-mail: info@scottish-tartans-society. co.uk
President: Duncan W Paisley of Westerlea
Register of all publicly known tartans worldwide. Archive; library; research; museums in Edinburgh, Franklin (USA).

TELEVISION AND RADIO

BBC SCOTLAND
Broadcasting House, Queen Margaret Drive, Glasgow G12 8DG
Tel: 0141-338 2000
e-mail: enquiries.scot@bbc.co.uk
web: www.bbc.co.uk/scotland
Controller: John McCormick; *National Governor and Chairman, Broadcasting Council for Scotland:* Sir Robert Smith
BBC Scotland is the only national broadcaster in Scotland, with an annual income of £120 million in 2001-02, and a diverse output providing Scotland and the national networks with drama, light entertainment, children's and leisure programming as well as documentaries, religion, education, arts, music, special events and

political coverage.

BBC Radio Scotland is a speech-led service broadcasting daily from 6am to midnight, while the separate service Radio nan Gaidheal transmits over 1,800 hours a year, reaching more than 90% of Scotland's Gaelic-speaking population. Radio Scotland broadcasts nearly 7,000 hours of output each year.

BBC Scotland produces more than 1,100 hours of television for the local and national networks, of which 900 hours are provided specifically for viewers in Scotland.

The advent of the Scottish Parliament has seen a large investment in devolution programming, with a range of television, radio and on-line services attracting healthy audiences.

Over 1,200 people are employed across 10 centres.

INDEPENDENT TELEVISION COMMISSION
123 Blythswood Street, Glasgow G2 4AN
Tel: 0141-226 4436
Head of ITC Scotland: Alan Stewart
Public body responsible for licensing and regulating all non-BBC television services operating in or for the UK. These include ITV, Channel 4, Channel 5, digital services, and a range of cable, satellite, text and data services. The national office in Scotland has a particular responsibility to liaise with the licensees in Scotland and to promote awareness and understanding of the ITC's functions.

MORAY FIRTH RADIO
PO Box 271, Inverness IV3 8UJ
Tel: 01463 224433
Fax: 01463 243224

e-mail: mfr@mfr.co.uk
web: www.morayfirth.co.uk
Managing Director: Gary Robinson

NORTH SOUND RADIO
45 Kings Gate, Aberdeen AB15 4EL
Tel: 01224 337000
Managing Director: Adam Findlay

RADIO BORDERS
Tweedside Park, Galashiels TD1 3TD
Tel: 01896 759444
Fax: 01896 759494
web: www.radioborders.com
Managing Director: Danny Gallagher

RADIO CLYDE
Clydebank Business Park, Glasgow G81 2RX
Tel: 0141-565 2200
Managing Director: Paul Cooney

RADIO FORTH
Forth House, Forth Street, Edinburgh EH1 3LE
Tel: 0131-556 9255
Managing Director: Sandy Wilkie

SCOT FM
Albert Quay, Leith EH6 7DN
Tel: 0131-625 8400
Managing Director: Mick Hall

SMG PLC
Chief Executive: Andrew Flanagan
Media company providing information and entertainment services to audiences across the UK. Operations include television (see below), radio (Virgin Radio, the national AM and London FM broadcaster of pop and rock music), newspapers (*The Herald, Sunday Herald, Evening Times*), SMG Magazines (consumer and business

titles), an internet business, and cinema and outdoor advertising (Pearl & Dean, and Primesight).

SMG TELEVISION
Chief Executive: Donald Emslie
Two ITV franchies in Scotland (Scottish Television and Grampian Television), broadcasting to 95% of the Scottish public. SMG Network Productions produces network television programmes for ITV, BBC, Channel 4, Sky and overseas broadcasters.
SCOTTISH TELEVISION
200 Renfield Street, Glasgow G2 3PR
Tel: 0141-300 3000
GRAMPIAN TELEVISION
Queen's Cross, Aberdeen AB15 4XJ
Tel: 01224 846846

TAY FM AND RADIO TAY AM
P O Box 123, Dundee DD1 9UF
Tel: 01382 200800
Managing Director: Arthur Ballingall

WEST SOUND
54a Holmston Road, Ayr KA7 3BE
Tel: 01292 283662
Fax: 01292 283665
web: www.west-sound.co.uk
Managing Director: Sheena Borthwick

TENNIS

TENNIS SCOTLAND
177 Colinton Road, Edinburgh EH14 1BZ
Tel: 0131-444 1984
Fax: 0131-444 1973
e-mail: gloria.duncan@ tennisscotland.org
web: www.tennisscotland.org
Secretary and Director of Tennis: Gloria Duncan

THEATRE (AMATEUR)

SCOTTISH COMMUNITY DRAMA ASSOCIATION
5 York Place, Edinburgh EH1 3EB
Tel: 0131-557 5552
Fax: 0131-557 5552
e-mail: headquarters@scda.org.uk
web: www.scda.org.uk
Administrative Assistant: Richard Kay; *Chairperson:* Richard Mackintosh
Development of amateur drama in Scotland. Binds together amateur societies throughout the country and offers them advice, encouragement and practical help.

SCOTTISH YOUTH THEATRE
3rd Floor, Forsyth House, 111 Union Street, Glasgow G1 3TA
Tel: 0141-221 5127
Director: Mary McCluskey; *Chair of Board:* Harry Warnock
Enables, stimulates and directly provides a quality theatre arts experience to young people in Scotland.

THEATRE (PROFESSIONAL)
Listed is a selection of the larger professional theatre companies.
See also: Theatres and Concert Halls

ARCHES THEATRE COMPANY
253 Argyle Street, Glasgow G2 8DL
Tel: 0141-565 1000
Artistic Director: Andy Arnold; *Chair, Board of Directors:* Lesley Thomson

BORDERLINE THEATRE COMPANY
North Harbour Street, Ayr KA8 8AA
Tel: 01292 281010
Producer: Eddie Jackson
One of Scotland's leading touring theatre companies.

BRUNTON THEATRE COMPANY
Ladywell Way, Musselburgh EH21 6AA
Tel: 0131-665 9900
Artistic Director: Mark Thomson; *General Manager*: Lesley Smith

BYRE THEATRE
36 South Street, St Andrews KY16 9JT
Tel: 01334 476288
Box Office: 01334 475000
e-mail: enquiries@byretheatre.com
web: www.byretheatre.com
Artistic Director: Ken Alexander
The only repertory theatre in Fife. The programme includes contemporary and classic drama, dance, concerts, opera, comedy and innovative education and community events.

CITIZENS THEATRE
Gorbals, Glasgow G5 9DS
Tel: 0141-429 5561
Director: Giles Havergal; *Chair*: Professor Jan McDonald
Founded in 1943 by James Bridie, who intended it to be a home of the Scottish theatre with a policy of positive encouragement for native dramatists and actors. The company was set up in a 19th-century music hall in Glasgow Gorbals, where it remains to the present day.

The present company was formed in 1970 under the direction of Giles Havergal and bases its repertoire on British and foreign classics. Since 1992 the company has operated in three theatres: the 600-seat main theatre and two smaller studio theatres. The company has toured extensively abroad and has been widely acclaimed for its innovative work as well as for important translations of modern and classical European drama.

DUNDEE REP
Tay Square, Dundee DD1 1PB
Tel: 01382 227684
Artistic Director: Hamish Glen
Established in 1939 and moved to a new purpose-built theatre in 1983. Operating as a producing house and home to Scotland's only full-time company of 14 actors, it stages an average of six of its own productions every season. As a receiving house, it hosts work from visiting companies. The theatre increases access to performing arts through an extensive community drama programme. It is also the home of Scottish Dance Theatre, founded in 1986, a contemporary dance company with a national remit.

MULL THEATRE
Dervaig, Isle of Mull, Argyll PA75 6QW
Tel: 01688 302673
Artistic Director: Alasdair McCrone

PERTH THEATRE
185 High Street, Perth PH1 5UW
Tel: 01738 621031
Fax: 01738 624576
e-mail: theatre@perth.org.uk
web: www.perth.org.uk/perth/theatre
Artistic Director: Michael Winter
Repertory theatre founded in 1935 by David Steuart and Marjorie Dence. In 1939 the first Scottish Theatre Festival was launched there. In 1946 the theatre became a non-profit-making organisation with financial support from the Arts Council, and after Marjorie Dence's death in 1966 it was bought by the local authority. Iain Cuthbertson, its director in the 1967-68 season, mounted an ambitious programme of Scottish plays. Since then, the theatre has presented a broader repertoire of home-produced theatre.

PITLOCHRY FESTIVAL THEATRE
Port-na-Craig, Pitlochry PH16 5DR
Tel: 01796 484600
Box Office: 01796 484626
Fax: 01796 484616
e-mail: admin@pitlochry.org.uk
web: www.pitlochry.org.uk
Festival Director: Clive Perry; *Chairman of Board*: Robin Douglas
The inspiration of John Stewart, who conceived the idea of a "theatre in the hills" for the presentation of a festival of plays in repertory. In May 1951 the theatre opened in a marquee housing a fan-shaped auditorium and an unusually large stage.

The early Pitlochry seasons presented six plays running from the spring to the early autumn, typically including one Scottish play, a work by a foreign author, a classic, a new play and one or popular favourites. In a modified fashion this pattern has been maintained to the present day, with the addition of concerts, art exhibitions, cinema, literary events and lectures.

In 1981, the company moved to a purpose-built theatre on the outskirts of the small Highland town where it is based. An unusually high proportion of its turnover is generated through ticket sales.

ROYAL LYCEUM THEATRE COMPANY
Grindlay Street, Edinburgh EH3 9AX
Tel: 0131-248 4800
Artistic Director: Kenny Ireland; *Chairman*: Dr Michael Shea
Launched in 1965 as the Edinburgh Civic Theatre Company at the Royal Lyceum, under the artistic direction of Tom Fleming. Bill Bryden, while associate director of the company between 1971 and 1975, presented new work by Scottish writers, including himself. Each year the present company produces between eight and 10 plays representative of both contemporary and classical theatre, and runs an education programme and Youth Theatre.

7:84 THEATRE COMPANY
333 Woodlands Road, Glasgow G3 6NG
Tel: 0141-334 6686
Fax: 0141-334 3369
e-mail: admin@784theatre.fsnet.co.uk
Artistic Director: Gordon Laird; *Chair of Board*: Chris Bartter
Touring theatre company with a 27-year history of presenting challenging theatre that explores current social, cultural and political issues.

TAG THEATRE COMPANY
18 Albion Street, Glasgow G1 1LH
Tel: 0141-552 4949
Artistic Director: James Brining; *Chairperson*: Professor Jan McDonald
Scotland's national theatre for young people, with a vision to allow every young person in Scotland the opportunity to see and participate in the excitement of live theatre.

THEATRE WORKSHOP
34 Hamilton Place, Edinburgh EH3 5AX
Tel: 0131-225 7942
e-mail: info@twe.org.uk
Artistic Director: Robert Rae

TOSG THEATRE COMPANY
Sabhal Mor Ostaig, Teangue, Sleat, Isle of Skye IV44 8RQ
Tel: 01471 888542
Fax: 01471 888541
e-mail: tosg@tosg.org
web: www.tosg.org
Artistic Director: Simon Mackenzie; *Chairperson:* Maggie Cunningham
Scotland's only professional Gaelic theatre company.

TRAMWAY
25 Albert Drive, Pollokshields, Glasgow G41 2PE
Tel: 0141-422 2023

TRAVERSE THEATRE
10 Cambridge Street, Edinburgh EH1 2ED
Tel: 0131-228 3223
Artistic Director: Philip Howard; *Chair*: Stuart Hepburn
Established in 1963 as a private club in a former lodging house in Edinburgh. Its first auditorium held 60 spectators on either side of the acting area. It has moved premises twice. From the start, it has championed the cause of new and experimental work, including plays by Scottish writers.

TRON THEATRE
63 Trongate, Glasgow G1 5HB
Tel: 0141-552 3748
Fax: 0141-552 6657
e-mail: neil@tron.co.uk
web: www.tron.co.uk
Administrator: Neil Murray; *Chair:* Peter Lawson
Produces and presents a varied programme of contemporary and classical drama, comedy, music and dance from Scotland and abroad.

THEATRES AND CONCERT HALLS

Listed is a selection of the larger theatres and a few others of special interest

CUMBERNAULD THEATRE
Braehead Road, Kildrum, Cumbernauld
G67 2BN
Tel: 01236 737235

EDEN COURT THEATRE
Bishop's Road, Inverness IV3 5SA
Tel: 01463 239841

Fax: 01463 713810
e-mail: admin@eden-court.co.uk
Theatre Director: Colin Marr

EDINBURGH FESTIVAL THEATRE
13/29 Nicolson Street, Edinburgh EH8 9FT
Tel: 0131-662 1112

EDINBURGH PLAYHOUSE
18/22 Greenside Place, Edinburgh EH1 3AA
Tel: 0131-557 2692
General Manager: Andrew Lyst

GLASGOW ROYAL CONCERT HALL
2 Sauchiehall Street, Glasgow G2 3NY
Tel: 0141-353 8000
e-mail: grch@grch.com
web: www.grch.com
Director: Louise Mitchell

HIS MAJESTY'S THEATRE
Rosemount Viaduct, Aberdeen AB25 1GL
Tel: 01224 637788

KING'S THEATRE (EDINBURGH)
Administration Offices: 13/29 Nicolson Street, Edinburgh EH8 9FT
Tel: 0131-662 1112

KING'S THEATRE (GLASGOW)
294 Bath Street, Glasgow G2 4JN
Tel: 0141-248 5153

MITCHELL THEATRE
3 Granville Street, Glasgow G3 7DR
Tel: 0141-287 4855

PAVILION THEATRE
121 Renfield Street, Glasgow G2 3AX
Tel: 0141-332 1846

QUEEN'S HALL
Clerk Street, Edinburgh EH8 9JG
Tel: 0131-668 3456
General Manager: Beth Cavanagh
Georgian church converted into a concert hall in 1979, featuring classical, jazz, folk, rock and comedy.

THEATRE ROYAL (GLASGOW)
282 Hope Street, Glasgow G2 3QA
Tel: 0141-332 3321
Theatre Manager: Martin Ritchie

TOURIST BOARDS

VISITSCOTLAND
23 Ravelston Terrace, Edinburgh EH4 3TP
Tel: 0131-332 2433
Fax: 0131-343 1513
web: www.visitsscotland.com
Chief Executive: Philip Riddle; *Chairman:* Peter J Lederer
Established as the Scottish Tourist Board under the Development of Tourism Act 1969 to attract visitors to Scotland and encourage them to travel widely within Scotland. Its mission is the generation of jobs and wealth. It aims to promote the highest standards of service and hospitality. Financed by government, through the Scottish Executive.

Local tourist boards:

ABERDEEN AND GRAMPIAN TOURIST BOARD
27 Albyn Place, Aberdeen AB10 1YL
Tel: 01224 288800
Chief Executive: Alan Clarke

ANGUS & CITY OF DUNDEE TOURIST BOARD
21 Castle Street, Dundee DD1 3AA
Tel: 01382 527527
Chief Executive: Dr Colin Smith

ARGYLL, THE ISLES, LOCH LOMOND, STIRLING, & TROSSACHS TOURIST BOARD
Old Town Jail, St John Street, Stirling FK8 1EA
Tel: 01786 445222

web: www.visitscottishheartlands.com
Chief Executive: James Fraser

AYRSHIRE & ARRAN TOURIST BOARD
15A Skye Road, Prestwick KA9 2TA
Tel: 01292 470700
Chief Executive: Janet Reuben

DUMFRIES AND GALLOWAY TOURIST BOARD
64 Whitesands, Dumfries DG1 2RS
Tel: 01387 245550
Chief Executive: Norma Hart

EDINBURGH & LOTHIANS TOURIST BOARD
4 Rothesay Terrace, Edinburgh EH3 7RY
Tel: 0131-473 3600
Chief Executive: Jack Munro

GREATER GLASGOW & CLYDE VALLEY TOURIST BOARD
11 George Square, Glasgow G2 1DY
Tel: 0141-204 4480
web: www.seeglasgow.com
Chief Executive: Eddie Friel

HIGHLANDS OF SCOTLAND TOURIST BOARD
Peffery House, Strathpeffer IV14 9HA
Tel: 01997 421160
Chief Executive: David Noble

KINGDOM OF FIFE TOURIST BOARD
Haig House, Haig Business Park, Balgonie Road, Markinch KY7 6AQ
Tel: 01592 750066
Chief Executive: Patrick Laughlin

ORKNEY TOURIST BOARD
6 Broad Street, Kirkwall, Orkney KW15 1NX
Tel: 01856 872856
Chief Executive: Barbara Foulkes

PERTHSHIRE TOURIST BOARD
Lower City Mills, West Mill Street,
Perth PH1 5QP
Tel: 01738 627958
Chief Executive: John L Grainger, MBE

SCOTTISH BORDERS TOURIST BOARD
Shepherds Mill, Whinfield Road,
Selkirk TD7 5DT
Tel: 01750 20555
Fax: 01750 21886
e-mail: sbtb@scot-borders.co.uk
Chief Executive: Riddell Graham

SHETLAND ISLANDS TOURISM
Market Cross, Lerwick, Shetland ZE1
0LU
Tel: 01595 693434
Chief Executive: Maurice Mullay

WESTERN ISLES TOURIST BOARD
4 South Beach, Stornoway, Isle of
Lewis
HS1 2XY
Tel: 01851 701818
Chief Executive: Angus MacMillan

TRADE ORGANISATIONS

HARRIS TWEED AUTHORITY
6 Garden Road, Stornoway HS1 2QJ
Tel: 01851 702269
Fax: 01851 702600
e-mail: enquiries@harristweed.org
web: www.harristweed.org
Chief Executive: Ian A Mackenzie
Promotion and authentication of
Harris Tweed.

SCOTCH MALT WHISKY SOCIETY
The Vaults, 87 Giles Street, Edinburgh
EH6 6BZ
Tel: 0131-554 3451
Fax: 0131-553 1003
e-mail: enquiries@smws.com
web: www.smws.com
Managing Director: Richard Gordon;

Chairman: Willie Phillips
Club for anyone who enjoys good
malt.

SCOTCH WHISKY ASSOCIATION
20 Atholl Crescent, Edinburgh EH3
8HF
Tel: 0131-222 9200
Chief Executive: Hugh Morison;
Chairman: Ian Good

**SCOTTISH ASSOCIATION OF MASTER
BAKERS**
4 Torphichen Street, Edinburgh EH3
8JQ
Tel: 0131-229 1401
Chief Executive: Kirk Hunter;
Chairman: Ian Hay

SCOTTISH BUILDING
Carron Grange, Carrongrange
Avenue, Stenhousemuir FK5 3BQ
Tel: 01324 555550
Fax: 01324 555551
e-mail: info@scottish-building.co.uk
web: www.scottish-building.co.uk
Chief Executive: S C Patten; *President*: J
Walker
Employers' federation for the
building industry in Scotland.

SCOTTISH DAILY NEWSPAPER SOCIETY
48 Palmerston Place, Edinburgh EH12
5DE
Tel: 0131-220 4353
Director: Jim Raeburn; *President*: Des
Hudson

SCOTTISH DECORATORS' FEDERATION
Federation House, 222 Queensferry
Road, Edinburgh EH4 2BN
Tel: 0131-343 3300
Chief Executive: Ian H Rogers;
President: W McEwan

SCOTTISH ENGINEERING
105 West George Street, Glasgow G2
1QL
Tel: 0141-221 3181
Chief Executive: P T Hughes, OBE

SCOTTISH FOOD TRADE ASSOCIATION
GCFT Business Enterprises, 230 Cathedral Street, Glasgow G1 2TG
Tel: 0141-552 1655

SCOTTISH GROCERS' FEDERATION
222-224 Queensferry Road, Edinburgh EH4 2BN
Tel: 0131-343 3300
Fax: 0131-343 6147
Chief Executive: Scott Landsburgh;
President: Douglas Edgar

SCOTTISH LICENSED TRADE ASSOCIATION
10 Walker Street, Edinburgh EH3 7LA
Tel: 0131-225 5169
Secretary: Colin A Wilkinson;
President: Maureen McKerrow

SCOTTISH MOTOR TRADE ASSOCIATION
3 Palmerston Place, Edinburgh EH12 5AF
Tel: 0131-225 3643
Fax: 0131-220 0446
e-mail: info@smta.co.uk
web: www.smta.co.uk
Executive Director: Douglas Robertson; *President*: John Chessor

SCOTTISH NEWSPAPER PUBLISHERS ASSOCIATION
48 Palmerston Place, Edinburgh EH12 5DE
Tel: 0131-220 4353
Fax: 0131-220 4344
e-mail: info@snpa.org.uk
web: www.snpa.org.uk
Director: Jim Raeburn; *President*: Alex Cargill

SCOTTISH AND NORTHERN IRELAND PLUMBING EMPLOYERS' FEDERATION
2 Walker Street, Edinburgh EH3 7LB
Tel: 0131-225 2255
Fax: 0131-226 7638
e-mail: info@snipef.org
web: www.snipef.org
Director and Secretary: R D Burgon

SCOTTISH PHARMACEUTICAL FEDERATION
135 Wellington Street, Glasgow G2 2XD
Tel: 0141-221 1235
Fax: 0141-248 5892/0141-226 5047
e-mail: spf@npanet.co.uk
web: www.npa.co.uk
Secretary/Treasurer: F E J McCrossin;
Chairman: I J Johnstone

SCOTTISH PRINT EMPLOYERS FEDERATION
48 Palmerston Place, Edinburgh EH12 5DE
Tel: 0131-220 4353
Fax: 0131-220 4344
e-mail: info@spef.org.uk
web: www.spef.org.uk
Director: Jim Raeburn; *President*: Gordon Cunningham

TRANSPORT OPERATORS

BAA SCOTTISH AIRPORTS
St Andrew's Drive, Glasgow Airport, Paisley PA3 2SW
Tel: 0141-887 1111
Fax: 0141-887 1699
web: www.baa.co.uk
Managing Director: Donal Dowds
Handling 15 million passengers every year through its airports at Edinburgh, Glasgow and Aberdeen, Scottish Airports is part of BAA plc, the world's leading international airports operator. A major contributor to the Scottish economy, BAA Scottish Airports has invested more than £400 million in Scotland since 1990. The company directly employs more than 1,000 people out of nearly 10,000 who work at its airports.

CALEDONIAN MACBRAYNE
The Pier, Gourock PA19 1QP
Tel: 01475 650100
Managing Director: Lawrie Sinclair;

Chairman: Harold Mills
Passenger and vehicle ferry services
to Clyde and Western Isles islands.

RAILTRACK PLC
Buchanan House, 58 Port Dundas
Road, Glasgow G4 0LQ
Tel: 0141-332 9811
Director Scotland Zone: Janette
Anderson
Owners of Britain's tracks, signals,
and stations, maintaining the
infrastructure of the railway.

SCOTRAIL RAILWAYS
Caledonian Chambers, 87 Union
Street, Glasgow G1 3TA
Tel: 08700 005151
Fax: 0141-335 4791
e-mail: john.yellowlees@scotrail.co.uk
web: www.scotrail.co.uk
Managing Director: Alastair
McPherson; *Group Chief Executive*:
Phil White
Scotland's national rail operator,
providing 95% of passenger train
services north of the border. Runs
suburban, inter-urban and rural
services in Scotland and the
Caledonian sleeper service to and
from London. In April 1997 the
National Express Group began a
seven-year franchise for the operation
of ScotRail and is investing £200
million in new and refurbished trains
for ScotRail.

STAGECOACH HOLDINGS PLC
10 Dunkeld Road, Perth PH1 5TW
Tel: 01738 442111
Fax: 01738 643648
web: www.stagecoachplc.com
Chief Executive: Keith Cochrane;
Chairman: Brian Souter
International bus and rail operator.

STRATHCLYDE PASSENGER TRANSPORT
Consort House, 12 West George
Street, Glasgow G2 1HN

Tel: 0141-333 6811
web: www.spt.co.uk
Director General: Dr Malcolm Reed;
Chair: Councillor Eric Ross
SPT is the marketing label for
Strathclyde Passenger Transport
Authority and Executive. It plans and
operates public transport services in
west central Scotland, including the
SPT Underground in Glasgow, some
ferries and subsidised buses. Rail
services in Strathclyde are provided
by ScotRail on SPT's behalf.

TRANSPORT ORGANISATIONS

SCOTTISH ASSOCIATION FOR PUBLIC TRANSPORT
5 St Vincent Place, Glasgow G1 2HT
Tel: 0141-639 3697
Hon Secretary: Alastair Reid; *Chair*: Dr
John McCormick
Campaigns for integrated transport
in, to, and from Scotland,
improvements in public passenger
transport, and shifts from roads to rail
and water-borne freight.

SCOTTISH RAILWAY PRESERVATION SOCIETY
The Station, Union Street, Bo'ness
EH51 9AQ
Tel: 01506 822298
web: www.srps.org.uk
General Secretary: Iain Gent; *Chairman*:
W Peddie
Aims to establish the Scottish Railway
Museum. Volunteer members operate
the Bo'ness and Kinneil Railway,
SRPS Railtours and the Scottish
Railway Exhibition.

SCOTTISH TRAMWAY AND TRANSPORT SOCIETY
PO Box 78, Glasgow G3 6ER

General Secretary: Hugh McAulay
Publication of books and videos on
Scottish tramway history and support
for preservation schemes.

UNIONS

SCOTTISH TRADES UNION CONGRESS
333 Woodlands Road, Glasgow G3
6NG
Tel: 0141-337 8100
Fax: 0141-337 8101
e-mail: info@stuc.org.uk
General Secretary: Bill Speirs;
Chairperson: David Bleiman
First convened in Glasgow in 1897.
Initially 30 of the 45 affiliated unions
were small independent Scottish
unions which then existed in such
industries as textiles and engineering
(although a number, like the
railwaymen, were always nationally
organised). Over the years, the
number of separate Scottish unions
declined through successive
amalgamations, until today there are
only six out of an affiliate
membership of 46. The number of
members rose from 76,000 in 1898 to
1,050,000 in 1978, from which peak it
has declined to just under 630,000.
Congress meets annually for a
week in April, the venue varying
from year to year. It is completely
independent (not a Scottish regional
organisation of the TUC) and is
financed from the subscriptions of
affiliated unions. Hours and
conditions of work have remained a
central preoccupation, but the STUC
has played a wider role by
campaigning for new industry and
from time to time has organised mass
demonstrations against unemploy-
ment, closures, and cuts in public
expenditure.

*Listed is a selection of the largest unions
and a few others of special interest*

**AMALGAMATED ENGINEERING &
ELECTRICAL UNION**
145/165 West Regent Street, Glasgow
G2 4RZ
Tel: 0141-248 7131
Scottish Regional Secretary: Danny
Carrigan

BRITISH ACTORS' EQUITY ASSOCIATION
114 Union Street, Glasgow G1 3QQ
Tel: 0141-248 2472

**BROADCASTING, ENTERTAINMENT,
CINEMATOGRAPH AND THEATRE UNION**
114 Union Street, Glasgow G2 3QQ
Tel: 0141-248 9558

FIRE BRIGADES UNION
4th Floor, 52 St Enoch Square,
Glasgow G1 4AA
Tel: 0141 221 2309

GMB
Fountain House, 1/3 Woodside
Crescent, Glasgow G3 7UJ
Tel: 0141-332 8641
e-mail: robert.parker@gmb.org.uk
Regional Secretary: Robert Parker

GPMU
Graphical House, 222 Clyde Street,
Glasgow G1 4JT
Tel: 0141-221 7730

**INSTITUTION OF PROFESSIONALS,
MANAGERS AND SPECIALISTS**
18 Melville Terrace, Stirling FK8 2NQ
Tel: 01786 465999
National Officer: Alan Denney

**MANUFACTURING, SCIENCE AND
FINANCE**
145-165 West Regent Street, Glasgow
G2 4RZ
Tel: 0141-229 6100
National Secretary Scotland: John Wall

Musicians' Union
11 Sandyford Place, Sauchiehall Street, Glasgow G3 7NB
Tel: 0141-248 3723

National Union of Journalists
114 Union Street, Glasgow G1 3QQ
Tel: 0141-248 7748
Scottish Organiser: Paul Holleran

National Union of Rail, Maritime and Transport Workers
180 Hope Street, Glasgow G2 2UE
Tel: 0141-332 1117

Prison Officers Association (Scotland)
21 Calder Road, Edinburgh EH11 3PF
Tel: 0131-443 8105
Assistant Secretary: Derek Turner

Public and Commercial Services Union
6 Hillside Crescent, Edinburgh EH7 5DY
Tel: 0131-556 0407
Scottish Secretary: Eddie Reilly

Transport and General Workers' Union
290 Bath Street, Glasgow G2 4LD
Tel: 0141-332 7321

Unifi
146 Argyle Street, Glasgow G2 8BL
Tel: 0141-221 6475

Union of Construction, Allied Trades and Technicians
53 Morrison Street, Glasgow G5 8LB
Tel: 0141-420 2880
Fax: 0141-420 2881
Scottish Secretary: A S Ritchie

Union of Shop, Distributive and Allied Workers
Muirfield, 342 Albert Drive, Glasgow G41 5PG
Tel: 0141-427 6561

Unison
14 West Campbell Street, Glasgow G2 6RX
Tel: 0141-332 0006
Scottish Secretary: Matt Smith

UNIVERSITIES

University of Aberdeen
Aberdeen AB24 3FX
Tel: 01224 272000
Fax: 01224 272086
e-mail: pubrel@abdn.ac.uk
web: www.abdn.ac.uk
Principal and Vice-Chancellor: Professor C Duncan Rice
History: Founded in 1495 as King's College. A second university, Marischal College, was founded in 1593. They merged in 1860. *Faculties:* Arts and Divinity; Medicine and Medical Sciences; Social Sciences and Law; Science and Engineering; Education. *Number of students:* 11,000. *Main undergraduate awards:* MA, BSc, BD, BTh, LTh, LLB, BLE, MB, ChB, BMedBiol, BEng, MEng, BScEng, BEd. *Key features:* Merged with Northern College of Education in 2001. Increase of 16.9% in applications for September 2001 entry put Aberdeen in second place (behind St. Andrews) in the UK.

University of Abertay, Dundee
Bell Street, Dundee DD1 1HG
Tel: 01382 308000
Fax: 01382 308877
e-mail: iro@abertay.ac.uk
web: www.abertay.ac.uk
Principal and Vice-Chancellor: Professor B King
History: Established as a university in 1994, with origins in the foundation of Dundee Technical Institute in 1888. *Schools:* Computing; Dundee Business School; Science and Engineering; Social and Health Sciences. *Number of*

students: 5,500. *Main undergraduate awards:* BA (Hons), BSc (Hons). *Key features:* Specialism in computer games technology and computer arts; innovative sports coaching degrees, internet degrees, biotechnology degrees. Award-winning library.

UNIVERSITY OF DUNDEE
Dundee DD1 4HN
Tel: 01382 344000
Fax: 01382 201604
e-mail: secretary@dundee.ac.uk
web: www.dundee.ac.uk
Principal and Vice-Chancellor: Sir Alan Langlands
History: Founded in 1967, the successor to University College, Dundee, which had been part of the University of St Andrews since 1881. *Faculties:* Medicine, Dentistry and Nursing; Science and Engineering; Law and Accounting; Arts and Social Sciences; Duncan of Jordanstone College. *Number of students:* 12,000. *Main undergraduate awards:* BA, BAcc, BArch, BDes, BDS, BEng, BFin, BMSc, BSc, LLB, MA, MB, ChB. *Key features:* International centre for cancer research and keyhole surgery. Also internationally-rated for research in civil engineering, computing, fine art and design; currently has a "live" patent portfolio of 115 projects; has granted licences for exploitation of a further 163. Two thirds of its departments received "Excellent" or "Highly satisfactory" ratings for teaching quality.

UNIVERSITY OF EDINBURGH
Old College, South Bridge,
Edinburgh EH8 9YL
Tel: 0131-650 1000
Fax: 0131-650 2253
e-mail: communications.office@ed.ac.uk
web: www.ed.ac.uk
Principal and Vice-Chancellor: Lord

Sutherland of Houndwood
History: Granted a charter by James VI in 1582, the Town Council providing the necessary finances. *Faculties:* Divinity; Law; Medicine; Arts; Education; Science and Engineering; Music; Social Sciences; Veterinary Medicine. *Number of students:* 20,000. *Main undergraduate awards:* BA, BCom, BD, BEng, BMus, BSc, BV&MS, LLB, MA, MB, ChB, MEng, MChem, MChemPhys, MPhys. *Key features:* 30% of all students in university accommodation. Alumni include David Hume, Walter Scott, J M Barrie, R L Stevenson.

UNIVERSITY OF GLASGOW
Glasgow G12 8QQ
Tel: 0141-339 8855
web: www.gla.ac.uk
Principal and Vice-Chancellor: Professor Sir Graeme Davies
History: Founded in 1451. Moved in 1871 from the city centre to the present campus in the West End. *Faculties:* Arts; Medicine; Law and Financial Studies; Divinity; Engineering; Veterinary Medicine; Social Sciences; Education; Physical Sciences; Biomedical and Life Sciences; Computing Science; Maths and Statistics. *Number of students:* 17,700. *Main undergraduate awards:* BA, BAcc, BArch, BD, BDS, BEd, BMus, BN, BSc, BEng, MEng, LLB, MA, MB, ChB, MSci, BVMS, BTechEd, BTheol, BTechnol. *Key features:* During 1999-2000, the university secured new grants and contracts worth more than £100 million. The university has the highest number of excellence awards for teaching quality in Scotland.

GLASGOW CALEDONIAN UNIVERSITY
Cowcaddens Road, Glasgow G4 0BA
Tel: 0141-331 3000
Fax: 0141-331 3005
web: www.caledonian.ac.uk
Principal: Dr Ian Johnston, CB

History: Founded in 1993 from the merger of the former Glasgow Polytechnic and the Queen's College, Glasgow. *Faculties:* Caledonian Business School; Health; Science and Technology. *Number of students:* 14,500. *Main undergraduate awards:* BA, BSc, BEng. *Key features:* most modern campus in Scotland. Leading provider of applied research for business and the professions.

HERIOT-WATT UNIVERSITY
Edinburgh EH14 4AS
Tel: 0131-451 3444
Fax: 0131-451 3441
e-mail: pr@hw.ac.uk
web: www.hw.ac.uk
Principal and Vice-Chancellor: Professor John S Archer
History: Founded in 1966, but tracing its origins to the foundation of Edinburgh School of Arts in 1821. In 1998 the University merged with the Scottish College of Textiles to form the Scottish Borders Campus in Galashiels which is home to the university's School of Textiles. *Faculties:* Science; Engineering; Economics and Social Studies; Environmental Studies; Art and Design; Textiles; Edinburgh Business School. *Number of students:* 6,000 on campus; 9,000 distance learning. *Main undergraduate awards:* BA, BArch, BEd, BEng, BSc, MEng. *Key features:* modern technological university specialising in applied sciences and mathematics, engineering and design, textiles, business management and languages. Centres of Excellence in Petroleum Engineering, and Brewing and Distilling. One of the top UK universities for income from business and industry. Has one of the highest graduate employment rates in the country.

NAPIER UNIVERSITY
219 Colinton Road, Edinburgh EH14 1DJ
Tel: 0131-444 2266
e-mail: info@napier.ac.uk
web: www.napier.ac.uk
Principal: Professor John Mavor
History: Opened in 1964 as Napier College of Science and Technology, acquiring full degree-awarding powers in 1992. *Faculties:* Health and Life Sciences; Arts and Social Science; Engineering and Computing; Napier Business School. *Number of students:* 12,500. *Main undergraduate awards:* BA, BEng, BSc. *Key features:* Four main campuses linked by an hourly bus service. New study programmes: e-Business; Sport and Exercise Science; Cultural Studies; Photojournalism; Psychology; Popular Music; Building Surveying with Computing.

OPEN UNIVERSITY IN SCOTLAND
10 Drumsheugh Gardens, Edinburgh EH3 7QJ
Tel: 0131-226 3851
Fax: 0131-220 6730
e-mail: rll@open.ac.uk
web: www.open.ac.uk/scotland
Director: Peter Syme
History: Established by royal charter in 1969. *Faculties:* Arts, Education, Health and Social Welfare, Law, Management, Maths and Computing, Modern Languages, Science, Social Sciences, Technology. *Number of students:* 13,000 in Scotland, 200,000 in the UK as a whole. *Main undergraduate awards:* BA, BSc. *Key features:* part-time open learning with extensive tutor support and opportunities for regular contact with fellow students. No qualifications required to study at undergraduate level. Courses taught using a variety of multi-media course materials, from written texts to videos and computer software.

UNIVERSITY OF PAISLEY
Paisley PA1 2BE
Tel: 0141-848 3000
e-mail: uni-direct@paisley.ac.uk

web: www.paisley.ac.uk
Principal and Vice-Chancellor: Professor John Macklin
History: Founded in 1897 as Paisley Technical College and School of Art. Given university status in 1992. Merged with former Craigie College of Education in 1993. Faculties: Business; Education and Media; Communications, Engineering and Science; Health and Social Sciences. Number of students: 10,500. Main undergraduate awards: BA, BAcc, BEd, BEng, BSc. Key features: Main campus in Paisley offers science, engineering, business, computing and IT, social sciences, nursing and health. Campus in Ayr specialises in education, media, nursing, tourism, midwifery. Third campus in Dumfries created through partnership arrangement with Glasgow University and Dumfries and Galloway College. 20% of all students in university accommodation.

ROBERT GORDON UNIVERSITY
Schoolhill, Aberdeen AB10 1FR
Tel: 01224 262000
Fax: 01224 262185
e-mail: i.centre@rgu.ac.uk
web: www.rgu.ac.uk
Principal and Vice-Chancellor: Professor William Stevely
History: Started as Robert Gordon's Hospital in 1750. Acquired central institution status in 1903, awarded university title in 1992. Faculties: Science and Technology; Health and Social Care; Design; Management. Number of students: 10,000. Main undergraduate awards: BA, BSc, BEng. Key features: Semester system. 25% of all students in university accommodation.

UNIVERSITY OF ST ANDREWS
College Gate, St Andrews KY16 9AJ
Tel: 01334 476161

e-mail: proffice@st-andrews.ac.uk
web: www.st-andrews.ac.uk
Principal and Vice-Chancellor: Dr Brian Lang
History: Founded in 1410, Scotland's oldest university and third oldest in UK. Faculties: Arts; Divinity; Science (including Medical Science). Number of students: 6,000. Main undergraduate awards: MA, BD, BSc, MChem, MSci, MTheol, MPhys. Key features: Top rated for teaching quality in Scotland; strong research profile; diverse and international student body, mainly residential university.

UNIVERSITY OF STIRLING
Stirling FK9 4LA
Tel: 01786 473171
e-mail: admissions@stir.ac.uk
web: www.stir.ac.uk
Principal and Vice-Chancellor: Professor C Bell
History: Founded in 1967. Faculties: Arts; Human Sciences; Management; Natural Sciences. Number of students: 8,500. Main undergraduate awards: BA, BSc, BAcc. Key features: Two semesters, each of 15 weeks. 60% of all students in university accommodation.

UNIVERSITY OF STRATHCLYDE
16 Richmond Street, Glasgow G1 1XQ
Tel: 0141-552 4400
web: www.strath.ac.uk
Principal and Vice-Chancellor: Professor Andrew Hamnett
History: Formed as Anderson's Institution in 1796, became Royal Technical College in 1912, Royal College of Science and Technology in 1956. Full university status was granted in 1964. Merged with Jordanhill College of Education in 1993. Faculties: Science; Engineering; Arts and Social Sciences; Strathclyde Business School (incorporating the Graduate School of Business);

Education. *Number of students:* 14,000. *Main undergraduate awards:* BA, BArch, BSc, MSci, BEng, MEng, MPharm, BEd, LLB. *Key features:* 19% of all students in university accommodation. 57% first degree students live at home.

VOLLEYBALL

SCOTTISH VOLLEYBALL ASSOCIATION
48 The Pleasance, Edinburgh EH8 9TJ
Tel: 0131-556 4633
Fax: 0131-557 4314
e-mail: sva@callnetuk.com
Director: Nick Moody

VOLUNTEERING

CSV SCOTLAND (COMMUNITY SERVICE VOLUNTEERS SCOTLAND)
Wellgate House, 200 Cowgate, Edinburgh EH1 1NQ
Tel: 0131-622 7766
Director Scotland: Claire Stevens; *Chairperson:* John Pulford
Promotes active citizenship through a nationwide programme of volunteering, training and community action opportunities.

EDINBURGH VOLUNTARY ORGANISATIONS COUNCIL
14 Ashley Place, Edinburgh EH6 5PX
Tel: 0131-555 9100
Fax: 0131-555 9101
e-mail: dianne.evoc@ukonline.co.uk
web: www.evoc.org.uk
Director: Shulah Allan; *Chairperson:* Maureen O'Neill
Umbrella body for the voluntary sector in Edinburgh.

GLASGOW COUNCIL FOR THE VOLUNTARY SECTOR
11 Queens Crescent, Glasgow G4 9AS
Tel: 0141-332 2444
Fax: 0141-332 0175
e-mail: information@gcvs.org.uk
Director: Helen Macneil
An umbrella body for the voluntary sector in Glasgow. Over 400 member organisations.

SCOTTISH COUNCIL FOR VOLUNTARY ORGANISATIONS
18/19 Claremont Crescent, Edinburgh EH7 4QD
Tel: 0131-556 3882
web: www.scvo.org.uk
Chief Executive: Martin Sime; *Convener:* Neil McIntosh
Established in 1936 as an umbrella body for voluntary organisations in Scotland, of which almost 1,200 are members. Works to promote and advocate the interests of the voluntary sector, publishing a weekly newspaper, handling 5,000 inquiries a year, maintaining a database of potential sources of charitable funding, running training courses, conferences and seminars, and undertaking specialist analysis of public policy as it affects voluntary bodies.

Its European unit is the first point of contact for charities wishing to gain access to European funds.

VOLUNTEER DEVELOPMENT SCOTLAND
Stirling Enterprise Park, Springbank Road, Stirling FK7 7RP.
Tel: 01786 479593
Fax: 01786 449285
e-mail: vds@vds.org.uk
web: www.vds.org.uk
Director: Liz Burns, OBE; *Chair:* W Ian Ball
National centre for volunteering and community involvement.

WATER

EAST OF SCOTLAND WATER
55 Buckstone Terrace, Edinburgh
EH10 6XH
Tel: 0131-445 4141
Fax: 0131-445 5040
web: www.esw.co.uk
Chief Executive: Jon Hargreaves;
Chairperson: Councillor Robert Cairns

NORTH OF SCOTLAND WATER
Cairngorm House, Beechwood Park
North, Inverness IV2 3ED
Tel: 01463 245400
web: www.noswa.co.uk
Chief Executive: Katharine Bryan

WEST OF SCOTLAND WATER
419 Balmore Road, Glasgow G22 6NU
Tel: 0808 100 5333
Fax: 0141-355 5146
e-mail: customer.service@
  westscotlandwater.org.uk
web: www.westscotlandwater.org.uk
Chief Executive: Charlie Cornish;
Chairman: Professor Alan Alexander

WOMEN

CHURCH OF SCOTLAND GUILD
121 George Street, Edinburgh EH2
4YN
Tel: 0131-225 5722
e-mail: guild@cofscotland.org.uk
web: www.cos-guild.org.uk
General Secretary: Alison M Twaddle;
National Convener: Elspeth Kerr
Invites women to commit their lives
to Christ and enables them to express
their faith in worship, prayer and
action through various projects.

**ROYAL SOCIETY FOR THE RELIEF OF
INDIGENT GENTLEWOMEN OF
SCOTLAND**
14 Rutland Square, Edinburgh EH1
2BD

Tel: 0131-229 2308
Fax: 0131-229 0956
e-mail: admin@igfund.freeserve.
  co.uk
Secretary and Cashier: George F
Goddard; *Chairman*: D H Galbraith
Offers financial assistance to ladies of
Scottish birth or background with
professional   or   business
backgrounds.

SCOTTISH WOMEN'S AID
Norton Park, 57 Albion Road,
Edinburgh EH7 5QY
Tel: 0131-475 2372
Text Tel: 0131-475 2389
Fax: 0131-475 2384
e-mail: swa@swa-1.demon.co.uk
web: www.scottishwomensaid.co.uk
National office for Women's Aid in
Scotland. Feminist organisation
aiming to end violence against
women. With affiliated local Women's
Aid groups in Scotland, exists to
promote the interests of women and
children who have experienced
domestic abuse, and to provide an
accessible and effective network and
service.

**SCOTTISH WOMEN'S RURAL
INSTITUTES**
42 Heriot Row, Edinburgh EH3 6ES
Tel: 0131-225 1724
Fax: 0131-225 8129
e-mail: swri@swri.demon.co.uk
General Secretary: Anne Peacock;
National Chairman: Kay Wragg
Educational and social opportunities
for women – handcrafts, cookery,
sport, drama, etc.

WOMEN'S ROYAL VOLUNTARY SERVICE
Edinburgh Administration Centre,
Clerwood House, Clermiston Road,
Edinburgh EH12 6UT
Tel: 0131-314 0600/0845 601 4670
Fax: 0131-334 6813
e-mail: volunteer@wrvs.org.uk
web: www.wrvs.org.uk

Volunteering Manager: Linda Hamilton Provides services for those in need in the community through 20,000 volunteers.

YOUTH

DUKE OF EDINBURGH'S AWARD
69 Dublin Street, Edinburgh EH3 6NS
Tel: 0131-556 9097
Secretary for Scotland: Janet Shepherd
Young people aged 14-25 undertake a challenging programme of leisure pursuits involving service in the community, skills, physical recreation and expeditions. Three levels of award – Bronze, Silver and Gold. Non-competitive and available to all.

FAIRBRIDGE IN SCOTLAND
57 Albion Road, Edinburgh EH7 5QY
Tel: 0131-475 2303
Director: Tom Watson

SCOTTISH YOUTH HOSTELS ASSOCIATION
7 Glebe Crescent, Stirling FK8 2JA
Tel: 01786 891400
Fax: 01786 891333
e-mail: syha@syha.org.uk
web: www.syha.org.uk
General Secretary: W B Forsyth;
Chairman: J P Lawson
To help all, but especially young people of limited means to know, use and appreciate the Scottish countryside and places of historic and cultural interest in Scotland, particularly by providing simple hostel accommodation for them on their travels.

YMCA SCOTLAND
James Love House, 11 Rutland Street, Edinburgh EH1 2AE
Tel: 0131-228 1464
Fax: 0131-228 5462

e-mail: info@ymcascotland.org
National General Secretary: Peter Crory;
President: Lord Hogg of Cumbernauld
Provides quality educational, training, support and recreational programmes aimed at physical, social, mental and spiritual development, especially for young people.

YOUTH CLUBS SCOTLAND
Balfour House, 19 Bonnington Grove, Edinburgh EH6 4BL
Tel: 0131-554 2561
Fax: 0131-555 5223
e-mail: office@ycs.org.uk
Chief Executive: Carol Downie
National voluntary youth organisation with an affiliated membership of more than 650 Scottish youth groups.

YOUTHLINK SCOTLAND
Central Halls, West Tollcross, Edinburgh EH3 9BP
Tel: 0131-229 0339
Chief Executive: Simon Jacquet;
President: Ian Fiddes
Exists to support and promote the work and collective aspirations of voluntary youth organisations in the interests of young people.

YWCA
7B Randolph Crescent, Edinburgh EH3 7TH
Tel: 0131-225 7592
Fax: 0131-467 7008
e-mail: info@ywcascotland.org
web: www.ywcascotland.org
Chief Executive: Elaine Samson
Enables young women, particularly those under 30, to develop their full potential in mind, body and spirit, and to participate at all levels of society worldwide. Delivers services locally, mainly in disadvantaged communities.

People

Royal appointments

Order of The Thistle

Order of chivalry consisting of the sovereign and 16 knights. May have existed under James V. Disappeared at the time of the Reformation. Revived by James VII in 1687.

Knights

1966 Earl of Wemyss and March
1973 Sir Donald Cameron of Lochiel
1978 Duke of Buccleuch and Queensberry
1981 Earl of Elgin and Kincardine
1981 Lord Thomson of Monifieth
1985 Earl of Airlie
1986 Captain Sir Iain Tennant
1995 Viscount Younger of Leckie
1996 Viscount Arbuthnot
1996 Earl of Crawford and Balcarres
1996 Lady Marion Fraser
1996 Lord Macfarlane of Bearsden
1997 Lord Mackay of Clashfern
2000 Lord Wilson of Tillyorn

Lords Lieutenant

Aberdeenshire A D M Farquharson, OBE
Angus Mrs G L Osborne
Argyll and Bute vacant
Ayrshire and Arran Major R Y Henderson, TD
Banffshire J A S McPherson, CBE
Berwickshire Major A Trotter
Caithness Major G T Dunnett, TD
Clackmannan Mrs S G Cruickshank

Dumfries Captain R C Cunningham-Jardine
Dunbartonshire Brigadier D D G Hardie, TD
East Lothian W Garth Morrison, CBE
Fife Mrs C M Dean
Inverness Lord Gray of Contin, PC
Kincardineshire J D B Smart
Lanarkshire G Cox, MBE
Midlothian Captain G W Burnet, LVO
Moray Air Vice-Marshal G A Chesworth, CB, OBE, DFC
Nairn Ewen J Brodie
Orkney G R Marwick
Perth and Kinross Sir David Montgomery, Bt
Renfrewshire C H Parker, OBE
Ross and Cromarty Captain R W K Stirling of Fairburn, TD
Roxburgh, Ettrick and Lauderdale Dr June Paterson-Brown, CBE
Shetland J H Scott
Stirling and Falkirk Lt-Col J Stirling of Garden, CBE, TD
Sutherland Major-General D Houston, CBE
Stewartry of Kirkcudbright Lt-Gen Sir Norman Arthur, KCB
Tweeddale Captain J D B Younger
West Lothian vacant
Western Isles A Matheson, OBE
Wigtown Major E S Orr-Ewing

The Lord Provosts of the four cities are Lords Lieutenant for those cities ex officio.
Edinburgh: Eric Milligan
Glasgow: Alex Mosson
Aberdeen: Margaret Smith
Dundee: John Letford

The Peerage

* denotes title designated as Scottish (pre-Union of the Parliaments)

Dukes

1701	*Argyll (13th), Torquhil Campbell; b 1968; s 2001
1703	*Atholl (11th), John Murray; b 1929; s 1996
1663	*Buccleuch (9th) and Queensberry (11th), Walter Francis John Montagu Douglas Scott, KT, VRD; b 1923; s 1973
1900	Fife (3rd), James George Alexander Bannerman Carnegie; b 1929; s 1959
1643	*Hamilton (15th) and Brandon (12th), Angus Alan Douglas Douglas-Hamilton; b 1938; s 1973 *Premier Peer of Scotland*
1707	*Montrose (8th), James Graham; b 1935; s 1992
1707	*Roxburghe (10th), Guy David Innes-Ker; b 1954; s 1974 *Premier Baronet of Scotland*

Marquesses

1916	Aberdeen and Temair (6th), Alastair Ninian John Gordon, b 1920; s 1984
1831	Ailsa (8th), Archibald Angus Charles Kennedy; b 1956; s 1994
1796	Bute (7th), John Colum Crichton-Stuart; b 1958; s 1993
1599	*Huntly (13th), Granville Charles Gomer Gordon; b 1944; s 1987 *Premier Marquess of Scotland*
1784	Lansdowne (9th), Charles Maurice Mercer Nairne Petty-Fitzmaurice; b 1912; s 1999
1902	Linlithgow (4th), Adrian John Charles Hope; b 1946; s 1987
1701	*Lothian (12th), Peter Francis Walter Kerr, KCVO; b 1922; s 1940
1682	*Queensberry (12th), David Harrington Angus Douglas; b 1929; s 1954
1694	*Tweeddale (13th), Edward Douglas John Hay; b 1947; s 1979
1892	Zetland (4th), Lawrence Mark Dundas; b 1937; s 1989

Earls

1639	Airlie (13th), David George Coke Patrick Ogilvy, KT, GCVO, PC; b 1926; s 1968
1662	*Annandale and Hartfell (11th), Patrick Andrew Wentworth Hope Johnstone; b 1941; claim established 1985
1922	Balfour (4th), Gerald Arthur James Balfour; b 1925; s 1968
1469	*Buchan (17th), Malcolm Harry Erskine; b 1930; s 1984
1455	*Caithness (20th), Malcolm Ian Sinclair; b 1948; s 1965
1827	Cawdor (7th), Colin Robert Vaughan Campbell; b 1962; s 1993
1398	*Crawford (29th) and Balcarres (12th), Robert Alexander Lindsay, KT PC; b 1927; s 1975
1861	Cromartie (5th), John Ruaridh Blunt Grant Mackenzie; b 1948; s 1989
1633	*Dalhousie (17th), James Hubert Ramsay; b 1948; s 1999
1660	*Dundee (12th), Alexander Henry Scrymgeour; b 1949; s 1983
1669	*Dundonald (15th), Iain Alexander Douglas Blair Cochrane; b 1961; s 1986
1686	*Dunmore (12th), Malcolm Kenneth Murray; b 1946; s 1995
1507	*Eglinton (18th) and Winton (9th), Archibald George Montgomerie; b 1939; s 1966
1633	*Elgin (11th) and Kincardine (15th), Andrew Douglas Alexander Thomas Bruce, KT; b 1924; s 1968

1452	*Erroll (24th), Merlin Sereld Victor Gilbert Hay; b 1948; s 1978
	Hereditary Lord High Constable and Knight Marischal of Scotland
1623	*Galloway (13th), Randolph Keith Reginald Stewart; b 1928; s 1978
1703	*Glasgow (10th), Patrick Robin Archibald Boyle; b 1939; s 1984
1619	*Haddington (13th), John George Baillie-Hamilton; b 1941; s 1986
1919	Haig (2nd), George Alexander Eugene Douglas Haig, OBE; b 1918; s 1928
1605	*Home (15th), David Alexander Cospatrick Douglas-Home, CVO; b 1943; s 1995
1633	*Kinnoull (15th), Arthur William George Patrick Hay; b 1935; s 1938
1677	*Kintore (13th), Michael Canning William John Keith; b 1939; s 1989
1624	*Lauderdale (17th), Patrick Francis Maitland; b 1911; s 1968
1641	*Leven (14th) and Melville (13th), Alexander Robert Leslie Melville; b 1924; s 1947
1633	*Lindsay (16th), James Randolph Lindesay-Bethune; b 1955; s 1989
1838	Lovelace (5th), Peter Axel William Locke King; b 1951; s 1964
1776 and 1792	Mansfield and Mansfield (8th), William David Mungo James Murray; b 1930; s 1971
1565	*Mar (14th) and Kellie (16th), James Thorne Erskine; b 1949; s 1994
1813	Minto (6th), Gilbert Edward George Lariston Elliot-Murray-Kynynmound, OBE; b 1928; s 1975
1562	*Moray (20th), Douglas John Moray Stuart; b 1928; s 1974
1458	*Morton (22nd), John Charles Sholto Douglas; b 1927; s 1976
1660	*Newburgh (12th), Don Filippo Giambattista Camillo Francesco Aldo Maria Rospigliosi; b 1942; s 1986
1647	*Northesk (14th), David John MacRae Carnegie; b 1954; s 1994
1696	*Orkney (9th), (Oliver) Peter St John; b 1938; s 1998
1605	*Perth (17th), John David Drummond, PC; b 1907; s 1951
1703	*Rosebery (7th), Neil Archibald Primrose; b 1929; s 1974
1457	*Rothes (21st), Ian Lionel Malcolm Leslie; b 1932; s 1975
1701	*Seafield (13th), Ian Derek Francis Ogilvie-Grant; b 1939; s 1969
1646	*Selkirk. Disclaimed for life, 1994, by Rt Hon Lord James Douglas-Hamilton, now Lord Selkirk of Douglas; b 1942
1703	*Stair (14th), John David James Dalrymple; b 1961; s 1996
1606	*Strathmore and Kinghorne (18th), Michael Fergus Bowes Lyon; b 1957; s 1987
1633	*Wemyss (12th) and March (8th), Francis David Charteris, KT; b 1912; s 1937

Countesses in their own right

1643	*Dysart (11th in line), Rosamund Agnes Greaves, b 1914; s 1975
1633	*Loudoun (13th in line), Barbara Huddleston Abney-Hastings; b 1919; s 1960
1115c	*Mar (31st in line), Margaret of Mar; b 1940; s 1975
1235c	*Sutherland (24th in line), Elizabeth Millicent Sutherland; b 1921; s 1963

Viscounts

1642	*of Arbuthnott (16th), John Campbell Arbuthnott, KT, CBE, DSC; b 1924; s 1966
1902	Colville of Culross (4th), John Mark Alexander Colville, QC; b 1933; s 1945
1620	*Falkland (15th), Lucius Edward William Plantagenet Cary; b 1935; s 1984. *Premier Scottish Viscount on the Roll*

1651	*of Oxfuird (13th), George Hubbard Makgill, CBE; b 1934; s 1986
1959	Stuart of Findhorn (3rd), James Dominic Stuart; b 1948; s 1999
1952	Thurso (3rd), John Archibald Sinclair; b 1953; s 1995
1938	Weir (3rd), William Kenneth James Weir; b 1933; s 1975
1923	Younger of Leckie (4th), George Kenneth Hotson Younger, KT, KCVO, TD, PC; b 1931; s 1997

Barons/Lords

1607	*Balfour of Burleigh (8th), Robert Bruce; b 1927; s 1967
1647	*Belhaven and Stenton (13th), Robert Anthony Carmichael Hamilton; b 1927; s 1961
1903	Biddulph (5th), (Anthony) Nicholas Colin Maitland Biddulph; b 1959; s 1988
1452	*Borthwick (24th), John Hugh Borthwick; b 1940; s 1997
1942	Bruntisfield (2nd), John Robert Warrender, OBE, MC, TD; b 1921; s 1993
1948	Clydesmuir (3rd), David Ronald Colville; b 1949; s 1996
1919	Cochrane of Cults (4th), (Ralph Henry) Vere Cochrane; b 1926; s 1990
1509	*Elphinstone (19th), Alexander Mountstuart Elphinstone; b 1980; s 1994
1627	*Fairfax of Cameron (14th), Nicholas John Albert Fairfax; b 1956; s 1964
1445	*Forbes (22nd), Nigel Ivan Forbes, KBE; b 1918; s 1953 *Premier Lord of Scotland*
1917	Forteviot (4th), John James Evelyn Dewar; b 1938; s 1993
1918	Glenarthur (4th), Simon Mark Arthur; b 1944; s 1976
1445	*Gray (22nd), Angus Diarmid Ian Campbell-Gray; b 1931; s 1946
1902	Kinross (5th), Christopher Patrick Balfour; b 1949; s 1985
1458	*Lovat (16th), Simon Fraser; b 1977; s 1995
1914	Lyell (3rd), Charles Lyell; b 1939; s 1943
1776	Macdonald (8th), Godfrey James Macdonald of Macdonald; b 1947; s 1970
1951	Macpherson of Drumochter (2nd), (James) Gordon Macpherson; b 1924; s 1965
1873	Moncreiff (5th), Harry Robert Wellwood Moncreiff; b 1915; s 1942
1627	*Napier (14th) and Ettrick (5th), Francis Nigel Napier, KCVO; b 1930; s 1954
1690	*Polwarth (10th), Henry Alexander Hepburne-Scott, TD; b 1916; s 1944
1932	Rankeillour (4th), Peter St Thomas More Henry Hope; b 1935; s 1967
1628	*Reay (14th), Hugh William Mackay; b 1937; s 1963
1651	*Rollo (14th), David Eric Howard Rollo; b 1943; s 1997
1911	Rowallan (4th), John Polson Cameron Corbett; b 1947; s 1993
1489	*Sempill (21st), James William Stuart Whitemore Sempill; b 1949; s 1995
1449	*Sinclair (17th), Charles Murray Kennedy St Clair, CVO; b 1914; s 1957
1955	Strathclyde (2nd), Thomas Galloway Dunlop du Roy de Blicquy Galbraith, PC; b 1960; s 1985
1564	*Torphichen (15th), James Andrew Douglas Sandilands; b 1946; s 1975

Baronesses/Ladies in their own right

1490	*Herries of Terregles (14th in line), Anne Elizabeth Fitzalan-Howard; b 1938; s 1975
1602	*Kinloss (12th in line), Beatrice Mary Grenville Freeman-Grenville; b 1922; s 1944
1445	*Saltoun (20th in line), Flora Marjory Fraser; b 1930; s 1979
1628	Strange (16th in line), (Jean) Cherry Drummond of Megginch; b 1928; title called out of abeyance, 1986

Life Peers

1974	Balniel, Earl of Crawford and Balcarres. *See Earls.*
1977	Cameron of Lochbroom, Kenneth John Cameron, PC; b 1931
1981	Campbell of Alloway, Alan Robertson Campbell, QC; b 1917
1974	Campbell of Croy, Gordon Thomas Calthrop Campbell, MC, PC; b 1921
1996	Clyde, James John Clyde, b 1932
1980	Emslie, George Carlyle Emslie, MBE, PC; b 1919
2000	Erskine of Alloa Tower, Earl of Mar and Kellie
1992	Ewing of Kirkford, Harry Ewing; b 1931
1999	Forsyth of Drumlean, Michael Bruce Forsyth; b 1954
1989	Fraser of Carmyllie, Peter Lovat Fraser, PC, QC; b 1945
1997	Gordon of Strathblane, James Stuart Gordon, CBE; b 1936
1983	Gray of Contin, James (Hamish) Hector Northey Gray, PC; b 1927
1997	Hardie, Andrew Rutherford Hardie, QC, PC; b 1946
1997	Hogg of Cumbernauld, Norman Hogg; b 1938
1995	Hope of Craighead (James Arthur) David Hope, PC; b 1938
1997	Hughes of Woodside, Robert Hughes; b 1932
1987	Irvine of Lairg, Alexander Andrew Mackay Irvine, PC, QC; b 1940
1975	Kirkhill, John Farquharson Smith; b 1930
1991	Laing of Dunphail, Hector Laing; b 1923
1997	Lang of Monkton, Ian Bruce Lang, PC; b 1940
1984	Macaulay of Bragar, Donald Macaulay, QC; b 1933
1976	McCluskey, John Herbert McCluskey; b 1929
1998	Macdonald of Tradeston, Angus John Macdonald, CBE; b 1940
1991	Macfarlane of Bearsden, Norman Somerville Macfarlane, KT; b 1926
1979	Mackay of Clashfern, James Peter Hymers Mackay, PC; b 1927
1995	Mackay of Drumadoon, Donald Sage Mackay, b 1946
1974	Mackie of Benshie, George Yull Mackie, CBE, DSO, DFC; b 1919
2001	Maclennan of Rogart, Robert Adam Ross; b 1936
1997	Monro of Langholm, Hector Monro; b 1922
1994	Nickson, David Wigley Nickson, KBE; b 1929
1990	Pearson of Rannoch, Malcolm Everard MacLaren Pearson; b 1942
1999	Robertson of Port Ellen, George Islay MacNeill Robertson, PC; b 1946
1992	Rodger of Earlsferry, Alan Ferguson Rodger, PC, QC; b 1944
1997	Russell-Johnston, David Russell Russell-Johnston; b 1932
1985	Sanderson of Bowden, Charles Russell Sanderson; b 1933
1997	Selkirk of Douglas, James Alexander Douglas-Hamilton; b 1942
1997	Steel of Aikwood, David Martin Scott Steel, KBE, PC; b 1938
1981	Stodart of Leaston, James Anthony Stodart, PC; b 1916
2001	Sutherland of Houndwood, Stewart Ross Sutherland; b 1941
1977	Thomson of Monifieth, George Morgan Thomson, KT, PC, b 1921
1997	Watson of Invergowrie, Michael Goodall Watson; b 1949
1992	Wilson of Tillyorn, David Clive Wilson, GCMG; b 1934
1992	Younger of Prestwick. *See Viscounts.*

Baronesses

1982	Carnegy of Lour, Elizabeth Patricia Carnegy of Lour; b 1925
1997	Linklater of Butterstone, Veronica Linklater; b 1943
2001	Michie of Gallanach, Janet Rae Michie; b 1934
1995	Smith of Gilmorehill, Elizabeth Margaret Smith; b 1940

The Judiciary

Judges of Court of Session

Lord President and Lord Justice General
Rt Hon Lord Rodger of Earlsferry (Adam Ferguson Rodger), b 1944

Lords of Session
First Division, Inner House
Rt Hon Lord Prosser (William Prosser), b 1934
Rt Hon Lord Cameron of Lochbroom (Kenneth John Cameron), b 1931
Rt Hon Lord Marnoch (Michael Bruce), b 1938

Lords of Session
Second Division, Inner House
Rt Hon Lord Cullen (William Cullen), *Lord Justice Clerk,* b 1935
Rt Hon Hon Lord Kirkwood (Ian Kirkwood), b 1932
Rt Hon Lord Coulsfield (John Cameron), b 1934
Rt Hon Lord MacLean (Ronald MacLean), b 1938
Rt Hon Lord Osborne (Kenneth Osborne), b 1937
Rt Hon Lord Penrose (George Penrose), b 1938

Lords of Session
Outer House
Hon Lord Abernethy (Alistair Cameron), b 1938
Hon Lord Johnston (Alan Johnston), b 1942
Hon Lord Gill (Brian Gill), b 1942
Hon Lord Hamilton (Arthur Hamilton), b 1942
Hon Lord Dawson (Thomas Dawson), b 1948
Hon Lord Macfadyen (Donald Macfadyen), b 1945
Hon Lady Cosgrove (Hazel Aronson), b 1946
Hon Lord Nimmo Smith (William Nimmo Smith), b 1942
Hon Lord Philip (Alexander Philip), b 1942
Hon Lord Kingarth (Derek Emslie), b 1949
Hon Lord Bonomy (Iain Bonomy), b 1946
Hon Lord Eassie (Ronald Mackay), b 1945

Hon Lord Reed (Robert Reed), b 1956
Hon Lord Wheatley (John Wheatley), b 1941
Hon Lady Paton (Ann Paton), b 1952
Hon Lord Carloway (Colin Sutherland), b 1954
Hon Lord Clarke (Matthew Clarke), b 1947
Rt Hon Lord Hardie (Andrew Hardie), b 1946
Rt Hon Lord Mackay of Drumadoon (Donald Mackay), b 1946
Hon Lord McEwan (Robin McEwan), b 1943
Hon Lord Menzies (Duncan Menzies), b 1953
Hon Lord Drummond Young (James Drummond Young), b 1950

Sheriffs

Grampian, Highland and Islands
Sir Stephen Young, *Sheriff Principal*

Aberdeen and Stonehaven
A S Jessop
A Pollock
Mrs A M Cowan
C J Harris, QC
P M Bowman
G K Buchanan

Peterhead and Banff
K A McLernan
D J Cusine

Elgin
I A Cameron

Inverness, Lochmaddy, Portree, Stornoway, Dingwall, Tain, Wick and Dornoch
W J Fulton
D Booker-Milburn
J O A Fraser
D O Sutherland

Kirkwall and Lerwick
C S Mackenzie

Fort William
W D Small (also *Oban*)

Tayside, Central and Fife
R A Dunlop, QC, *Sheriff Principal*

Arbroath and Forfar
K A Veal
C N R Stein

Dundee
R A Davidson
A L Stewart, QC
J P Scott
G J Evans (also *Cupar*)
P P Davies
F R Crowe

Falkirk
A V Sheehan
A J Murphy
C Caldwell

Perth
M J Fletcher
J K Tierney
D Pyle
L D R Foulis

Stirling
Hon R E G Younger
W Robertson
W M Reid

Alloa
W M Reid

Cupar
G J Evans (also Dundee)

Dunfermline
J S Forbes
G W M Liddle
Mrs I G McColl
R J Macleod
N C Stewart

Kirkcaldy
F J Keane
Mrs L G Patrick
B G Donald

Lothian and Borders
C G B Nicholson, QC, *Sheriff Principal*

Edinburgh
R G Craik, QC (also *Peebles*)
Miss I A Poole
R J D Scott (also *Peebles*)
A M Bell
J M S Horsburgh, QC
G W S Presslie (also *Haddington*)
J A Farrell
A Lothian
I D MacPhail, QC
C N Stoddart
M McPartlin
J D Allan
N M P Morrison, QC
Miss M M Stephen

Mrs M L E Jarvie, QC
Mrs K E C Mackie
N J MacKinnon
D W M McIntyre

Peebles
R G Craik, QC (also *Edinburgh*)
R J D Scott (also *Edinburgh*)

Linlithgow
H R MacLean
G R Fleming
P Gillam
W D Muirhead

Haddington
G W S Presslie (also *Edinburgh*)

Jedburgh and Duns
T A K Drummond, QC

North Strathclyde
B A Kerr, QC, *Sheriff Principal*

Oban
W D Small (also *Fort William*)

Dumbarton
J T Fitzsimons
T Scott
S W H Fraser

Paisley
J Spy
C K Higgins
N Douglas
D J Pender
W Dunlop
G C Kavanagh (also *Campbeltown*)
Mrs I S McDonald

Greenock
J P Herald (also *Rothesay*)
V Canavan
Mrs R Swanney

Kilmarnock
T M Croan
D B Smith
T F Russell
Mrs I S Donald

Dunoon
Mrs C M A F Gimblett

Campbeltown
W Dunlop (also *Paisley*)

Rothesay
J P Herald (also *Greenock*)

Glasgow and Strathkelvin
E F Bowen, QC, *Sheriff Principal*

Glasgow
B Kearney
B A Lockhart
Mrs A L A Duncan
A C Henry
J K Mitchell
A G Johnston
Miss S A O Raeburn, QC
D Convery
I A S Peebles, QC
C W McFarlane, QC
K M Maciver
H Matthews, QC
J A Baird
Miss R E A Rae, QC
A W Noble
J D Friel
Mrs D M MacNeill, QC
J A Taylor
C A L Scott
S Cathcart
Ms L M Ruxton
I H L Miller
Mrs F L Reith
W J Totten
M G O'Grady

South Strathclyde, Dumfries and Galloway
J C McInnes, QC, *Sheriff Principal*

Hamilton
L Cameron
D C Russell
W E Gibson
J H Stewart
Miss J Powie
H S Neilson
S C Pender

Lanark
Ms N C Stewart

Ayr
N Gow, QC
J McGowan
C B Miller

Stranraer and Kirkcudbright
J R Smith

Dumfries
K G Barr
K A Ross

Airdrie
R H Dickson
I C Simpson
J C Morris, QC

The Churches

Church of Scotland
Moderator 2001: Rt Rev John Miller, b 1941
Moderator Designate: Rev Finlay Macdonald, b 1945

Free Church of Scotland
Moderator 2001: Rev William M Mackay, b 1934
Moderator Designate: Rev John Maclean, b 1946

United Free Church of Scotland
Moderator 2001: Rev A M Ford, b 1954
Moderator Designate: Rev Colin Brown, b 1954

Free Presbyterian Church of Scotland
Moderator 2001: Rev Donald J MacDonald, b 1931
Moderator Designate: not yet selected

Roman Catholic Church
Archbishops
St Andrews and Edinburgh Most Rev Keith Patrick O'Brien, b 1938
Glasgow Most Rev Mario Conti, b 1934

Bishops
Aberdeen vacant
Argyll and the Isles Rt Rev Ian Murray, b 1932
Dunkeld Rt Rev Vincent Logan, b 1941
Galloway Rt Rev Maurice Taylor, b 1926
Motherwell Rt Rev Joseph Devine, b 1937
Paisley Rt Rev John A Mone, b 1929

Scottish Episcopal Church
Bishops
Edinburgh Rt Rev Brian Smith, b 1943
Aberdeen and Orkney Most Rev Andrew Bruce Cameron (Primus), b 1941
Argyll and the Isles Rt Rev Douglas MacLean Cameron, b 1935
Brechin Rt Rev Neville Chamberlain, b 1939
Glasgow and Galloway Rt Rev Dr Idris Jones, b 1943
Moray, Ross and Caithness Rt Rev John Michael Crook, b 1940
St Andrews, Dunkeld and Dunblane Rt Rev Michael Harry George Henley, b 1938

Chiefs of Clans and Names

*denotes living outside Scotland

Agnew Sir Crispin Agnew of Lochnaw, Bt, QC

Anstruther Sir Ralph Anstruther of that Ilk, Bt, GCVO, MC

Arbuthnott Viscount of Arbuthnott, KT, CBE, DSC

Barclay *Peter C Barclay of Towie Barclay and of that Ilk

Borthwick Lord Borthwick

Boyd *Lord Kilmarnock

Boyle Earl of Glasgow

Brodie Ninian Brodie of Brodie

Bruce Earl of Elgin and Kincardine, KT

Buchan David S Buchan

Burnett J C A Burnett of Leys

Cameron Sir Donald Cameron of Lochiel, KT, CVO, TD

Campbell Duke of Argyll

Carmichael Richard J Carmichael of Carmichael

Carnegie Duke of Fife

Cathcart Earl Cathcart

Charteris Earl of Wemyss and March, KT

Clan Chattan *M K Mackintosh of Clan Chattan

Chisholm *Hamish Chisholm of Chisholm (The Chisholm)

Cochrane Earl of Dundonald

Colquhoun Sir Ivar Colquhoun of Luss

Cranstoun David A S Cranstoun of that Ilk

Crichton vacant

Cumming Sir William Cumming of Altyre, Bt

Darroch *Captain Duncan Darroch of Gourock

Davidson *Alister G Davidson of Davidston

Dewar Michael Dewar of that Ilk and Vogrie

Drummond Earl of Perth, PC

Dunbar *Sir James Dunbar of Mochrum, Bt

Dundas *David D Dundas of Dundas

Durie Andrew Durie of Durie, CBE

Elliott Mrs Margaret Eliott of Redheugh

Erskine Earl of Mar and Kellie

Farquharson Captain A Farquharson of Invercauld, MC

Fergusson Sir Charles Fergusson of Kilkerran, Bt

Forbes Lord Forbes, KBE

Forsyth Alistair Forsyth of that Ilk

Fraser Lady Saltoun

Fraser (of Lovat) Lord Lovat

Gayre R Gayre of Gayre and Nigg

Gordon Marquess of Huntly

Graham Duke of Montrose

Grant Lord Strathspey

Grierson *Sir Michael Grierson of Lag, Bt

Haig Earl Haig, OBE

Haldane Martin Haldane of Gleneagles

Hannay Ramsey Hannay of Kirkdale and of that Ilk

Hay *Earl of Erroll

Henderson *John Henderson of Fordell

Hunter *Pauline Hunter of Hunterston

Irvine of Drum David C Irvine of Drum

Jardine *Sir Alexander Jardine of Applegirth, Bt

Johnstone Earl of Annandale and Hartfell

Keith Earl of Kintore

Kennedy Marquess of Ailsa

Kerr Marquess of Lothian, KCVO

Kincaid *Arabella Kincaid of Stoneyeld

Lamont *Peter N Lamont of that Ilk

Leask *Madam Leask of Leask

Lennox *Edward J H Lennox of that Ilk

Leslie *Earl of Rothes

Lindsay Earl of Crawford and Balcarres, KT, PC

Lockhart Angus H Lockhart of the Lee

Lumsden *Gillem Lumsden of that Ilk and Blanerne

MacAlester *William St J S McAlester of Loup and Kennox

McBain *J H McBain of McBain

Macdonald Lord Macdonald (The Macdonald of Macdonald)

Macdonald of Clanranald Ranald A Macdonald of Clanranald

Macdonald of Sleat (Clan Husteain) *Sir Ian M Macdonald of Sleat, Bt

MacDonell of Glengarry Ranald MacDonell of Glengarry

MacDougall vacant

Macdowall *Fergus D H Macdowall of Garthland

MacGregor Sir Gregor MacGregor of MacGregor, Bt

MacIntyre *James W MacIntyre of Glenoe

Mackay *Lord Reay

Mackenzie Earl of Cromartie

Mackinnon *Madam Anne Mackinnon of Mackinnon

Mackintosh The Mackintosh of Mackintosh

MacLaren Donald MacLaren of MacLaren and Achleskine

Maclean Hon Sir Lachlan Maclean of Duart, Bt, CVO

MacLennan Ruaraidh MacLennan of MacLennan

MacLeod John MacLeod of MacLeod

MacMillan George MacMillan of MacMillan

Macnab J C Macnab of Macnab *(The Macnab)*

Macnaghten *Sir Patrick Macnaghten of Macnaghten and Dundarave, Bt

Macneacail *Iain Macneacail of Macneacail and Scorrybreac

MacNeil of Barra Ian R Macneil of Barra *(The Macneil of Barra)*

Macpherson Hon Sir William Macpherson of Cluny, TD

MacTavish E S Dugald MacTavish of Dunardry

MacThomas Andrew P C MacThomas of Finegand

Maitland Earl of Lauderdale

Makgill *Viscount of Oxfuird

Malcolm (MacCallum) Robin N L Malcolm of Poltalloch

Mar *Countess of Mar

Marjoribanks Andrew Marjoribanks of that Ilk

Matheson *Major Sir Fergus Matheson of Matheson, Bt

Menzies David R Menzies of Menzies

Moffat *Madam Moffat of that Ilk

Moncreiffe Peregrine Moncreiffe of Moncreiffe

Montgomerie *Earl of Eglinton and Winton

Morrison *Dr Iain M Morrison of Ruchdi

Munro Hector W Munro of Foulis

Murray Duke of Atholl

Nesbitt (or Nisbet) *Robert Nesbitt of that Ilk

Nicolson *Lord Carnock

Ogilvy Earl of Airlie, KT, GCVO, PC

Ramsay Earl of Dalhousie

Rattray James S Rattray of Rattray

Riddell *Sir John Riddell of Riddell, CB, CVO

Robertson *Alexander G H Robertson of Struan

Rollo Lord Rollo

Rose Miss Elizabeth Rose of Kilravock

Ross David C Ross of that Ilk and Balnagowan

Ruthven *Earl of Gowrie PC

Scott Duke of Buccleuch and Queensberry, KT, VRD

Scrymgeour Earl of Dundee

Sempill Lord Sempill

Shaw John Shaw of Tordarroch

Sinclair *Earl of Caithness

Skene Danus Skene of Skene

Stirling *Fraser J Stirling of Cader

Strange *Major Timothy Strange of Balcaskie

Sutherland Countess of Sutherland

Swinton *John Swinton of that Ilk

Trotter Alexander Trotter of Mortonhall

Urquhart *Kenneth T Urquhart of Urquhart

Wallace Ian F Wallace of that Ilk

Wedderburn of that Ilk The Master of Dundee

Wemyss David Wemyss of that Ilk

Prominent People

Sovereigns

c 843–58	Kenneth I
858–62	Donald I
862–77	Constantine I
877–88	Aed
878–89	Giric
	Eochaid
889–900	Donald II
900–943	Constantine II
943–54	Malcolm I
954–62	Indulf
962–66	Dubh
966–71	Culen
971–95	Kenneth II
995–97	Constantine III
?997–1005	Kenneth III
	Giric?
1005–34	Malcolm II
1034–40	Duncan I
1040–57	Macbeth
1057–58	Lulach
1058–93	Malcolm III
1093–94	Donald III
1094	Duncan II
1094–97	Donald III (restored)
1097–1107	Edgar
1107–24	Alexander I
1124–53	David I
1153–65	Malcolm IV
1165–1214	William I
1214–49	Alexander II
1249–86	Alexander III
1286–90	Margaret
1290–92	interregnum
1292–96	John
1296–1306	interregnum
1306–29	Robert I
1329–71	David II
1371–90	Robert II
1390–1406	Robert III
1406–37	James I
1437–60	James II
1460–88	James III
1488–1513	James IV
1513–42	James V
1542–67	Mary I
1567–1625	James VI
1625–49	Charles I
1649–85	Charles II (exiled 1651–60)
1685–89	James VII
{1689–1702	William II
1689–94	Mary II}
1702–07	Anne

Secretary of State for Scotland

Holders of the office, and its predecessor titles, since 1707

Secretary of State, Scottish Department

1707	Earl of Loudon and Earl of Mar
1707	Duke of Queensberry, until his death in 1711
1713	Earl of Mar, again
1714	Duke of Montrose
1716	Duke of Roxburghe, until 1725
1741	Marquess of Tweeddale, until 1746

Secretary for Scotland

1885	Duke of Richmond and Gordon, KG
1886	G O Trevelyan (later Sir G O Trevelyan, Bt)
1886	Earl of Dalhousie, KT
1886	A J Balfour (later Earl of Balfour)
1887	Marquess of Lothian
1892	Sir G O Trevelyan, Bt, again
1895	Lord Balfour of Burleigh
1903	A Graham Murray (later Viscount Dunedin)
1905	2 Feb Marquess of Linlithgow, KT, GCVO, GCMG
1905	10 Dec J Sinclair (later Lord Pentland)
1912	T McKinnon Wood
1916	9 Jul H J Tennant
1916	10 Dec R Munro (later Lord Alness)
1922	Viscount Novar, GCMG
1924	22 Jan W Adamson
1924	6 Nov Sir John Gilmour, Bt, DSO

Secretary of State for Scotland

1926	Sir John Gilmour, Bt, DSO
1929	W Adamson

1931	Sir Archibald Sinclair, Bt, CMG (later Viscount Thurso)
1932	Sir Godfrey Collins
1936	Walter E Elliot, MC
1938	D J Colville (later Lord Clydesmuir)
1940	Ernest Brown, MC
1941	Thomas Johnston
1945	25 May Earl of Rosebery, DSO, MC
1945	3 Aug Joseph Westwood
1947	Arthur Woodburn
1950	Hector McNeil
1951	James Stuart, MVO, MC (later Viscount Stuart of Findhorn)
1957	John S Maclay, CH, CMG (later Viscount Muirshiel)
1962	Michael A C Noble (later Lord Glenkinglas)
1964	William Ross, MBE (later Lord Ross of Marnock)
1970	Gordon T C Campbell, MC (later Lord Campbell of Croy)
1974	William Ross, MBE (later Lord Ross of Marnock)
1976	Bruce Millan
1979	George Younger, TD (later Viscount Younger of Leckie, KT)
1986	Malcolm Rifkind (later Sir Malcolm Rifkind, KCMG)
1990	Ian Lang (later Lord Lang of Monkton)
1995	Michael Forsyth (later Sir Michael Forsyth)
1997	Donald Dewar
1999	John Reid
2001	Helen Liddell

Lord Advocate

Holders of the office since 1709

1709	Sir David Dalrymple of Hailes, Bt
1711	Sir James Stewart
1714	Thomas Kennedy
1714	Sir David Dalrymple of Hailes, Bt
1720	Robert Dundas, yr, of Arniston
1725	Duncan Forbes of Culloden
1737	Charles Erskine of Tinwald
1742	Robert Craigie of Glendoick
1746	William Grant of Prestongrange
1754	Robert Dundas of Arniston
1760	Thomas Miller of Barskimming and Glenlee
1766	James Montgomery of Stanhope
1775	Henry Dundas
1783	Henry Erskine
1784	Hay Campbell of Succoth
1789	Robert Dundas of Arniston
1801	Charles Hope of Granton
1804	Sir James Montgomery, Bt
1806	Henry Erskine
1807	Archibald Campbell (afterwards Colquhoun)
1816	Alexander Maconochie
1819	Sir William Rae, Bt
1830	Francis Jeffrey
1834	John Archibald Murray
1834	Sir William Rae, Bt
1835	John Archibald Murray
1839	Andrew Rutherfurd
1841	Sir William Rae, Bt
1842	Duncan McNeill
1846	Andrew Rutherfurd
1851	James Moncreiff
1852	Adam Anderson
1852	John Inglis
1853	James Moncreiff
1858	John Inglis of Glencorse
1858	Charles Baillie
1859	David Mure
1859	James Moncreiff
1866	George Patton
1867	Edward Strathearn Gordon
1868	James Moncreiff
1869	George Young
1874	Edward Strathearn Gordon
1876	William Watson
1880	John McLaren
1881	John Blair Balfour
1885	John Hay Athole Macdonald
1886	John Blair Balfour
1886	John Hay Athole Macdonald
1888	James Patrick Bannerman Robertson
1891	Sir Charles John Pearson
1892	John Blair Balfour
1895	Sir Charles John Pearson
1896	Andrew Graham Murray
1903	Charles Scott Dickson
1905	Thomas Shaw
1909	Alexander Ure
1913	Robert Munro
1916	James Avon Clyde
1920	Thomas Brash Morison
1922	Charles David Murray
1922	Hon William Watson
1924	Hugh Pattison Macmillan
1924	Hon William Watson

1929   Alexander Munro MacRobert
1929   Craigie Mason Aitchison
1933   Wilfred Guild Normand
1935   Douglas Jamieson
1935   Thomas Mackay Cooper
1941   James Scott Cumberland Reid
1945   George Reid Thomson
1947   John Wheatley
1951   James Latham McDiarmid Clyde
1955   William Rankine Milligan
1960   William Grant
1962   Ian Hamilton Shearer
1964   George Gordon Stott
1967   Henry Stephen Wilson
1970   Norman Russell Wylie
1974   Ronald King Murray
1979   James Peter Hymer Mackay
1984   Kenneth John Cameron
1989   Peter Lovat Fraser
1992   Alan Ferguson Rodger
1995   Donald S Mackay
1997   Andrew Hardie
2000   Colin Boyd

Solicitor General for Scotland

Holders of the office since 1960

1960   David Colville Anderson
1964   Norman Russell Wylie
1964   James Graham Leechman
1965   Henry Stephen Wilson
1967   Ewan George Francis Stewart
1970   David William Robert Brand
1972   William Ian Stewart
1974   John Herbert McCluskey
1979   Nicholas Hardwick Fairbairn
1982   Peter Lovat Fraser
1989   Alan Ferguson Rodger
1992   Thomas Cordner Dawson
1995   Donald S Mackay
1997   Colin D Boyd
2000   Neil Davidson
2001   Elish Angiolini

Queen's Counsel

Holders of the office at present
Douglas Reith (1957); D M Walker (1958); Sir Frederick O'Brien (1960); Neil Macvicar (1960); G S Gimson (1961); A A Bell (1961); Isabel L Sinclair (1964); R D Ireland (1964); A M G Russell (1965); J G Mitchell (1970); James Law (1970); Neil Gow (1970); W M Walker (1971); Gavin Douglas (1971); G H Gordon (1972); W G Stevenson (1973); D B Robertson (1973); T G Coutts (1973); Professor John Murray (1974); Rt Hon Lord Macaulay of Bragar (1975); William C Galbraith (1977); N J Adamson (1979); J M S Horsburgh (1980); Ian R Hamilton (1980); R G Craik (1981); R E Henderson (1982); A G C McGregor (1982); C N McEachran (1982); Rt Hon W M Campbell (1982); Rt Hon Lord Fraser of Carmyllie (1982); C P C Boag-Thomson (1982); P K Vandore (1982); C G B Nicholson (1982); H H Campbell (1983); J F Wallace (1985); C S Haddow (1985); Rt Hon Malcolm L Rifkind (1985); G N H Emslie (1986); R R Dalgety (1986); B A Kerr (1986); W J Taylor (1986); N D MacLeod (1986); T A K Drummond (1987); J L Mitchell (1987); M G Thomson (1987); P H Brodie (1987); Professor Robert Black (1987); W T Hook (1988); A C Horsfall (1988); Angus Stewart (1988); D R Findlay (1988); P G B McNeill (1988); I S Forrester (1988); R F Macdonald (1988); N M P Morrison (1988); J E Drummond Young (1988); R L Martin (1988); J S Mowat (1988); N D Shaffer (1989); E G M Targowski (1989); K N Mure (1989); M S Jones (1989); Douglas May (1989); C W McFarlane (1989); M Lynda Clark (1989); C J MacAulay (1989); I D MacPhail (1990); J C McInnes (1990); J C McCluskie (1990); G R Fleming (1990); C M Campbell (1990); R A Dunlop (1990); W G Jackson (1990); J J Maguire (1990); J W McNeill (1991); A F Wylie (1991); G C Bell (1991); Susan A O Raeburn (1991); D S Burns (1991); D A Y Menzies (1991); M C N Scott (1991); J Irvine Smith (1992); H A Kerrigan (1992); H W Currie (1992); Hugh Matthews (1992); N D Murray (1992); E F Bowen (1992); I G Mitchell (1992); Alexander Bolland (1992); J J Mitchell (1992); Rita E A Rae (1992); D J Risk (1992); C J Harris (1992); I A S Peebles (1993); R S Keen (1993); Anne Smith (1993); D I Mackay (1993); J Gordon Reid (1993); A B Wilkinson (1993); E Prais (1993); N F Davidson (1993); W S Gale (1993); G L Cox (1993);

S N Brailsford (1994); Leeona J Dorrian (1994); A M Hajducki (1994); J A Peoples (1994); I R Abercrombie (1994); Deirdre M MacNeill (1994); C D Boyd (1995); Elizabeth Jarvie (1995); Sir Crispin Agnew (1995); A P Campbell (1995); P B Cullen (1995); A L Stewart (1995); Earl of Ancram (1996); P S Hodge (1996); J N Wright (1996); G R Steele (1996); A D Turnbull (1996); Fiona L Reith (1996); J C Morris (1996); Rt Hon Lord Selkirk of Douglas (1996); J R Doherty (1997); T Welsh (1997); J R Campbell (1997); J R Wallace (1997); G J Davidson (1997); G J B Moynihan (1997); I D Truscott (1997); J D Campbell (1998); Mungo Bovey (1998); Frances J McMenamin (1998); Susan J O'Brien (1998); D W Batchelor (1998); C J Tyre (1998); S E Woolman (1998); A J S Glennie (1998); R A Smith (1999); R Gilmour Ivey (1999); J G Sturrock (1999); A M O'Neill (1999); Valerie E Stacey (1999); M G O'Grady (1999); D A Ogg (1999); Ruth A Anderson (1999); P J Layden (2000), J M W Thomson (2000), I G Armstrong (2000), Marion A Caldwell (2000), R B M Howie (2000), Scott Brady (2000), I W F Ferguson (2000), I M Duguid (2000), P G McBride (2000), R W J Anderson (2000), Laurence Murphy (2000), D P Sellar (2000).

Moderator, General Assembly, Church of Scotland

Holders of the office since 1980
William B Johnston, Edinburgh Colinton, 1980; Andrew B Doig, National Bible Society of Scotland, 1981; John McIntyre, CVO, University of Edinburgh, 1982; J Fraser McLuskey, MC, London St Columba's, 1983; John M K Paterson, Milngavie St Paul's, 1984; David M B A Smith, Logie, 1985; Robert Craig, CBE, Emeritus of Jerusalem, 1986; Duncan Shaw, JP, Edinburgh Craigentinny St Christopher's, 1987; James A Whyte, University of St Andrews, 1988; William J G McDonald, Edinburgh Mayfield, 1989; Robert Davidson, University of Glasgow, 1990; William B R Macmillan, Dundee St Mary's, 1991; Hugh Wyllie, Hamilton

Old, 1992; James L Weatherhead, Principal Clerk of Assembly, 1993; James A Simpson, Dornoch Cathedral, 1994; James Harkness, CB, OBE, Chaplain General (Emeritus), 1995; John H McIndoe, London: St Columba's lw Newcastle: St Andrew's, 1996; Alexander McDonald, General Secretary, Board of Ministry, 1997; Rev Professor Alan Main, University of Aberdeen, 1998; Rev John B Cairns, Dumbarton Riverside, 1999; Rev Dr Andrew McLellan, St Andrew's and St George's, Edinburgh, 2000; Rt Rev John Miller, Castlemilk East, 2001

Royal Scottish Academy

Holders of offices at present
Senior Academicians: William J.L. Baillie, CBE; Ellen Malcolm; R Ross Robertson; Sir Anthony Wheeler, OBE.
Academicians: Elizabeth Blackadder, OBE; Gordon Bryce; Dennis Buchan; Frederick Bushe, OBE; Vincent Butler; Joyce Cairns; Alexander Campbell; Peter Collins; George Donald; David Evans; Alexander Fraser; Jake Harvey; John Houston, OBE; Ian Howard; Jack Knox; William Littlejohn; William Maclean; Andrew MacMillan, OBE; Andrew Merrylees; Isi Metzstein; David Michie, OBE; James Morris; James Morrison; Frances Pelly; Frank Pottinger; Barbara Rae; Philip Reeves; Stuart Renton, MBE; John Richards, CBE; James D Robertson; Bill Scott; Duncan Shanks; Ian McKenzie Smith, OBE; Michael Snowden; Robert R Steedman, OBE; Frances Walker
Senior Associates: A Buchanan Campbell; Derek Clarke; Earl Haig; Bet Low; Geoffrey Squire; George Wyllie
Associates: James Fairgrieve; John G Clifford; Kirkland Main; William Brotherston; Alastair Ross; Iain R McIntosh; Michael Docherty; John Mooney; Glen Onwin; Douglas Cocker; Arthur Watson; Roland Wedgwood; John Busby; Victoria Crowe; George MacPherson; Andrew Stenhouse; Ian Arnott; Fiona Dean; Ian McCulloch; Robert Black; Beth Fisher; Willie Rodger; Lennox Dunbar; Elspeth Lamb; Sylvia

Wishart; David Page; Frank Convery; Adrian Wiszniewski; Martin Rayner; Robin Webster; Alfons Bytautas; Ronald Forbes; Edward Summerton; Ric W L Russell; Stuart Duffin; Eileen Lawrence; Gordon Mitchell; Richard Murphy; Marion Smith

Chairmen, Royal Fine Art Commission

Sir John M Stirling-Maxwell, 1927-32
Lord Hamilton of Dalzell, 1932-52
Rt Hon Earl of Rosebery, 1952-56
Sir Hector Hetherington, 1957-65
Hon Lord Johnston, 1965-78
Professor Sir Robert Grieve, 1978-83
Professor A J Youngson, 1983-90
Hon Lord Prosser, 1990-95
Rt Hon Lord Cameron of Lochbroom, since 1995

Fellows, Scottish Council for Development and Industry

Sir Kenneth Alexander, 1991; P E G Balfour, CBE, 1991; Professor C Blake, CBE, 1992; Hon J M E Bruce, CBE, 1993; Campbell Christie, 1998; Ian Christie, 1997; Sir William Coats, 1985; A R Cole-Hamilton, CBE, 1995; Sir James Duncan, 1992; Dr T L Johnston, 1990; J Langan, 1987; Sir William Lithgow, Bt, 1985; I H Macdonald, OBE, 1991; Sir James Marjoribanks, KCMG, 1985; Sir Donald McCallum, CBE, 1993; Duncan McPherson, CBE, 1991; George Menzies, 1999; W C C Morrison, CBE, 1993; Brian Nicholls, 1997; Rt Hon Lord Polwarth, TD, DL, 1985; Dr Ian Preston, CBE, 1999; D S Reid, OBE, 1985; Dr W S Robertson, CBE, 1985; D A Ross Stewart, OBE, 1990; Lord Taylor of Gryfe, DL, 1985; Rt Hon Viscount Younger of Leckie, KCVO, TD, 2000

Astronomers Royal for Scotland

Thomas Henderson, 1834-44
Charles Piazzi Smyth, 1846-88
Ralph Copeland, 1889-1905
Sir Frank Watson Dyson, 1905-10
Ralph Allen Sampson, 1910-37

Michael Greaves, 1938-55
Hermann Alexander Brück, 1957-75
Vincent Cartledge Reddish, 1975-80
Malcolm Sim Longair, 1980-90
Title in abeyance, 1991-95
John Campbell Brown, 1995-

Presidents, National Trust for Scotland

Since foundation in 1931
Duke of Atholl
Sir John Stirling Maxwell
Earl of Wemyss and March
Marquis of Bute
Duke of Atholl
Earl of Airlie

Presidents, Royal College of Surgeons of Edinburgh

Holders of the office since 1861

1861	Patrick Small Keir Newbigging
1863	Benjamin Bell
1865	James Dunsmure
1867	James Spence
1869	James Donaldson Gillespie
1871	William Walker
1873	James Simson
1875	Sir Henry Duncan Littlejohn
1877	Sir Patrick Heron Watson
1879	Francis Brodie Imlach
1882	Sir William Turner
1883	John Smith
1885	Douglas Moray Cooper Lamb Argyll Robertson
1887	Joseph Bell
1889	John Duncan
1891	Robert James Blair Cunynghame
1893	Peter Hume Maclaren
1895	Sir John Struthers
1897	John Chiene
1899	James Dunsmure
1901	Sir John Halliday Croom
1903	Sir Patrick Heron Watson
1905	Charles Watson MacGillivray
1907	Sir Joseph Montagu Cotterill
1910	Sir George Andreas Berry
1912	Francis Mitchell Caird
1914	Sir James William Beeman Hodson
1917	Robert McKenzie Johnston
1919	George Mackay
1921	Sir David Wallace
1923	Sir Harold Jalland Stiles

1925	Arthur Logan Turner
1927	Alexander Miles
1929	James Haig Ferguson
1931	John Wheeler Dowden
1933	Arthur Henry Havens Sinclair
1935	Sir Henry Wade
1937	William James Stuart
1939	Harry Moss Traquair
1941	John William Struthers
1943	Robert William Johnstone
1945	James Methuen Graham
1947	Francis Evelyn Jardine
1949	Walter Quarry Wood
1951	Sir Walter Mercer
1957	Sir John Bruce
1962	James Johnston Mason Brown
1964	George Ian Scott
1967	James Roderick Johnston Cameron
1970	Sir Donald Douglas
1973	James Alexander Ross
1976	Andrew Wood Wilkinson
1979	Francis John Gillingham
1982	Sir James David Fraser
1985	Thomas Jaffrey McNair
1988	Geoffrey Duncan Chisholm
1991	Patrick Stewart Boulter
1994	Sir Robert Shields
1997	Arnold G D Maran
2000	John Temple

Presidents, Royal College of Physicians of Edinburgh

Holders of the office since 1937

1937	Alexander Goodall
1940	Charles McNeil
1943	Andrew Fergus Hewat
1945	David Murray Lyon
1947	William Douglas Denton Small
1949	David Kennedy Henderson, Kt
1951	William Alister Alexander
1953	Leybourne Stanley Patrick Davidson, Kt
1957	Andrew Rae Gilchrist
1960	James Davidson Stuart Cameron
1963	Ian George Wilson Hill, Kt
1966	Christopher William Clayson
1970	John Halliday Croom
1973	John Wenman Crofton, Kt
1976	Ronald Foote Robertson
1979	John Anderson Strong
1982	Ronald Haxton Girdwood
1985	Michael Francis Oliver
1988	John Richmond

1991	Anthony Toft
1994	John D Cash
1997	James C Petrie
2001	Dr Niall D C Finlayson

Presidents, Royal College of Physicians and Surgeons of Glasgow

Holders of the office since 1937

1937	John Henderson
1939	John Souttar McKendrick
1940	Roy Frew Young
1942	James Hogg MacDonald
1944	William Alexander Sewell
1946	Geoffrey Balmanno Fleming
1948	William Robertson Snodgrass
1950	Walter Weir Galbraith
1952	Andrew Allison
1954	Stanley Galbraith Graham
1956	Stanley Alstead
1958	Arthur Henry Jacobs
1960	Joseph Houston Wright
1962	Sir Charles Illingworth
1964	Archibald Brown Kerr
1966	James Holmes Hutchison
1968	Sir Robert Brash Wright
1970	Edward McCombie McGirr
1972	Sir Andrew Watt Kay
1974	Sir Ferguson Anderson
1976	Thomas Gibson
1978	Gavin Brown Shaw
1980	Douglas H Clark
1982	Thomas J Thomson
1984	Ian A MacGregor
1986	Arthur C Kennedy
1988	James McArthur
1990	Robert Hume
1992	Sir Donald Campbell
1994	Norman MacKay
1997	Colin MacKay
2000	Professor A Ross Lorimer

St Andrews University

Principals since 1859

1859	Sir David Brewster
1859	John Tulloch
1886	Sir James Donaldson
1915	Sir John Herkless
1921	Sir James Colquhoun Irvine
1953	Sir Thomas Malcolm Knox
1966	John Steven Watson
1986	Professor Struther Arnott
2001	Dr Brian Lang

Glasgow University

Principals since 1858
1858 Thomas Barclay
1873 John Caird
1898 Robert Herbert Story
1907 Sir Donald MacAlister of Tarbert
1929 Sir Robert Sangster Rait
1936 Sir Hector James Wright Hetherington
1961 Sir Charles Haynes Wilson
1976 Alywn Williams
1988 Sir William Fraser
1995 Sir Graeme Davies

Edinburgh University

Principals since 1859
1859 Sir David Brewster
1868 Sir Alexander Grant
1885 Sir William Muir
1903 Sir William Turner
1916 Sir James Ewing
1929 Sir Thomas Holland
1944 Sir John Fraser
1948 Sir Edward Appleton
1965 Sir Michael Swann
1974 Professor Sir Hugh Robson
1979 Sir John Burnett
1987 Sir David Smith
1994 Lord Sutherland of Houndwood

Aberdeen University

Principals since 1860
1860 Peter Colin Campbell
1876 William Robertson Pirie
1885 William Duguid Geddes
1900 John Marshall Lang
1909 George Adam Smith
1935 William Hamilton Fyfe
1948 Thomas Murray Taylor
1962 Edward Maitland Wright
1976 Fraser Noble
1981 George Paul McNicol
1991 John Maxwell Irvine
1996 C Duncan Rice

Strathclyde University

Principals
1964 Sir Samuel Curran
1980 Sir Graham Hills
1991 Sir John Arbuthnott
2001 Professor Andrew Hamnett

Stirling University

Principals
1965 Dr Tom Cottrell
1975 Dr William Cramond
1981 Sir Kenneth Alexander
1986 Professor A J Forty
1994 Professor A Miller
2001 Professor Colin Bell

Heriot-Watt University

Principals
1966 Dr Hugh B Nisbet
1968 Dr Robert A Smith
1974 Professor George M Burnett
1981 Dr Thomas L Johnston
1989 Professor Alistair G J MacFarlane
1997 Professor John S Archer

Dundee University

Principals
1967 James Drever
1978 Adam Matthew Neville
1987 Michael J Hamlin
1994 Dr Ian Graham-Bryce
2000 Sir Alan Langlands

Robert Gordon University

Principals
1992 Dr David Kennedy
1997 Professor William Stevely

Napier University

Principals
1992 Professor William Turmeau
1994 Professor John Mavor

Paisley University

Principals
1992 Professor Richard W Shaw
2001 Professor John Macklin

Glasgow Caledonian University

Principals
1993 Professor J Stanley Mason
1998 Dr Ian Johnston

University of Abertay Dundee

Principal
1994 Professor Bernard King

Compendium

Almanac

January

1	James Stuart (Old Pretender) died 1766
	Glasgow Chamber of Commerce incorporated 1783
2	Ibrox Park disaster, 66 supporters killed, 1971
3	O H Mavor (James Bridie) born 1888
7	Glasgow University founded 1450
8	Lord Hardie of Blackford, Lord Advocate, born 1946
10	Rod Stewart born 1945
13	Keir Hardie founded Independent Labour Party 1893
17	Compton Mackenzie born 1883
19	James Watt born 1736
20	Benny Lynch crowned world flyweight champion 1937
22	Ramsay MacDonald first Labour Prime Minister 1924
24	First train over Forth Bridge 1890
25	Robert Burns born 1759
27	Glasgow Herald first published 1783
	First public demonstration of TV by John Logie Baird 1926
28	William Burke, body snatcher, executed 1829
29	Greenwich Mean Time adopted by Scotland 1848
31	Charles Edward Stuart died 1788
	Princess Victoria, Stranraer-Larne ferry, sank 1953

February

5	Thomas Carlyle died 1881
8	Mary, Queen of Scots, beheaded 1587
9	Sandy Lyle born 1958
10	Lord Darnley, Mary Stuart's consort, assassinated 1567
11	John Buchan died 1940
13	Massacre of Glencoe 1692
20	James I assassinated 1437
	Gordon Brown, Chancellor of the Exchequer, born 1951
22	Robert II acceded to Scottish throne 1370
24	Flying Scotsman went into service 1923
	Denis Law born 1940
26	Harry Lauder died 1950
28	Robin Cook, Foreign Secretary, born 1946

March

1	Scots voted in favour of devolution, but failed to reach 40% threshhold 1979
3	Alexander Graham Bell born 1847
7	Alexander Graham Bell patented the telephone 1876
9	David Rizzio murdered 1566
11	Alexander Fleming died 1955
13	Clydeside blitz 1941
	Sixteen primary school children and their teacher murdered in Dunblane 1996

14	First television programmes broadcast in Scotland 1952
17	cotland won Grand Slam for first time in 59 years 1984
19	Tobias Smollett born 1721
	David Livingstone born 1813
	Billy Graham began All-Scotland Crusade 1955
24	Crowns of England and Scotland united 1603
25	Bruce crowned king of Scotland 1306
27	First Scotland/England rugby international 1871
31	David Steel born 1938

April

1	Robert III died 1406
2	George MacDonald Fraser born 1925
4	James VII deprived of throne 1689
	John Napier, inventor of logarithms, died 1617
6	Declaration of Arbroath 1320
7	Jim Clark killed in crash 1968
9	Lord Lovat beheaded on Tower Hill for high treason 1747
10	James V born 1512
16	Charles Edward Stuart defeated at Culloden 1746
24	Mary, Queen of Scots, married French dauphin 1558
27	Scots defeated by Edward I at Dunbar 1296
29	Andrew Cruickshank died 1988

May

1	Union of England and Scotland proclaimed 1707
	David Livingstone died 1873
5	Sir Hugh Fraser died 1987
6	Elections for Scottish Parliament 1999
7	David Hume born 1711
9	J M Barrie born 1860
10	Rudolf Hess, Hitler's deputy, descended by parachute into Scotland 1941
12	John Smith died 1994
13	Mary, Queen of Scots, defeated at Battle of Langside 1568
15	Mary, Queen of Scots, married Bothwell 1567
21	James, Marquess of Montrose, died 1650
24	Malcolm IV acceded to Scottish throne 1153
	First circulating library opened in Edinburgh 1726
	Stanley Baxter born 1928
25	John Stuart, Earl of Bute, Britain's first Scottish Prime Minister, born 1713
	Oscar Slater found guilty of murder 1909
	Celtic won European Cup 1967
28	Cheapside docks fire, Glasgow, 19 firemen killed, 1960
29	Peter Manuel sentenced to death at the High Court in Glasgow for seven murders 1958

June

1	Covenanters defeated Claverhouse at Dumclog 1679
	Pope John Paul II in Glasgow 1982
2	Helicopter crash on Mull of Kintyre, 29 anti-terrorism experts killed, 1994

4	Peru defeated Scotland 3-1 in World Cup 1978
5	HMS Hampshire sank off Orkney 1916
	Adam Smith born 1723
7	James Young Simpson born 1811
	Robert the Bruce died 1329
10	James Stuart (Old Pretender) born 1688
11	James III assassinated 1488
	Empress of Britain launched from Clydebank 1930
13	James Clerk Maxwell born 1831
14	John Logie Baird died 1946
16	Mary, Queen of Scots, recognised Philip II of Spain as her heir 1586
	Lord Reith died 1971
17	Articles of religion, introducing Anglican principles into Scottish worship, endorsed by Scottish parliament 1617
19	James VI of Scotland and I of England born 1566
	J M Barrie died 1937
20	New Tay rail bridge opened 1887
21	German fleet scuttled in Scapa Flow 1919
22	Duke of Monmouth subdued insurrection of Covenanters at Bothwell Bridge 1679
23	Mass protest in West of Scotland against closure of John Brown's shipyard 1971
24	Robert the Bruce defeated Edward II at Bannockburn 1314
25	Crofters Act passed 1886
30	Jack McConnell born 1960

July

1	Queen opened new Scottish Parliament 1999
	Craig Brown born 1940
2	Lord Home of the Hirsel born 1903
	Erskine Bridge opened 1971
3	Robert Adam born 1728
	John Logie Baird transmitted first colour television 1928
6	Explosion aboard North Sea oil rig Piper Alpha, 166 lives lost, 1988
7	Kelvin Hall exhibition building, Glasgow, destroyed by fire 1925
	David Steel became Liberal leader 1976
9	Madeleine Smith acquitted of murder 1857
11	Robert the Bruce born 1274
	Eric Liddell won Olympic 400 metres in Paris 1924
12	Sir Alastair Burnet born 1928
13	Scottish Reform Act passed 1868
16	Commonwealth Games opened in Edinburgh 1970
17	Adam Smith died 1790
18	John Smith became Labour leader 1992
20	Lord Reith born 1889
	Oscar Slater's conviction quashed 1928
21	Robert Burns died 1796
	Maurice Lindsay born 1918
	Sandy Lyle won Open Golf Championship 1985

22	English defeated Scots at Battle of Falkirk 1298
23	Charles Edward Stuart landed on Eriskay 1745
24	James VI acceded to Scottish throne 1567
	David Wilkie won Olympic 200 metres breaststroke 1976
25	Annie Ross, singer, born 1930
	Alan Wells won Olympic 100 metres 1980
26	Ill-fated Darien expedition sailed from Scotland 1698
28	Forth and Clyde canal opened 1790
29	Mary, Queen of Scots, married Lord Darnley 1565
	Jo Grimond born 1913

August

3	James II killed 1460
4	Harry Lauder born 1870
5	Wallace captured by the English 1305
6	Sir Alexander Fleming born 1881
11	C M Grieve (Hugh MacDiarmid) born 1892
13	John Logie Baird born 1888
15	Macbeth killed in battle 1057
	Sir Walter Scott born 1771
	Keir Hardie born 1856
17	Royal visit of George IV to Edinburgh began 1822
18	Tay Road Bridge opened 1966
21	Donald Dewar, Scotland's first First Minister, born 1937
23	Wallace executed 1305
25	David Hume died 1776
	James Watt died 1819
	Sean Connery born 1930
	Ramsay MacDonald formed a National Government 1931
27	First balloon ascent in Britain by James Tytler, at Edinburgh, 1784

September

3	Cromwell defeated Scots at Battle of Dunbar 1650
4	Forth Road Bridge opened 1964
5	Robert Fergusson born 1750
9	James IV killed in battle at Flodden 1513
	C M Grieve (Hugh MacDiarmid) died 1978
10	English defeated Scots at Battle of Pinkie 1547
	Mungo Park born 1771
11	James Thomson, author of *Rule Britannia*, born 1700
	Referendum on Scottish Parliament 1997
13	Montrose defeated by Covenanters at Battle of Philiphaugh 1645
	John Smith born 1938
15	Charles Edward Stuart occupied Edinburgh 1745
18	Lord Rodger of Earlsferry, Lord Justice General, born 1944
20	Queen Elizabeth II launched from Clydebank 1966
21	John Home born 1722
	Charles Edward Stuart victorious at Prestonpans 1745
	John McAdam born 1756
22	Viscount Younger of Leckie (George Younger) born 1931
27	Barbara Dickson born 1948

October

2	United Free Church merged with Church of Scotland 1929
4	Boys' Brigade founded in Glasgow 1883
9	Lord Home of the Hirsel died 1995
10	Hugh Miller born 1802
12	Ramsay MacDonald born 1866
13	Allan Ramsay, painter, born 1713
14	German submarine sank Royal Oak in Scapa Flow, 1939
15	Allan Ramsay, poet, born 1686
16	James II born 1430
17	George Mackay Brown born 1921
21	Clarkston Toll disaster, 12 killed, 1971
29	James Boswell born 1740
30	Caledonian Canal opened 1822
31	Alastair Hetherington born 1919

November

1	Bank of Scotland founded 1695
	Naomi Mitchison born 1897
3	Ludovic Kennedy born 1919
8	John Duns Scotus died 1308
	Neil Gunn born 1891
12	Sir James Young Simpson first used chloroform as an anaesthetic 1847
13	Malcolm III killed 1093
	Robert Louis Stevenson born 1850
17	John Baliol acceded to Scottish throne 1292
22	Tom Conti born 1942
24	John Knox died 1572
	Billy Connolly born 1942
25	Andrew Carnegie born 1835
27	Oscar Slater released from prison 1927
	First deaths from E-coli outbreak in Scotland 1996
29	Margaret, Queen of Scotland, born 1489

December

3	Robert Louis Stevenson died 1894
4	Thomas Carlyle born 1795
6	Charles Edward Stuart's entry into Derby 1745
8	Mary, Queen of Scots, born 1542
10	Charles Rennie Mackintosh died 1928
14	Mary, Queen of Scots, acceded to Scottish throne 1542
20	First General Assembly of Church of Scotland ratified Confession of Faith 1560
21	Lockerbie disaster, 270 killed, 1988
23	Hugh Miller died 1856
25	Stone of Destiny removed from Westminster Abbey 1950
26	Sir Alastair Dunnett born 1908
28	Rob Roy died 1734
	Tay Bridge disaster 1879
31	Charles Edward Stuart died 1720
	Alex Salmond born 1954

Awards and Honours

Thistle Awards

Recognises and celebrates excellence in Scottish tourism.

2001 Awards

Large Company Training: Peebles Hotel Hydro
Small Company Training: The Lodge, Carfraemill
Tourism and the Environment: BressaBoats, Shetland
Cultural Tourism: Mercat Tours Ltd.
Travel Journalism: Tom Bruce-Gardyne, Sunday Telegraph articles
Flavour of Scotland: Monachyle Mhor Hotel, Balquhidder
Customer Care, Hotel: Highland Cottage, Tobermory
Customer Care, Guesthouse/BB: East Lochhead Country House, Cottages and Gardens, Lochwinnoch
Customer Care Self-catering: Crosswoodhill Farm Holiday Cottages, West Calder
Customer Care, Camping and Caravan Park: Lomond Woods Holiday Park, Tullichewan, Balloch
Customer Care, Visitor Attraction: Gordon Highlanders Museum, Aberdeen
Area Tourism Initiative: Scottish Borders Tourist Board, Land of Creativity
Individual Excellence Award: Damian Forster, Off Beat Bikes, Fort William
Scotland Year-Round: Scottish Youth Hostels Association, RentaHostel.com
Small Business Marketing Initiative: 5pm.co.uk
Marketing Initiative: British Trust Hotels, Easy Breaks
Business Tourism Initiative: Our Dynamic Earth
IT Initiative: The Big Idea, Irvine
The Silver Thistle: Peter Taylor, Town House Company, Edinburgh

Beautiful Scotland in Bloom

2001 Awards

Premier Awards

The Rosebowl: Aberdeen
Rosebowl Reserve Trophy: Perth
Best Village Shield: Comrie

Class Awards

City: Aberdeen
Large Town: Perth
Medium Town: Hawick
Small Town: Alness
Country Town: Pitlochry
Urban Community: Dyce
Large Village: Comrie
Small Village: Rowanburn

Entrant Awards

Lady Jane Grosvenor Wee Village Trophy: Balmerino
New Entrant Trophy: Kiltarlity
Horticultural Award: Perth
Permanent Landscaping Award: Comrie
Cleanliness Award: Edzell
David Welch Memorial Award: Alness

Local Authority Awards

Royal Caledonian Horticultural Society Trophy: Aberdeen City Council
ILAM Scotland Trophy: Perth and Kinross Council
IWM Scottish Centre Trophy: Highland Council
Wright Sustainable Development Award: Dumfries and Galloway Council

Royal British Legion – Best Kept War Memorials

Champion of Champions: Carnoustie
Large Community: Pitlochry
Small Community: Millport
Memorials without Gardens: Cupar

Taste of Scotland Awards

Set up to encourage the pursuit of excellence and by so doing to encourage others to emulate the winners.

1995

Hotel: Balmoral Hotel, Edinburgh; *Restaurant:* Green Inn, Ballater; *Country House Hotel:* Flodigarry Country House Hotel, Staffin, Skye; *Special Merit Award for Newcomers:* Braidwoods Restaurant, near Dalry; *Special Merit Award for Achievement:* Loch Fyne Oyster Bar, Cairndow; *Macallan Personality of the Year:* Christine Morrison, Handa, Lochs, Isle of Lewis

1996

Hotel: Balbirnie House Hotel, Glenrothes; *Restaurant:* Symphony Room at Beardmore Hotel, Clydebank; *Country House Hotel:* Ardsheal House, Kentallen; *Special Merit Award for Best Informal Lunch:* East Haugh Country House Hotel and Restaurant, Pitlochry; *Special Merit Award for Hospitality:* Little Lodge, Gairloch; *Macallan Personality of the Year:* Stewart Cameron, Turnberry Hotel

1997

Hotel: Wheatsheaf Hotel, Swinton; *Restaurant:* Let's Eat, Perth; *Country House Hotel:* Knockinaam Lodge, Portpatrick; *Special Merit Award for Best Lunch:* Ballathie House Hotel, Perth; *Special Merit Award for Best Tea-room:* Kind Kyttock's Kitchen, Falkland; *Macallan Personality of the Year:* Alan Craigie, Creel Restaurant and Rooms, St Margaret's Hope, Orkney

1998

Hotel: Crinan Hotel, Crinan; *Restaurant (jointly):* Let's Eat, Perth, Three Chimneys Restaurant, Isle of Skye; *Country House Hotel:* Kilmichael Country House Hotel, Isle of Arran; *Best Breakfast:* Kinloch Lodge, Isle of Skye;

Best Child Friendly Establishment: Old Pines Restaurant, Spean Bridge; *Overall Excellence Award and Best Restaurant with Rooms:* The Albannach, Lochinver

1999

Hotel Dining: Balmoral Hotel, Edinburgh; *Restaurant with Rooms Award and Overall Excellence Award:* Three Chimneys Restaurant, Isle of Skye; *City Restaurant Award:* Stravaigin, Glasgow; *Country Lunch Award:* Greywalls, Gullane; *Rural Restaurant with Rooms Award:* Gordon's Restaurant, Inverkeilor; *Small Residence Award:* Old Smiddy Guest House, Laide

2000

Overall Excellence: Braidwoods, Dalry; *City Restaurant:* Ubiquitous Chip, Glasgow; *Country House:* Auchterarder House; *Out of Town:* Livingston's Restaurant, Linlithgow; *Chef Proprietor, Fine Dining in a Rural Setting:* Braidwoods, Dalry; *Dedication to Use of Local Seasonal Produce:* Auchendean Lodge Hotel, Dulnain Bridge; *Small Residence:* Cosses Country House, Ballantrae

2001

Overall Excellence: Kinloch House, Blairgowrie; *Bed and Breakfast Award:* Craigadam, Castle Douglas; *Light Bite Award:* Coach House, Luss; *Out of Town Restaurant Award:* Monachyle Mhor, Balquidder; *Country House Award:* Kinloch House, Blairgowrie; *Restaurant Award:* The Witchery by the Castle, Edinburgh; *Best Newcomer Award:* 63 Tay Street, Perth

The Queen's Awards for Enterprise 2001

Instituted by royal warrant in 1976 as the Queen's Award for Export Achievement (now International Trade) and the Queen's Award for

Technological Achievement (now Innovation) and taking the place of the Queen's Award to Industry, which was instituted in 1965. A third award, the Queen's Award for Environmental Achievement (now Sustainable Development), was instituted in 1992. The Scottish winners in 2001 were as follows:

International Trade

Aortech Europe Ltd, Bellshill (replacement heart valves)
Scottish Biomedical, Glasgow (biomedical consultancy services)
M&A Thomson Litho Ltd, East Kilbride (printing material and software)
John Wood Group PLC, Aberdeen (new generation contracting, solutions and services to global energy industries)

Innovation

Silberline Ltd, Leven ("silvet" metal pigment in novel granular form)
Tritech International Ltd, Westhill, Aberdeenshire (SeaKing range of networked subsea tools and sensors)

Sustainable Development

ScottishPower plc, Generation Division, Glasgow (gas reburn, cost effective NO_x reduction technology)

Vibes Awards 2001

(Vision in Business for the Environment)

New competition being held to encourage and reward Scotland's business community for environmental best practice.

National Winners:

Small Business:
Encore Environmental Aggregates, East Calder

Medium Size Business:
McKechnie Plastic Components, Beith
Large Business:
Tayside Contracts

North of Scotland Winners: REBUS Project Management, Orkney Herring Company, Tayside Contracts
East of Scotland Winners: Encore Environmental Aggregates, GR Advanced Materials, SCA Packaging
West of Scotland Winners: The Scottish Nappy Company, McKechnie Plastic Components, Hydro Seafood

Scottish Business Insider Corporate Elite Awards 2001

Recognising exceptional achievement and leadership by the people leading Scotland's major companies and public sector bodies.

Business Achievement Award: Fred Goodwin, Group Chief Executive, Royal Bank of Scotland Group plc
Business Ambassador for Scotland Award: Sir Ian Wood, Chairman and Managing Director, John Wood Group plc
Lifetime Achievement Award: Sir Angus Grossart, Chairman and Managing Director, Noble Grossart Ltd
Most Promising Young Business Leader Award: Paul Muir, Chief Executive Officer, McLaren plc
Insider Readers' Award: Steve Remp, Chairman and Chief Executive, Ramco Energy plc
IT Achievement Award: Alastair Wilkie, Managing Director, Vision Consulting Ltd
Corporate Elite Leader of the Year Award: Fred Goodwin, Group Chief Executive, Royal Bank of Scotland Group plc

Scottish Press Awards 2001

sponsored by Bank of Scotland, Standard Life, BAA Scottish Airports, Virgin Trains, Royal Mail

Journalist of the Year: Alastair McKay, The Scotsman
Scoop of the Year: Lorna Martin, The Herald (location of Madonna's wedding)
Reporter of the Year: Bob Dow, Daily Record
Journalist Team of the Year: Viv Aitken, Mark Daly, Mark McGivern, Keith McLeod, Anna Smith, Daily Record
Feature Writer of the Year: Catherine Deveney, Scotland on Sunday
Columnist of the Year: Muriel Gray, Sunday Herald
Campaigning Journalist of the Year: Emma Nugent/Andrea Tuckerman, Evening Times
Financial/Business Writer of the Year: Kenny Kemp, Sunday Herald
IT/New Media Writer of the Year: Iain Bruce, Sunday Herald
Political Journalist of the Year: Ken Farquharson, Sunday Times
Sports Journalist of the Year: Richard Bath, Sunday Herald
Arts/Entertainment Writer of the Year: Alastair McKay, The Scotsman
Cartoonist of the Year: Bill Caldwell, Sunday Mail
Young Journalist of the Year: Derek Alexander, Sunday Mail
Weekly Newspaper Journalist of the Year: James Doherty, The Big Issue
David Boyle Erskine Hospital Memorial Award: James Doherty, The Big Issue
Gaelic Journalist of the Year: Roddy Maclean, Inverness Courier
Scottish Lifetime Achievement Award: Alex Cameron, former chief sports writer, Daily Record

Quality Scotland

The Quality Scotland Award for Business Excellence, instituted in 1994, is based on the belief that the promotion of quality and the achievement of excellence can be sustained in Scotland through the existence of a prestigious quality award.

Awards

1995   Aviall Caledonian Engine Services, Prestwick
O.I.L. Ltd, Aberdeen
Rank-Xerox (Scotland), Glasgow
1996   Inland Revenue Accounts, Cumbernauld
TSB Homeloans, Glasgow
Vesuvius, Newmilns
1997   ICI Explosives Europe
Aberdeen College
Govan Initiatives Ltd
1998   Honeywell Control Systems Ltd, Motherwell
Scottish Homes
1999   St Ninian's High School, East Renfrewshire
2000   Bekaert Handling
Scottish Courage Brands
2001   Edinburgh International Conference Centre
Currie Community High School

Calor Gas Scottish Community of the Year 2001

Presented in collaboration with the Association of Scottish Community Councils. The awards aim to develop awareness of community councils and highlight work being undertaken by communities throughout Scotland.

Scottish Community of the Year:
Whitehills Community Council

Environment:
Winner: Uig Community Council; *Highly Commended:* Deskford and District Community Council

Business:
Winner: Whitehills Community Council; *Highly Commended:* Callander Community Council

Young People:
Winner: Tain Community Council; *Highly Commended:* Milngavie Community Council

Older People:
Winner: Bo'ness Community Council; *Highly Commended:* Uig Community Council

Community Life:
Winner: Whitehills Community Council; *Highly Commended:* Newcastleton and District Community Council

Community Enhancement through IT – Community Website Proposal
Winner: Lochwinnoch Community Council

Community Enhancement through IT – Community Website
Winner: Gavinton, Fogo and Polwarth Community Council

Association for Protection of Rural Scotland

Annual award scheme, instituted in 1975, encourages good planning, architecture and landscaping and recognises particularly fine examples of structures in a rural setting. It is thought essential that each work be seen to be making a definite contribution to the rural scene in Scotland. To celebrate 25 years of these awards, APRS made a special Award of Awards to a previous winner in 2001.

A new competition was initiated in 2001 with the title Creative, Native and Innovative for new, converted or renovated buildings utilising native hardwood.

Annual Award Winners

1975   The Smiddy Bothy, Dundonell, Wester Ross

1976   Torridon Youth Hostel, Wester Ross
1977   Gigha Hotel, Isle of Gigha
1978   Little Carbeth, Killearn, Stirlingshire
1979   Parton Village, near Castle Douglas
1980   Boathouse, Loch Marlich, Inverness-shire
1981   Corrigill Farm Museum, Harray, Orkney
1982   Flotta Oil Terminal, Orkney
1983   Easter Society, Hopetoun, West Lothian
1984   Fowler Croft, Straiton, Ayrshire
1985   The Old Castle, East Saltoun, East Lothian
1986   Salen Primary School, Mull
1987   The Hanseatic Booth, Symbister, Whalsay, Shetland; Fort George, Inverness
1988   Kylesku Bridge, Sutherland
1989   Muir of Blebo, near Cupar
1990   Aonach Mor, near Fort William
1991   The Auld Haa, Fair Isle, Shetland; Shirgarton Farmhouse, Kippen, Stirling
1992   Gesto, Isle of Skye
1993   Doctor's surgery, Ballachulish, near Fort William
1994   Six cottages, Balmacara, Kyle of Lochalsh
1995   Ardgour Primary School, near Fort William; Cantraybridge Rural Skills Cottage, Cawdor; Inverewe Garden Restaurant, Wester Ross; Old Seminary, The Scalan, Glenlivet; Moray District Local Plan, 1993-98 (Housing in the Countryside)
1996   Craigend Visitor Centre, Mugdock Country Park; The Mews and Courtyard, Sundrum Castle, Ayrshire; Scalpay Community Centre
1997   Glenmore Visitors Centre, Cairngorm
1998   Conversion of stables to a dwelling at Easter Tullybannocher, Comrie; Pentlands Science Park, Penicuik
1999   Clanland and Seal Point Visitor Centre, Foulis Ferry, Evanton; new house at Ardblair, near Beauly; new artist's studio, Tulliepowrie,

Strathtay
2000   Two new houses at Houss,
Eastburra, Shetland; The Millennium
Link, Central Scotland (restoration of
Union Canal); Eilean Bar Project,
Kyleakin, Isle of Skye
2001 Award of Awards:
Parton Village, near Castle Douglas

Creative, Native and Innovative Award

2001   New office building being built
for Natural Power at Forrest Estate, near
Dalry.

Scottish Arts Council

(1) Creative Scotland Awards 2002

The largest arts awards of their kind in
the UK. Fourteen of Scotland's leading
artists receive £25,000 each to help them
carry out a major new work, to develop
their skills, or to move their work in a
new direction.

Visual Arts:
   Christine Borland
   Gina Czarnecki
   Louise Hopkins
   Wendy McMurdo
Cross-media:
   Angus Farquhar
Literature:
   Gillian Ferguson
   Janice Galloway
   Don Paterson
   Ian Stephen
Crafts/Music:
   Alison Kinnaird
Drama:
   Stewart Laing
Music:
   Dick Lee
   Alistair MacDonald
Dance/Film:
   Katrina McPherson

(2) Spring 2001 Book Awards

Douglas Dunn for *The Year's Afternoon*

Alan Spence for *Seasons of the Heart*
Margaret Elphinstone for *The Sea Road*
Alasdair Campbell for *The Nessman*
Christopher Whyte for *The Cloud
Machinery*

(3) Children's Book Awards 2001

Julie Lacome for *Ruthie's Big Old Coat*
Tom Pow and (illustration) Robert
Ingpen for *Who is the World For?*
Diana Hendry for *Harvey Angell Beats
Time*
J K Rowling for *Harry Potter and the
Goblet of Fire*
Lindsay MacRae for *How to Avoid
Kissing your Parents in Public*
Alison Prince for *Second Chance*

Saltire Society

Housing Design Awards 2001

Awards

New housing at Locharthur. Architect:
   Crallan & Winstanley. Builder: T
   Graham & Son Ltd
Crown Street 2A, Gorbals, Glasgow.
   Architect: Page & Park. Builder: John
   Dickie Construction Ltd
Crown Street 3A, Gorbals, Glasgow.
   Architect: Elder & Cannon. Builder:
   John Dickie Construction Ltd
New Build 3, Graham Square, Glasgow.
   Architect: McKeown Alexander.
   Builder: John Dickie Construction
   Ltd

Commendations
Terrace and Object Building, Homes for
   the Future, Lanark Street, Glasgow
Stanley Mills, near Perth

Scottish Science Award

1990 (Physics) Professor Peter Ware
   Higgs, Department of Physics,
   Edinburgh University

1991 (Earth) Professor Brian Bluck, Department of Geology and Applied Geology, Glasgow University
1992 (Medicine) Professor Kenneth Murray, Department of Molecular Biology, Edinburgh University
1993 (Physics) Professor Malcolm Sim Longair, Jackson Professor of Natural Philosophy, Cambridge University
1994 (Biology) Dr John D Oldham, Scottish Agricultural College
1995 (Earth) Professor Colin Ballantyne, Professor of Physical Geography, St Andrews University
1996 (Medicine) Professor Christopher Haslett, Professor of Respiratory Medicine and Director of the Rayne Laboratories
1997 (Physics) Professor Bernard Roberts, Professor of Solar Megnetohydrodynamics,St Andrews University
1998 (Biology) Professor Niel Gow, Department of Molecular and Cell Biology, Aberdeen University
1999 (Earth) Robert Stuart Haszeldine, Reader in Geology, Edinburgh University
2000 (Veterinary Science) Professor Quintin A. McKellar, Chief Executive and Scientific Director, Moredun Research Institute

Literary awards

A. Book of the Year

1996 *The Kiln* by William McIlvanney
1997 *Grace Notes* by Bernard MacLaverty
1998 *The Sopranos* by Alan Warner
1999 *Pursuits* by George Bruce
2000 *The Lantern Bearers* by Ronald Frame
2001 *Medea* by Liz Lochhead

B. Best First Book of the Year

1996 *Slattern* by Kate Clanchy
1997 *A Painted Field* by Robin Robertson
1998 *The Pied Piper's Poison* by Christopher Wallace; *Two Clocks Ticking* by Dennis O'Donnell
1999 *Some Rain Must Fall* by Michael Faber

2000 *The Rising Sun* by Douglas Galbraith
2001 *In the Bluehouse* by Meaghan Delahunt

C. Scottish History Book of the Year
(in memory of Dr Agnes Muir MacKenzie)

1997 *The Early Stewart Kings, Robert II and Robert III 1371-1406* by Dr Stephen Boardman
1998 *The Identity of the Scottish Nation* by Dr William Ferguson
1999 *Patrick Sellar and The Highland Clearances, Homicide Eviction and the Price of Progress*, by Eric Richards
2000 *The Rough Wooings of Mary Queen of Scots 1542-1551*, by Marcus Merriman

D. Research Book of the Year

1998 *The Edinburgh History of the Scots Language*, edited by Charles Jones
1999 *The Poems of William Dunbar, Vols. I and II*, edited by Priscilla Bawcutt; special commendation: *Scottish Education*, by TGK Bryce and WM Humes
2000 *Jessie Kesson, Writing her Life*, by Isobel Murray
2001 *The Scottish Book Trade 1500–1720*, by Alastair J Mann

John Grierson Award for Young Filmmakers 2001

Cars and Stripes, by Susan Cassidy, Sheila MacKie, Pamela Nelson, Diego Rincon, Jo-anne Storrar

Scottish Museums Council

Scottish Museum of the Year Awards 2001

Scottish Museum of the Year: Kirriemuir Gateway to the Glens Museum (*highly commended:* Museum of Islay Life)
Countess of Perth Trophy: Auld Kirk Museum, Kirkintilloch

Publications Award: Fergusson Gallery, Perth, for *Living Paint*
Cramond Award: Inverness Museum
Educational Initiative Award: National Museums of Scotland

Scottish Writer of the Year

McVitie's Prize

1987   David Thomson for *Nairn in Darkness and Light*
1988   Bernard MacLaverty for *The Great Profundo & Other Stories;* and Edwin Mickleburgh for *Antarctica: Beyond the Frozen Sea*
1989   Alan Bold for *MacDiarmid*
1990   Sorley MacLean for *From Wood to Ridge*
1991   William Boyd for *Brazzaville Beach*
1992   John Purser for *Scotland's Music*
1993   John Prebble for *Landscapes and Memories*
1994   Janice Galloway for *Foreign Parts*
1995   Frank Kuppner for *Something Very Like Murder*
1996   Alan Spence for *Stone Garden and other stories*

Stakis Prize

1997   Aongoas MacNeacail for *A Proper Schooling and other poems*
1998   Edwin Morgan for *Virtual and Other Realities;* James Kelman for *The Good Times*
1999 Award discontinued

Royal Scottish Academy

Annual Exhibition Awards 2001

RSA Guthrie Award: Kevin Dagg for Dystopia
RSA Latimer Awards: Neal Macdonald for Cave-in (Twin Peaks – Homage to Hargreaves in Blue and Fiona

Macaulay for Eriskay
RSA Benno Schotz Prize: Dugald Peters, untitled
RSA Keith Prize: Brian Koelz for ...in the brisk air
RSA Ottillie Helen Wallace Prize: Geraldine Knight for Lost Sheep
RSA Medal for Architecture: Mick Duncan, RMJM Architects for Oslo Opera House Competition
Meyer Oppenheim Prize: Tomoyuki Shimadate for Love Seat
John Murray Thomson Award: Amanda Phillips for Painted Desert, Arizona
Maude Gemmell Hutchison Prizes: Brent Millar for Self Portrait with Hare and Adrian O'Donnell for Hybrid
N S Macfarlane Charitable Trust Award (Painting): Lachlan Goudie for Nocturne
N S Macfarlane Charitable Trust Award (Sculpture): Natalie Taylor for Extensions
Dunfermline Building Society Prize: James D Robertson for Argyll Landscape
Highland Society of London Award: Arthur Watson for Sweeping Through (The Gates of New Jerusalem)
William J Macaulay/Scottish Gallery Award: Barbara Balmer for Ravine
Scottish Arts Club Prize: Ian Robertson for Gondwana
Glasgow Art Club Prize: Stuart T Mackenzie for Kirkaig

Royal Scottish Society of Painters in Watercolour

Award Winners 2002

Alexander Graham Munro Travel Award: Stephanie Dees for Twilight
RSW Council Award: Dawson Murray for Through to the Paddock
Alexander Graham Munro Award: Simon Laurie for Red Earth

Sir William Gillies Award: Emma S Davis for Paddy's Milestone
May Marshall Brown Award: Will Maclean for Rituals of Myth
John Gray Award: Marian Leven for Coastal Marks
Winsor & Newton Award: Claire Harkess for Gannets, Bass Rock
Betty Davies SFI Award: Delia Baillie for Deceivement
Scottish Arts Club Award: Ann Ross for Pienza, Altarpiece
Glasgow Art Club Fellowship: Jennifer McRae for In the Studio – Camel Coat
Dundee Arts & Heritage Purchase Prize: Delia Baillie for Deceivement
Hospitalfield Residency in Visual Arts: Michael Durning

An Comunn Gaidhealach

Winners of the Royal National Mod Gold Medal 1991-2001

1991 Wilma Kennedy, Glasgow
      Donald Murray, Insch
1992 Katrina MacKellar, Auldearn
      George Gunn, Inbhir Nis
1993 Mairead Stiubhart-Harding, Am Bac
      Seumas Gunna, Inbhir Nis
1994 Maggie MacDonald, Inverness
      Norman MacKinnon, Campbeltown
1995 Margaret J MacLellan, Mingarry
      Fionnlagh MacAoidh, Goilspidh
1996 Joanne Murray, Lewis
      Alasdair Barnett, Oban
1997 Alyth McCormack, Glasgow
      Grahma Neilson, Edinburgh

1998 Barbara Smith, Dornie
      Angus Smith, Oban
1999 Joyce Murray, Lewis
      Raymond Bremner, Caithness
2000 Judith Peacock, Milngavie
      Innes Macleod, Lewis
2001 Riona Whyte, Mull
      Archie MacLean, Glasgow

Winners of the Lovat & Tullibardine Choral Competition, 1991-2001

1991 Largs Gaelic Choir
1992 Glasgow Hebridean Choir
1993 Glasgow Gaelic Musical Assoc
1994 Oban Gaelic Choir
1995 Coisir Ghaidhlig Inbhirnis
1996 Dingwall Gaelic Choir
1997 Glasgow Islay Gaelic Choir
1998 Inverness Gaelic Choir
1999 Lothian Gaelic Choir
2000 Inverness Gaelic Choir
2001 Glasgow Islay Gaelic Choir

Scottish Community Drama Association

Scottish Finals 2001

1, Wick Players; 2, Forfar Dramatic Society; 3, Stewarton Drama Group; Best Stage Decor: Clachan Players; Best Original Play: *Uncle Jimmy* by Harry Glass

Scottish Youth One Act Festival Finals 2001

Lochside Youth Theatre

The Towns of Scotland

In official statistics prepared from the 1991 census, there appear such "towns" as Clarkston and Polmont which are suburbs rather than towns. Compiling a list of genuine towns, we have chosen to return to the self-governing structure of burghs which existed until the mid 1970s. We think we have caught all of them – but there were rather a lot! Population figure as shown.

Aberchirder *Aberdeenshire* 1,098
Aberdeen *Aberdeen* 189,707
Aberfeldy *Perth and Kinross* 1,748
Aberlour *Moray* 821
Abernethy *Perth and Kinross* 895
Airdrie *North Lanarkshire* 36,998
Alloa *Clackmannan* 18,842
Alva *Clackmannan* 5,201
Alyth *Perth and Kinross* 2,383
Annan *Dumfries and Galloway* 8,930
Anstruther *Fife* 3,650
Arbroath *Angus* 23,474
Ardrossan *North Ayrshire* 10,750
Armadale *West Lothian* 8,958
Auchterarder *Perth and Kinross* 3,549
Auchtermuchty *Fife* 1,932
Ayr *South Ayrshire* 47,962
Ballater *Aberdeenshire* 1,362
Banchory *Aberdeenshire* 6,230
Banff *Aberdeenshire* 4,110
Barrhead *East Renfrewshire* 17,252
Bathgate *West Lothian* 13,819
Bearsden *East Dunbartonshire* 27,806
Biggar *South Lanarkshire* 1,994
Bishopbriggs *E Dunbartonshire* 23,825
Blairgowrie *Perth and Kinross* 8,001
Bo'ness *Falkirk* 14,595
Bonnyrigg and Lasswade *Midlothian* 13,696
Brechin *Angus* 7,655
Bridge of Allan *Stirling* 4,864
Buckhaven and Methil *Fife* 17,069
Buckie *Moray* 8,425
Burghead *Aberdeenshire* no pop count
Burntisland *Fife* 5,951
Callander *Stirling* 2,622
Campbeltown *Argyll and Bute* 5,722
Carnoustie *Angus* 10,673
Castle Douglas *Dumfries and Galloway* 3,697
Clydebank *West Dunbartonshire* 29,171
Coatbridge *North Lanarkshire* 43,617
Cockenzie and Port Seton *East Lothian* 4,235

Coldstream *Borders* 1,746
Coupar Angus *Perth and Kinross* 2,223
Cove and Kilcreggan *Argyll and Bute* 1,586
Cowdenbeath *Fife* 12,126
Crail *Fife* 1,449
Crieff *Perth and Kinross* 6,023
Cromarty *Highland* 721
Cullen *Moray* 1,430
Culross *Fife* 470
Cumbernauld *North Lanarkshire* 48,762
Cumnock *East Ayrshire* 9,607
Cupar *Fife* 7,545
Dalbeattie *Dumfries and Galloway* 4,421
Dalkeith *Midlothian* 11,567
Darvel *East Ayrshire* 3,759
Denny and Dunipace *Falkirk* 13,481
Dingwall *Highland* 5,224
Dollar *Clackmannan* 2,670
Dornoch *Highland* 1,196
Doune *Stirling* 1,213
Dufftown *Moray* 1,750
Dumbarton *West Dunbartonshire* 21,962
Dumfries *Dumfries and Galloway* 31,136
Dunbar *East Lothian* 6,518
Dunblane *Stirling* 7,368
Dundee *Dundee* 158,981
Dunfermline *Fife* 55,083
Dunoon *Argyll and Bute* 9,038
Duns *Borders* 2,444
East Kilbride *South Lanarkshire* 70,422
East Linton *East Lothian* 1,422
Edinburgh *Edinburgh* 401,910
Elgin *Moray* 19,027
Elie and Earlsferry *Fife* 903
Ellon *Aberdeenshire* 8,627
Eyemouth *Borders* 3,473
Falkirk *Falkirk* 35,610
Falkland *Fife* 1,197
Findochty *Moray* 1,100
Forfar *Angus* 12,961
Forres *Moray* 8,531
Fortrose *Highland* 1,319
Fort William *Highland* 10,391
Fraserburgh *Aberdeenshire* 12,843
Galashiels *Borders* 13,753
Galston *East Ayrshire* 5,154
Gatehouse of Fleet *Dumfries and Galloway* 919
Girvan *South Ayrshire* 7,449
Glasgow *Glasgow* 662,954
Glenrothes *Fife* 38,650
Gourock *Inverclyde* 11,743
Grangemouth *Falkirk* 18,739

Grantown on Spey *Highland* 2,391
Greenock *Inverclyde* 50,013
Haddington *East Lothian* 8,844
Hamilton *South Lanarkshire* 49,991
Hawick *Borders* 15,812
Helensburgh *Argyll and Bute* 15,852
Huntly *Aberdeenshire* 4,230
Innerleithen *Borders* 2,515
Inveraray *Argyll and Bute* 512
Inverbervie *Aberdeenshire* 1,879
Invergordon *Highland* 3,929
Inverkeithing *Fife* 6,001
Inverness *Highland* 41,234
Inverurie *Aberdeenshire* 9,567
Irvine *North Ayrshire* 32,988
Jedburgh *Borders* 4,118
Johnstone *Renfrewshire* 18,635
Keith *Moray* 4,793
Kelso *Borders* 5,989
Kilmarnock *East Ayrshire* 44,307
Kilsyth *North Lanarkshire* 9,918
Kilwinning *North Ayrshire* 15,479
Kinghorn *Fife* 2,931
Kingussie *Highland* 1,296
Kinross *Perth and Kinross* 4,552
Kintore *Aberdeenshire* 4,347
Kirkcaldy *Fife* 47,155
Kirkcudbright *Dumfries and Galloway* 3,588
Kirkintilloch *E Dunbartonshire* 20,780
Kirkwall *Orkney* 6,469
Kirriemuir *Angus* 5,571
Ladybank *Fife* 1,373
Lanark *South Lanarkshire* 8,877
Langholm *Dumfries and Galloway* 2,538
Largs *North Ayrshire* 10,925
Lauder *Borders* 1,064
Laurencekirk *Aberdeenshire* 1,611
Lerwick *Shetland* 7,336
Leslie *Aberdeenshire* 3,062
Leven *Fife* 8,317
Linlithgow *West Lothian* 11,866
Livingston *West Lothian* 41,647
Loanhead *Midlothian* 5,659
Lochgelly *Fife* 7,044
Lochgilphead *Argyll and Bute* 2,441
Lochmaben *Dumfries and Galloway* 2,024
Lockerbie *Dumfries and Galloway* 3,982
Lossiemouth *Moray* 7,184
Macduff *Aberdeenshire* 3,894
Markinch *Fife* 2,176
Maybole *South Ayrshire* 4,737
Melrose *Borders* 2,270
Millport *North Ayrshire* 1,340
Milngavie *East Dunbartonshire* 12,592
Moffat *Dumfries and Galloway* 2,342

Monifieth *Angus* 7,900
Montrose *Angus* 11,440
Motherwell *North Lanarkshire* 30,717
Musselburgh *East Lothian* 20,630
Nairn *Highland* 7,892
Newburgh *Fife* 1,401
New Galloway *Dumfries and Galloway*
Newmilns *East Ayrshire* 3,436
Newport on Tay *Fife* 4,343
Newton Stewart *Dumfries and Galloway* 3,673
North Berwick *East Lothian* 5,687
Oban *Argyll and Bute* 8,203
Oldmeldrum *Aberdeenshire* 1,976
Paisley *Renfrewshire* 75,526
Peebles *Borders* 7,065
Penicuik *Midlothian* 17,173
Perth *Perth and Kinross* 41,453
Peterhead *Aberdeenshire* 18,674
Pitlochry *Perth and Kinross* 2,541
Pittenweem *Fife* 1,561
Port Glasgow *Inverclyde* 19,693
Portknockie *Moray* 1,296
Portsoy *Aberdeenshire* 1,822
Prestonpans *East Lothian* 7,014
Prestwick *South Ayrshire* 13,705
Queensferry *Edinburgh* 8,887
Renfrew *Renfrewshire* 20,764
Rosehearty *Aberdeenshire* no pop count
Rothes *Moray* 1,345
Rothesay *Argyll and Bute* 5,264
Rutherglen *Glasgow*
St Andrews *Fife* 11,136
St Monance *Fife* 1,373
Saltcoats *North Ayrshire* 11,865
Sanquhar *Dumfries and Galloway* 2,095
Selkirk *Borders* 5,922
Stevenston *North Ayrshire* 10,153
Stewarton *East Ayrshire* 6,481
Stirling *Stirling* 30,515
Stonehaven *Aberdeenshire* 9,445
Stornoway *Western Isles* 5,975
Stranraer *Dumfries and Galloway* 11,348
Stromness *Orkney* 1,890
Tain *Highland* 3,715
Tayport *Fife* 3,346
Thurso *Highland* 8,488
Tillicoultry *Clackmannan* 5,269
Tobermory *Argyll and Bute* 825
Tranent *East Lothian* 8,316
Troon *South Ayrshire* 15,231
Turriff *Aberdeenshire* 3,951
Whitburn *West Lothian* 11,511
Whithorn *Dumfries and Galloway* 949
Wick *Highland* 7,681
Wigtown *Dumfries and Galloway* 1,117

The Islands of Scotland

Population 5 or more in 1991

Shetland Islands

Mainland	17,560
Yell	1,080
Unst	1,060
Whalsay	1,040
West Burra	817
Bressay	352
Trondra	117
Muckle Roe	115
Fetlar	90
Out Skerries	85
East Burra	72
Fair Isle	67
Foula	40
Papa Stour	33

Orkney Islands

Mainland	15,120
South Ronaldsay	943
Westray	704
Sanday	533
Hoy	450
Stronsay	382
Burray	363
Shapinsay	322
Rousay	217
Eday	166
Flotta	126
North Ronaldsay	92
Papa Westray	85
Egilsay	46
Wyre	28
Graemsay	27

Clyde

Bute	7,350
Arran	4,470
Great Cumbrae	1,390
Little Cumbrae	6

Inner Hebrides

Skye	8,840
Islay	3,540
Mull	2,680
Tiree	768
Seil	506
Jura	196
Luing	179
Coll	172
Raasay	163
Gigha	143
Lismore	140
Colonsay	133
Iona	130
Eigg	69
Easdale	41
Kerrera	39
Ulva	30
Rum	26
Muck	24
Canna	20
Soay	14
Isle of Ewe	12
Holy Island	10
Shona	9
Scalpay	7

Outer Hebrides

Lewis and Harris	21,680
South Uist	2,110
Benbecula	1,830
North Uist	1,400
Barra	1,240
Scalpay	382
Great Bernera	262
Grimsay (North Uist)	215
Eriskay	179
Berneray	141
Vatersay	72
Baleshare	55
St Kilda	25
Grimsay (Benbecula)	24
Flodday	8

The Scottish Weather

Coldest day: Minimum air temperature recorded: -27.2 degrees C at Braemar, 11 February 1895

Windiest day: Fastest gust recorded: 173 mph at Cairngorm, 20 March 1986.

Wet, wet, wet: Scotland's average rainfall ranges from 22 inches to 40 inches a year, typically about 15 inches higher than England's.

Hot stuff?: Average temperature of the coldest month in Lerwick is 3 degrees C compared to -10 degrees C in Moscow, which is several hundred miles to the south of Lerwick.

The Geography of Scotland

10 highest mountains and their height in feet
Ben Nevis, 4,406
Ben Macdhui, 4,300
Braeriach, 4,248
Cairn Toul, 4,241
Cairngorm, 4,084
Aonach Beag (Lochaber), 4,060
Carn Mor Dearg, 4,012
Aonach Mor (Highland), 3,999
Ben Lawers, 3,984
Beinn a' Bhuird, 3,924

10 largest lochs and their size in square miles
Loch Lomond, 27.5
Loch Ness, 21.9
Loch Awe, 14.9
Loch Maree, 11.0
Loch Morar, 10.3
Loch Tay, 10.2
Loch Shin, 8.7
Loch Shiel, 7.6
Loch Rannoch, 7.4
Loch Ericht, 7.2

10 deepest lochs and their depth in feet
Loch Morar, 1,017
Loch Ness, 751
Loch Lomond, 623
Loch Lochy, 531
Loch Ericht, 512
Loch Tay, 508
Loch Katrine, 495
Rannoch, 440
Loch Treig, 436
Loch Sheil, 420

10 longest rivers and their length in miles
Tay, 119
Forth, 116
Clyde, 106
Spey, 96
Tweed, 96
Dee, 87
Don, 82
Nith, 70
Findhorn, 62
Deveron, 61

10 largest islands and their size in square miles
Lewis and Harris, 859
Skye, 643
Mainland Shetland, 373
Mull, 347
Islay, 247
Mainland Orkney, 207
Arran, 168
Jura, 143
North Uist, 136
South Uist, 128

5 highest waterfalls and their height in feet
Eas Coul Aulin, 658
Falls of Glomach, 370
Foyers, 205
Falls of Bruar, 200
Grey Mare's Tail, 200

The above information was compiled for us by the Royal Scottish Geographical Society

Other geographical facts

The greatest distance from north to south in mainland Scotland is 274 miles from Cape Wrath to the Mull of Galloway. The greatest width is 154 miles from Buchan Ness to Applecross. The width of the central belt between the Firths of Clyde and Forth measures 25 miles. The border with England runs 60 miles along the line of the Cheviot Hills.

Scotland has 790 islands, of which 130 are inhabited.

It has 31,460 lochs.

It has six mountains of more than 4,000 feet.

Distance in miles by road from Edinburgh
Aberdeen, 125; Ayr, 73; Berwick upon Tweed, 57; Birmingham, 292; Dundee, 56; Exeter, 450; Fort William, 144; Glasgow, 44; Land's End, 574; London, 378; Stranraer, 124; Swansea, 392; York, 194

Maximum length of the United Kingdom
787 miles from Unst to St Agnes, Isles of Scilly

Schools of Scotland

Figure in parentheses is school roll

ABERDEEN
Aberdeen Grammar School (1102)
Bankhead Academy (720)
Bridge of Don Academy (745)
Cults Academy (1100)
Dyce Academy (510)
Harlaw Academy (925)
Hazlehead Academy (996)
Kincorth Academy (837)
Linksfield Academy (401)
Northfield Academy (986)
Oldmachar Academy (1164)
St Machar Academy (1115)
Torry Academy (488)

ABERDEENSHIRE
Aboyne Academy (600)
Alford Academy (573)
Banchory Academy (918)
Banff Academy (1105)
Ellon Academy (1659)
Fraserburgh Academy (1216)
Gordon Schools (878)
Inverurie Academy (1210)
Kemnay Academy (534)
Mackie Academy (1173)
Mearns Academy (526)
Mintlaw Academy (976)
Peterhead Academy (1570)
Portlethen Academy (833)
Turiff Academy (713)
Westhill Academy (940)

ANGUS
Abroath Academy (651)
Arbroath High School (1108)
Brechin High School (609)
Carnoustie High School (980)
Forfar Academy (1151)
Monifieth High School (860)
Montrose Academy (1025)
Webster's High School (769)

ARGYLL AND BUTE
Campbeltown Grammar School (520)
Dunoon Grammar School (1000)
Hermitage Academy (1500)
Islay High School (270)
Lochgilphead High School (530)
Oban High School (1100)

Rothesay Academy (490)
Tarbert Academy (280)
Tiree High School (120)
Tobermory High School (250)

CLACKMANNANSHIRE
Alloa Academy (690)
Alva Academy (1210)
Lornshill Academy (1050)

DUNDEE
Baldragon Academy (745)
Braeview Academy (856)
Craigie High School (800)
Grove Academy (810)
Harris Academy (1351)
Lawside RC Academy (861)
Menzieshill High School (920)
Morgan Academy (1000)
St John's High School (901)
St Saviour's RC High School (643)

DUMFRIES AND GALLOWAY
Annan Academy (1041)
Castle Douglas High School (540)
Dalbeattie High School (399)
Dalry Secondary School (108)
Douglas-Ewart High School (766)
Dumfries Academy (864)
Dumfries High School (1102)
Kirkcudbright Academy (535)
Langholm Academy (258)
Lockerbie Academy (805)
Maxwelltown High School (381)
Moffat Academy (223)
Sanquhar Academy (310)
St Joseph's College (629)
Stranraer Academy (1200)
Wallace Hall Academy (433)

EAST AYRSHIRE
Auchinleck Academy (963)
Cumnock Academy (1020)
Doon Academy (396)
Grange Academy (1069)
James Hamilton Academy (886)
Kilmarnock Academy (824)
Loudoun Academy (1146)
St Joseph's Academy (835)
Stewarton Academy (888)

EAST DUNBARTONSHIRE
Bearsden Academy (1310)
Bishopbriggs High School (964)
Boclair Academy (1100)
Douglas Academy (945)
Kirkintilloch High School (764)
Lenzie Academy (1304)
St Ninian's High School (740)
Thomas Muir High School (740)
Turnbull High School (900)

EAST LOTHIAN
Dunbar Grammar School (570)
Knox Academy (828)
Musselburgh Grammar School (1073)
North Berwick High School (750)
Preston Lodge High School (920)
Ross High School (863)

EAST RENFREWSHIRE
Barrhead High School (620)
Eastwood High School (1030)
Mearns Castle High School (1000)
St Luke's High School (560)
St Ninian's High School (1360)
Williamwood High School (1300)
Woodfarm High School (820)

EDINBURGH
Balerno High School (880)
Boroughmuir High School (1060)
Broughton High School (1030)
Castlebrae Community High
   School (300)
Craigmount High School (1260)
Craigroyston Community High
   School (465)
Currie Community High School (900)
Drummond High School (430)
Firrhill High School (840)
Forrester High School (970)
Gracemount High School (550)
Holy Rood High School (900)
James Gillespie's High School (1100)
Leith Academy (964)
Liberton High School (798)
Portobello High School (1400)
Queensferry High School (800)
Royal High School (1075)
St Augustine's RC High School (760)
St Thomas of Aquin's RC High
   School (630)
Trinity Academy (920)

Tynecastle High School (808)
Wester Hailes Education Centre (566)

FALKIRK
Bo'ness Academy (836)
Denny High School (1237)
Falkirk High School (1353)
Graeme High School (1474)
Grangemouth High School (850)
Larbert High School (1502)
St Mungo's RC High School (850)
Woodlands High School (506)

FIFE
Auchmuty High School (1266)
Balwearie High School (1550)
Beath High School (1187)
Bell Baxter High School (1633)
Buckhaven High School (1221)
Dunfermline High School (1715)
Glenrothes High School (964)
Glenwood High School (1217)
Inverkeithing High School (1448)
Kirkcaldy High School (1509)
Kirkland High School and Community
   College (928)
Lochgelly High School (980)
Madras College (1754)
Queen Anne High School (1775)
St Andrew's RC High School (819)
St Columba's RC High School (928)
Viewforth High School (456)
Waid Academy (712)
Woodmill High School (850)

GLASGOW
All Saints Secondary School (850)
Bannerman High School (1353)
Bellahouston Academy (784)
Bellarmine Secondary School (580)
Castlemilk High School (630)
Cleveden Secondary School (1250)
Drumchapel High School (833)
Eastbank Academy (1099)
Govan High School (550)
Hillhead High School (1220)
Hillpark Secondary School (790)
Holyrood Secondary School (2247)
Hyndland Secondary School (906)
John Paul Academy (850)
King's Park Secondary School (1209)
Knightswood Secondary School (1000)
Lochend Secondary School (820)
Lourdes Secondary School (1350)

Notre Dame High School (821)
Penilee Secondary School (848)
Shawlands Academy (1392)
Smithycroft Secondary School (750)
Springburn Academy (568)
St Andrew's Secondary School (1115)
St Margaret Mary's Secondary
  School (611)
St Mungo's Academy (1000)
St Roch's Secondary School (655)
St Thomas Aquinas Secondary
  School (673)
Whitehill Secondary School (750)

HIGHLAND
Alness Academy (700)
Charleston Academy (900)
Culloden Academy (940)
Dingwall Academy (1170)
Dornoch Academy (157)
Farr High School (140)
Fortrose Academy (650)
Gairloch High School (212)
Glen Urquhart High School (150)
Golspie High School (520)
Grantown Grammar School (360)
Invergordon Academy (450)
Inverness High School (473)
Inverness Royal Academy (790)
Kilchuimen Academy (60)
Kingussie High School (400)
Kinlochbervie High School (92)
Kinlochleven High School (130)
Lochaber High School (1060)
Mallaig High School (154)
Millburn Academy (1070)
Nairn Academy (820)
Plockton High School (300)
Portree High School (670)
Tain Royal Academy (670)
Thurso High School (1004)
Ullapool High School (206)
Wick High School (900)

INVERCLYDE
Gourock High School (563)
Greenock Academy (960)
Greenock High School (587)
Notre Dame High School (847)
Port Glasgow High School (600)
St. Columba's High School (815)
St. Stephen's High School (830)
Wellington Academy (537)

MIDLOTHIAN
Beeslack Community High School (960)
Dalkeith High School (760)
Lasswade High School Centre (1200)
Newbattle High School (810)
Penicuik High School (850)
St. David's RC High School (910)

MORAY
Buckie High School (880)
Elgin Academy (1019)
Elgin High School (570)
Forres Academy (996)
Keith Grammar School (550)
Lossiemouth High School (690)
Milne's High School (547)
Speyside High School (460)
Tomintoul School (58)

NORTH AYRSHIRE
Ardrossan Academy (1207)
Arran High School (300)
Auchenharvie Academy (614)
Garnock Academy (1208)
Greenwood Academy (1233)
Irvine Royal Academy (1080)
Kilwinning Academy (1019)
Largs Academy (940)
St Andrew's Academy (700)
St Michael's Academy (795)

NORTH LANARKSHIRE
Abronhill High School (590)
Airdrie Academy (1120)
Bellshill Academy (750)
Braidhurst High School (450)
Brannock High School (770)
Calderhead High School (710)
Caldervale High School (900)
Cardinal Newman High School (1150)
Chryston High School (810)
Clyde Valley High School (980)
Coatbridge High School (800)
Coltness High School (850)
Columba High School (750)
Cumbernauld High School (870)
Dalziel High School (952)
Greenfaulds High School (1040)
Kilsyth Academy (810)
Our Lady's High School,
  Cumbernauld (1000)
Our Lady's High School,
  Motherwell (750)
Rosehall High School (520)

St Aidan's High School (1320)
St Ambrose High School (1300)
St Margaret's High School (1300)
St Maurice's High School (1160)
St Patrick's High School (994)
Taylor High School (830)

PERTH AND KINROSS
Auchterarder High School (345)
Blairgowrie High School (1050)
Breadalbane Academy (659)
Crieff High School (584)
Kinross High School (860)
Perth Academy (1349)
Perth Grammar School (963)
Perth High School (1438)
Pitlochry High School (145)
St. Columba's RC High School (469)

RENFREWSHIRE
Castlehead High School (1200)
Gleniffer High School (1150)
Gryffe High School (884)
Johnstone High School (1270)
Linwood High School (460)
Merksworth High School (390)
Paisley Grammar School (1100)
Park Mains High School (1500)
Renfrew High School (950)
St Andrews' Academy (890)
St Brendan' High School (400)
St Cuthbert's High School (460)
St Mirin's High School (450)
Trinity High School (940)

SCOTTISH BORDERS
Berwickshire High School (760)
Earlston High School (710)
Eyemouth High School (452)
Galashiels Academy (1030)
Hawick High School (1080)
Jedburgh Grammar School (390)
Kelso High School (650)
Peebles High School (1020)
Selkirk High School (600)

SOUTH AYRSHIRE
Ayr Academy (630)
Belmont Academy (1279)
Carrick Academy (645)
Girvan Academy (622)
Kyle Academy (886)
Mainholm Academy (477)

Marr College (1403)
Prestwick Academy (1120)
Queen Margaret Academy (715)

SOUTH LANARKSHIRE
Ballerup High School (555)
Biggar High School (600)
Blantyre High School (920)
Carluke High School (1375)
Cathkin High School (1000)
Claremont High School (1180)
Duncanrig Secondary School (1072)
Earnock High School (930)
Hamilton Grammar School (1150)
Holy Cross High School (1630)
Hunter High School (730)
John Ogilvie High School (1010)
Lanark Grammar School (1020)
Larkhall Academy (1100)
Lesmahagow High School (710)
St Andrew's High School (570)
St Bride's High School (860)
Stonelaw High School (1230)
Strathaven Academy (900)
Trinity High School (1085)
Uddingston Grammar School (1275)

STIRLING
Balfron High School (850)
Bannockburn High School (786)
Dunblane High School (780)
McLaren High School (650)
St. Modan's High School (801)
Stirling High School (890)
Wallace High School (925)

WEST DUNBARTONSHIRE
Braidfield High School (632)
Clydebank High School (1068)
Dumbarton Academy (823)
Our Lady and St. Patrick's High
    School (1518)
St Andrew's High School (770)
St Columba's RC High School (1043)
Vale of Leven Academy (1100)

WEST LOTHIAN
Armadale Academy (720)
Bathgate Academy (1020)
Broxburn Academy (800)
Deans Community High School (740)
Inveralmond Community High
    School (1030)
James Young High School (820)
Linlithgow Academy (1120)

St Kentigern's Academy (1030)
St Margaret's Academy (990)
West Calder High School (930)
Whitburn Academy (1000)

ORKNEY
Glaitness Aurrida School (19)
Kirkwall Grammar School (900)
North Walls Community School (50)
Pierowall Junior High School (90)
Sanday Junior High School (81)
Stromness Academy (450)
Stronsay Junior High School (51)

SHETLAND
Aith Junior High School (183)
Anderson High School (840)
Brae High School (420)
Skerries School (11)
Symbister House Junior High
   School (190)

WESTERN ISLES
Back School (240)
Bayble School (123)
Castlebay School (120)
Daliburgh School (160)
Eriskay School (20)
Leurbost School (80)
Lionel School (85)
Nicolson Institute (1030)
Paible School (37)
Sgoil Lionacleit (450)
Shawbost School (88)
Sir E Scott School (146)

INDEPENDENT SCHOOLS

ABERDEEN
Albyn School for Girls (410)
Hamilton School (240)
International School of Aberdeen (380)
Robert Gordon's College (962)
St Margaret's School for Girls (200)

ARGYLL AND BUTE
Lomond School (400)

CLACKMANNANSHIRE
Dollar Academy (749)

DUNDEE
High School of Dundee (720)

EAST LOTHIAN
Loretto School (275)

EAST RENFREWSHIRE
Belmont House School (341)

EDINBURGH
Edinburgh Academy (458)
Fettes College (401)
George Heriot's School (885)
George Watson's College (1273)
Mary Erskine School (685)
Merchiston Castle School (365)
Rudolf Steiner School (300)
St George's School for Girls (550)
St Margaret's School and St Denis and
   Cranley (370)
St Mary's Music School (67)
St Serf's School (170)
Stewart's Melville College (760)

FIFE
St Leonards School (270)

GLASGOW
Craigholme School (481)
Glasgow Academy (600)
High School of Glasgow (668)
Hutchesons' Grammar School (1250)
Jordanhill School (1100)
Kelvinside Academy (330)
St Aloysius College (837)

INVERCLYDE
St Columba's School (360)

MORAY
Gordonstoun School (430)

PERTH AND KINROSS
Glenalmond College (400)
Kilgraston School (200)
Morrison's Academy (362)
Rannoch School (200)
Strathallan School (400)

SOUTH AYRSHIRE
Wellington School (510)

SOUTH LANARKSHIRE
Fernhill School (327)

STIRLING
Beaconhurst School (280)
Queen Victoria School (270)

WEST DUNBARTONSHIRE
Keil School (220)

Index of Organisations

**The song often sung of which few can remember,
if they ever knew, the words**

Should auld acquaintance be forgot,
And never brought to min'?
Should auld acquaintance be forgot,
And auld lang syne?

For auld lang syne, my dear.
For auld lang syne,
We'll tak a cup o' kindness yet,
For auld lang syne.

We twa hae run about the braes,
And pu'd the gowans fine;
But we've wander'd mony a weary foot
Sin' auld lang syne.

We twa hae paidled i' the burn,
From morning sun till dine;
But seas between us braid hae roar'd
Sin' auld lang syne.

And there's a hand, my trusty fiere,
And gie's a hand o' thine;
And we'll tak a right guid-willie waught,
For auld lang syne.

And surely ye'll be your pint-stowp,
And surely I'll be mine;
And we'll tak a cup o' kindness yet
For auld lang syne

Editor's note: the word "syne" is pronounced with an s, not a z